The New Hebridean Kitchen

by

Murdo Alex Macritchie

The New Hebridean Kitchen

by

MURDO ALEX MACRITCHIE

Gaelic text by Jo MacDonald

HAAR

HAAR

HAAR

In memory of Murdo Alex Macritchie
Mar Chuimhneachan air Murdo Ailig Macrisnidh

1977-2019

Thou didst me answer in the day
when I to thee did cry;
And thou my fainting soul with strength
didst strengthen inwardly.
Psalm 138:3

San là a ghlaodh mi riut, a Dhè,
fhreagair thu mi gu luath;
Is thug thu spionnadh dhomh gu leòr,
le treòir, am anam truagh.
Salm 138:3

All royalties from the sale of this book will be donated to
Bethesda Hospice, Stornoway and Pancreatic Cancer UK.

HAAR

Haar Restaurant @ Gearrannan Blackhouse
Carloway, Isle of Lewis, Outer Hebrides

November 2016
7.30pm

Admits One

CONTENTS

Introduction
Facal-toisich
21

The New Hebridean Kitchen and the story of HAAR
Còcaireachd Ùr Innse-Gallach agus Sgeulachd HAAR
26

Small Bites
Blasadan Beaga
32

Rocks and Shore
Creagan is Cladach
62

The Guga
An Guga
88

Moor and Machair
Mòinteach is Machair
96

Eòin Fhiadhaich is Ainmhidhean
Wildfowl and Game
106

Sheiling
Àirigh
126

Sea and River
Muir is Abhainn
142

Creel Fishermen
Iasgairean Chlèibh
160

Hebridean Salmon Rivers
Aibhnichean Bhradan nan Eilean
168

A Good Catch
Deagh Iasgach
184

From the Croft
Bhon Lot
212

Highlander Beef
Mairtfheòil Crodh Gàidhealach
226

Polycrubs
Tunailean-fàis
232

Baking and Desserts
Bèicearachd agus Mìlsean
246

Sùlair
282

Suppliers
Solaraichean
288

Introduction Facal-toisich

Murdo Alex Macritchie, my brother, came up with the idea of a pop-up restaurant called HAAR, so that he could bring almost forgotten Hebridean dishes, not only to Lewis diners but also to other locations throughout the country. The HAAR pop-up was intended to be a complete dining experience, inspired by outstanding produce and by the natural and cultural history of the Hebridean Islands of Scotland. The islands' landscape and culture had a profound influence on the way we prepared and cooked each dish.

We brought traditional foods that were familiar to all islanders to our menus. Our suppliers and producers were crucial to our success – it was their produce that constantly inspired Murdo Alex to cook, as he explains in the following introduction he wrote for the book.

The HAAR pop-ups proved very popular, with all venues sold out. We were privileged to cook at Comunn Eachdraidh Nis, at Bogbain Farm in Inverness, in the iconic Duart Castle in Mull and at Gearrannan Blackhouses on the west coast of Lewis, a stunning venue which fitted in perfectly with what HAAR was all about. We also managed to showcase Hebridean produce with a three-day pop-up in Suffolk!

I worked alongside Murdo Alex at Sùlair, his first restaurant, and at HAAR. Chef Andrew Wallis, who worked with Murdo Alex in his first kitchen, has worked in some of the best kitchens in the UK as well as working as Sous Chef at the critically acclaimed AMASS in Copenhagen. We were the HAAR team!

But Murdo Alex had his own personal team - his wife Michelle, who always encouraged and supported him in all his ventures. Michelle was the friendly front of house in Sùlair; they made a great partnership which continued in their working lives in Suffolk. Along with my mam, dad and brother Iain, Michelle was determined that this book should be completed and published.

In 2016 Murdo Alex was diagnosed with pancreatic cancer. During his three-year battle with cancer he began work on this book, *HAAR The New Hebridean Kitchen*. Sadly, Murdo Alex was unable to complete the book before he passed away on 17th October 2019. To make Murdo Alex's vision a reality, Andrew and I, with help from my cousin Jo MacDonald, completed the book, as a tribute to Murdo Alex's amazing talent as a chef. Although some of his recipes are incomplete, the stunning photographs of his dishes are a reminder of what we lost.

We are so grateful for the immense support we received from suppliers and customers. They are too numerous to mention all by name. I would like to give special thanks to Murdo Murray and Donald 'Sweeny' Macsween who went out of their way to supply many ingredients while we were testing recipes. I would also like to thank Comunn Eachdraidh Nis for use of material from their archives.

All royalties from the sale of this book will be donated to Bethesda Hospice, Stornoway and Pancreatic Cancer UK.

Finally, I sincerely hope the book looks and feels similar to the book Murdo Alex had in mind.

Kathleen MacDonald
August 2022

THE HAAR MENU

Winter 2016

'Ceann Cropaig Cracker' – Cod's head, its liver & oatmeal, soused herring salad cream, sheep's sorrel

'Marag dhubh' – Stornoway black pudding, potato scone, last summer's gooseberry & elderflower jam

Langoustine roasted in chicken dripping, chicken skin crumble, prune & elderberry

Scotch pie made from Hebridean black sheep mutton, pickled onion, sheep's cheese, dried moorberries

Fried rabbit haggis, whipped pine oil & roasted leek and a light grating of dried rabbit heart

'Aran Eòrna' – beremeal bannock, fresh herb crowdie & cream

Salt mackerel, frozen buttermilk, celery jam fermented rhubarb

Croft potato cooked over a smouldering peat fire
Smoked herring roe, pickled kohlrabi

Diver caught scallop, smoked roe cream, the humble snèap, seaweed, dill

Highlander beef, barley & malted onion porridge, cabbage, barley vinegar, puffed barley

'Duff' – traditional Hebridean fruit pudding cooked in a cloth, Colonsay machair flower honey & buttermilk ice cream, dried raspberries from late last summer

Salted whey caramel, sheep's yoghurt, compressed apple, mint & Isle of Harris gin ice

Isle of Lewis blackhouse tea with a rosehip, oat & potato 'Scottish macaroon'

'Oidhche Mhath' – A dram of Bruichladdich 'The Classic Laddie' whisky from the Inner Hebridean Isle of Islay

POP-UP

BY THE GRAPEVINE + HAAR

CEANN CROPAIG
A traditional Hebridean dish of cod's head, liver & oatmeal, crab,
smoked scallop roe emulsion

MARAG DHUBH
Stornoway black pudding, potato scone

LAST SUMMERS GOOSEBERRY & ELDERFLOWER JAM

LANGOUSTINE
Roasted in chicken dripping, chicken skin crumble,
prune & elderberry

SCOTCH PIE
Pickled onion, sheep's cheese, dried moor berries

FRIED RABBIT HAGGIS
Pine oil & leek emulsion

Malted barley & dulse bread, seaweed butter

SALT MACKEREL
Frozen buttermilk, celery jam,
fermented rhubarb

CROFT POTATO
Cooked over a smouldering peat fire

SMOKED HERRING ROE
Pickled chive flowers

SCALLOP
Diver caught from the Isle of Lewis

BROTH
Hebridean sea lettuce & sugar kelp

WHITE FISH
The humble snèap, a sauce made from mussels & dill

HOGGET
Hebridean hogget from Sunhill Croft on the Isle of Berneray,
our own crowdie cheese, beetroot & barley porridge, dried rosehip

———

'Aran Corc agus Caise'- Isle of Mull blue cheese & oat crumble

'Duff' - traditional Hebridean fruit pudding cooked in a cloth

Colonsay machair flower honey & buttermilk ice cream, dried raspberries from late last summer

Salted whey caramel, sheep's yoghurt, compressed apple, mint & Isle of Harris gin

Isle of Lewis blackhouse tea with chocolates

The New Hebridean Kitchen and the Story of HAAR

The idea of 'The New Hebridean Kitchen' and 'New Hebridean Cuisine' began in 2007 when I had opened my first restaurant, Sùlair. Back then my food was heavily influenced by classical French and Italian cooking techniques and I had already begun to become obsessed with sourcing and using ingredients that came from the Hebridean Islands, particularly Lewis and Harris.

Beautiful hand dived scallops from Uig, creel-caught langoustines, squatties and lobsters from Harris, grouse, woodcock, snipe from the Barvas moor, wild red deer from Eishken Estate, Aberdeen Angus beef and Cheviot lamb from a family from the district of Ness, organically grown vegetables and salads from the west side of Lewis and fresh, locally caught fish from a number of different fishermen. I had discovered the abundant natural larder of the Hebridean Islands!

During the three years that Sùlair was open I had slowly started to incorporate my take on a few classic Island dishes onto the menu but it was still a menu that was heavily rooted in my classical French training. 'New Hebridean Cuisine' was still very much in its embryonic stage, though my dream at that time was to make Sùlair an exclusively Hebridean restaurant with its own distinct identity. Sadly, the recession of 2010 impacted us greatly as a fine dining restaurant so we took the difficult decision to close the restaurant. Sùlair was no more.

Fast forward to 2015. I had been working as a private chef to a family in the movie and fashion business for a number of years. I still had a passion for Hebridean produce and continued to work with a number of producers and suppliers from the Islands but the environment in which I was working was not suited to serving Hebridean inspired dishes, although I did have some guga sent down for my German boss to try and she loved it! Travelling abroad with work afforded me the opportunity to source food produce from the most amazing markets, farm shops and artisanal producers. Yet I became more and more convinced that the produce from the Hebrides was unrivalled anywhere in the world. I understand what a bold statement that is but I do genuinely believe that Scotland, and in particular the Hebrides, has the best larder in the world.

The 'New Heb' idea was taking shape. I was now being influenced by the whole New Nordic movement made famous by the Copenhagen restaurant Noma and its chef, Rene Redzepi. I began to notice the similarities between traditional Nordic food and the food I grew up eating on the Isle of Lewis. Smoking, salting, curing and fermenting were all important techniques used in both cultures. The eating of sea birds and their eggs was a familiar concept to me.

HAAR was intended to be a complete dining experience driven by outstanding produce and the natural and cultural history of the Hebridean Islands of Scotland. The landscape, along with the Gaelic culture, had a heavy influence in the way we prepared and cooked each dish. We wanted to bring something different to the Islands with the pop-ups – a dining experience showcasing the Hebrides.

We brought food traditions that are so familiar to us all on the Islands to our menus, but only taking them apart sympathetically and refining them to something more gastronomic, fusing traditional cooking methods with more modern techniques. The suppliers and producers that we used for HAAR were extremely important. It is their produce that inspired me to cook.

An Cidsin Ùr Innse-Gallach agus Sgeulachd HAAR

Thòisich mi a' beachdachadh air 'Cidsin Ùr Innse-Gallach' agus 'Còcaireachd Ùr Innse-Gallach' air ais ann an 2007, an dèidh dhomh mo chiad taigh-bìdh, Sùlair, fhosgladh. Aig an àm bha mo chòcaireachd gu mòr fo bhuaidh nòsan còcaireachd clasaigeach na Frainge agus na h-Eadailt ach bha mi cuideachd air mo bheò-ghlacadh le bhith a' lorg agus a' cleachdadh tàthchuidean eileanan Innse-Gall, gu h-àraid Leòdhas agus na Hearadh – creachain glacte le làimh ann an Ùig, muasgain-chaola, giomaich agus giomaich-thuathal air an glacadh ann an clèibh anns na Hearadh, cearcan-fraoich, coilich-coille agus naoisg bho mòinteach Bharabhais, sitheann fhèidh bho Oighreachd Èisgein, mairtfheòil Aberdeen Angus agus feòil uain Cheviot bho theaghlach ann an sgìre Nis, glasraich agus saileadan fàs-bheairteach bho thaobh siar Leòdhais agus pailteas de dh'iasg ùr bho ghrunn de dh'iasgairean an àite. Bha mi air seòmar-bìdh tairbheartach, nàdarra Innse-Gall a lorg!

Fad nan trì bliadhna a bha Sùlair fosgailte bha mi air mo shocair a' cur mo thionndadh fhèin de sheòrsachan bìdh clasaigeach nan Eilean air a' chlàr-bìdh ach, a dh'aindeoin sin, b' e clàr-bìdh a bha fhathast air a fhreumhachadh gu mòr nam thrèanadh clasaigeach Frangach a bha ann. Cha robh 'Còcaireachd Ùr Innse-Gallach' ach aig ìre glè thràth ged a bha mi a' bruadar mun àm a dhèanainn Sùlair na thaigh-bìdh Innse-Gallach a-mhàin, le dearbh-aithne soilleir aige. Gu duilich, thug seacadh eaconamach 2010 fìor dhroch bhuaidh oirnn mar thaigh-bìdh aig àrd-ìre agus b' fheudar dhuinn tighinn gu co-dhùnadh doirbh agus an taigh-bìdh a dhùnadh. Cha bhiodh Sùlair ann tuilleadh.

A' gluasad aig astar air adhart gu 2015. Fad grunn bhliadhnaichean bha mi air a bhith ag obair mar chòcaire prìobhaideach dha teaghlach a bha an sàs ann an gnìomhachasan filmichean agus fasain. Bha mi fhathast air mo bheò-ghlacadh le toradh Innse-Gallach agus bha mi air leantainn orm ag obair le cuid de sholairichean is builichearan às na h-eileanan. Ach cha robh an àrainneachd anns an robh mi ag obair freagarrach airson biadh stèidhte air dlùth-cheangal le Innse-Gall, ged a fhuair mi aon turas guga a bhruich mi dham fhastaiche Gearmailteach agus chòrd e gu mòr rithe. Thug a bhith a' siubhal thall thairis ri linn m' obair cothrom dhomh biadh a cheannach bho na margaidhean a b' iongantaiche, bho bhùithtean-tuathanais agus bho luchd-ciùird, ach a dh'aindeoin sin bha mi a' fàs nas cinntiche 's nas cinntiche nach robh samhail biadh Innse-Gall ann an àite sam bith air an t-saoghal. Tha mi a' tuigsinn gu bheil mi gu math dàna le sin a ràdh, ach tha mi dha-rìribh a' creidsinn gu bheil toradh nàdarra na mara 's na talmhainn ann an Alba, agus gu h-àraid ann an Innse Gall, nas fheàrr na tha ri fhaighinn ann an àite sam bith san t-saoghal.

Bha a' bheachd a bh' agam mu chòcaireachd ùr Innse-Gallach a' tòiseachadh a' tighinn gu ìre. Bha mi a-nise a' tighinn fo bhuaidh a' ghluasaid 'New Nordic' a dh'fhàs cho ainmeil mar thoradh air taigh-bìdh Noma ann an Copenhagen agus Rene Redzepi a bha a' còcaireachd ann. Thòisich mi a' mothachadh gu robh biadh traidiseanta Lochlannach agus am biadh air an robh mi eòlach a' fàs suas ann an Leòdhas caran coltach ri chèile. Bha smocadh, sailleadh, ciùradh agus brachadh cumanta san dà chultar agus cha robh càil annasach dhomh mu dhaoine a bhith ag ithe eòin-mhara agus an uighean.

Bha sinn airson gu faigheadh an neach a ghabhadh dìnneir ann an HAAR biadh coileanta, stèidhichte air toradh air leth, freumaichte ann an saoghal nàdarra agus eachdraidh chultarach eileanan Innse-Gall. Bha buaidh mhòr aig cruth na tìre agus cultar na Gàidhlig air an dòigh anns an robh sinn a' deasachadh agus a' còcaireachd gach grèim bìdh. Bha sinn airson rudeigin eadar-dhealaichte a thoirt dha na h-Eileanan le na *pop-ups*, biadh a bha a' taisbeanadh Innse-Gall.

Thug sinn traidiseanan bìdh air a bheil sinn uile eòlach sna h-Eileanan gu ar clàir-bìdh, ach an dèidh an toirt às a chèile le co-fhaireachdainn agus tuigse agus an ath-chruthachadh 's an lìomhadh gu ìre eile, a' cur dòighean còcaireachd traidiseanta agus dòighean nas ùire an ceann a chèile. Bha na solaraichean agus na builichearan a bha sinn a' cleachdadh airson HAAR air leth cudromach – b' e am biadh aca-san a bha gam bhrosnachadh gu còcaireachd.

Small Bites
Blasadan Beaga

At HAAR we always like our guests to begin their meal with five small delicious bites that come out in quick succession before the first plated dish is put down in front of them. In each of the *Blasadan Beaga* there must be an intense flavour explosion, one or two bites that leave the guests wanting more, leaving them with an anticipation of what is to come.

Aig HAAR bu mhath leinn gun tòisicheadh ar n-aoighean an dinnear le còig blasadan beaga, blasta a' tighinn thuca gu luath, fear an dèidh fir, mus tèid a' chiad thruinnsear bìdh a chur air am beulaibh. Feumaidh dìreach spreadhadh de bhlas a bhith anns gach 'Blasad Beag', grèim beag no dhà a dh'fhàgas aoighean ag iarraidh tuilleadh agus a' dèanamh fiughair ri na tha ri thighinn.

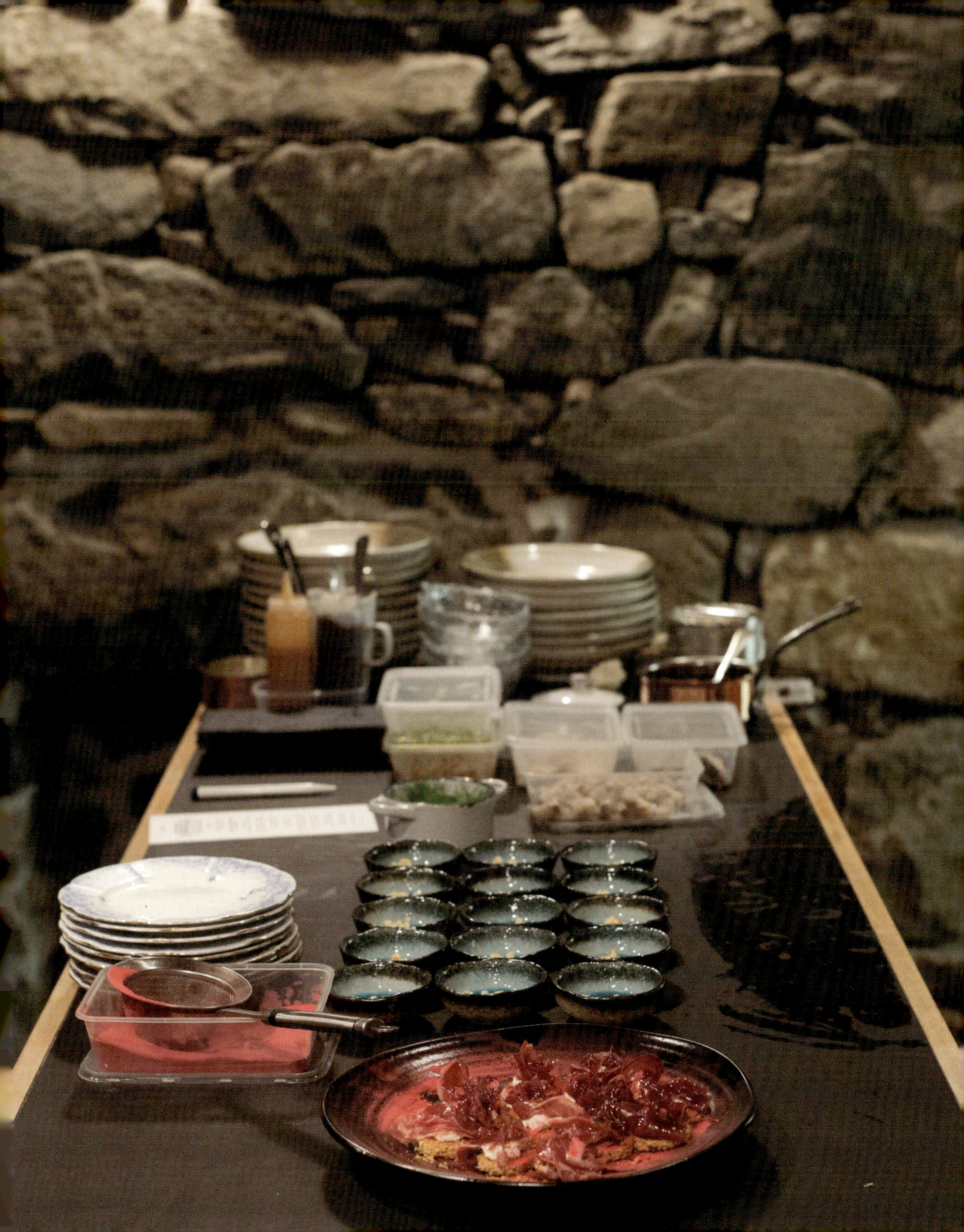

SMOKED MUTTON FLANK GLAZED IN MINT VINEGAR — ISLE OF MULL BLUE CHEESE — MARJORAM FLOWERS

Mutton or lamb with blue cheese may sound odd but they go wonderfully together and I would encourage you to try it. Chops with a blue cheese crust are absolutely delicious! For this recipe slowly braise the flank with lots of aromatics until it is almost falling off the bone. It's then pressed overnight under a heavy weight to compress the layers of fat. We then cut and trim the flank into little riblets and roast over hot coals until the skin is crispy, continuously glazing it with a home-made marjoram vinegar which adds a lovely acidic, floral note, helping to cut through the fatty meat. Serve with a blue cheese dip made simply by mixing blue cheese and cream together to keep the purity of its flavour. It's then finished with wild mint and marjoram flowers.

FLANC MUILTFHEÒIL SMOCTE, GLAINICHTE LE FÌON GEUR MEANNT — CÀIS GHORM À EILEAN MHUILE — FLÙRAICHEAN LUS-MARSAILIDH

'S dòcha gu saoil sibh gu bheil muiltfheòil no feòil uain le càis ghorm caran neònach ach tha iad a' tighinn air leth math air a chèile agus mholainn dhuibh fheuchainn. Tha sgineach uain le rùsg de chàis ghorm anabarrach blasta! Airson an reasabaidh seo bidh sinn a' bruich flanc gu slaodach, socair, le tòrr stuthan cùbhraidh gus a bheil e cha mhòr a' tuiteam far a' chnàimh. Tha e an uair sin air fhàgail fad oidhche fo chuideam trom gus na fillidhean geir a bhruthadh ri chèile. Bidh sinn an uair sin ga ghearradh gu grinn na asnaichean beaga agus gan ròstadh thairis air èibhlean teth gus a bheil an craiceann brisg, fad na h-ùine ga ghlainneachadh le fìon geur a rinn sinn le lus-marsailidh, a' toirt dha blas àlainn, geur ach flùranach, a tha a' gearradh tron fheòil gheireach. Tha e air ithe le diop de chàis ghorm air a dèanamh gu sìmplidh le dìreach uachdar a mheasgachadh leis a' chàis airson fìorghlaine a' bhlais a chumail. Tha e air a sgeadachadh an uair sin le meannt fiadhaich agus flùraichean lus-marsailidh.

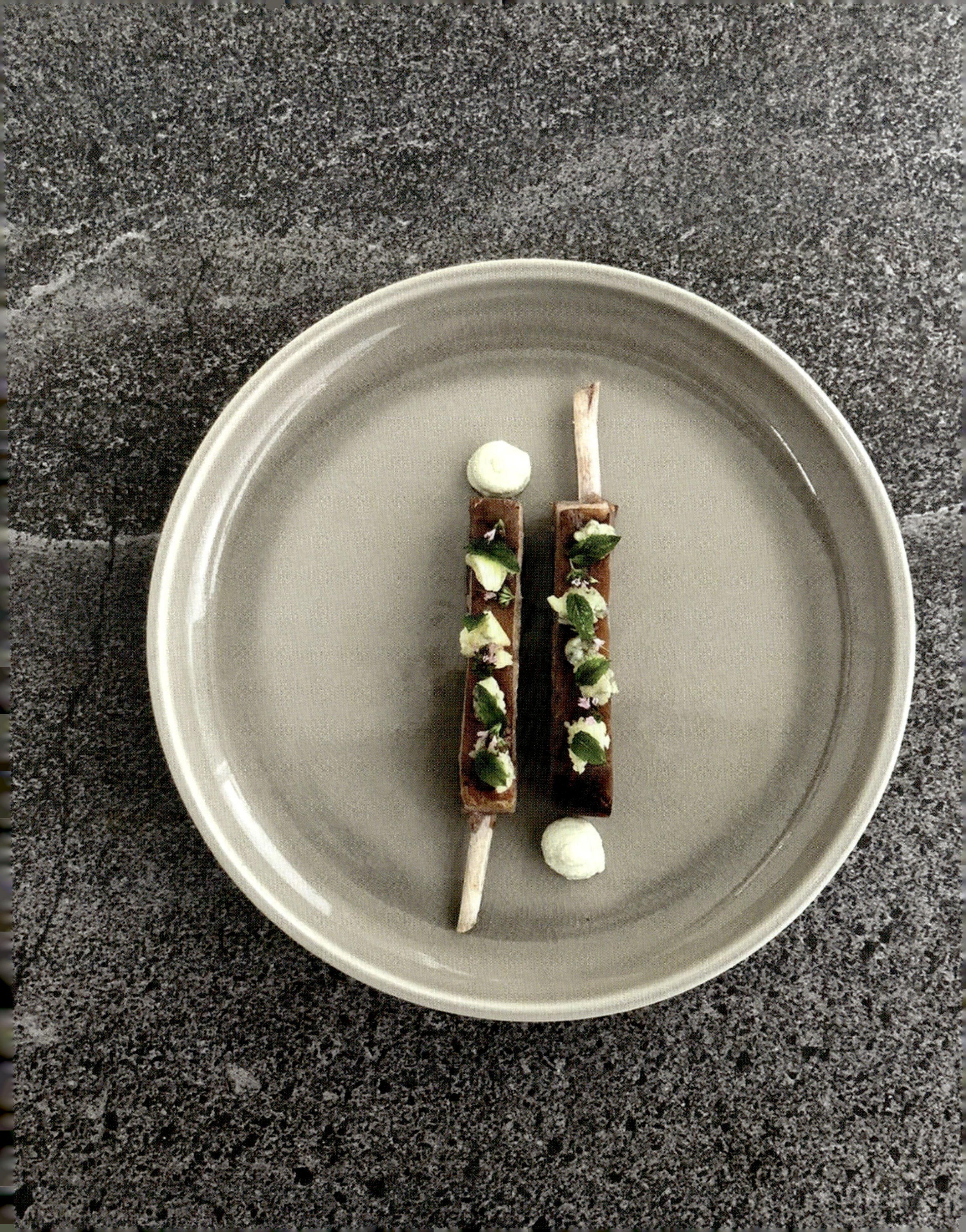

STEAMED MONKFISH LIVER BANNOCK — SMOKED MACKEREL BUTTER — FRESH HERBS

This is an interpretation of a cod liver bannock that is made on the Isle of Barra. Traditionally the bannock is made by soaking a cod liver overnight. The next day the liver would be chopped finely, discarding any stringy bits. It would then be mixed with some fine oatmeal, a little bicarbonate of soda, salt and pepper and finally shaped into little discs, ready to be steamed for 45 minutes. Here I have made the bannock with monkfish liver, barley flour, yeast, butter and sugar and shaped them into smaller bannocks. Then they are steamed for 6-8 minutes. These are delicious served with smoked mackerel butter.

BONNACH ADHA MUICE-LÀMHAICH CEÒ-THEASAICHTE — ÌM LE BLAS RIONNACH SMOCTE — LUSAN ÙRA

'S e tionndadh a tha seo de bhonnach adha truisg a thathar a' dèanamh ann am Barraigh. Gu traidiseanta, bha am bonnach air a dhèanamh le bhith a' fàgail an adha ann an uisge fad oidhche. An ath latha bhiodh an adha air a gearradh na pìosan mìn, a' faighinn cuidhteas pìosan sreangach sam bith. Bhiodh i an uair sin air a measgachadh le aran-coirce mìn, beagan sòda-arain, salainn agus piobar. Bhiodh sin an uair sin air a dhèanamh na bhonnaich bheaga, deiseil gu bhith air an ceò-theasachadh airson 45 mionaid. An seo tha mi air bonnaich nas lugha a dhèanamh le adha muice-làimhich, min-eòrna, beirm, ìm agus siùcar, air an ceò-theasachadh airson 6-8 mionaidean. Tha iad air leth blasta le ìm le blas rionnach smocte.

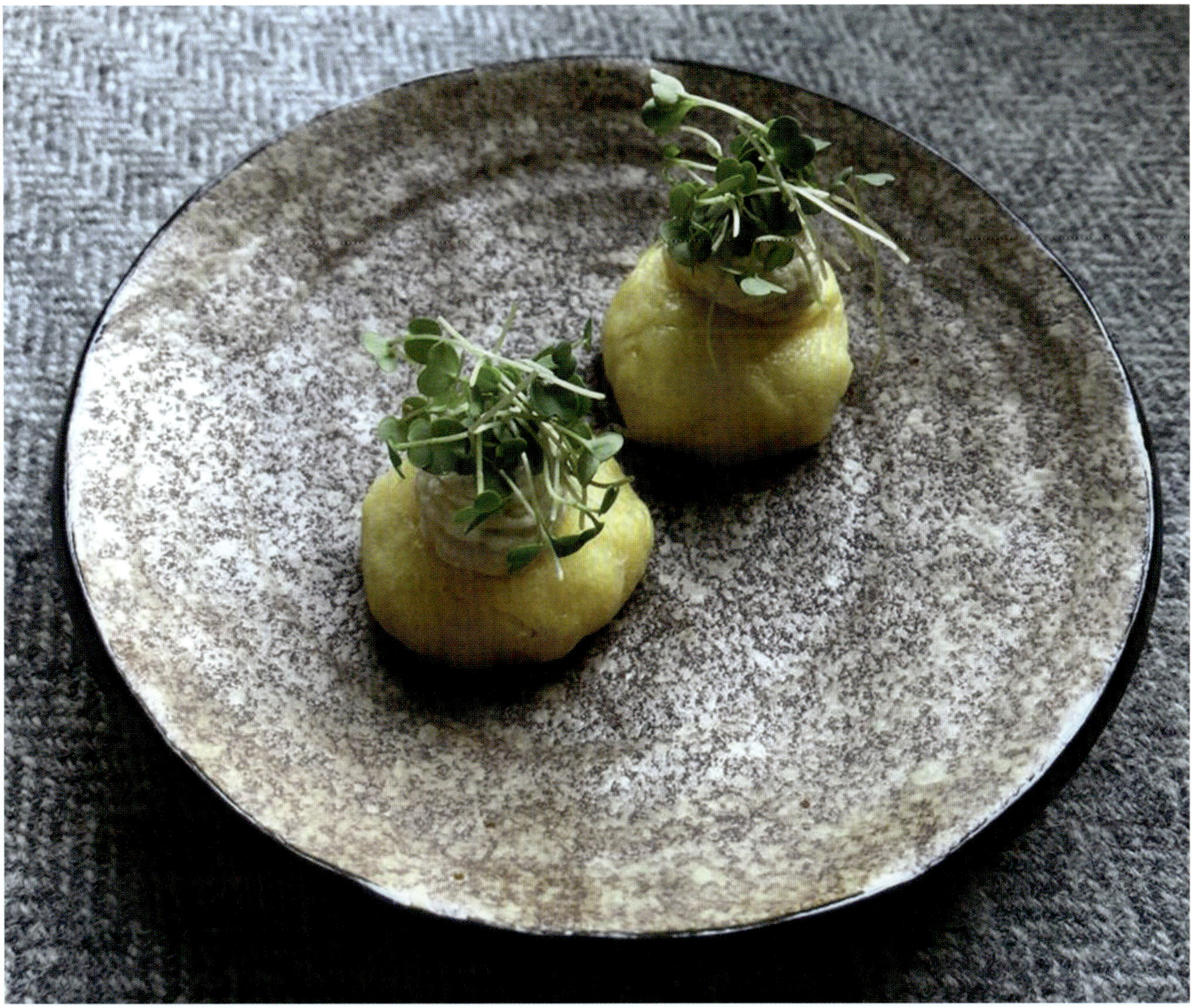

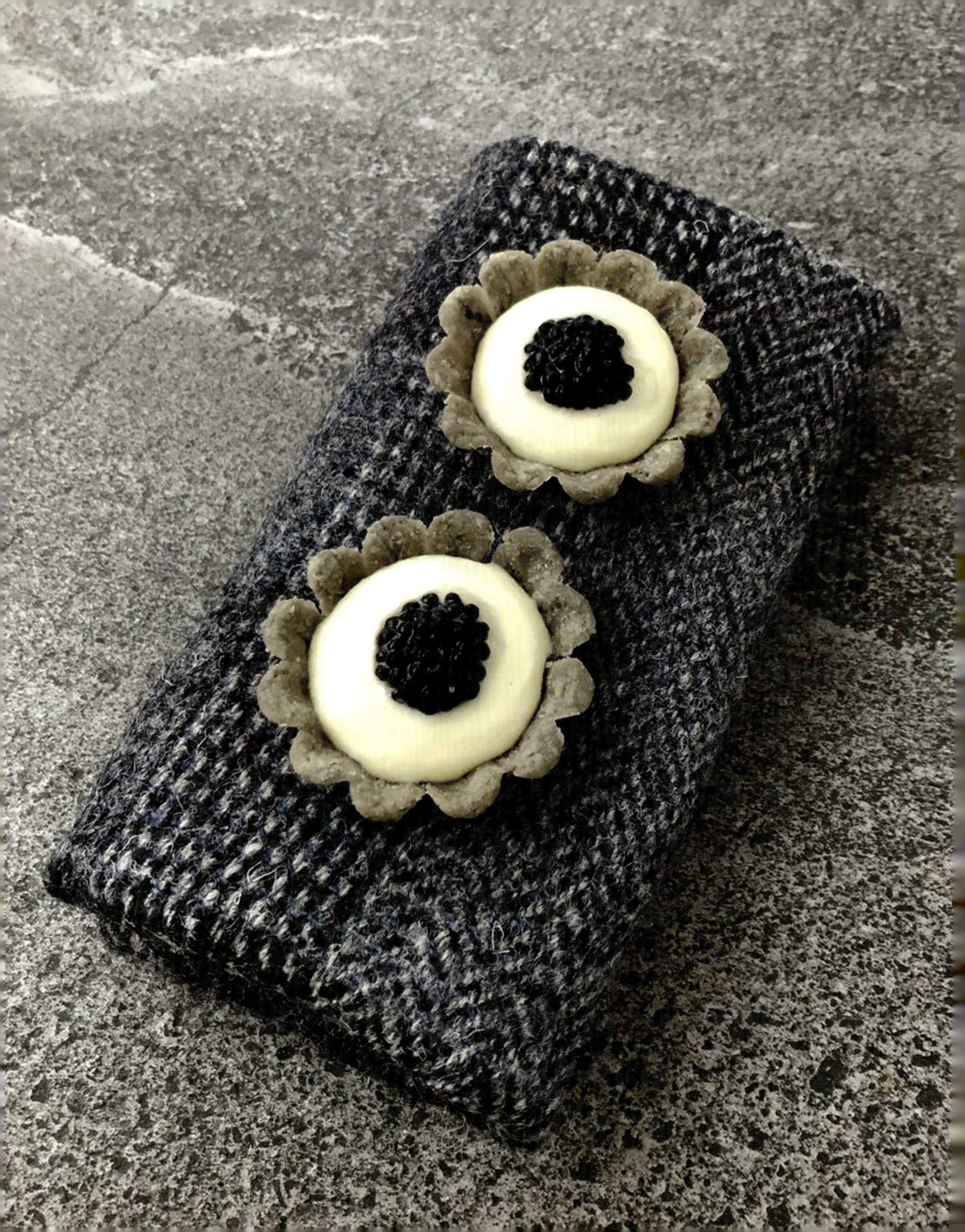

TARTLET OF SALT LING AND POTATO —
SMOKED HERRING ROE — SOUSED ONIONS

These little tartlets are made with a rich pastry that is flavoured with squid ink. The bottom of the tarts are filled with soused onions. The mousse is made by soaking a piece of dried salt ling overnight, draining it and placing it in a pan with equal quantities of small diced potatoes. The ling and potatoes are then covered with milk and cooked gently for 12-15 minutes until the potatoes are tender. The mix is then blitzed with some double cream and passed through a sieve. We then pour the mix into an ISI cream whipper, load it with two gas charges and fill the cases with the aerated mousse before topping with smoked herring roe.

TORTAN BEAGA DE LANGA SHAILLTE AGUS BUNTÀTA —
IUCHAIR SGADAIN SMOCTE — UINNEANAN PICILTE

Tha na tortan beaga seo air an dèanamh le pastraidh beairteach air a bhlasachadh le inc giobarnaich. Tha bonnan nan tortan air an còmhdach le uinnean picilte. Tha am mousse air a dhèanamh le pìos langa shaillt a bha am bogadh ann an uisge fad oidhche. Tha an t-uisge saillt air a thilgeil às agus tha an langa air a cur ann am poit còmhla ris an aon chuideam de bhuntàta air a ghearradh na phìosan beaga. Tha an langa 's am bùntata an uair sin air an còmhdach le bainne agus air am bruich gu socair airson 12-15 mionaid gus a bheil am buntàta bruich. Tha am measgachadh an uair sin air a bhleith le uachdar tiugh na cheann agus air a chur tro shìoltachan. Bhitheamaid an uair sin ga dhòrtadh ann am bualadair uachdar ISI, ga luchdachadh le dà urchair gas agus a' lìonadh nan tortan leis a' mhousse àilichte mus cuireamaid iuchair sgadain smocte air uachdar.

LANGOUSTINE — CHICKEN FAT — PRUNE — ELDERBERRY

The langoustines are gently grilled in rendered chicken fat to 42°C then brushed with an intense oil made with the shells. To cut through the richness of the shellfish a purée of fermented elderberry juice and prunes is piped on each langoustine.

GIOMACH NIRRIBHEACH — GEIR CIRCE — PRÙN — CAORA-DHROMAIN

Tha na giomaich Nirribheach air an còcaireachd gu socair gu 42 puing ann an geir circe leaghte agus an uair sin air an suathadh le dian-ola a rinneadh le na sligean. Airson gearradh tro bheairteas a' mhaoraich, tha purée de shùgh caora-dhromain tòirnichte agus prùnaichean air a chur air gach giomach Nirribheach.

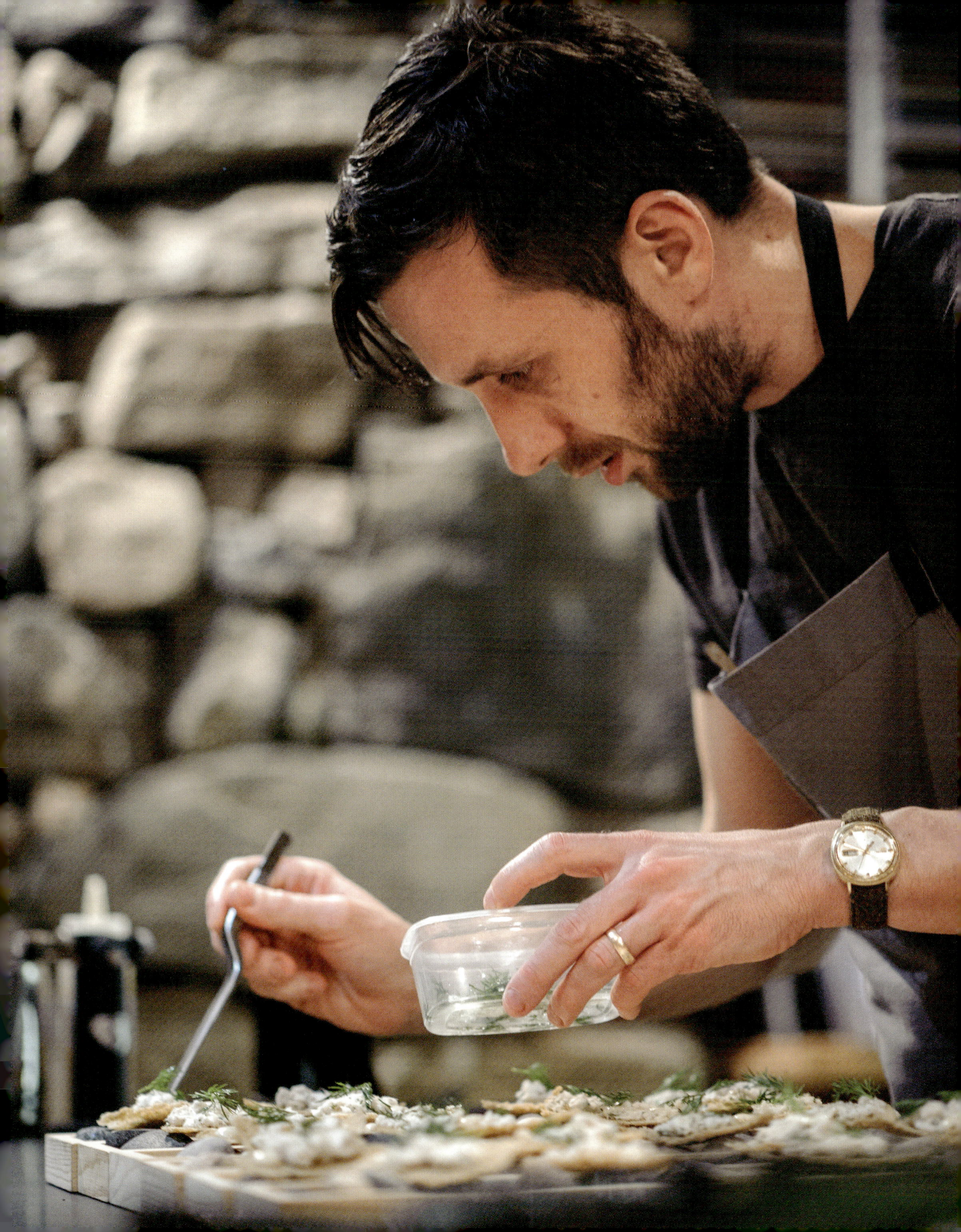

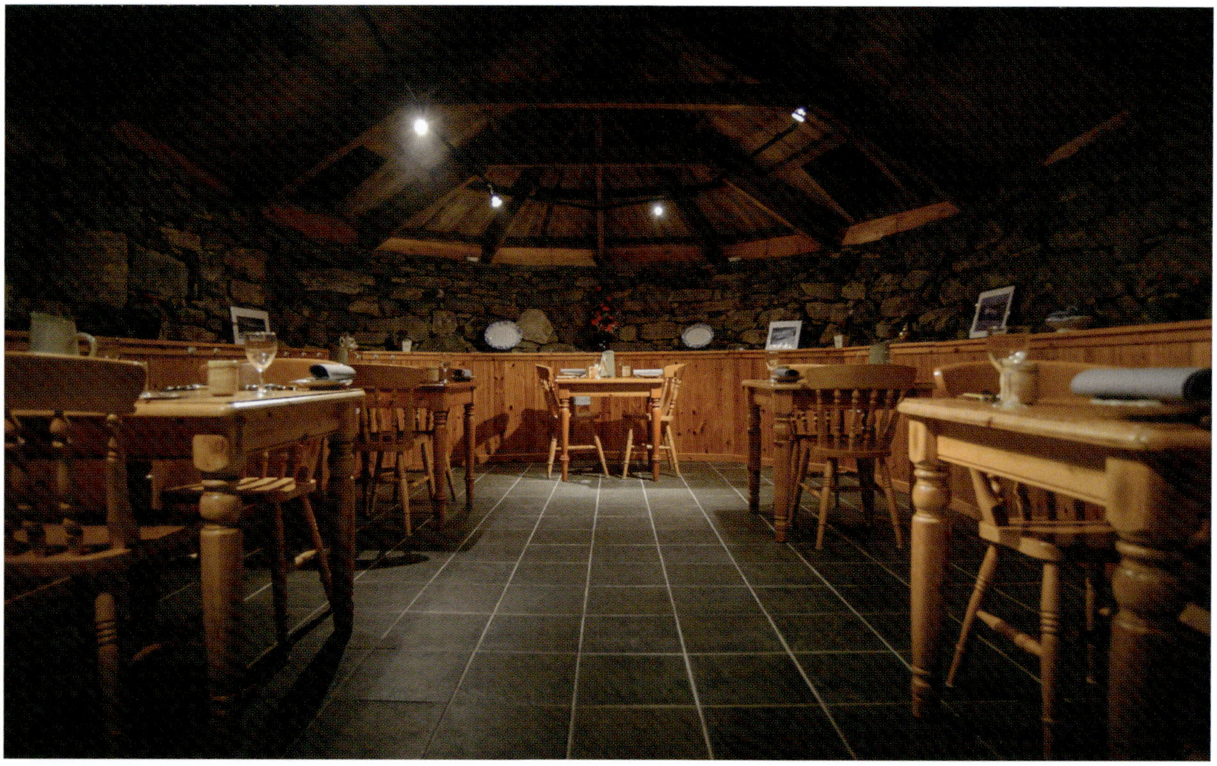

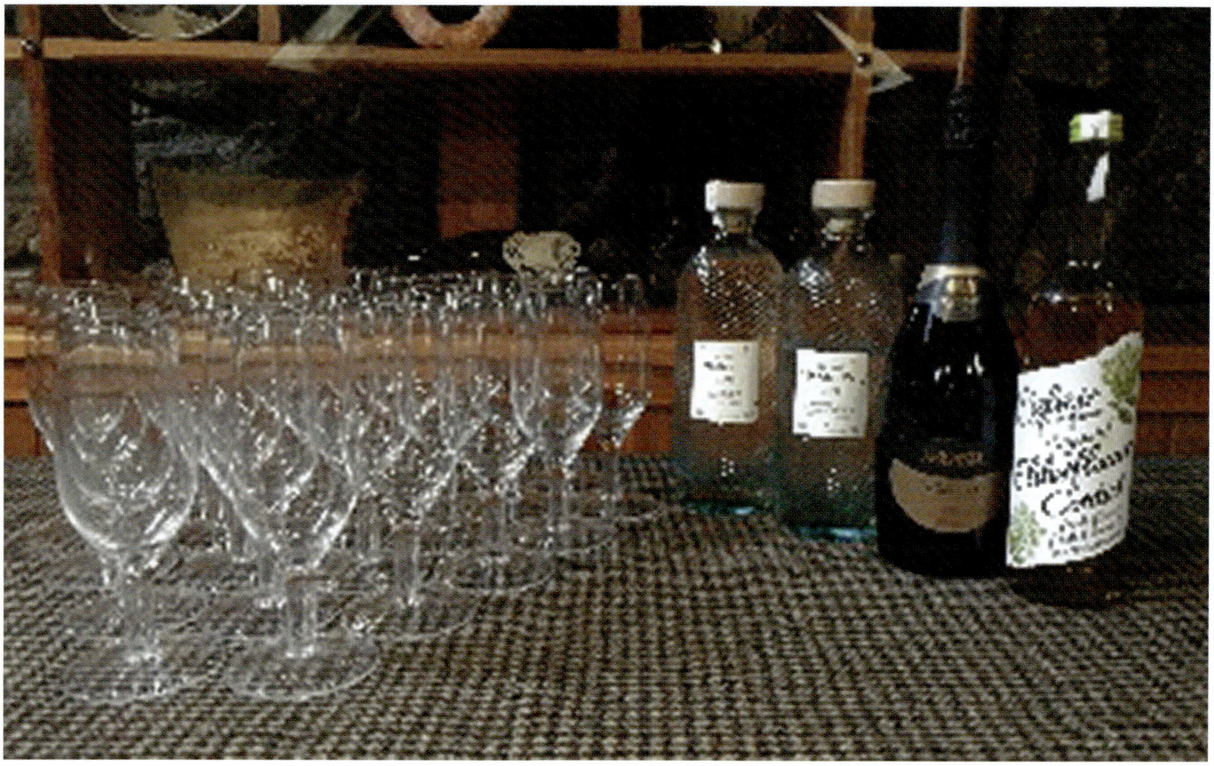

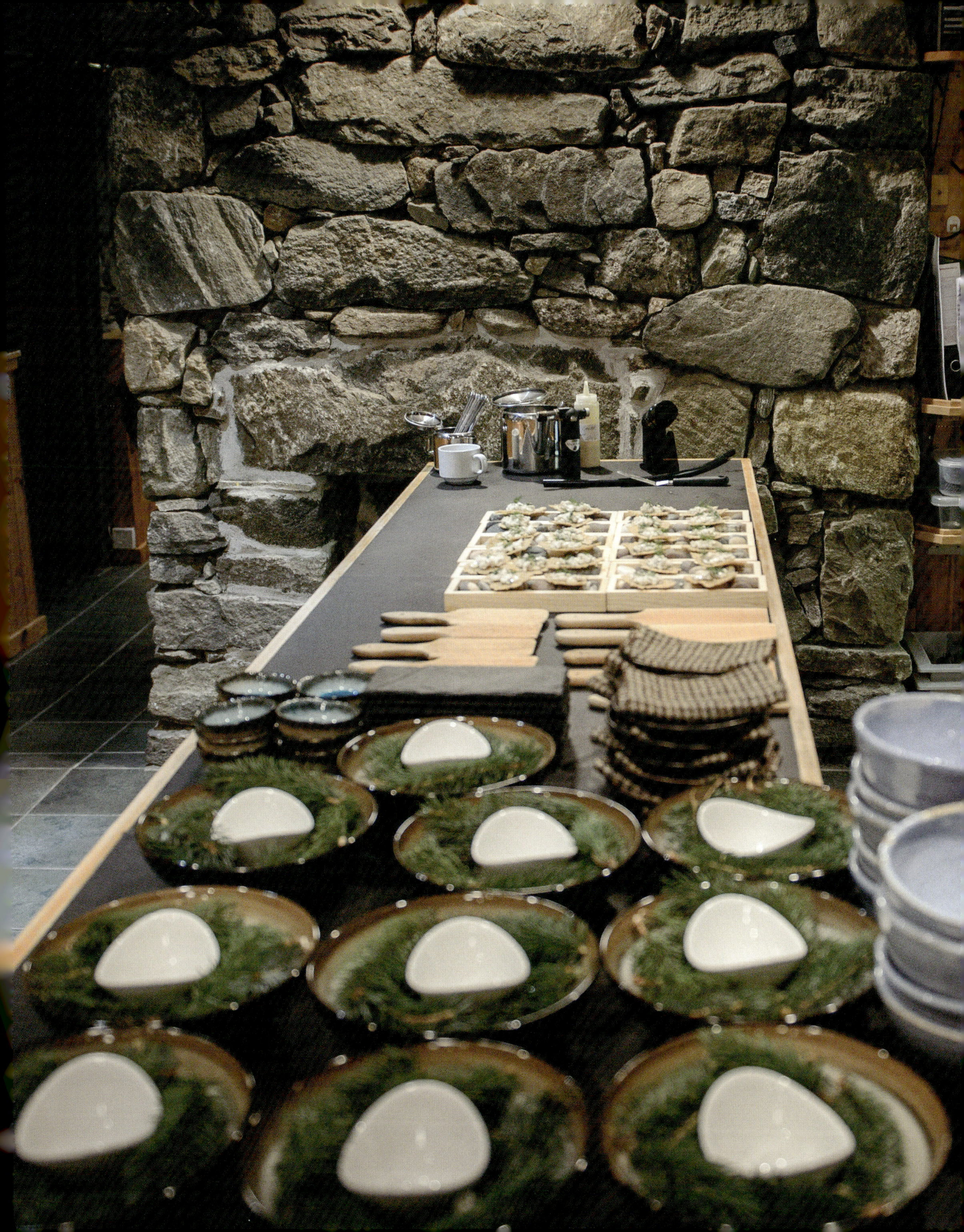

FRIED RABBIT HAGGIS — WHIPPED ROASTED LEEK — HIGHLAND RAPESEED AND PINE OIL

At HAAR we make our own haggis using 300g each of rabbit offal (heart, lungs and liver), boned out rabbit legs, streaky bacon and diced onions. We then mix that with 150g of pinhead oatmeal that has been soaked overnight, 7g of salt and a blend of spices that includes mace, ginger and allspice. The haggis mix is then wrapped in three layers of cling film, in a sausage shape, then tied off at both ends. We steam the haggis for 35 minutes. Once the haggis is cooked we mix it with rabbit shoulders that have been slowly cooked in a pine infused rapeseed oil then flaked off the bone. The haggis is shaped into small balls and coated in flour, egg and pine breadcrumbs and deep fried until golden and crispy. We serve the fried haggis with an emulsion of pine oil and leeks which have been wrapped in foil and roasted on an open fire until sweet and tender.

TAIGEIS COINEANAICH AIR A FHRAIDHIGEADH — CREAMH-GÀRRAIDH RÒSTA BUAILTE — OLA LUS-OLA GÀIDHEALACH AGUS GIUTHAIS

Ann an HAAR tha sinn a' dèanamh ar taigeis fhìn, a' cleachdadh 300g gach fear de anablach coineanaich (cridhe, sgamhain, adha), casan coineanaich gun chnàimh, muicfheòil gheireach, agus uinneanan air an gearradh beag. Tha sinn a' measgachadh sin le 150g min-choirce a tha air a bhith am bogadh fad oidhche, 7g salainn, agus measgachadh de spìosraidhean, nam measg mace, dinnsear agus allspice. Tha am measgachadh seo air a chòmhdach le trì fillidhean de dh'fhilm-còmhdachaidh agus air a thoirt gu cumadh isbein, ceangailte an uair sin aig gach ceann. Bidh sinn a' ceò-theasachadh na taigeis airson 35 mionaid. Aon uair 's gu bheil an taigeis bruich bidh sinn ga mheasgachadh le gualainnean coineanaich a tha air a bhith air an còcaireachd gu socair ann an ola lus-ola Gàidhealach agus giuthais agus an fheòil air a thoirt bhon chnàimh an uair sin. An dèidh sin tha sinn a' dèanamh bàlaichean beaga dhen taigeis, gan còmhdach ann am flùr, ugh agus criomagan arain le blas giuthais. Tha iad an uair sin air am fraidhigeadh gus am bheil iad òrbhuidhe agus brisg. Tha iad air an ithe le co-mheasgachadh de dh'ola giuthais agus creamh-gàrraidh a tha air a bhith air an còmhdach ann am foidhl agus air an ròstadh air teine fosgailte gus a bheil iad maoth agus milis.

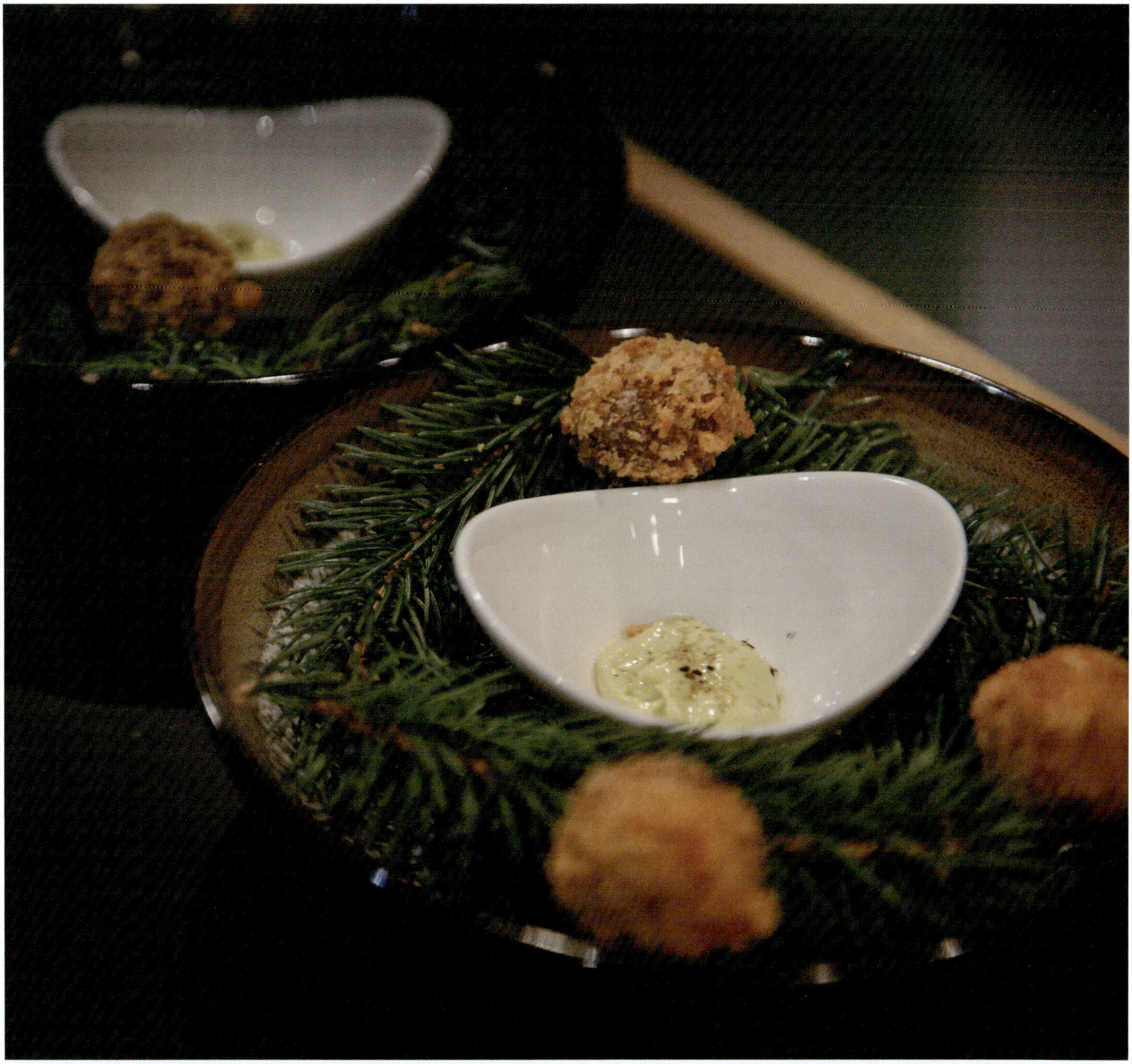

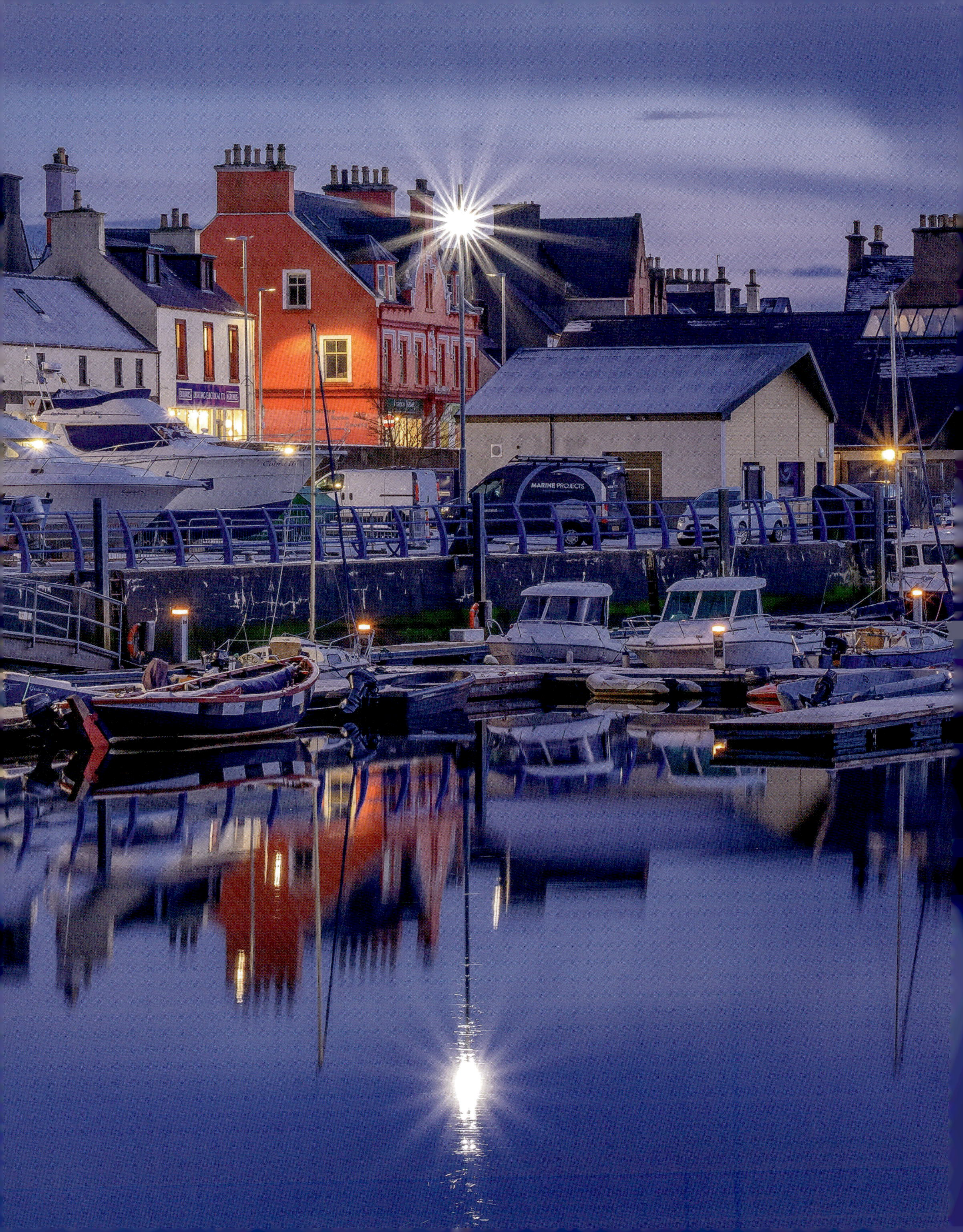
MARINE PROJECTS

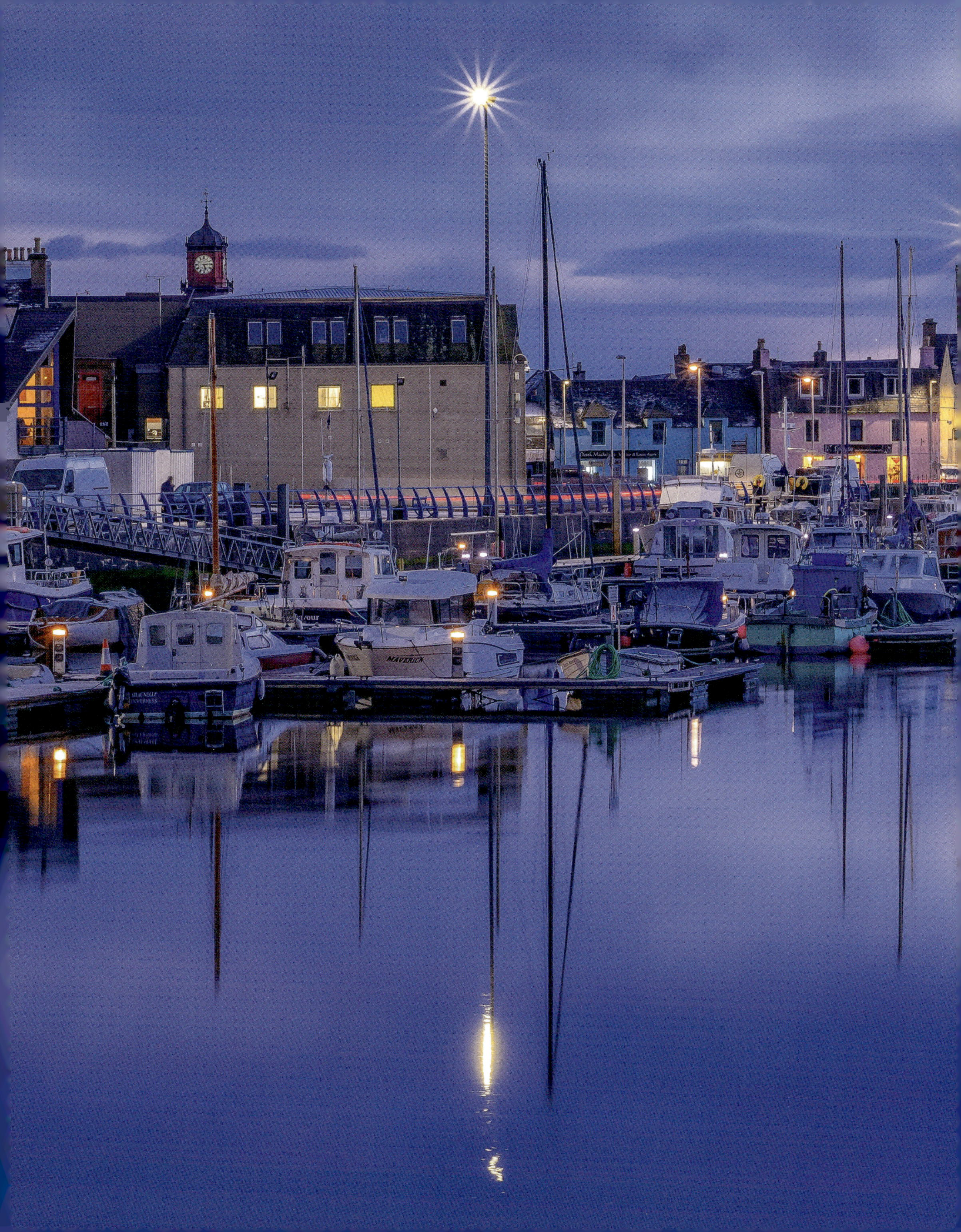
MAVERICK

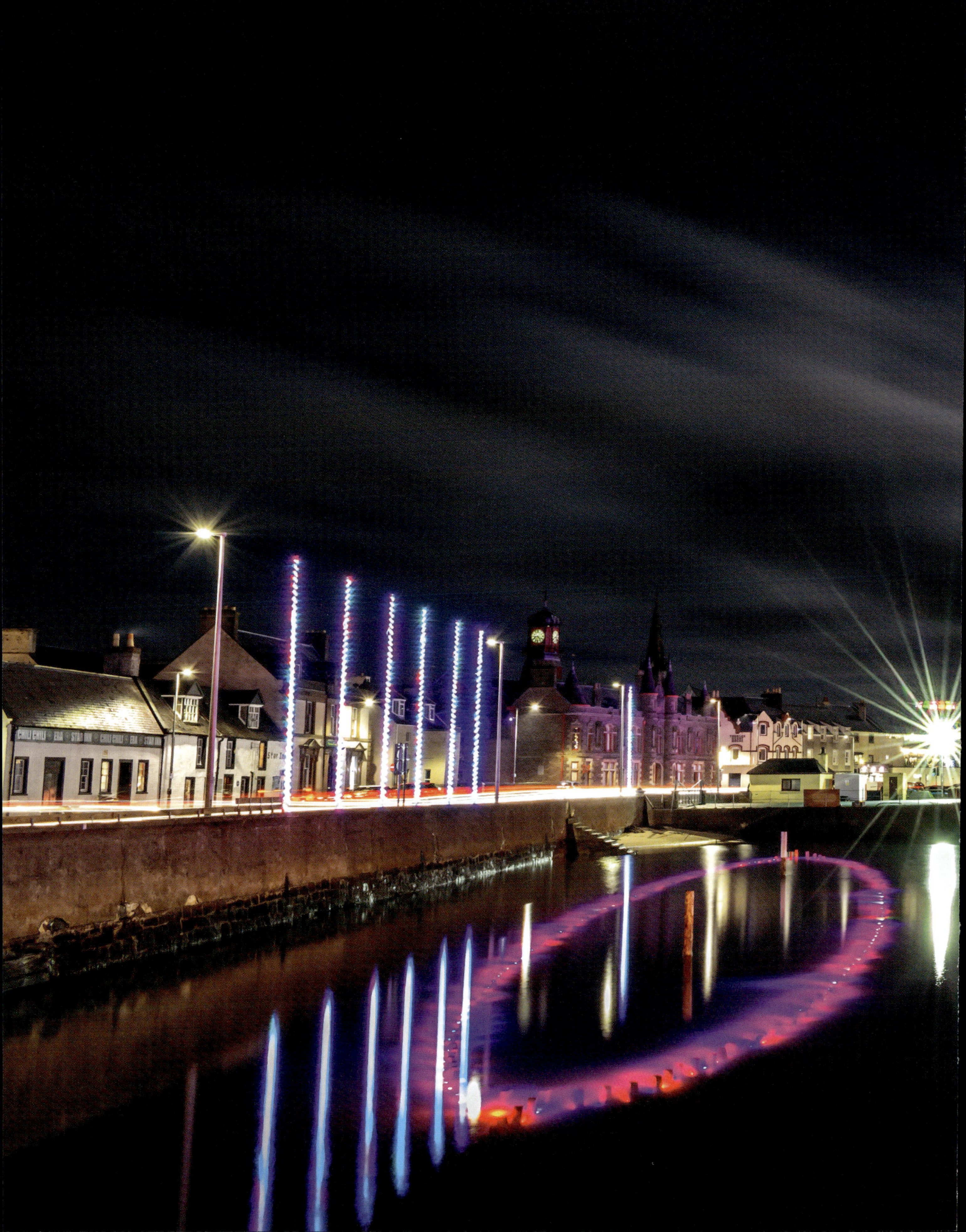

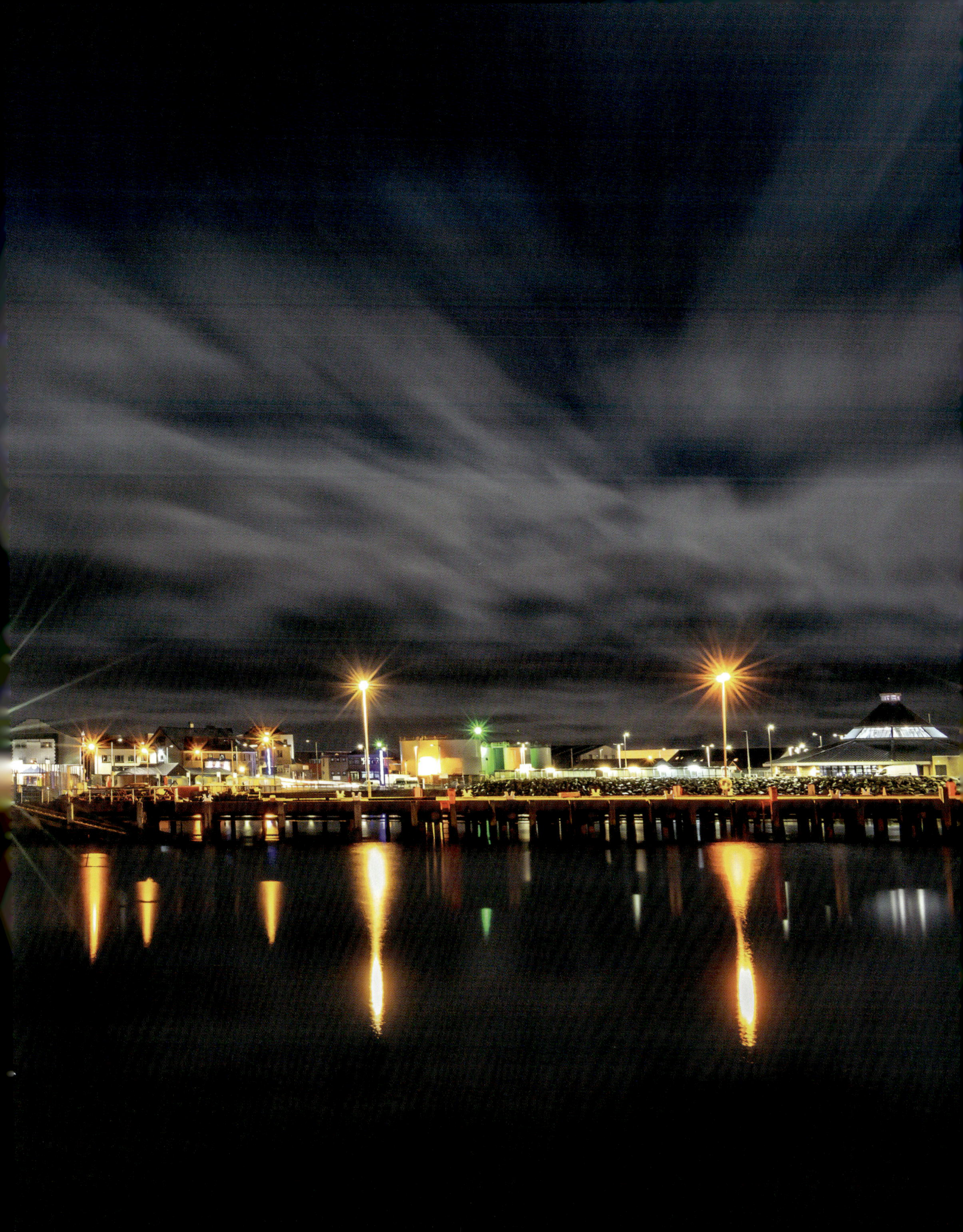

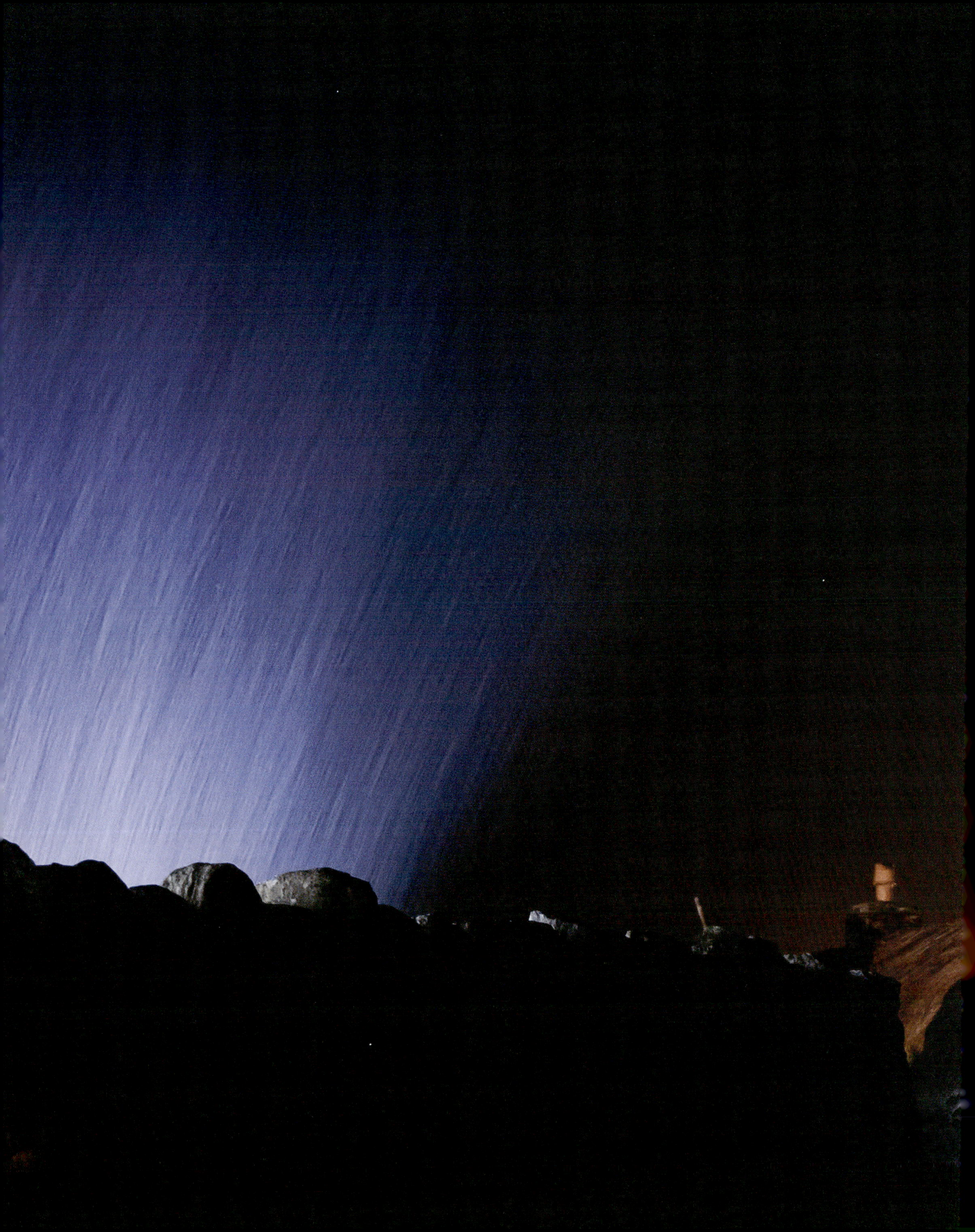

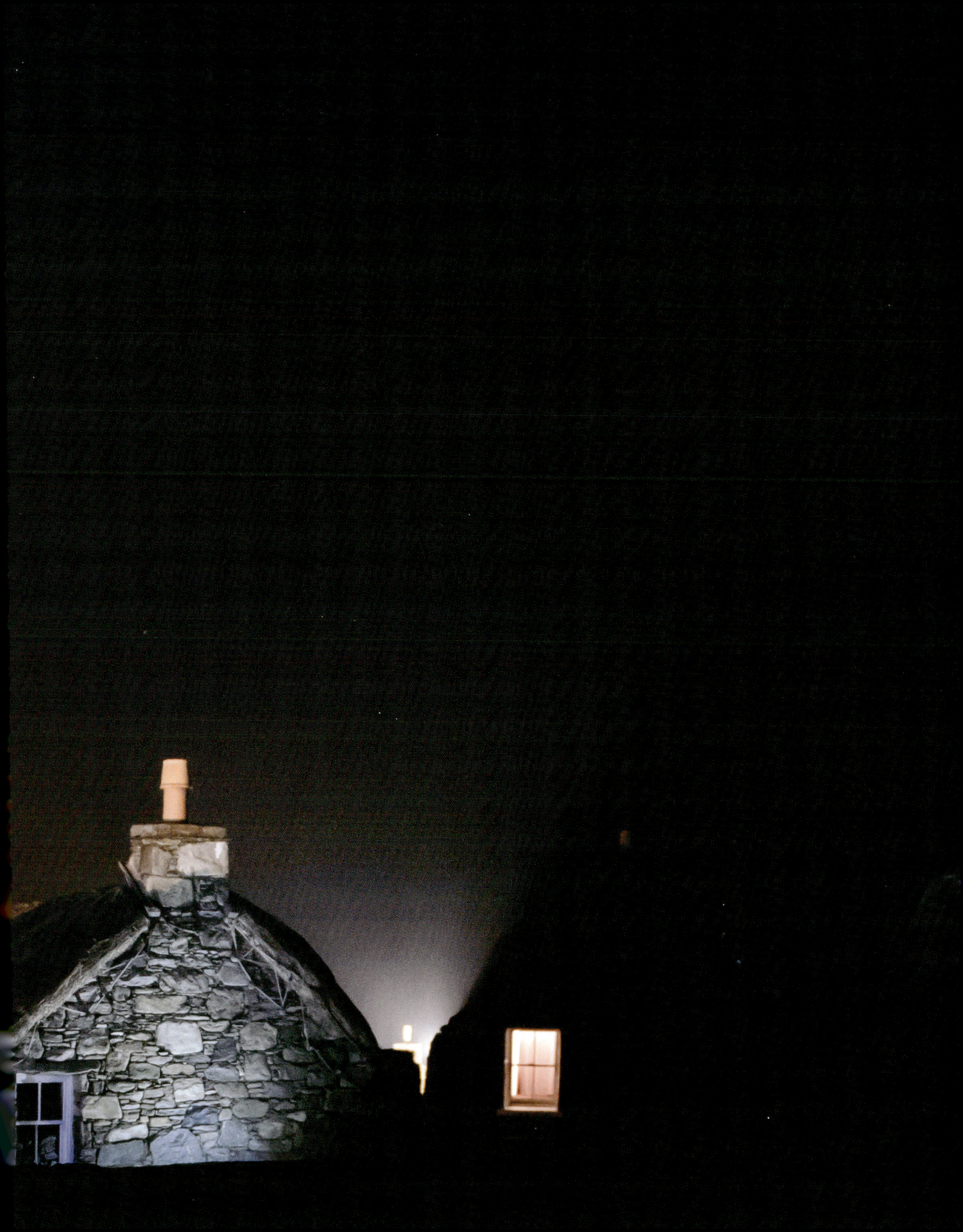

WILD TEAL HAM — DUCK EGG YOLK CURED IN PEAT SMOKE SALT — BEETROOT KETCHUP — LEMON THYME AND DUCK FAT OATCAKE

Duck Ham
6 teal breasts
(4 mallard or 2 farmed duck breasts)
280g Skye sea salt
280g golden caster sugar
1 chopped sprig of rosemary
1 chopped sprig of lemon thyme
4 crushed juniper berries
½ tsp cracked black pepper

Leave the skin and fat on the duck breast to add to the flavour of the final product and place them in a plastic container. Do not use metal. Mix together the dry ingredients and sprinkle over the duck breasts, cover and place in the fridge for three days. After three days of curing remove the duck and rinse well in cold water and dry off using a tea towel. Now wrap the duck in muslin cloth and tie the top with butcher's string, creating a loop to enable the ham to be hung. Hang the duck in a cool, airy place for a week to dry. A dry cellar or a shed would be ideal.

Beetroot Ketchup
1 tsp Highland rapeseed oil
1 onion, thinly sliced
1 large croft beetroot
230ml water
2 tbsp barley vinegar
(white or malt vinegar will suffice)
1 tbsp brown sugar
½ tsp Worcestershire sauce
⅛ tsp salt

Cook the onion gently in the rapeseed oil until it browns, around eight minutes. Grate the beetroot, then add to the onions. Add the water and continue cooking until the beets are soft and no liquid remains, about 12 minutes. Stir in vinegar, sugar, Worcestershire sauce and salt. Season with a little white pepper and transfer to a blender and blitz until smooth. Let it cool completely. Refrigerate and keep for up to two weeks.

Lemon Thyme and Duck Fat Oatcake
75g medium oatmeal
75g fine oatmeal
20g plain flour
1 tbsp finely chopped lemon thyme
1 tbsp melted duck fat
pinch of salt bicarbonate of soda
hot water to mix

Mix the oatmeal and flour with the salt, thyme and bicarbonate of soda. Pour in the melted fat and mix together. Add enough hot water to mix to a stiff paste. Working quickly before the paste cools, roll the mixture out on a floured board and cut into small rectangles. Either cook on a hot griddle or in an oven set at 180°C until the edges just begin to brown.

Cured Duck Egg Yolk
250g Skye sea salt
250g golden caster sugar
6 duck eggs
a little chopped lemon thyme

Pulse salt, sugar and thyme in food processor until evenly mixed and slightly ground. Add a layer of salt to the bottom of a plastic or glass tub. Using a whole, in-shell egg, make six evenly spaced indentations in the salt bed by pressing the bottom of an egg gently into the salt mixture. Transfer yolks to the indentations in the salt bed. Gently pour the remaining salt mixture evenly over the yolks. Wrap in cling film and refrigerate until the yolks are firm and dry throughout. This takes one week. Remove the yolks from the salt mixture and rinse gently in water. Pat the yolks dry with paper towels and transfer to a dehydrator or on to a tray in an oven that is set at 93°C. Bake for 30-40 minutes until the exteriors of the yolks are dry to touch. Wrap at intervals in muslin cloth, tying each interval with butcher's string until you have a chain of yolks (think onions tied in tights!). Place some beetroot ketchup on the oatcake, add some evenly chopped duck ham, grate over a generous amount of cured egg yolk using a microplane grater and finish with a few lemon thyme leaves.

AIR DRIED MUTTON — CROWDIE — OATCAKE — ROSEHIP

The mutton leg is simply cured with salt, sugar, some aromatics, then air dried for six months. After six months the leg is then lightly smoked and thinly sliced like an Italian prosciutto. We balance out the smoky, fatty, mutton flavour with an oatcake, freshly made *gruth* (crowdie cheese) and dried rosehip. The rosehip adds a wonderful acidic tang to this delicious mouthful.

FRIED HERRING — OATMEAL — SOUSED HERRING — SALAD CREAM — APPLE — DILL

Fried herring in oatmeal was, and still is, a staple in the Hebridean diet. This little bite incorporates a small piece of fresh herring, traditionally fried in oatmeal. We accompany this with an aerated sweet and sour herring salad cream, pickled herring, fresh apple and dill.

MUILTFHEÒIL AIR A THIORMACHADH — GRUTH — ARAN-COIRCE — MUCAGAN

Tha ceathramh muiltfheòil air a chiùradh le salainn, siùcar, spìosraidhean is eile, agus air a thiormachadh san èadhar airson sia mìosan. An dèidh sia mìosan tha an ceathramh air a smocadh gu h-aotrom agus air a ghearradh gu tana mar prosciutto Eadailteach. Tha sinn a' cothromachadh blas saillt, geireach a' mhuiltfheòil le aran-coirce, gruth ùr agus mucagan tioram. Tha na mucagan a' toirt blas mìorbhaileach, caran searbh, chun ghrèim bhlasta seo.

SGADAN AIR A FHRAIDHIGEADH — MIN-CHOIRCE — SGADAN PICILTE — UACHDAR SAILEAD — UBHAL — DILE

Bha sgadan le min-choirce air a fhraidhigeadh na bhiadh àbhaisteach aig eileanaich agus tha fhathast. Anns a' ghrèim seo tha pìos beag sgadain air a fhraidhigeadh gu traidiseanta le min-choirce, agus còmhla ris tha uachdar sailead àilichte le blas sgadain, sgadan picilte, ubhal ùr agus dile.

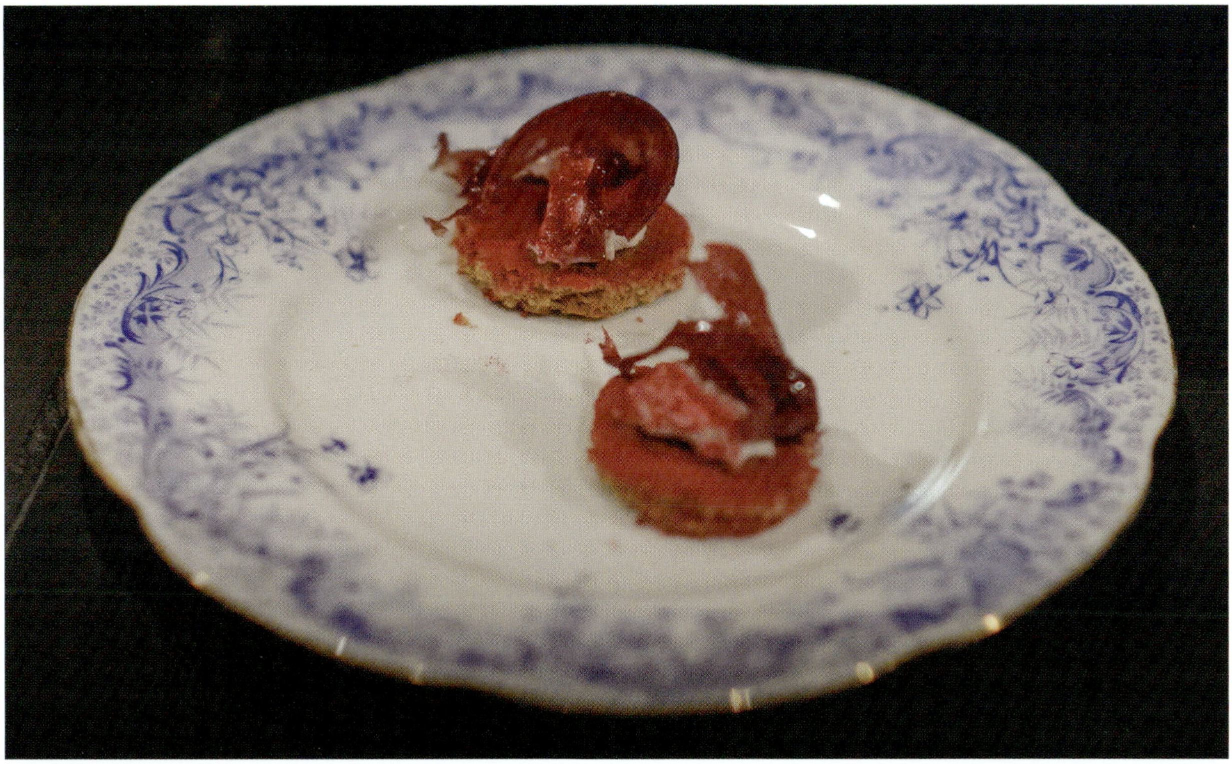

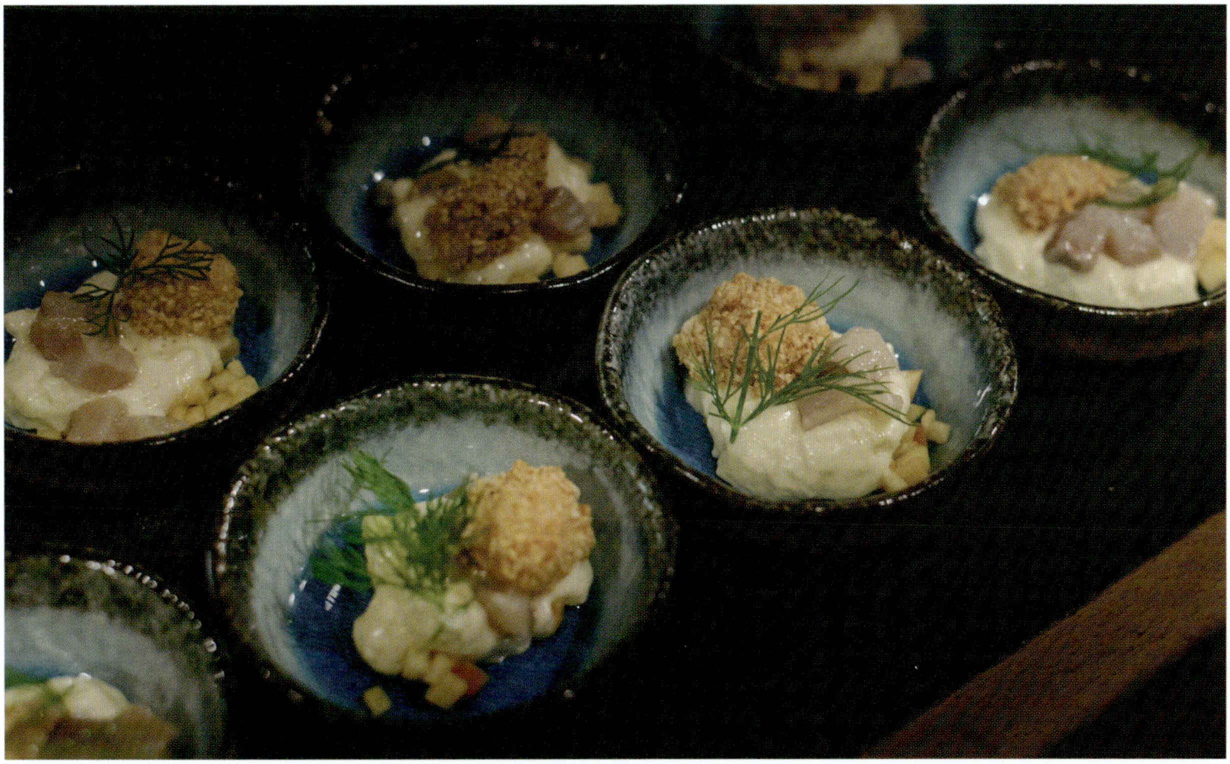

CEANN CROPAIG — COD'S HEAD — SMOKED SCALLOP ROE — DILL

Ceann cropaig is a dish that is widely eaten throughout the Hebrides. At HAAR we have refined this humble dish and made it more accessible to our diners by transforming it into these delicate little crackers. To make the crackers, a traditional *ceann cropaig* needs to be made using the pristine white livers from either freshly caught haddock, cod or ling. The livers are then de-veined, mixed with oatmeal and a little salt. The liver mix is then stuffed inside a cod's head, wrapped in cheesecloth and brought to the boil in a pan of cold water and sliced onions. The *sabhs*, the liquid that the heads were cooked in, would traditionally be drunk as an accompaniment to the *ceann cropaig*, along with pieces of boiled fish. This *sabhs* is used to make a porridge that is cooked for 40 minutes, then blended to a purée with a little barley vinegar, buttermilk and the *ceann cropaig*. We then spread the mix out thinly on dehydrator trays and dehydrate at 65°C for 12 hours.

The dried crackers are then dressed with the meat from the cod's head, an emulsion of smoked scallop roe and Highland rapeseed oil, and finally finished off with a dusting of dried dill powder.

CEANN CROPAIG — CEANN TRUISG — IUCHAIR CREACHAIN SMOCTE — DILE

Bha fèill mhòr air ceann cropaig am measg muinntir nan eilean. Aig HAAR tha sinn air am biadh iriosal seo a ghrinneachadh agus a dhèanamh nas fhasa dha ar n-aoighean le thionndadh na bhriosgaidean beaga mìn. Airson nam briosgaidean a dhèanamh feumar an toiseach ceann cropaig traidiseanta a dhèanamh, a' cleachdadh adhaichean glan, geal bho adag, trosg no langa ùr. Tha na cuislean air an toirt às na h-adhaichean agus tha iad an uair sin air am measgachadh le min-choirce agus beagan salainn. Tha seo air a bhruthadh a-steach do cheann truisg, air a shuaineadh ann an anart-càise agus air a thoirt chun na goil ann am poit uisge fuar agus slisean uinnein. Bhiodh an sabhs, an leann anns am biodh na cinn air am bruich, air òl còmhla ris a' cheann cropaig agus pìosan èisg bruich. Tha an sabhs air a chleachdadh airson lit a dhèanamh, a tha air a bhruich airson 40 mionaid agus an uair sin air a bhleith gu bhith na phurée le beagan fion geur eòrna, blàthach agus an ceann cropaig. Bidh sinn an uair sin a' sgaoileadh sin gu tana air trèidhichean ann an sgreubhadair agus gan sgreubhadh aig 65 puingean airson 12 uair a thìde.

Tha na briosgaidean tioram air an còmhdach leis an iasg à ceann an truisg, co-mheasgachadh de dh'ola lus-ola Gàidhealach agus iuchair creachain smocte agus, mu dheireadh, tha iad air an sgeadachadh le craiteachan de dh'fhùdar dile tioram.

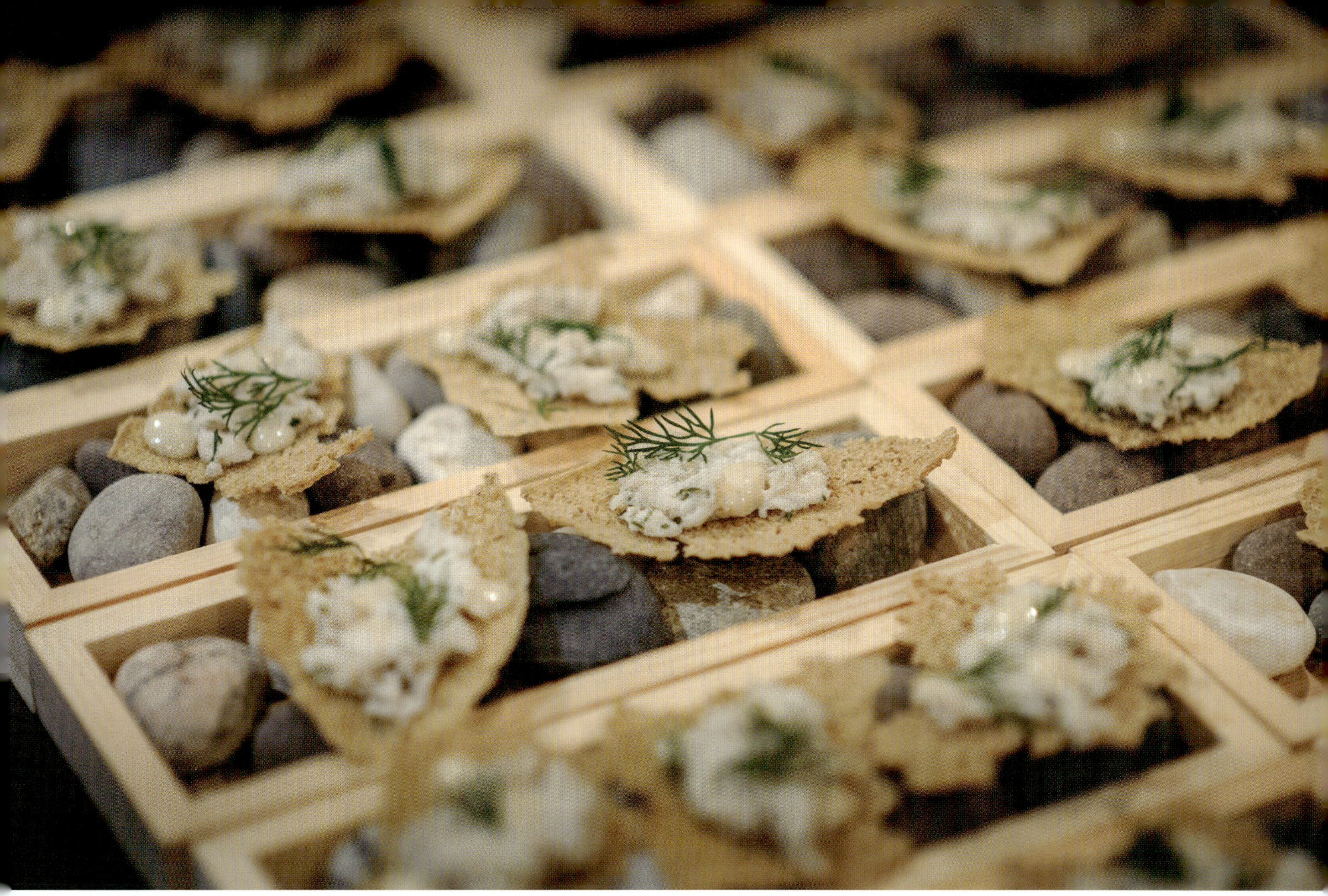

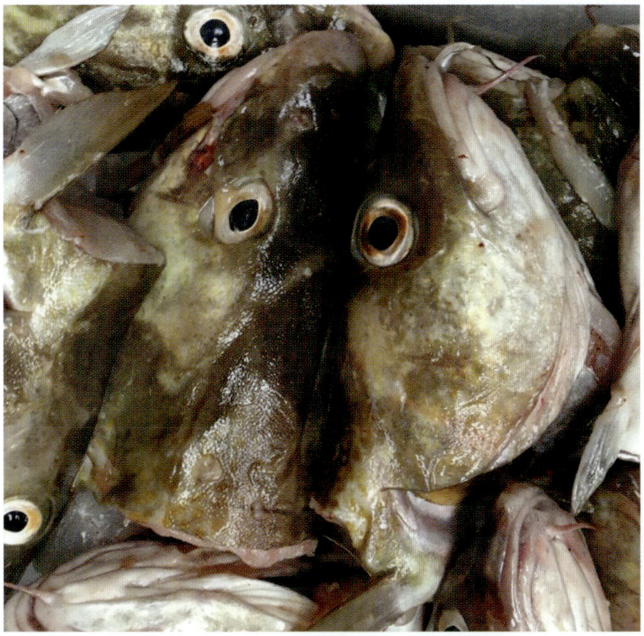

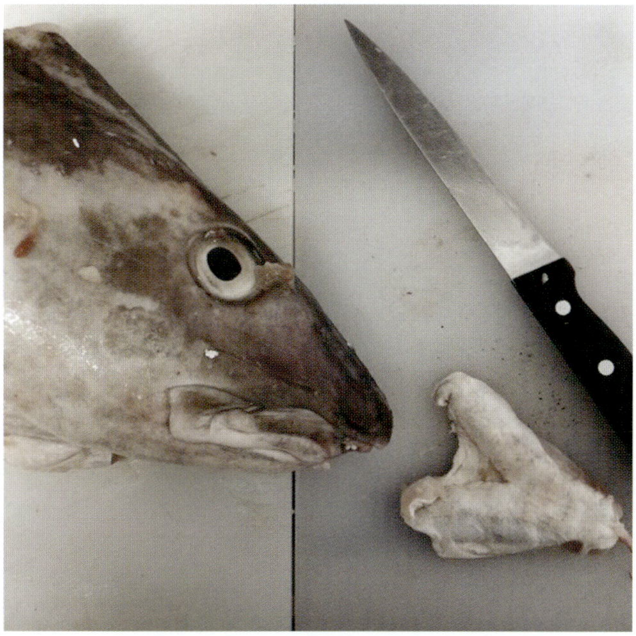

DEER NECK PIE — PICKLED ONION — FRESH CHEESE — DRIED MOORBERRY

These little pies are made using a Scotch pie hot water pastry with rendered pork fat. The necks are minced together with 20% pork fat. Venison is such a lean meat that it needs the additional fat to keep the pies moist. We season the meat with salt, black pepper, nutmeg and some reduced game gravy before filling the pies and baking until they are golden brown.

Before sending out to our guests, each pie is topped with a little fresh cheese, finely diced pickled onion and some tart dried moorberries.

PÀIDH AMHAICH FÈIDH — UINNEAN PICILTE — CÀIS ÙR — CORRA-MHITHEAGAN TIORAM

Tha na pàidhean beaga seo air an dèanamh a' cleachdadh an aon sheòrsa pastraidh uisge teth ri pàidh Albannach, le geir muicfheòil air a leaghadh. Tha na h-amhaichean air am mion-ghearradh còmhla ri 20% geir muicfheòil. Tha sitheann fèidh cho tioram 's gu feum e geir a bharrachd airson a chumail tais. Tha sinn a' blasachadh na feòla le salainn, piobar dubh, cnò-mheannt agus sùgh lùghdaichte sithinn, mus tèid na pàidhean a lìonadh agus an cur dhan àbhainn gu bheil iad òrbhuidhe donn.

Mus tèid iad air beulaibh aoighean tha beagan càis ùr, uinnean picilte air a ghèarradh mìn agus corra-mhitheagan tioram is geur air a chur air gach pàidh.

STORNOWAY BLACK PUDDING — POTATO SCONE — LAST YEAR'S GOOSEBERRY AND ELDERFLOWER JAM

This little snack proved to be a real favourite with our guests at the original HAAR pop-ups. It's simply made by warming up some Stornoway black pudding until it becomes pliable. Then it's rolled out thinly between two sheets of greaseproof paper and placed in the fridge to set. We then make potato scones using potatoes, cultured butter, flour and dried elderflower. Both the black pudding and scones are cut into small bite-size rounds and warmed up under the grill before being topped off with the previous year's gooseberry and elderflower jam.

MARAG DHUBH STEÒRNABHAIGH — SGONA BUNTÀTA — SILIDH GRÒSAID AGUS DROMAIN NA BLIADHNA 'N-UIRIDH

Bha ar n-aoidhean air leth measail air a' ghrèim bheag bhlasta seo aig a' chiad taighean-bidh sealach aig HAAR. Tha e air a dhèanamh gu sìmplidh le pìosan de mharag dhubh Steòrnabhaigh air a theasachadh gus am fàs iad bog. An uair sin tha iad air an roiligeadh eadar dà dhuilleag pàipear lìth-dhìonach agus air an cur dhan fhuaradair gus am fàs iad cruaidh. Tha sinn a' dèanamh sgonaichean a' cleachdadh buntàta, ìm geur, flùr agus flùraichean dromain air an tiormachadh. Tha na sgonaichean agus na pìosan maraig dhuibh air an gearradh ann an cumaidhean beaga cruinn agus air an teasachadh fon ghrìosaich mus eil iad air an crìochnachadh le silidh gròsaid agus dromain na bliadhna 'n-uiridh.

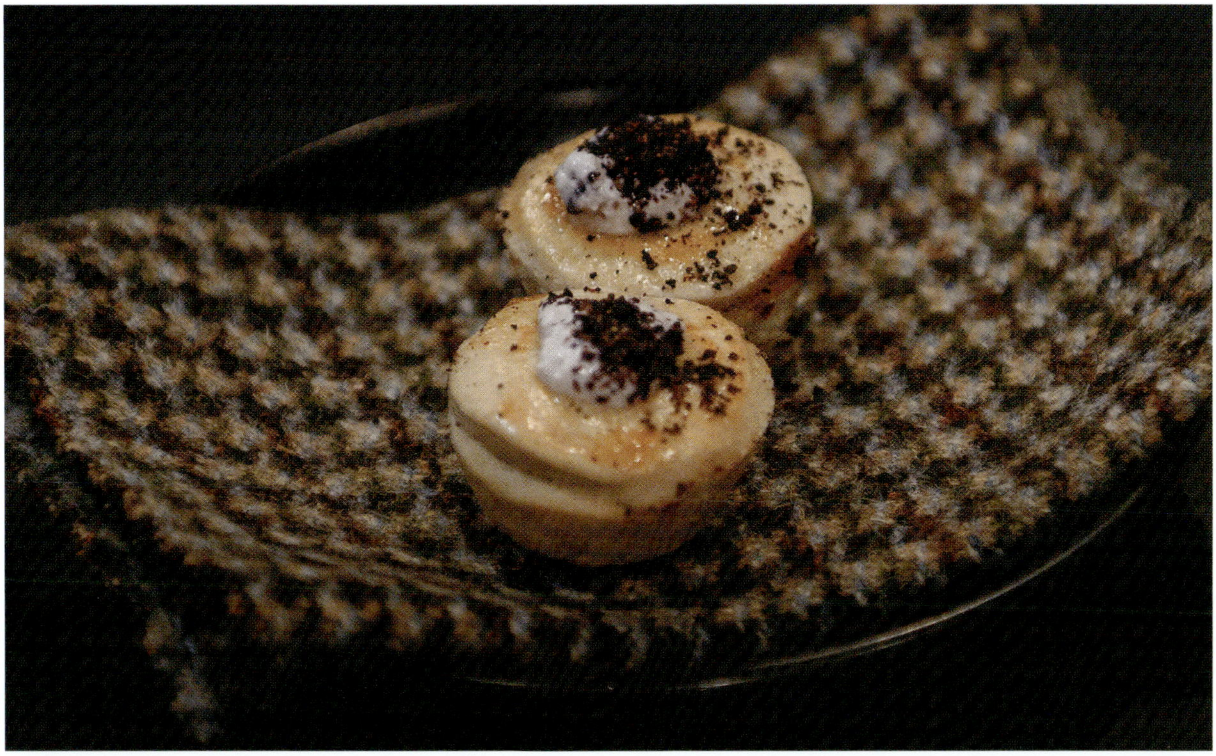

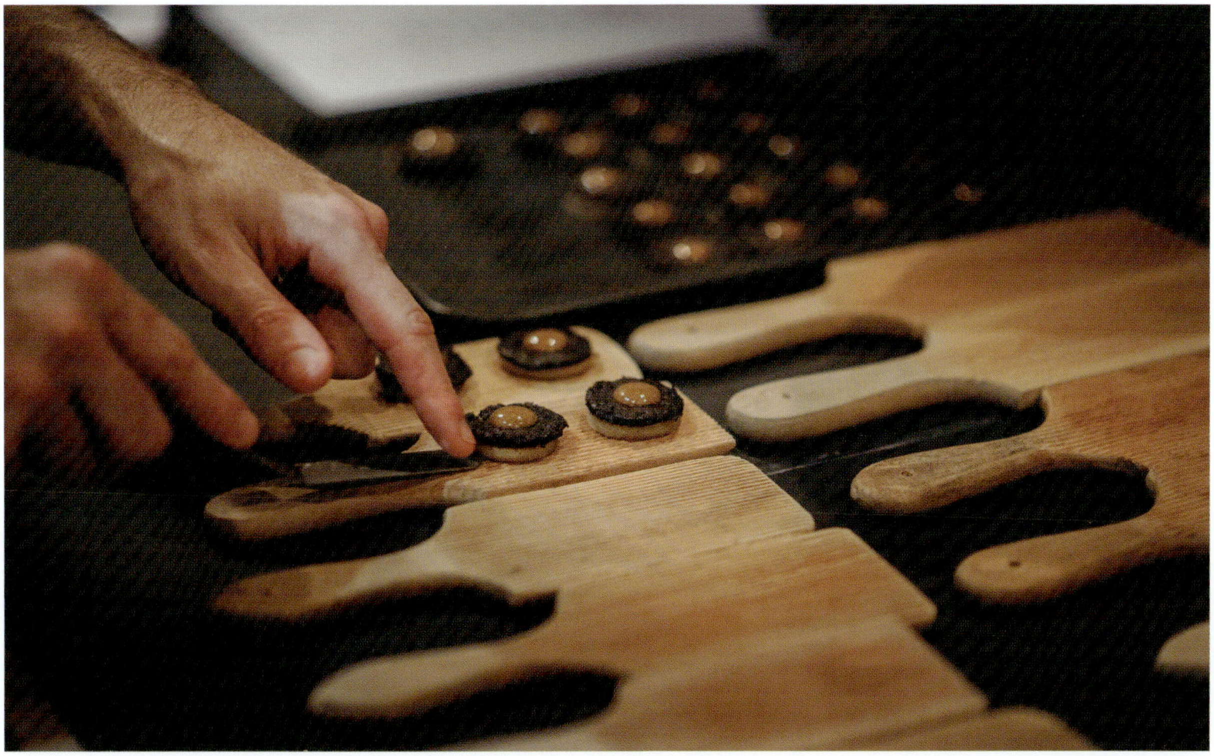

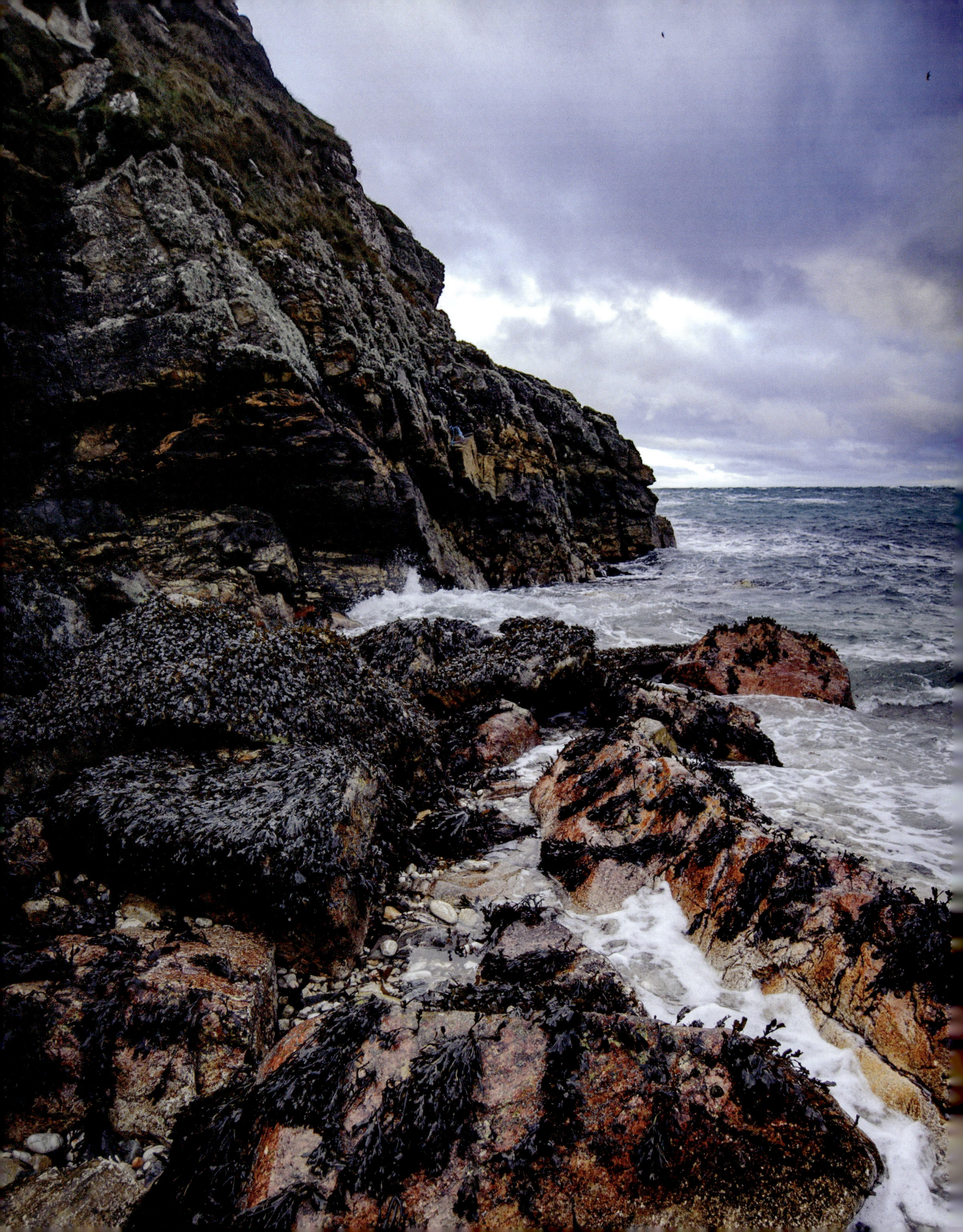

Rocks and Shore
Creagan is Cladach

PINE SMOKED MUSSELS — LEEKS BRAISED IN MUSSEL JUICE — BABY ANYA POTATOES — CULTURED CREAM — DILL OIL

Smoked Mussels
2kg Loch Leurbost mussels
knob of butter
white of one leek
60ml barley wine
(white wine will suffice)

Finely chop the white of one leek and sweat gently in the butter until soft. Add the mussels and wine, cover and cook for 2-3 minutes, shaking the pan after one minute. Strain the liquid through a sieve into a jug and set aside. Shell the mussels, discarding any that did not open and place evenly on a tray or plate. Place the tray of mussels in a tabletop smoker filled with fresh dried pine needles. Gently smoke to your desired taste. Cover the mussels and set aside in the fridge until needed.

Braised Leeks
2 whole leeks
reserved mussel cooking juices
fresh dill
knob of butter
salt

Finely chop the leeks to small brunoise and sweat gently in the butter, add the dill and cooking juices, cover with a lid and gently braise for 10-12 minutes until the leeks are very soft but retaining their colour.

Anya Potatoes
250g croft grown baby anya potatoes

Cook the potatoes in plenty of boiling water until tender. Dress with some dill oil.

Cultured Cream
250ml double cream
2 tbsp whey or buttermilk

Add your cream and whey to a sterilised glass jar, leaving an inch at the top. Mix to combine. Attach the lid and leave it in a warm place (22-25°C) to culture for 12-24 hours, until it has thickened. The cream will thicken from the top down, so use a spoon to make sure that most of the jar has cultured rather than simply the top layer. Transfer to the fridge, where it will keep for up to three weeks.

Dill Oil
25g fresh dill
50g rapeseed oil

Pick the dill leaves, removing the stalks. Blitz together in thermomix set at 90°C for six minutes then place in a metal bowl set over ice. Press through some muslin cloth and store in a small plastic squeezy bottle.

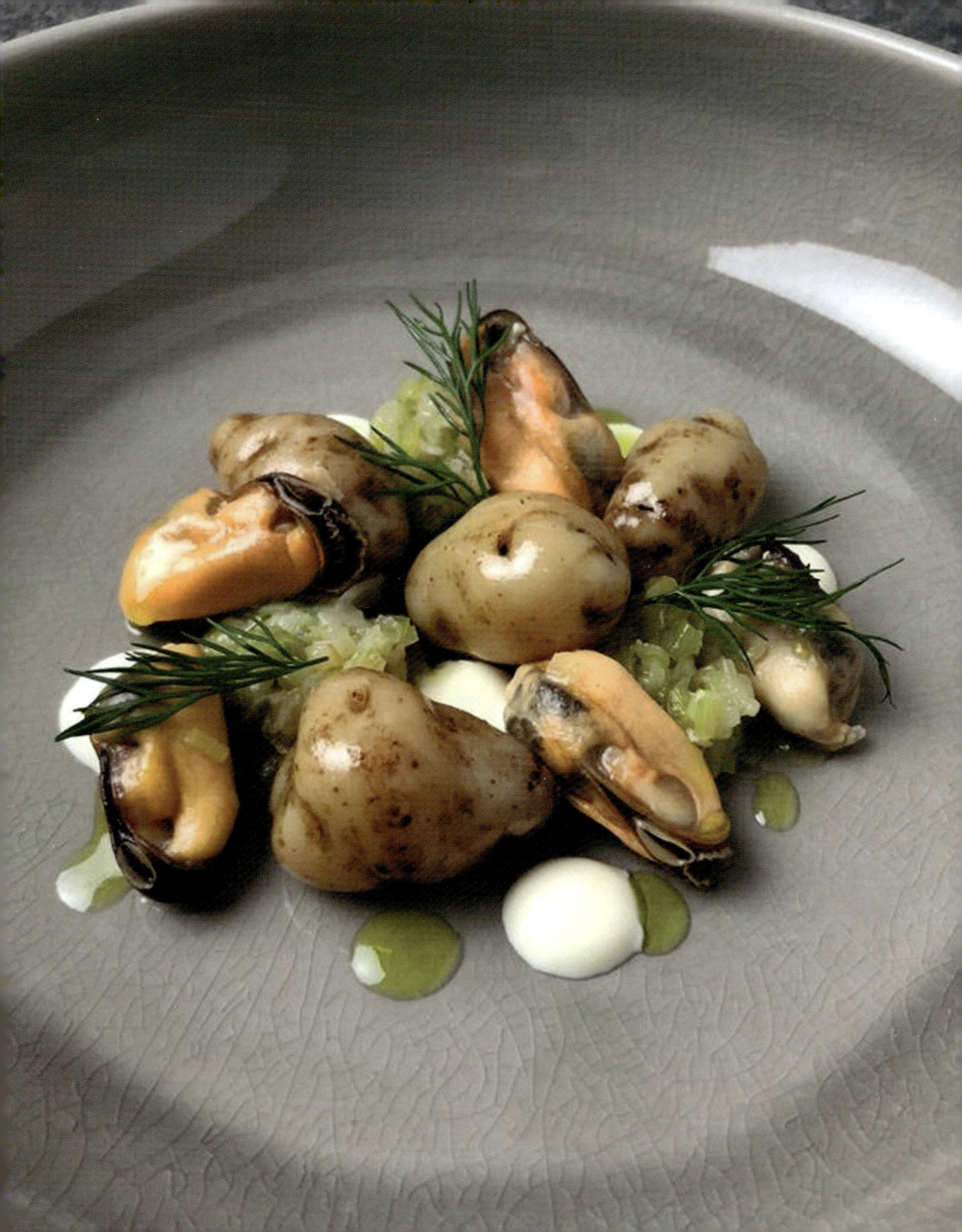

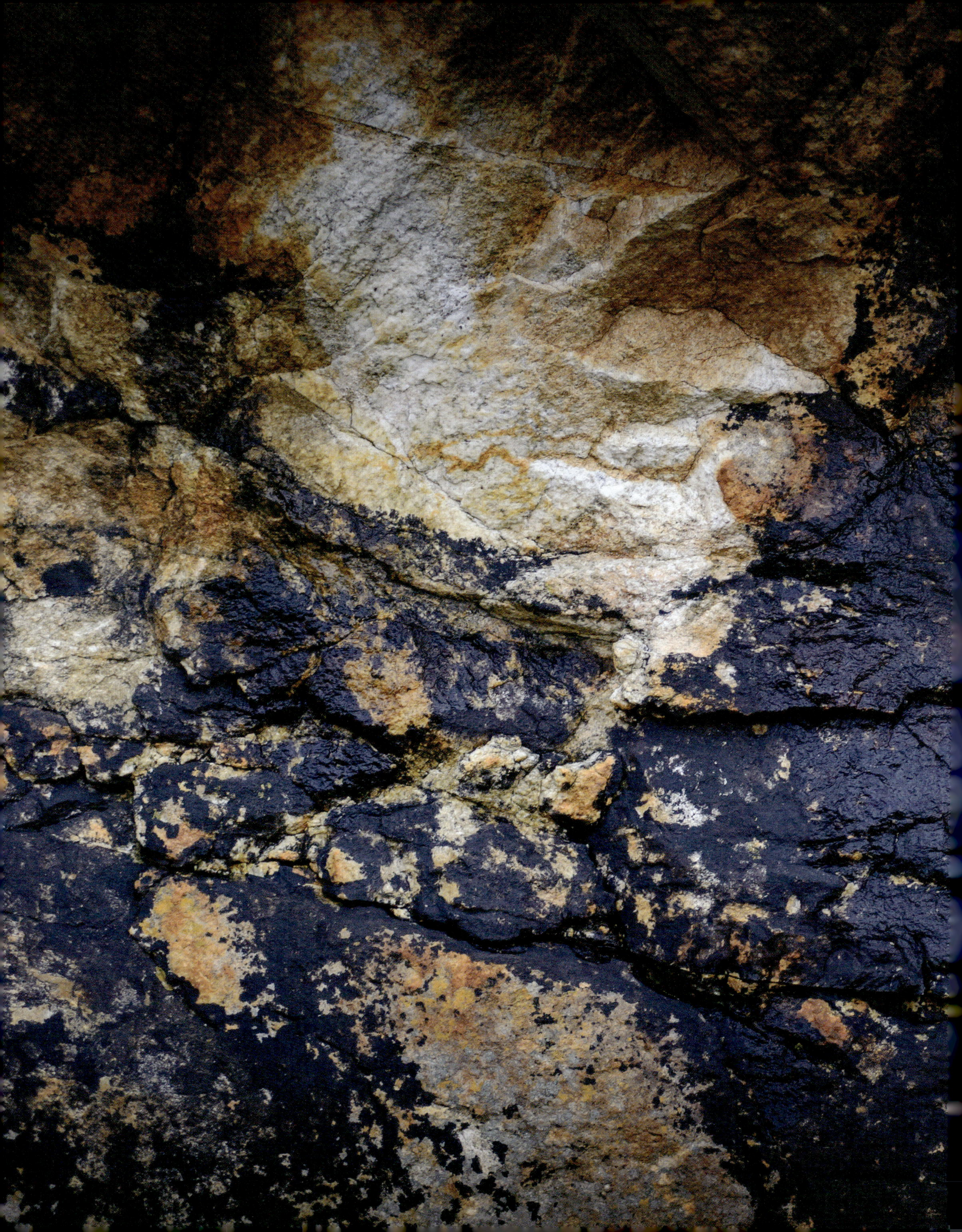

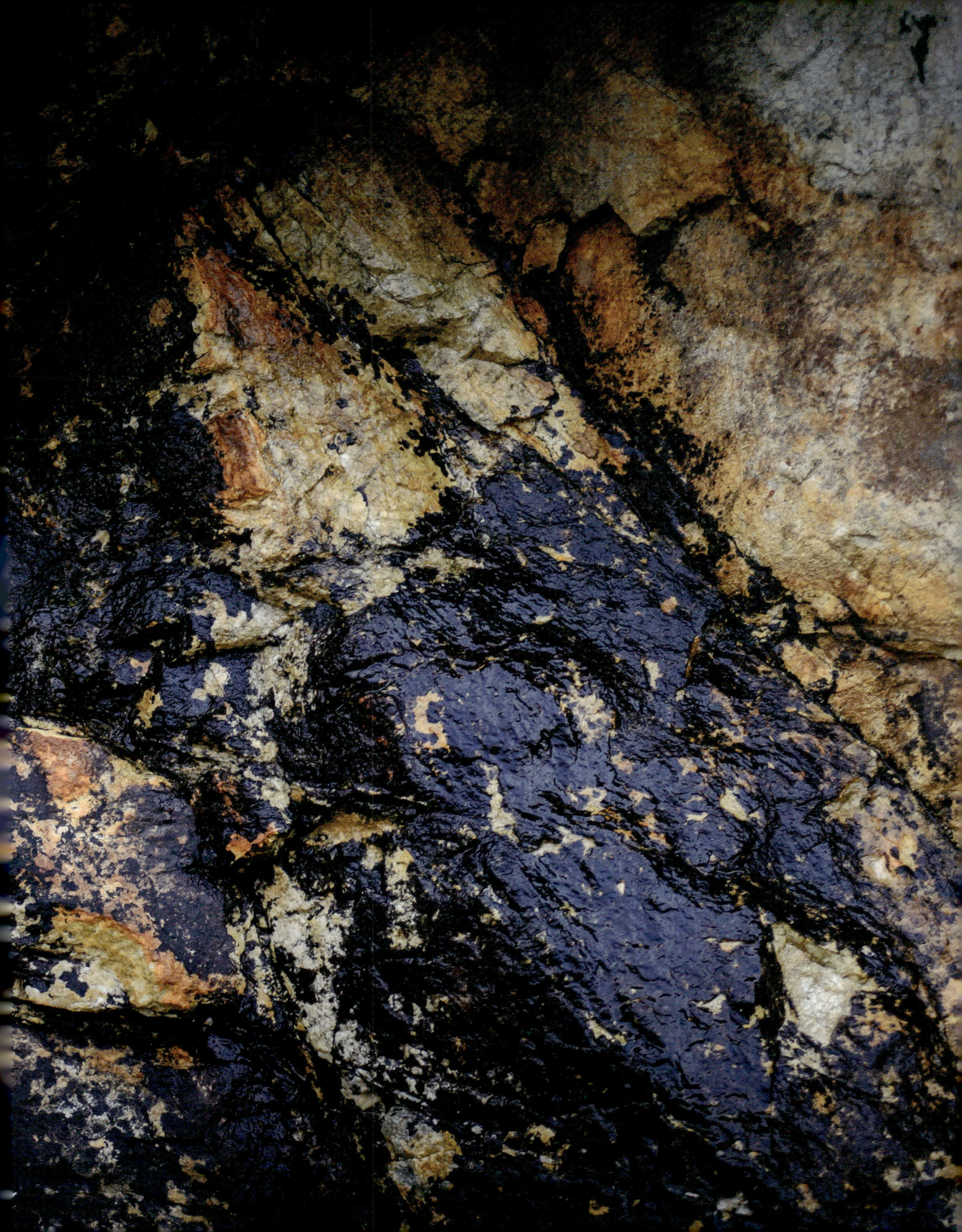

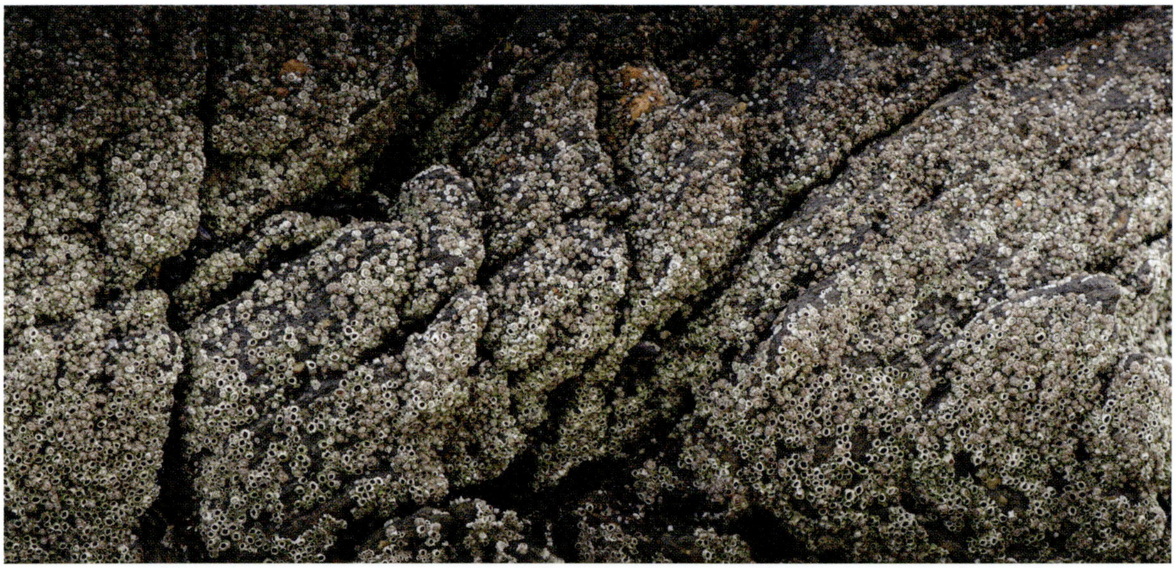
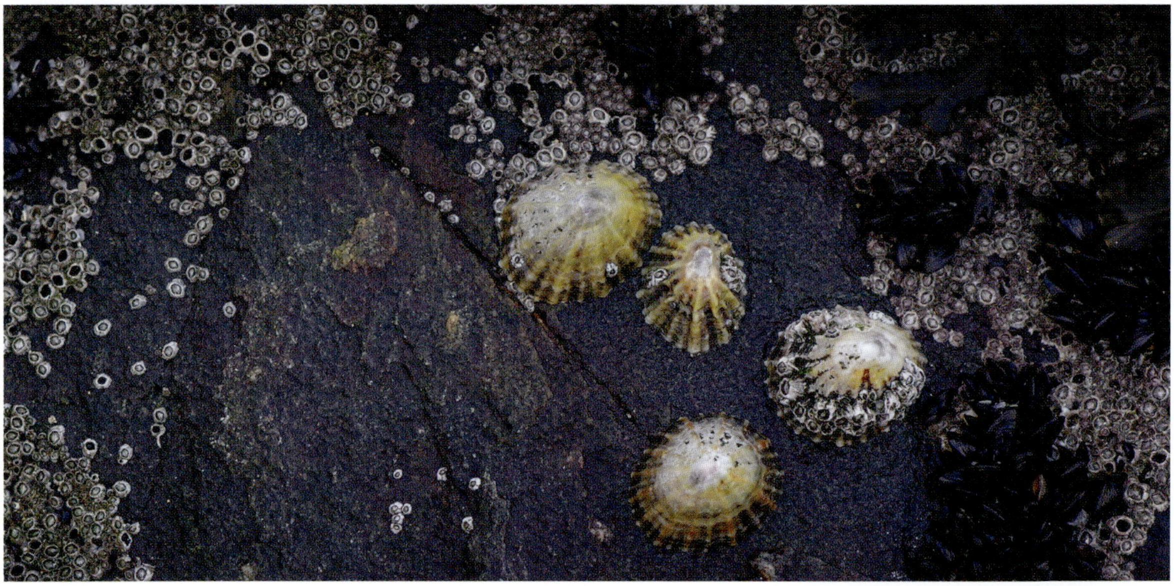
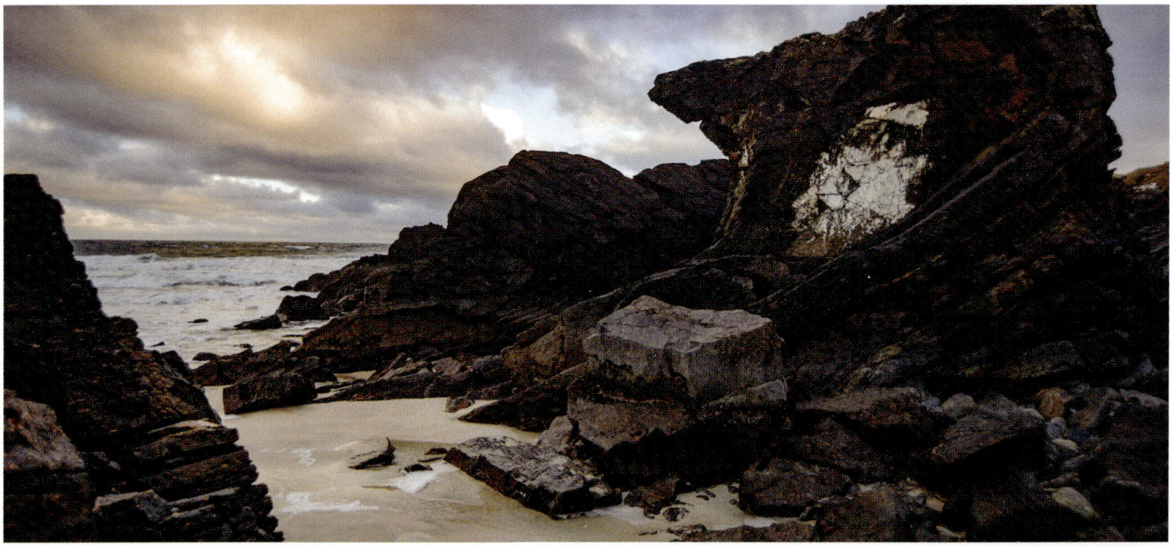

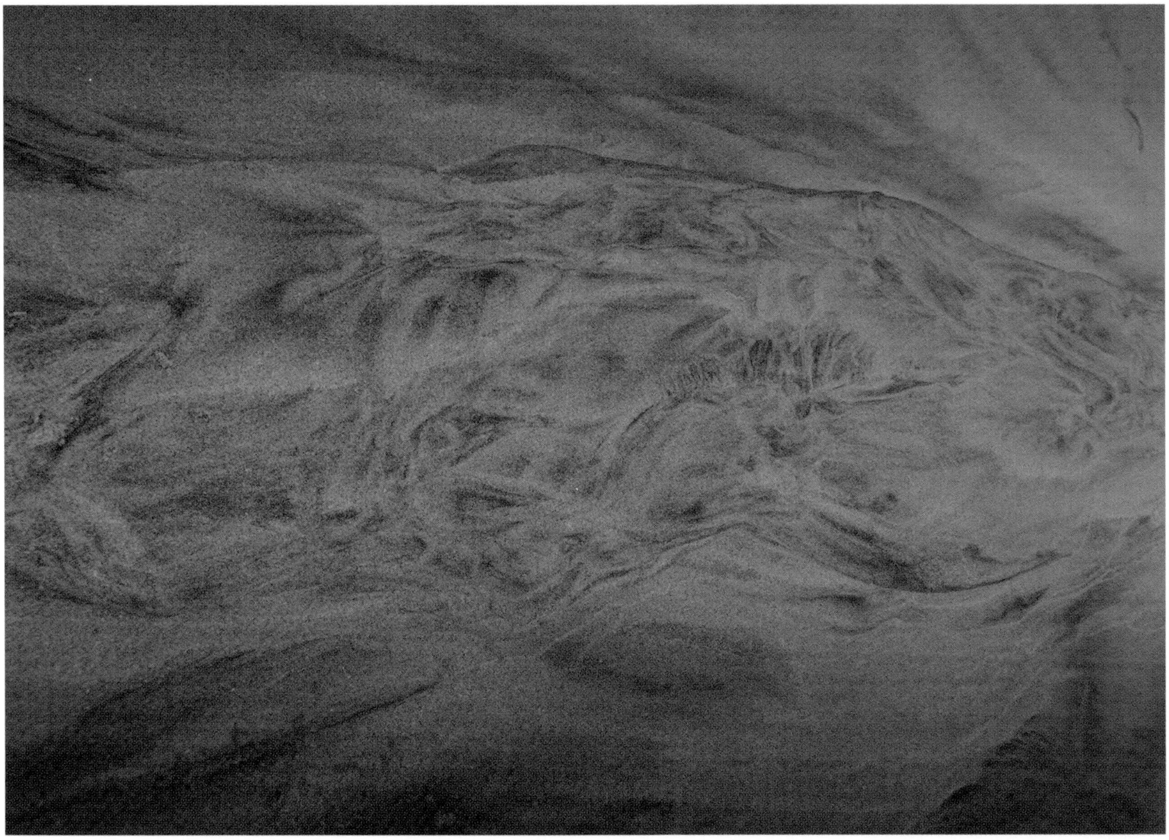

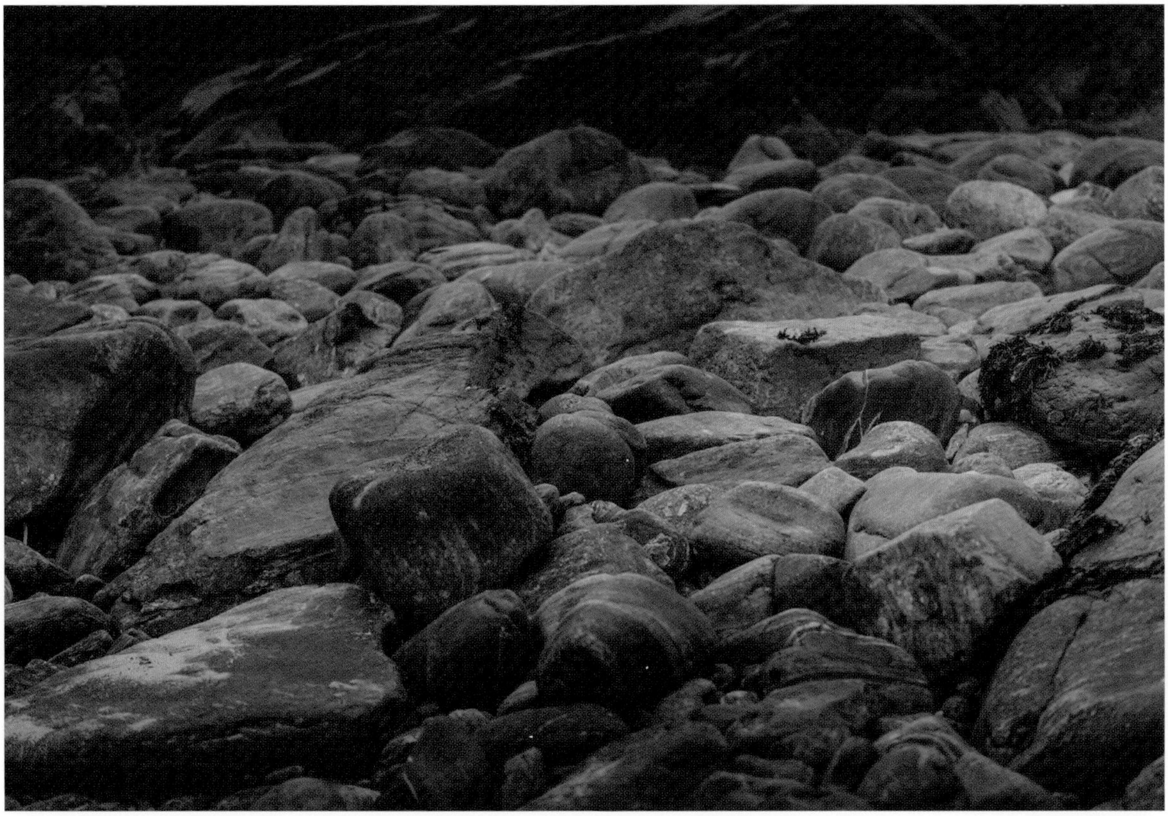

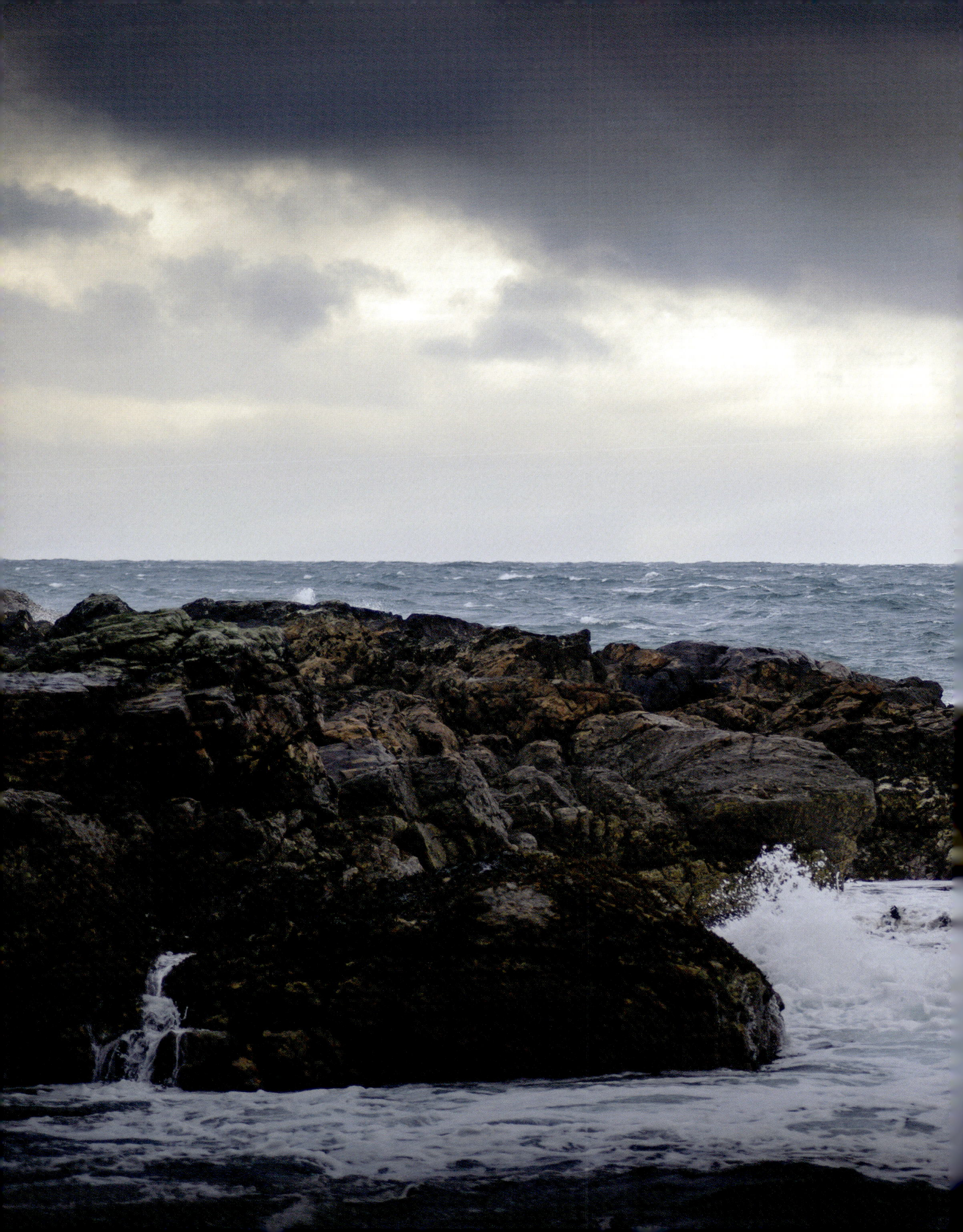

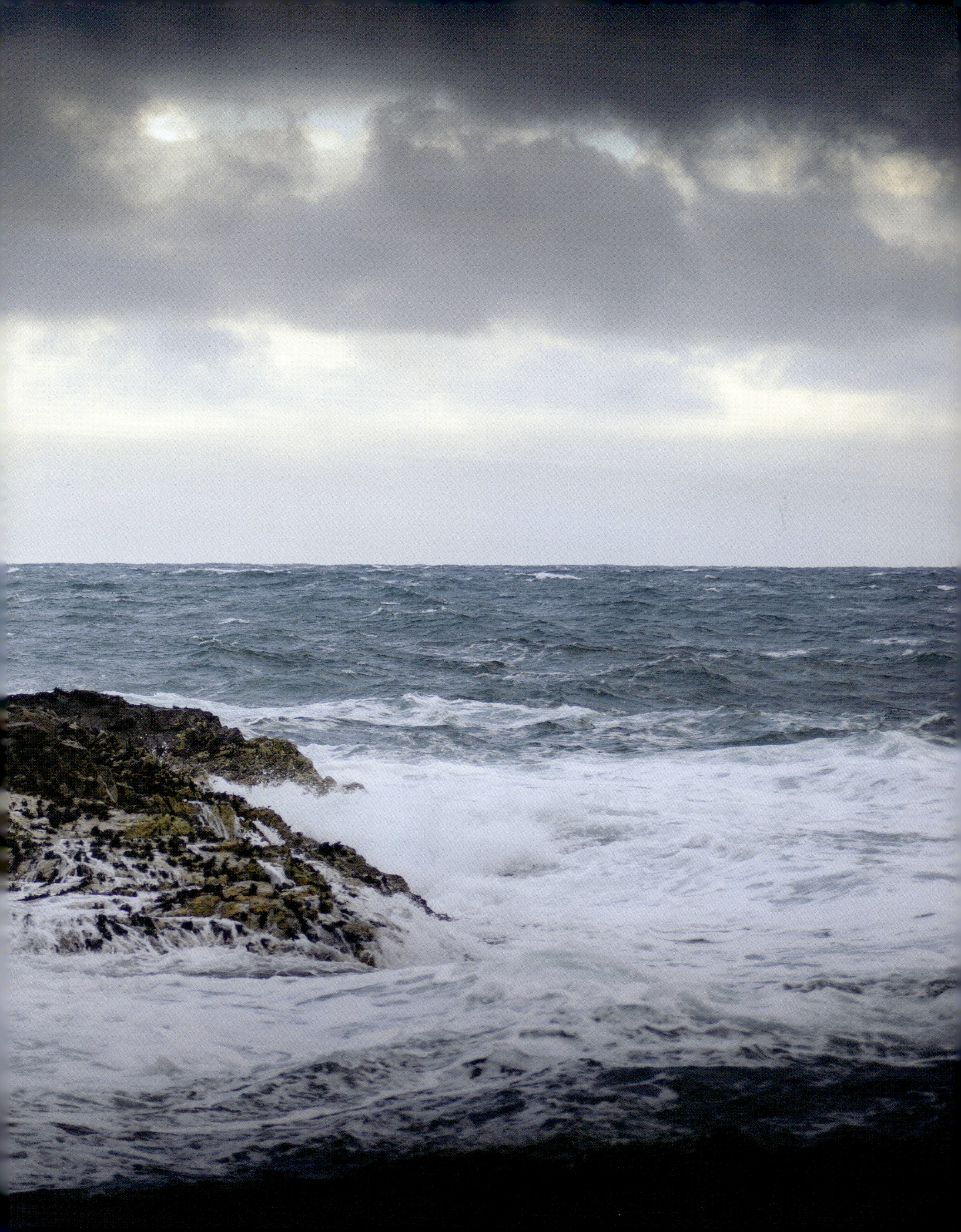

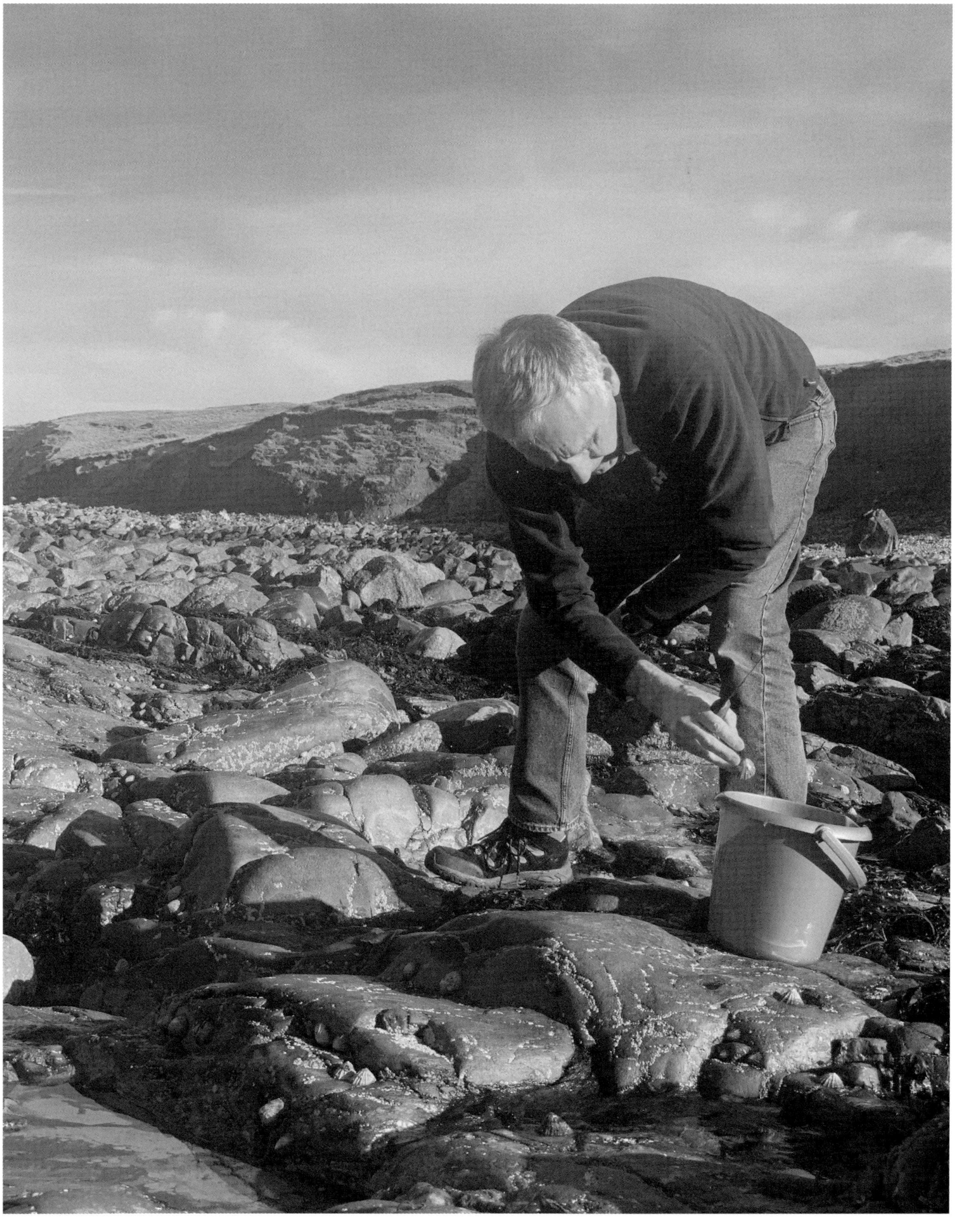

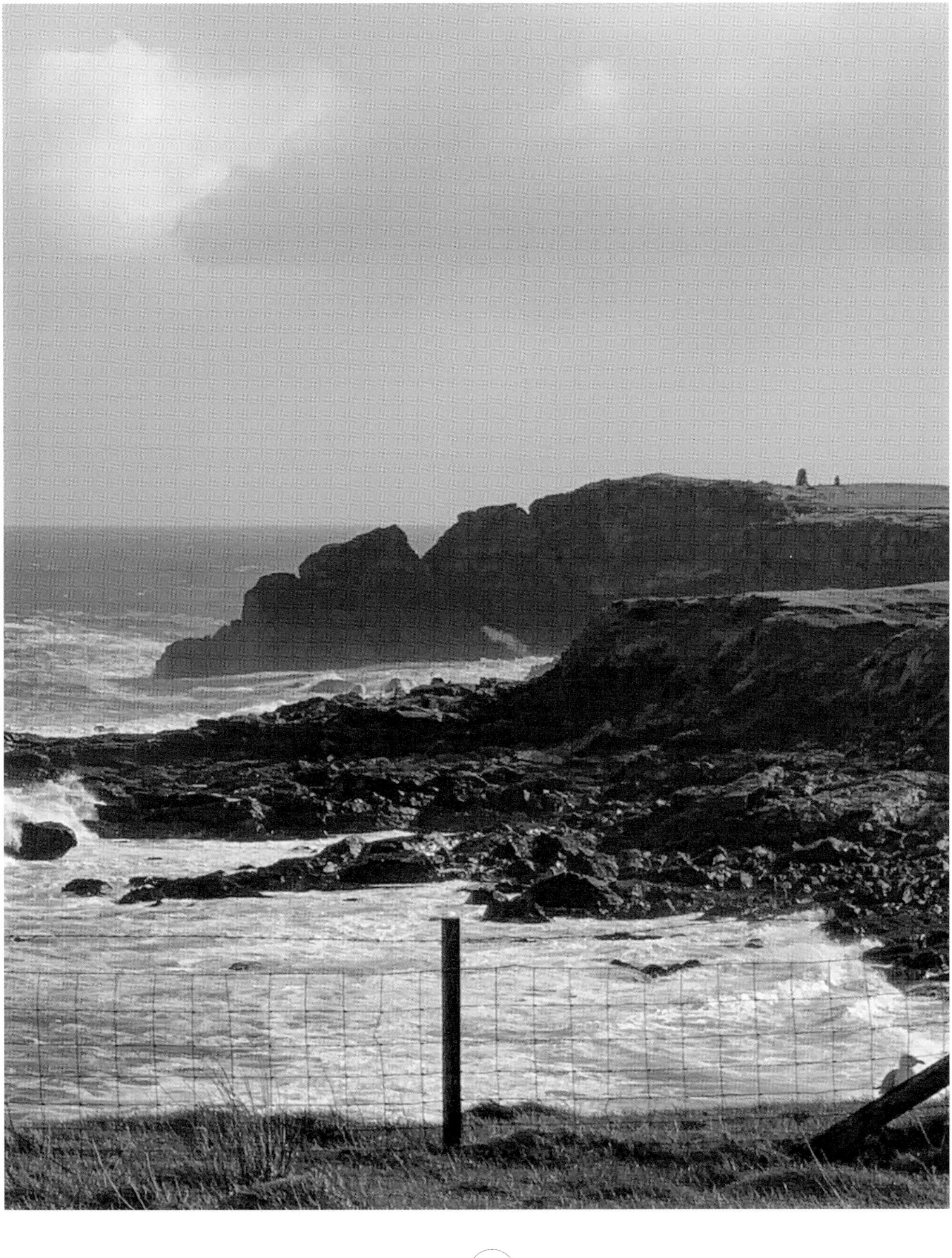

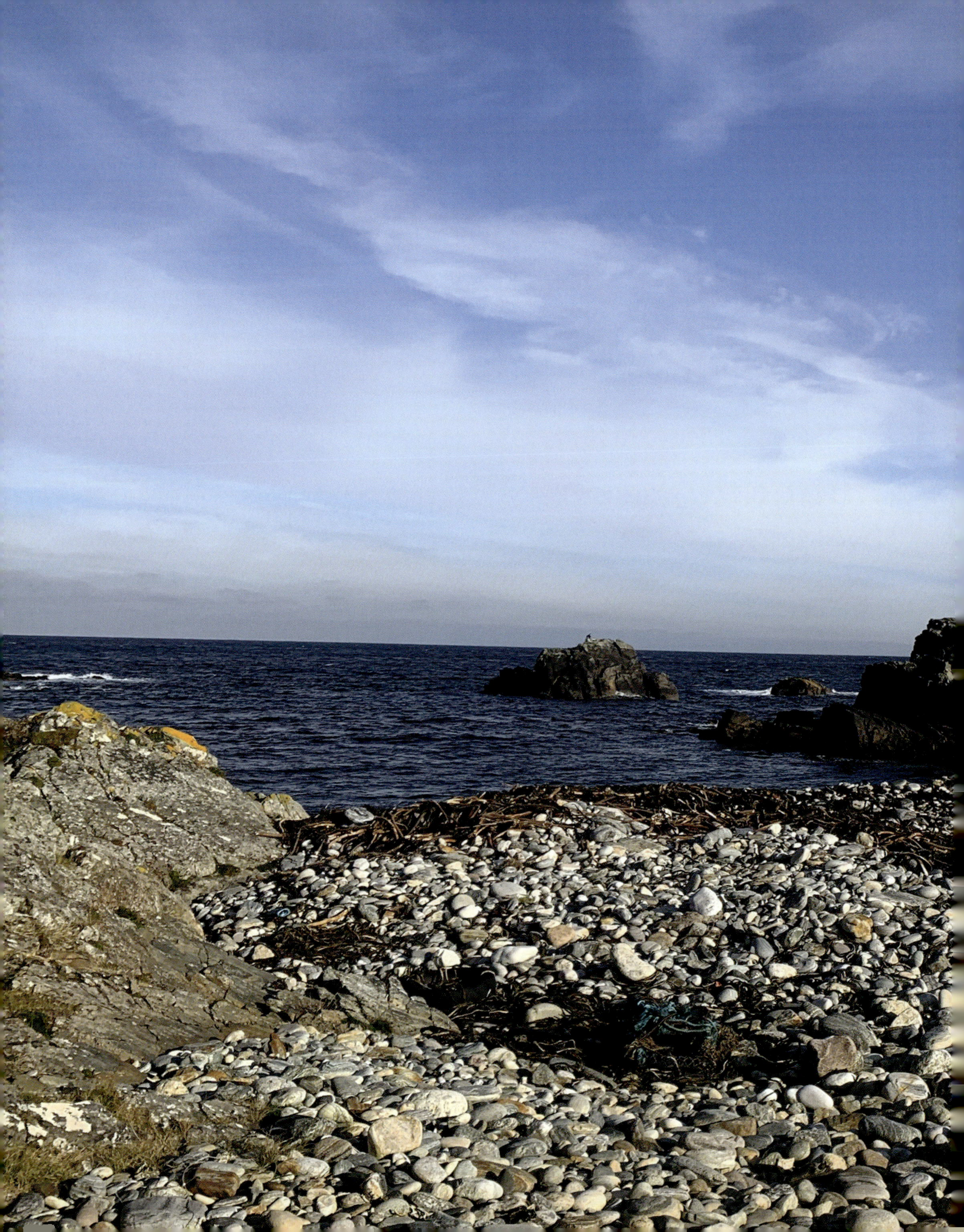

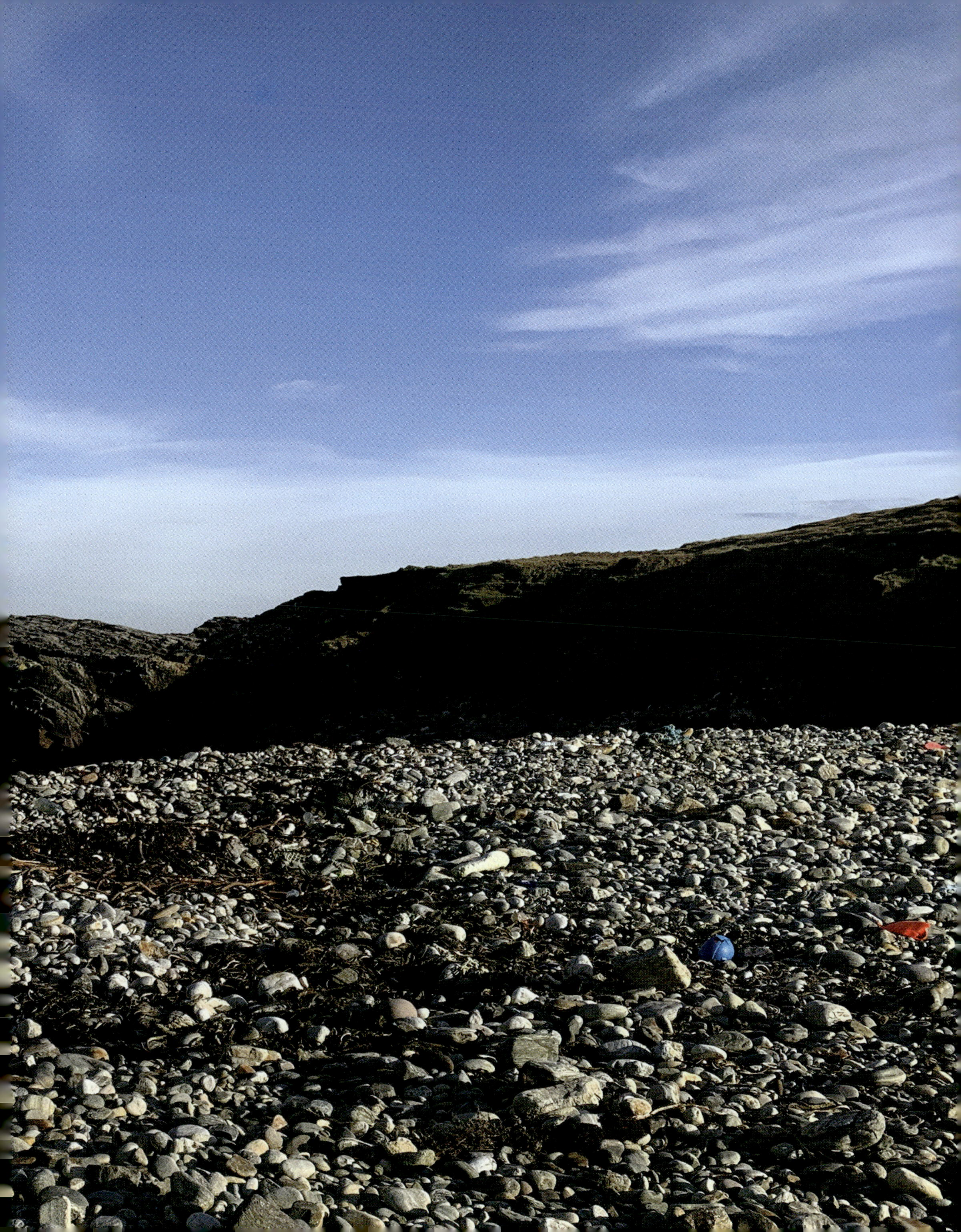

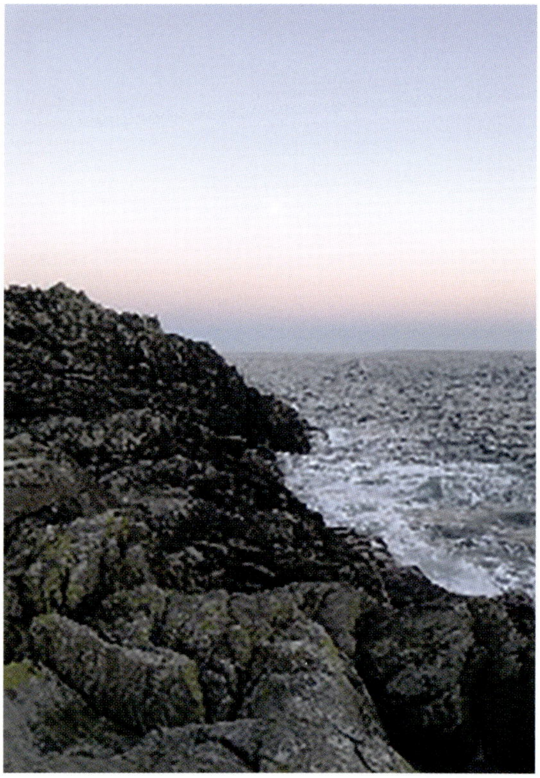
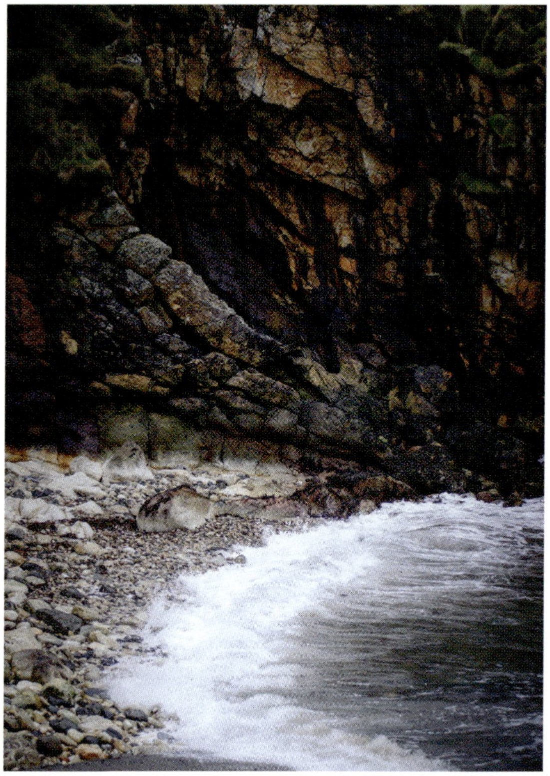
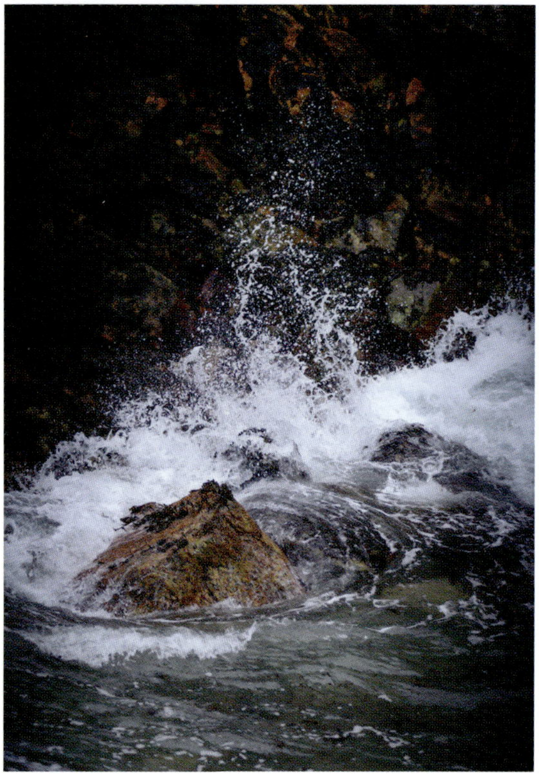
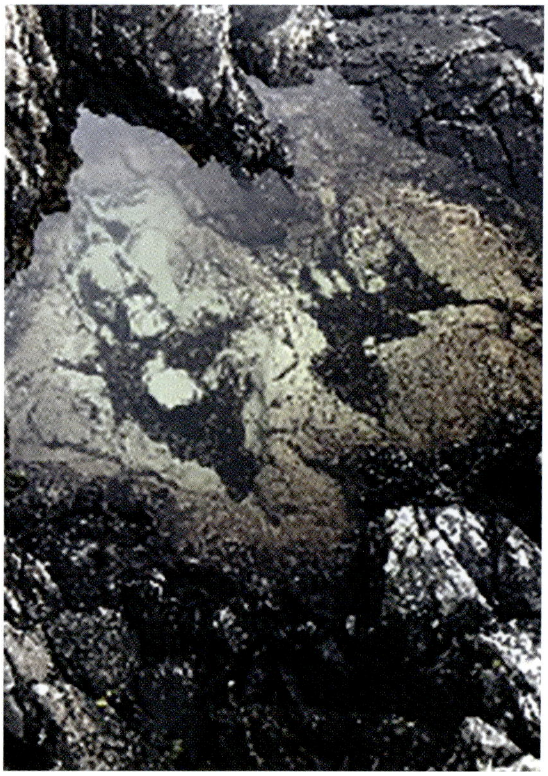

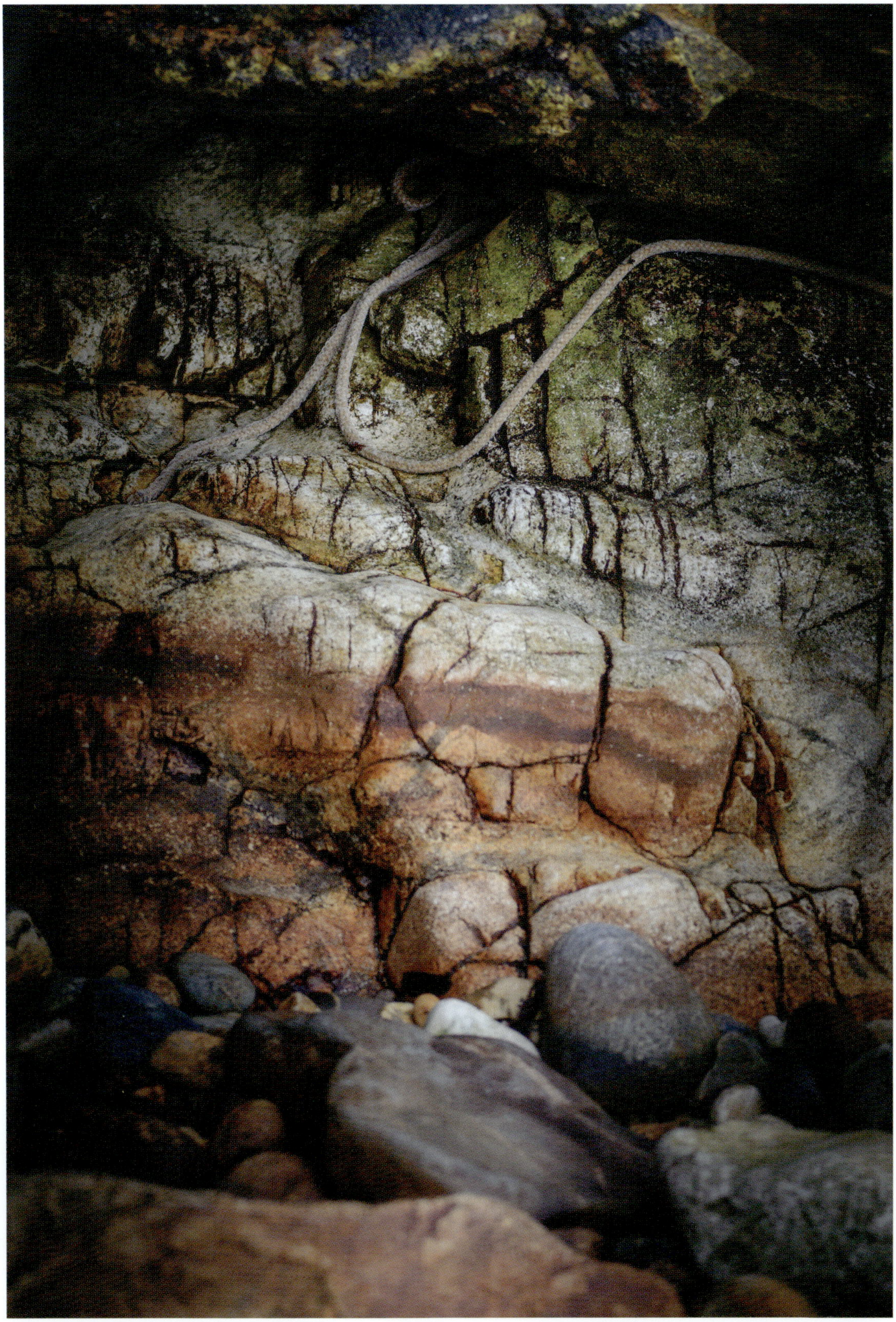

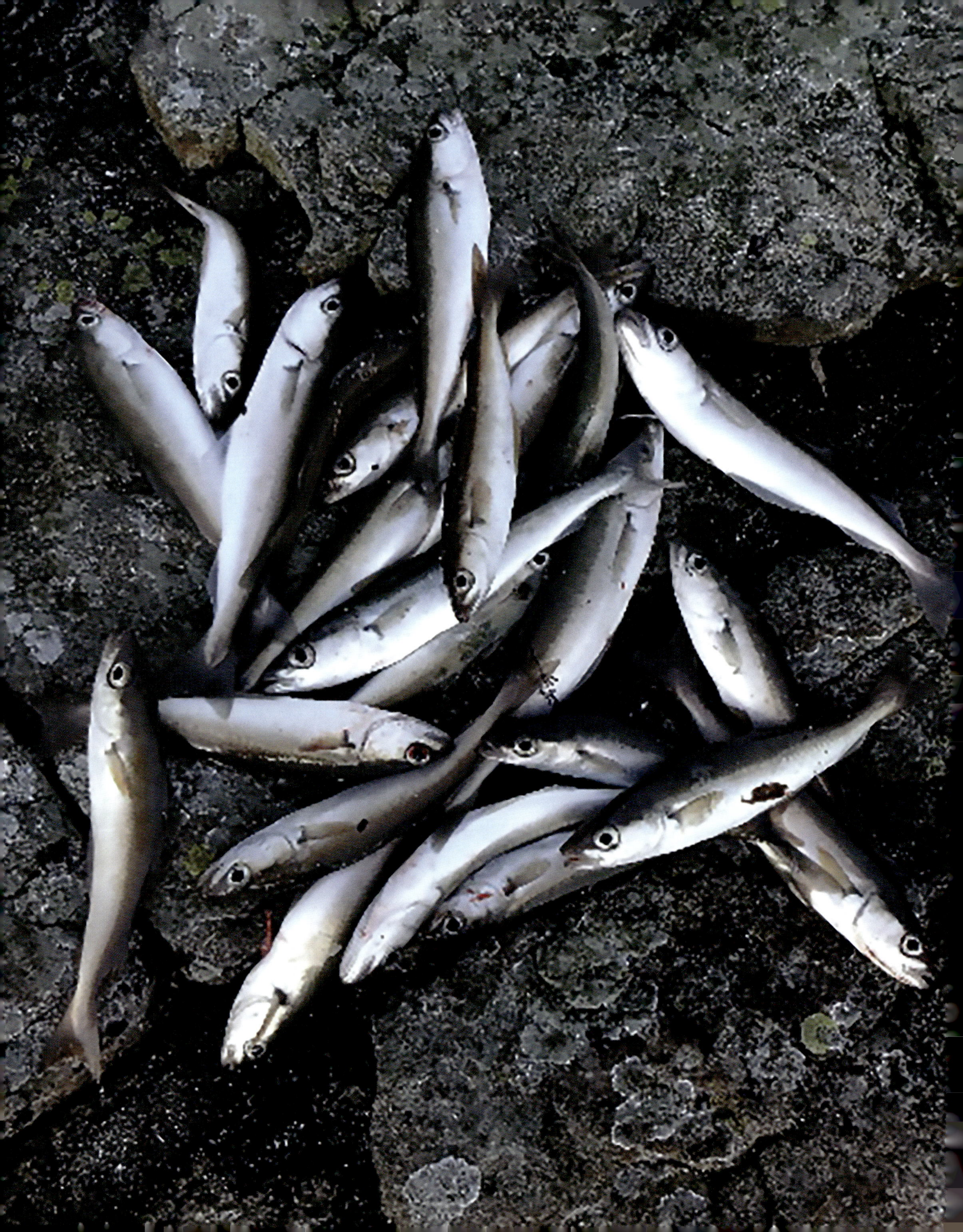

My favourite way of eating *cudaigean* (young saithe or cuddies as we called them) is simply fried in flour and butter. My grandfather used to catch them on a bamboo rod with orange cord, little white flies made from seagull feathers and a lead weight made by pouring molten lead into a carved out piece of peat. He made me a smaller bamboo rod, but I preferred using a big spinning rod. We would come home with a big black bin bag full of them. Traditionally *cudaigean* would be caught with a spoon-net called a *taigh-thàbhaidh*. The *taigh-thàbhaidh* was made with wooden rods, a net would then be fastened on the inside of the frame and weighted down with a stone. The handle, which was ten feet long, was made from an oar. It was used for fishing off the rocks and it could take up to 2-3 men to pull in a spoon-net full of cuddies.

'S ann air am fraidhigeadh le beagan flùr is ìm a b'fheàrr a bha saoidhein òga, no cudaigean mar a bh'againn orra, a' còrdadh rium. Bhiodh mo sheanair gan glacadh le slat bambù, le sreang orains, cuileagan beaga geala air an dèanamh le itean faoileig, agus cuideam luaidhe a bh'air a dhèanamh le bhith a' dòrtadh na luaidhe leaghte do mholldair a bh'air a ghearradh ann am fàd mònach. Rinn e slat bambù na bu lugha dhomhsa, ach b'fheàrr leam a bhith a' cleachdadh slat shnìomhadair mhòr. Thilleadh sinn dhachaigh le poca plastaig mòr, dubh, làn dhiubh. Chleachd cudaigean a bhith air an glacadh le seòrsa de lìon ris an canar taigh-thàbhaidh. Bha an taigh-thàbhaidh air a dèanamh le frèam fhiodh, le lìon air a cheangal ri a taobh a-staigh agus clach mar chuideam innte. Bhiodh suas ri deich troighean a dh'fhaid sa chas, air a dèanamh le ràmh. Bha i air a cleachdadh air a' chreagach agus dh'fhaodadh feum a bhith air neart dhithis no thriùir airson taigh-thàbhaidh làn chudaigean a thogail às an uisge.

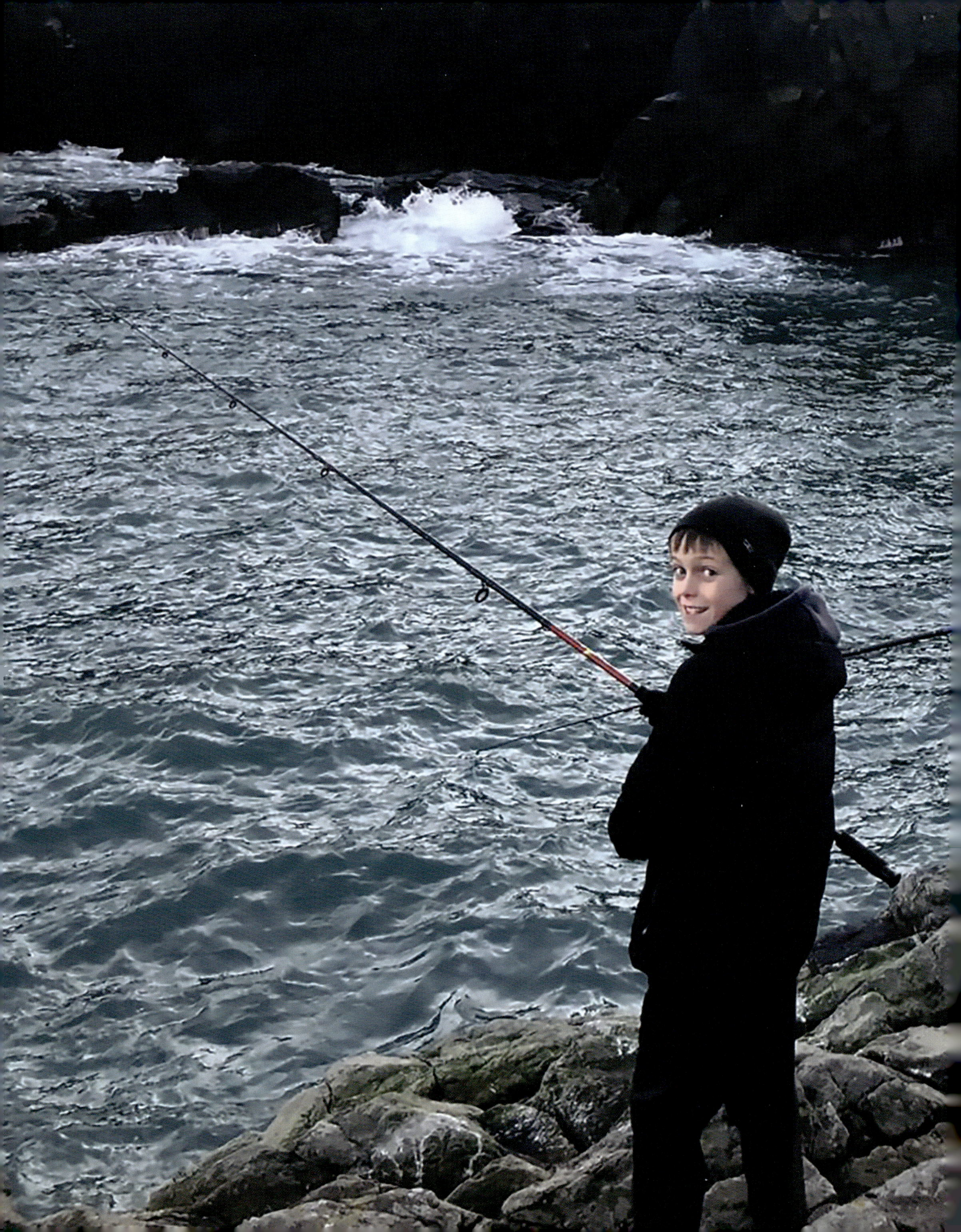

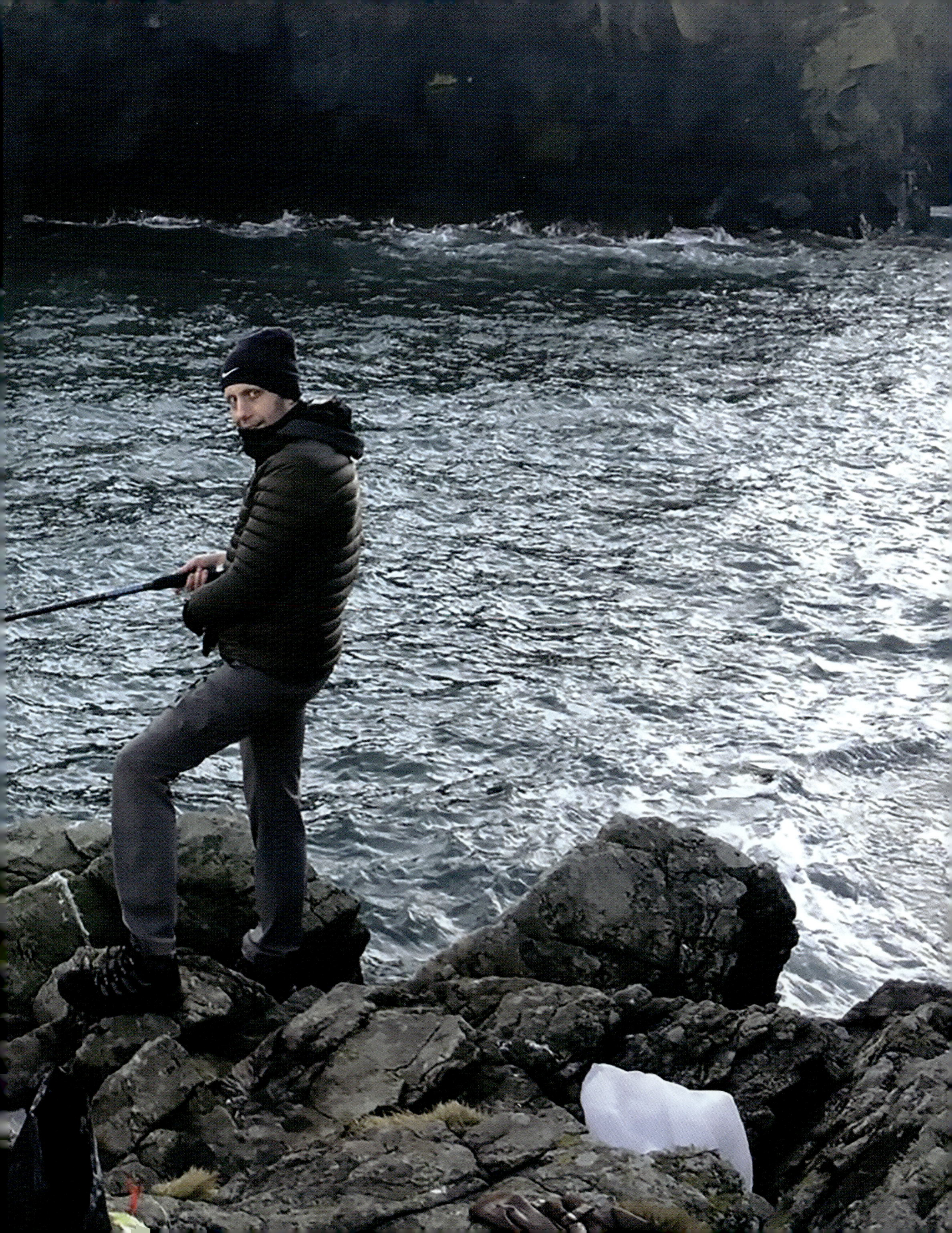

SEABIRD EGGS

Gulls' eggs were often eaten by the Hebrideans. From what I've heard, my grandfather would even take a few and eat them himself. The folk on Hiort, St Kilda, would leave the fulmar's eggs, as they only laid one egg – they would eat the birds once hatched and grown instead, and eat copious amounts of gannet and guillemot eggs as these birds would replace the stolen egg with another. They would simply boil them and eat them fresh. Any left over would then be preserved in the ashes of peat, giving an astringent taste to those who were not used to eating them. It is illegal to harvest gulls' eggs without a licence in the UK and the season is very short, being around three weeks in May. The eggs here are legally bought black-headed gulls' eggs. They have stunning green, speckled shells with sunset orange yolks and are the creamiest, richest eggs you will ever try!

UIGHEAN EÒIN-MHARA

Bhiodh muinntir nan eilean tric ag ithe uighean fhaoileagan. Bho na chuala mi, bhiodh fiùs mo sheanair a' faighinn dhà na thrì agus gan ithe e fhèin. Bha muinntir Hiort a' fàgail uighean an eòin-chruim no an fhulmair chionns nach robh iad a' breith ach aon ugh. Dh'itheadh iad a leòr de dh'uighean an t-sùlaire agus eòin dubh an sgadain, chionns gum breitheadh iadsan ugh eile an àite an fhir a chaill iad. Bha iad dìreach gam bruich 's gan ithe ùr. Nam biodh feadhainn air fhàgail bhiodh iad air an gleidheadh ann an luath na mònach, a' toirt blas caran teanndaigh dhaibhsan nach robh eòlach orra. Tha e mì-laghail falbh le uighean faoileig gun chead anns an RA agus tha an seusan goirid, dìreach mu thrì seachdainean sa Chèitean. Chaidh na h-uighean seo, uighean faoileig a' chinn duibh, a cheannach gu laghail. Tha sligean àlainn, breac-bhallach, uaine orra, le buidheagain cho orains ri dol fodha na grèine. Cha bhlais thu gu bràth air uighean a tha cho beairteach agus cho barragach riutha.

WILD GULLS' EGGS — HOT SMOKED SALMON — SEAWEED SALT — SALAD CREAM

4 Gulls' Eggs

Bring a small pan of water to the boil and add the eggs, cook for exactly four minutes, refresh in cold water, peel and cut the top off.

30g Hebridean Hot Smoked Salmon

Flake the salmon and gently place three pieces around the rim of the egg.

Salad Cream
1 tbsp plain flour
4 tbsp sugar
pinch of salt
2 free-range eggs
100ml white wine vinegar
150ml double cream
squeeze of barley vinegar (or lemon juice)

Whisk the flour, sugar, salt and eggs in a bowl set over a pan of simmering water until pale and thickened. Remove the pan from the heat and stir in the vinegar, cream and barley vinegar or lemon juice. Set aside to cool.

Seaweed Salt
50g Skye sea salt
20g dried kelp

Blitz the salt and dried seaweed together in a spice grinder and sprinkle over the egg.

BEACH CAUGHT FLOUNDER — ROASTED CAULIFLOWER — GRILLED SYBOES — SOUSED WINKLES

LEÒBAG NA TRÀGHAD — CÀL-COLAIG RÒSTA — SIOBAIDEAN GRÌOSAICHTE — FAOCHAGAN PICILTE

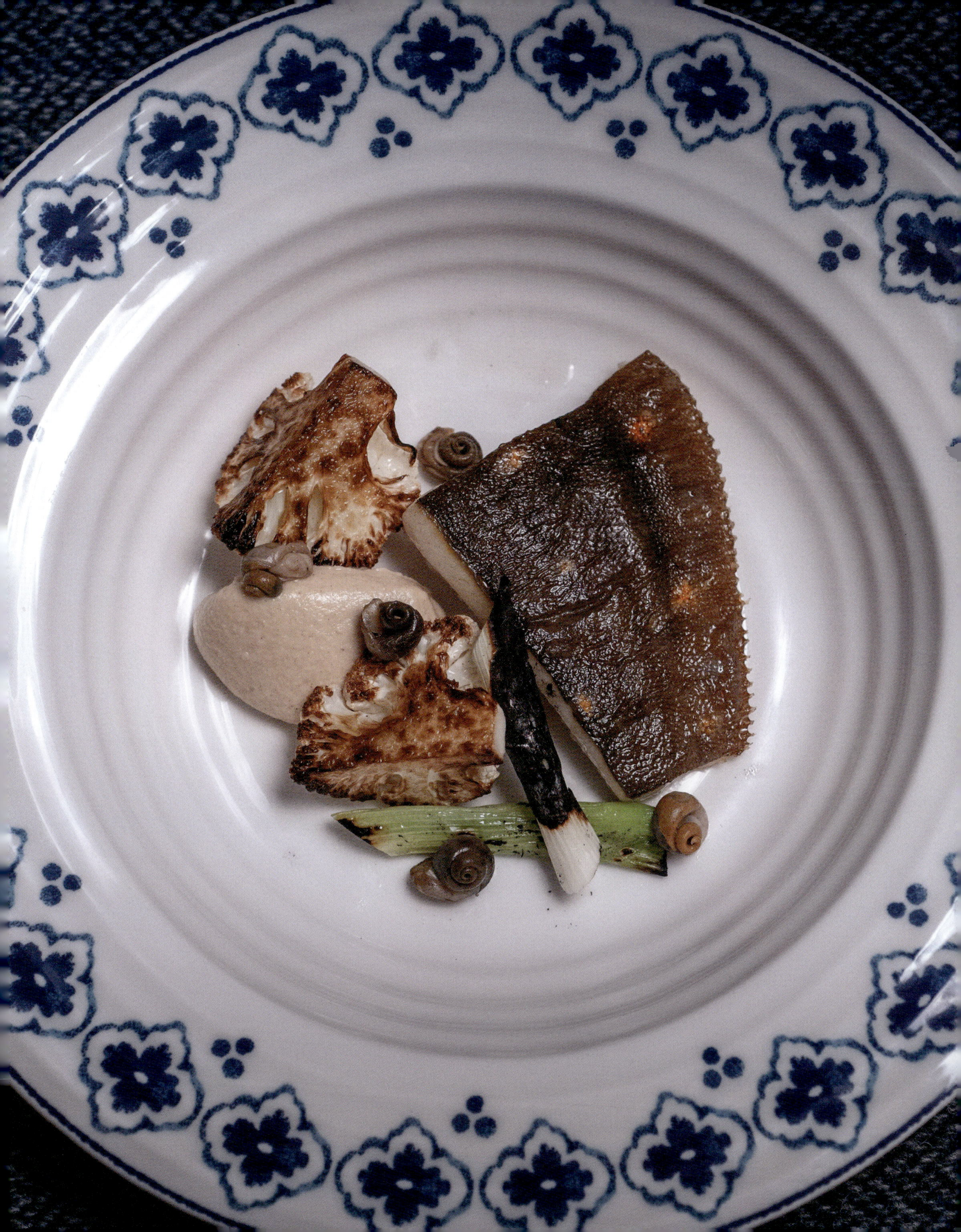

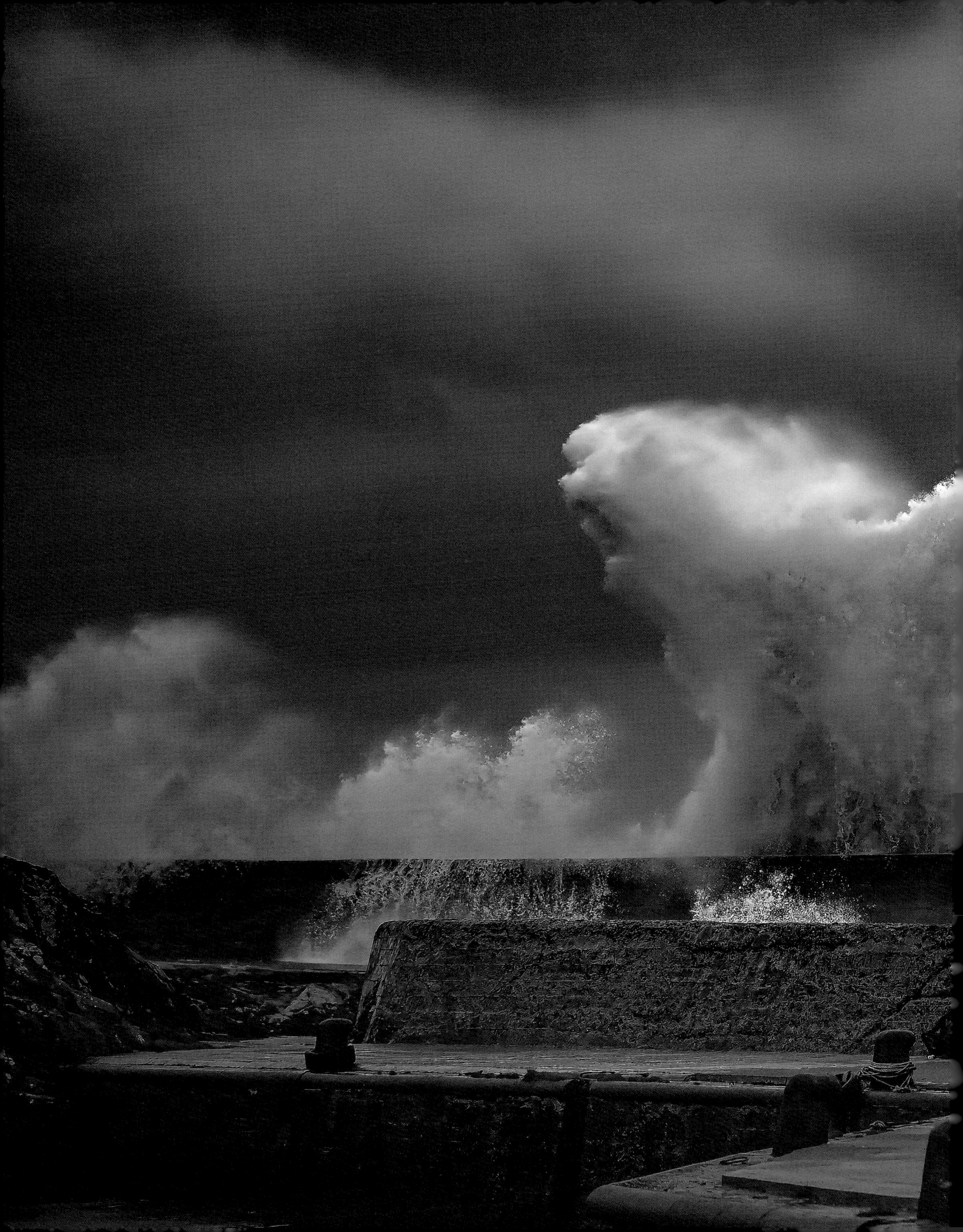

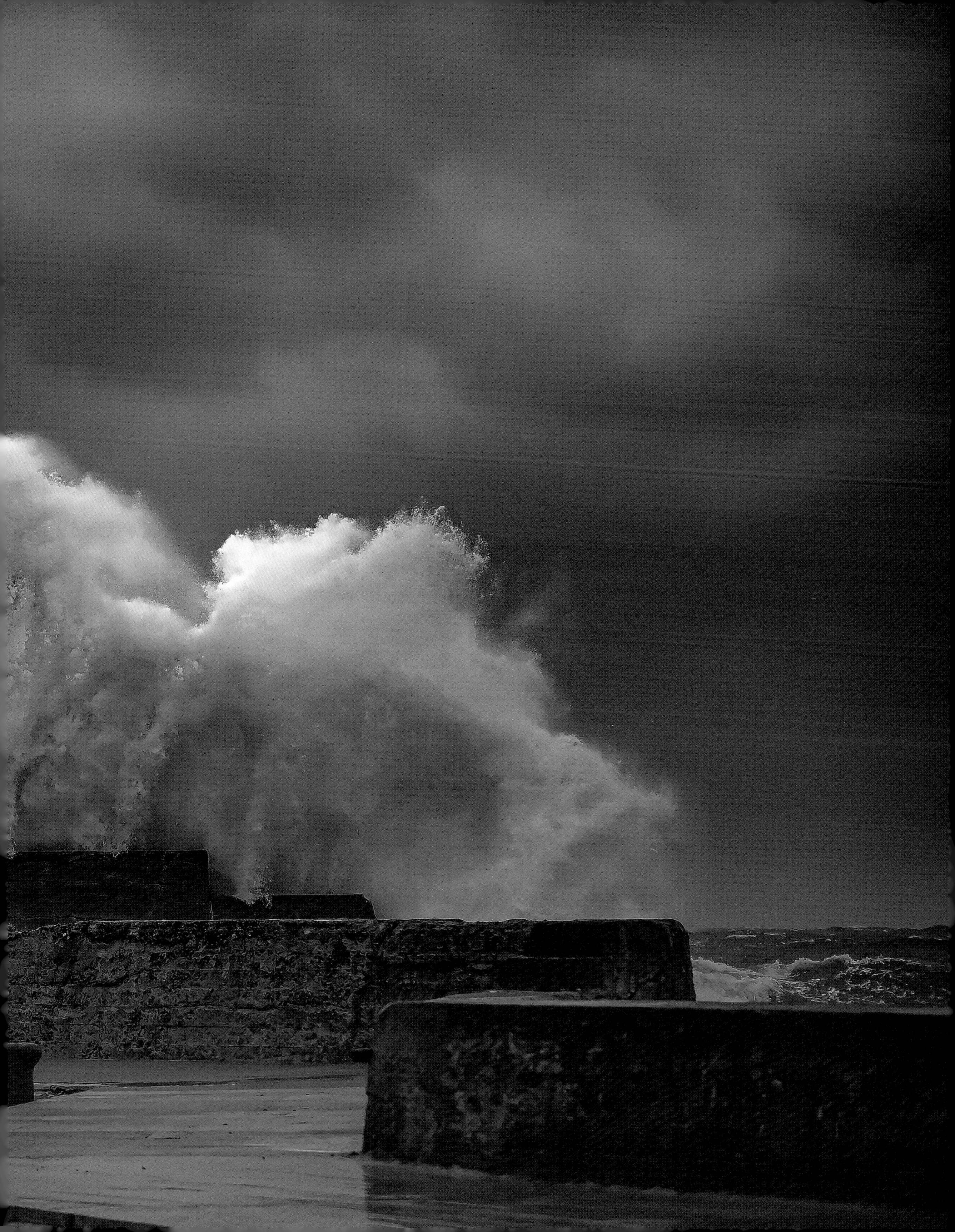

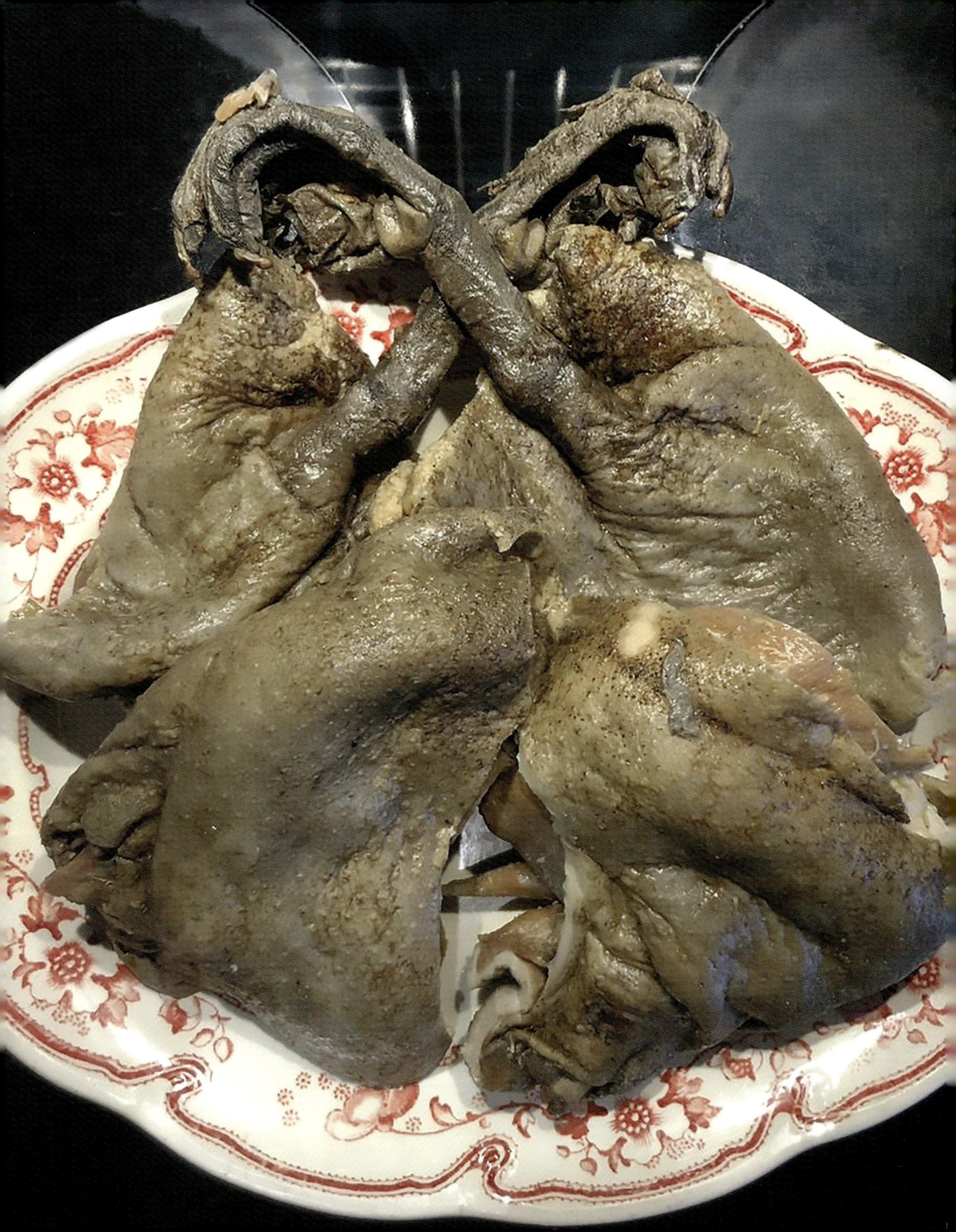

The Guga
An Guga

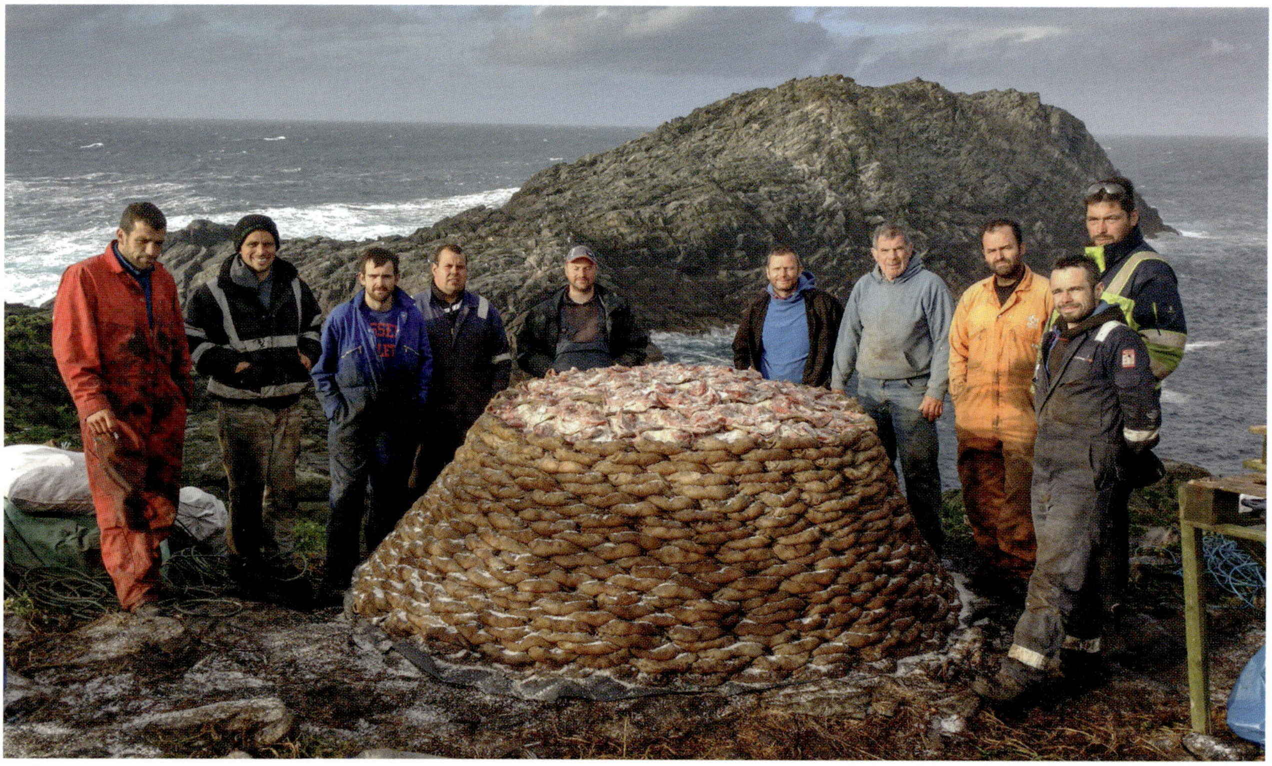

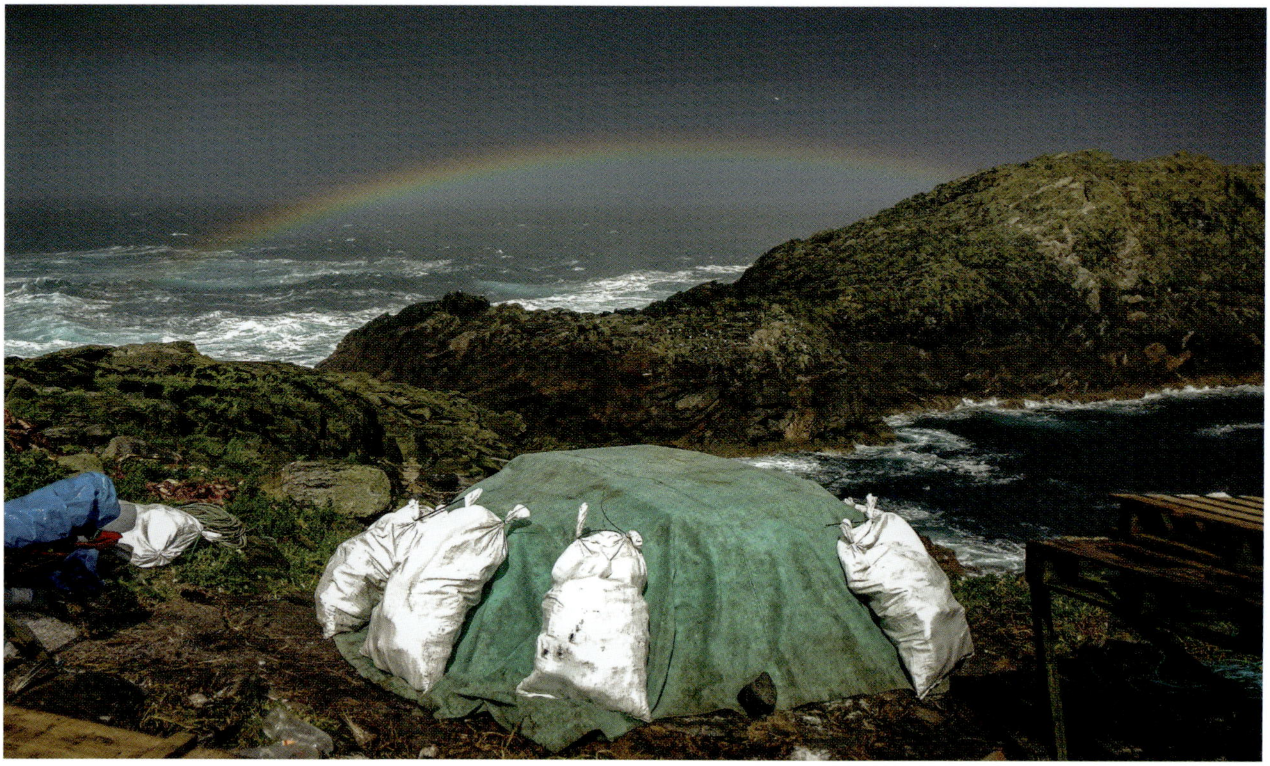

The salted young gannet has been traditionally eaten by the Ness folk on the Isle of Lewis since at least the 15th century. Men from Ness would sail out to an uninhabited island called Sùlaisgeir, located 40 miles out from Port of Ness. They would stay there for a number of weeks, culling the birds using a pole and noose. The *guga* would then be processed and salted. The salted bird was an important part of the winter diet. Under the Protection of Birds Act, 1954, the *guga* was protected, but with the inclusion of a clause to exempt the men from Ness and allow them annually to take 2000 birds from Sùlaisgeir. Pictured are the boys on the annual *guga* hunt on Sùlaisgeir. That time of year when those who love eating this salted delicacy get their hand on a bird or two, is also the time when those who can't stand it start running for the hills! The *guga* has an oily, fishy taste and is definitely an acquired taste. I absolutely love it!

Sadly in recent years Covid and Avian flu have prevented the annual trip to Sùlaisgeir.

Tha muinntir Nis ann an Eilean Leòdhais air a bhith ag ithe an t-sùlaire òg, saillte, bho co-dhiù an còigeamh linn deug. Bhiodh fir à Nis a' seòladh gu eilean iomallach air a bheil an t-ainm Sùlaisgeir, mu 40 mìle bho Phort Nis. Bhiodh iad a' fuireach air an eilean airson beagan sheachdainean, a' glacadh 's a' marbhadh nan eun le pòlaichean fada le dul orra. Bhiodh an guga an uair sin air a ghiullachd agus air a shailleadh. Bha an guga na phàirt cudromach de bhiadh a' gheamhraidh. Fo Achd Dìon nan Eun, 1954, bha dìon air a chur air a' ghuga ach tha cumha san achd a tha a' toirt cead do dh'fhir Nis 2000 eun a thoirt à Sùlaisgeir gach bliadhna. San dealbh tha an sgioba leis a' phile ghugaichean air an eilean. 'S e seo an t-àm dhen bhliadhna nuair a tha an fheadhainn a tha dèidheil air a' ghuga a' dèanamh fiughair ris, ach an t-àm nuair a tha feadhainn eile a' teiche bhuaidhe. Tha blas ùilleach, saillt an èisg air a' ghuga agus, gu cinnteach, feumaidh duine fàs suas ris. Tha mi-fhìn air leth dèidheil air!

Gu duilich, sna bliadhnaichean mu dheireadh tha Covid agus Flu nan Eun air bacadh a chur air an turas bhliadhnail gu Sùlaisgeir.

TRADITIONALLY COOKED GUGA — BOILED CROFT POTATOES — A GLASS OF MILK

To cook the *guga* the traditional way you would simmer it in a pan of boiling water for about one hour and five minutes, changing the water halfway through to make it less salty. Serve with croft potatoes boiled in their jackets and a glass of milk. No cutlery required!

GUGA AIR A BHRUICH GU TRAIDISEANTA — BUNTÀTA BRUICH NA CROIT — GLAINNE BAINNE

Airson guga a chòcaireachd san dòigh thraidiseanta bhruicheadh tu e ann am poit uisge goileach airson timcheall air uair a thìde agus còig mionaidean, ag atharrachadh an uisge mu letheach-slighe gus nach bi e cho saillte. Tha thu ga ithe le buntàta bruich len rùsg orra agus glainne bainne. Chan eil feum air forc no sgian!

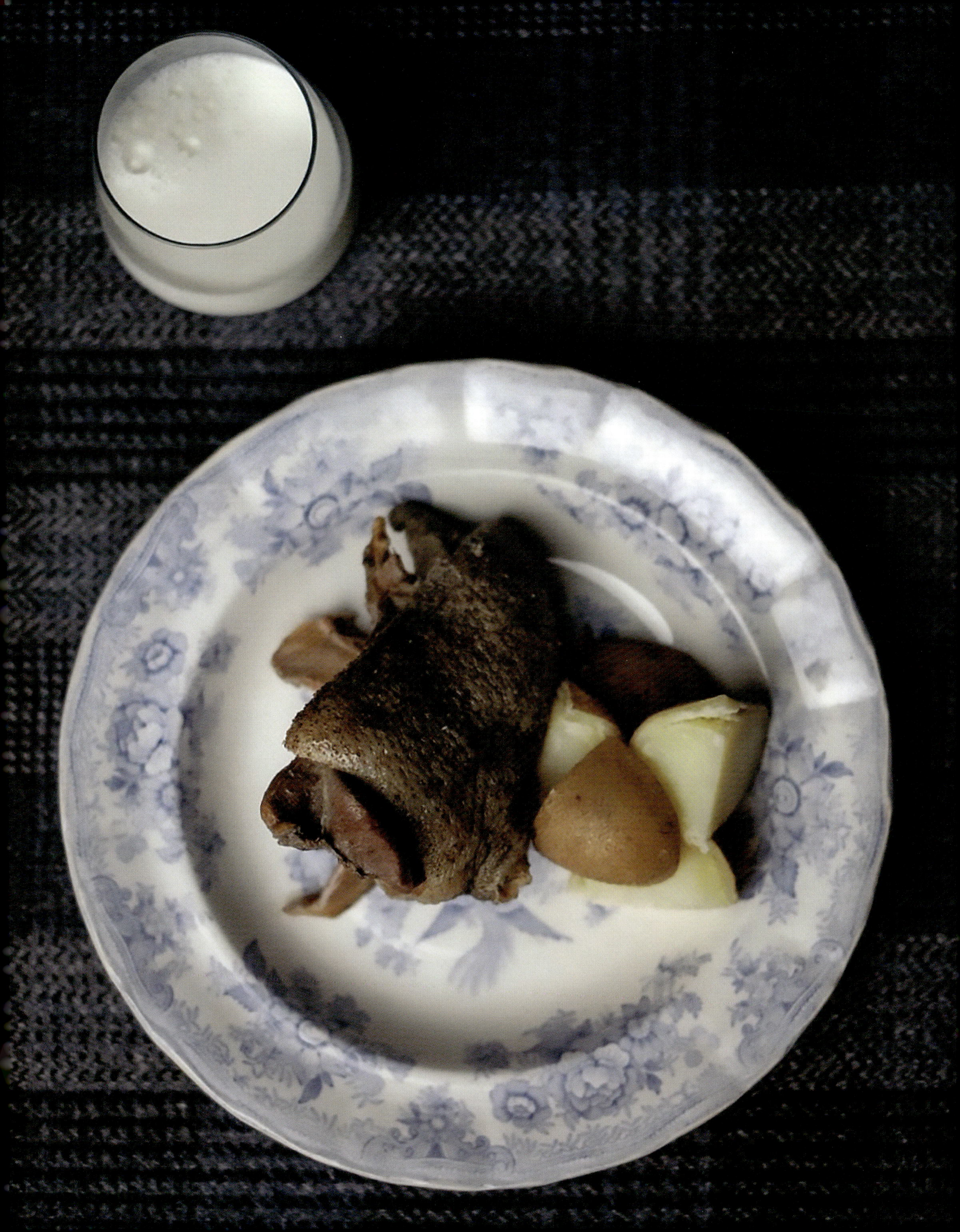

SALTED GUGA — POTATO SCONE — SOUSED GOOSEBERRIES — BUTTERMILK GEL — SEA ASTER

I've used some sliced salted young gannet breast, which is sat on a potato scone that is made with floury potatoes, wheat flour and cultured butter. To counter the salty meat there are some sharp fermented red gooseberries, sweet white gooseberry purée, buttermilk gel and some peppery baby mustard leaves. It's like a Hebridean taco that is salty, sweet, sour, hot and creamy! I have to say it is absolutely delicious and I'm convinced that even the guga haters would eat this and enjoy it.

Tha mi air sliseagan de bhroilleach guga saillte a chur air sgona buntàta a th'air a dèanamh le buntàta flùrach, flùr cruithneachd agus ìm geur. Airson leasachadh a dhèanamh air an fheòil shaillte tha gròsaidean dearga geura, tòirnichte, purée milis de ghròsaidean geala, gel blàthaich agus duilleagan òga piobaireach sgeallain. Tha e coltach ri taco Innse-Gallach a tha saillte, milis, geur, teth agus barragach. Dh'fheumainn aideachadh gu bheil e anabarrach blasta agus tha mi cinnteach gun itheadh 's gun còrdadh e fiùs riuthasan air a bheil sgàig ron ghuga.

Potato Scone
splash of vinegar
600g floury potatoes
60g butter
130-150g self-raising flour
pinch of salt

Line a baking tray with salt and bake the potatoes at 180°C until cooked. Scoop out the flesh (you should have 500g) and place in a pan and cook out as much of the moisture as you can. Heat a griddle or cast iron skillet over medium-high heat, grease with a little butter.
Mash potatoes with the flour, butter, and salt until a stiff dough forms. Turn the dough out onto a lightly-floured work surface. Knead dough lightly and roll it out to about ½ cm thick. Cut into rounds, working in batches. Cook the scones, turning once on the hot griddle until golden brown, four to five minutes per side.

Guga
breast of *guga*

Rinse the bird well in cold water, soak overnight if you find it too salty. Boil the *guga* for one hour and five minutes, remove the skin and fat and slice the breast into thin pieces.

Soused Gooseberries
200g green and red gooseberries
100g barley vinegar
25g malt extract

Top, tail, wash and dry the gooseberries and place in a sterilised kilner jar. Bring the vinegar and malt extract to the boil, allow to cool. Pour pickling liquid over the gooseberries and leave to pickle for at least 30 days.

Buttermilk Gel
200ml buttermilk
150ml double cream
2.5g agar agar
2g lecithin
splash of vinegar

Boil the buttermilk and cream until reduced by half. Add the vinegar, agar agar and lecithin and return to the boil and then blitz in a blender. Pour the mixture onto a tray and leave to set in the fridge. Once set, blitz until smooth in a blender and pass through a sieve. Garnish with sea aster.

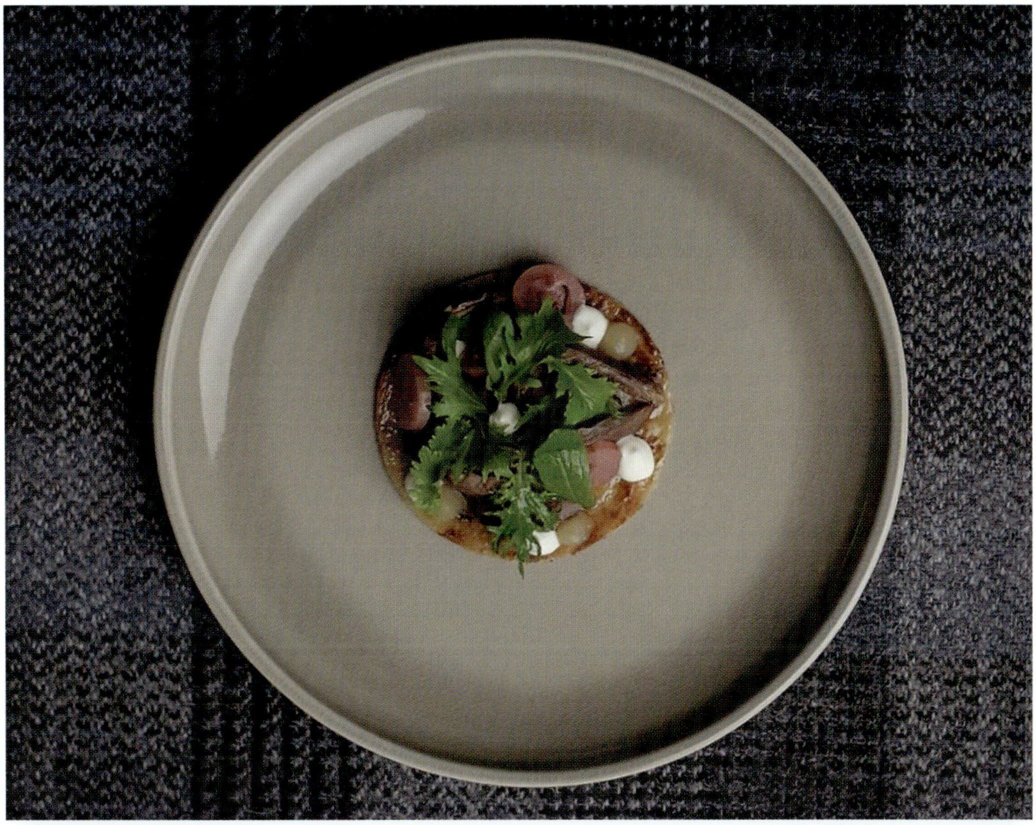

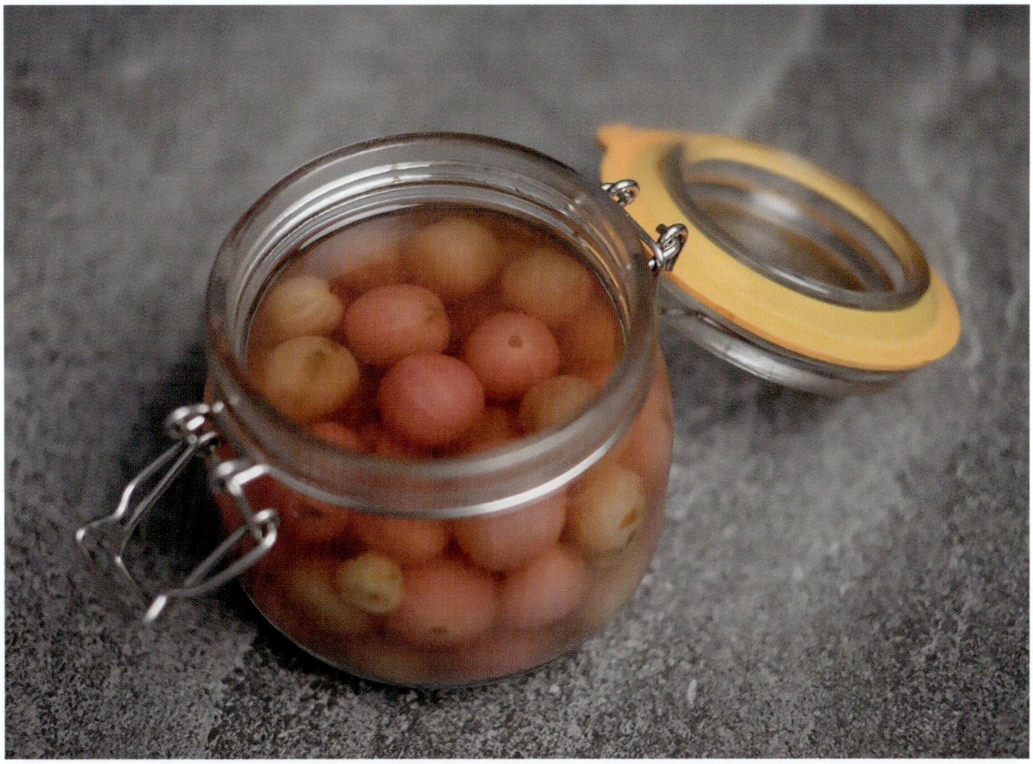

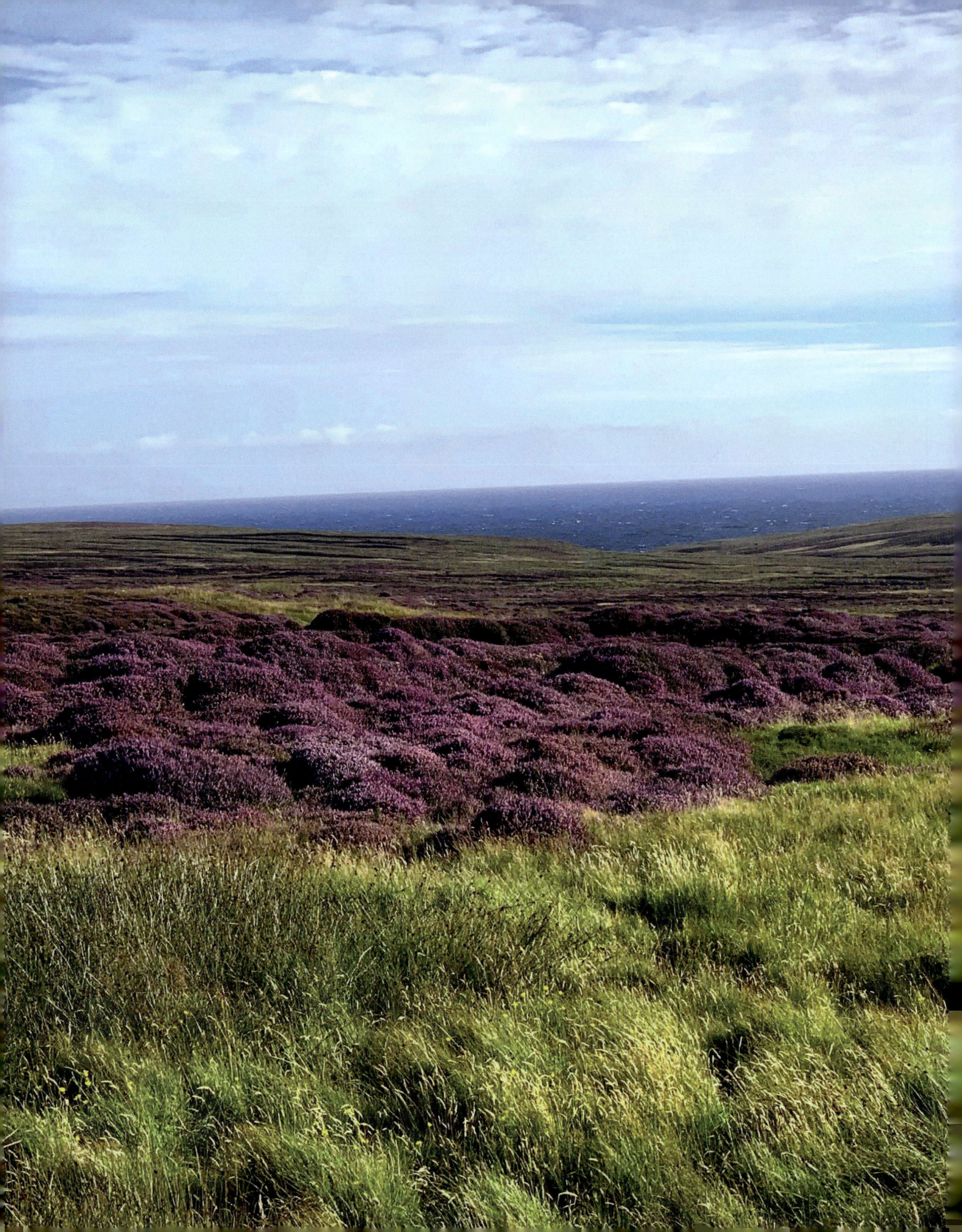

Moor and Machair
Mòinteach is Machair

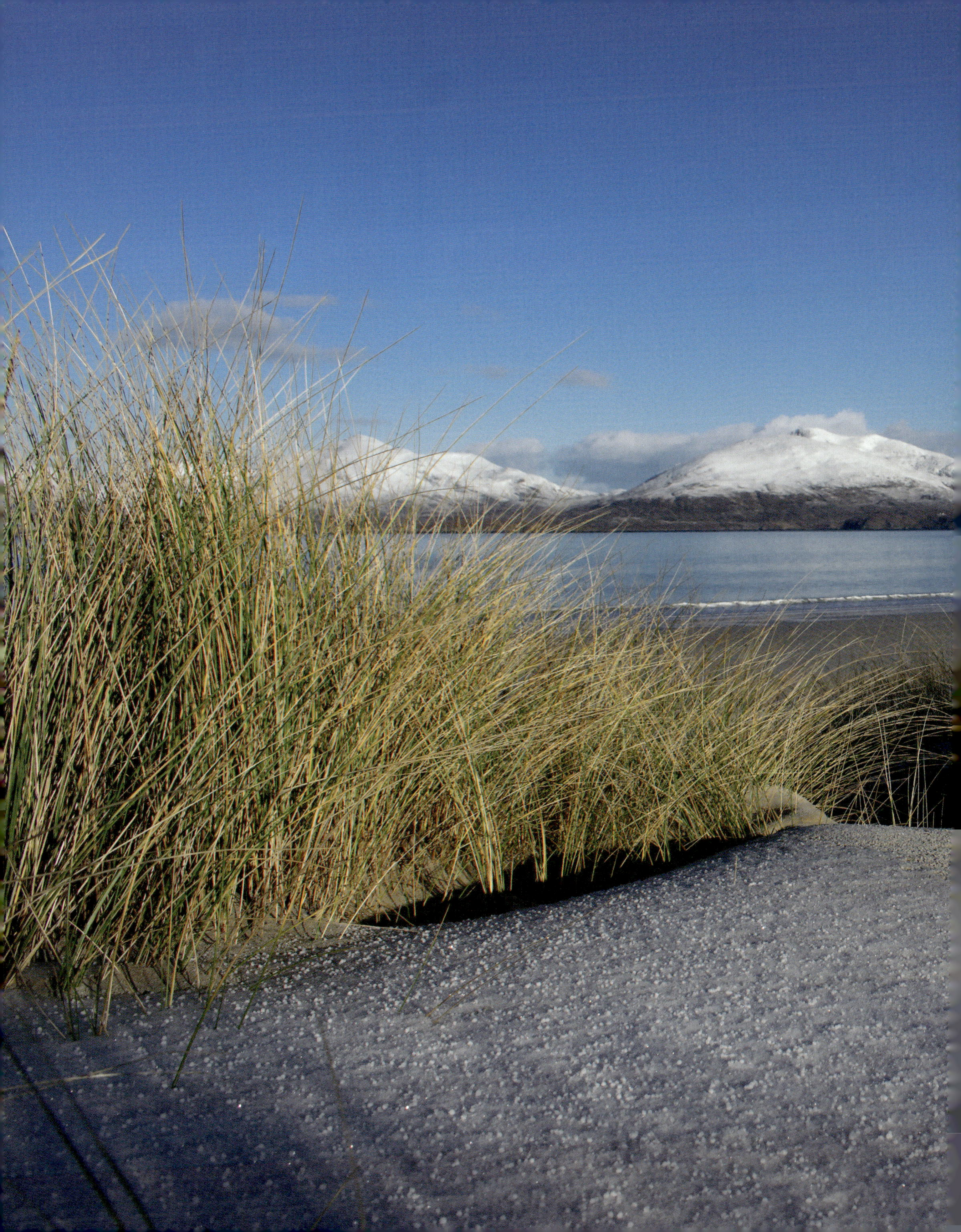

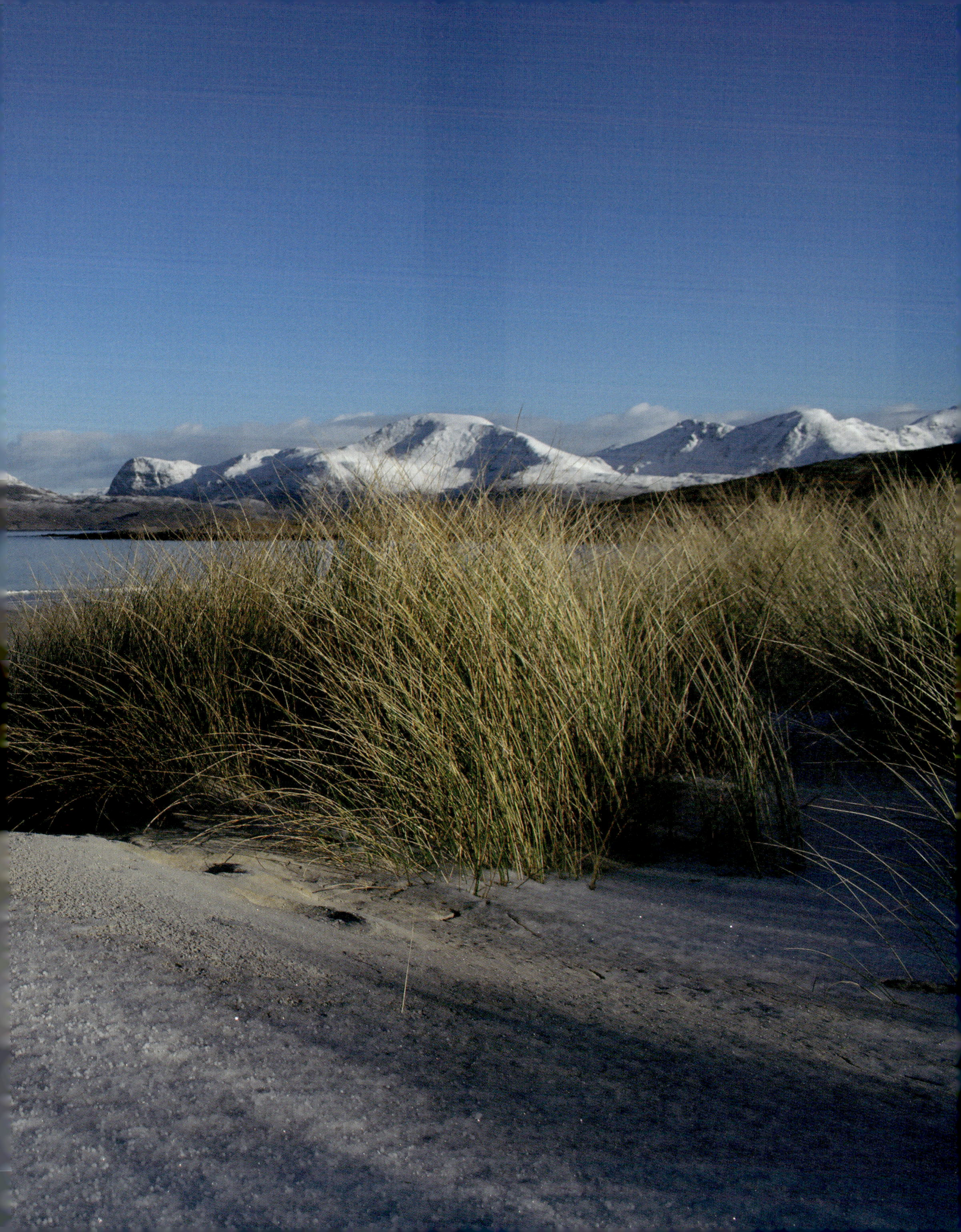

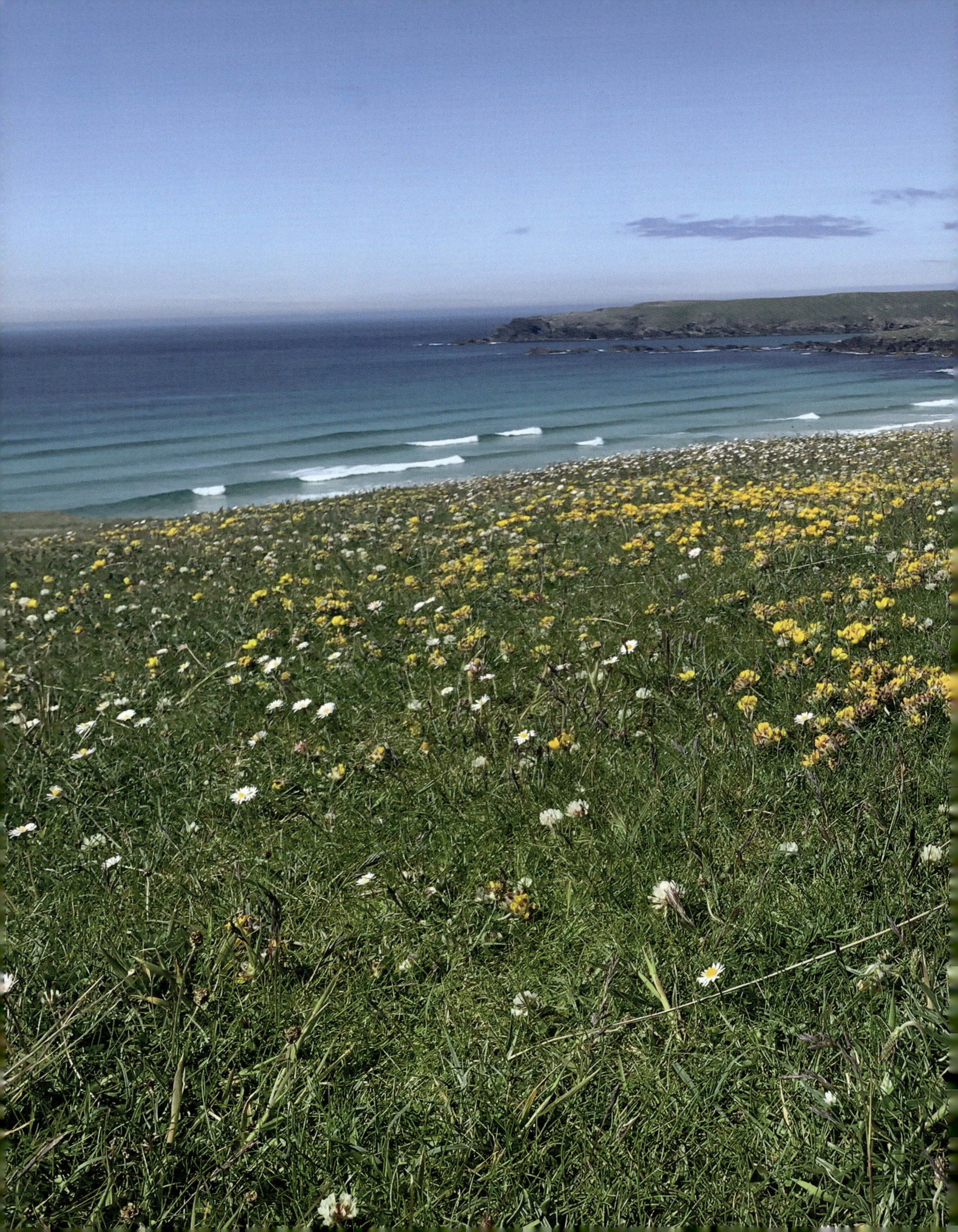

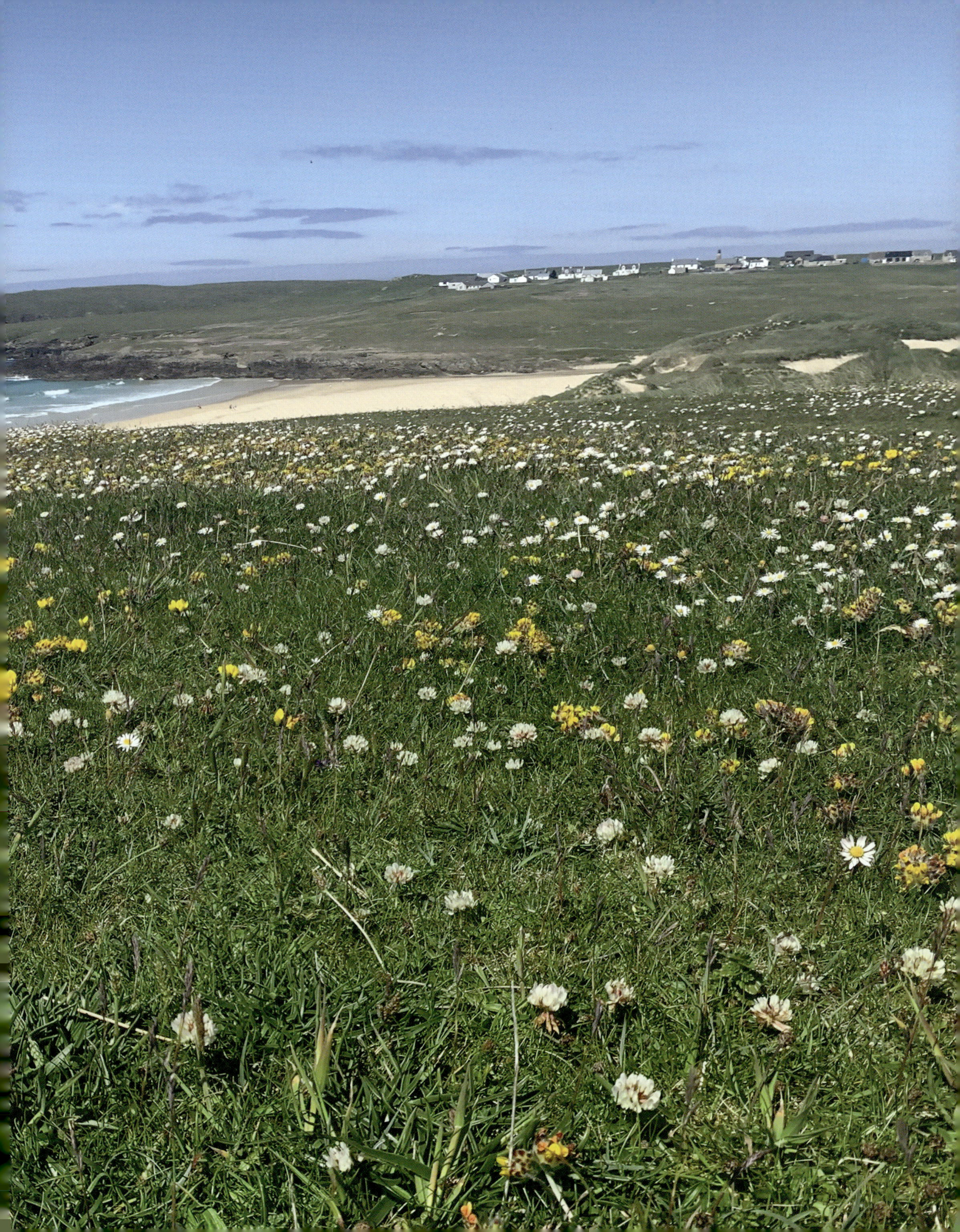

102

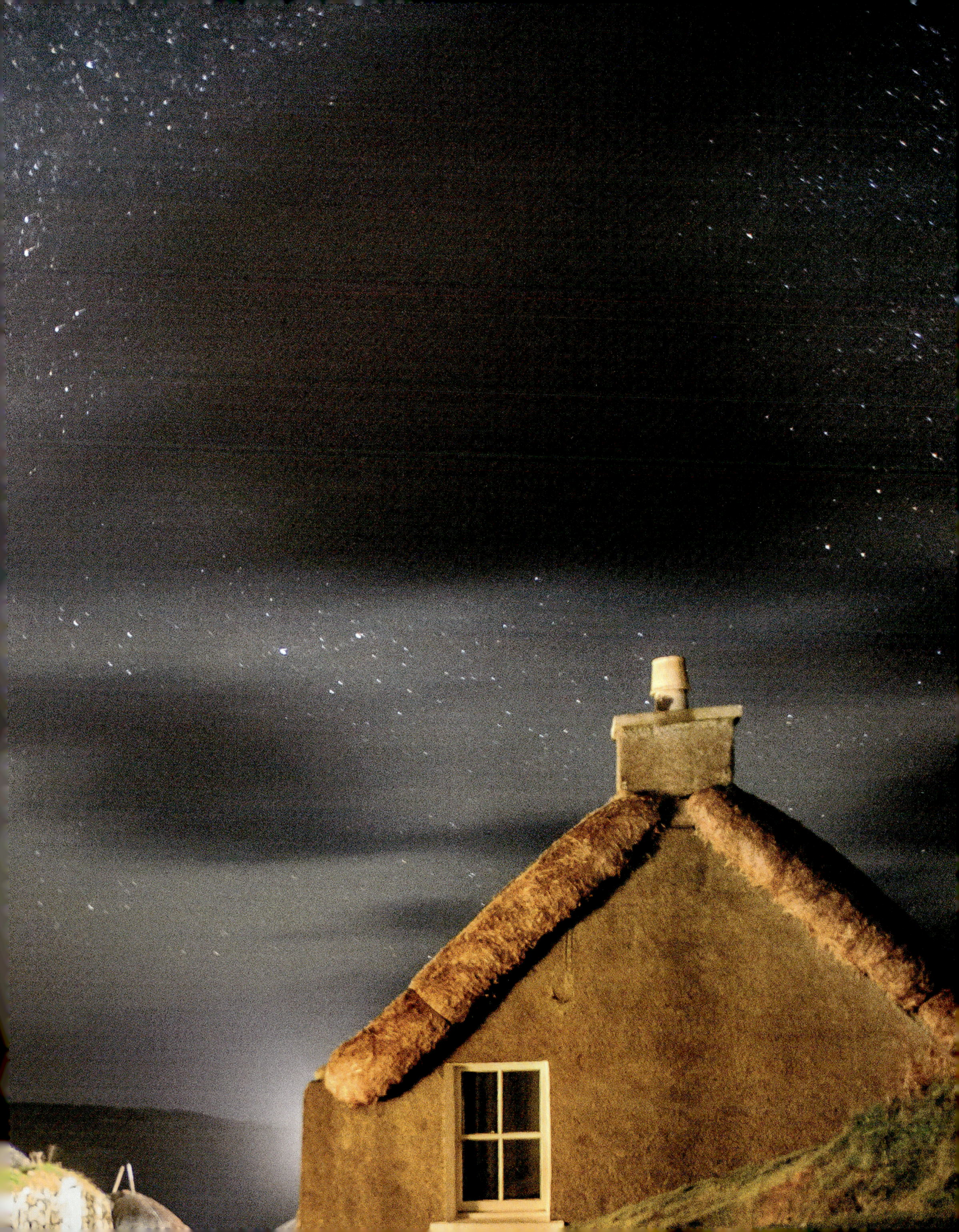

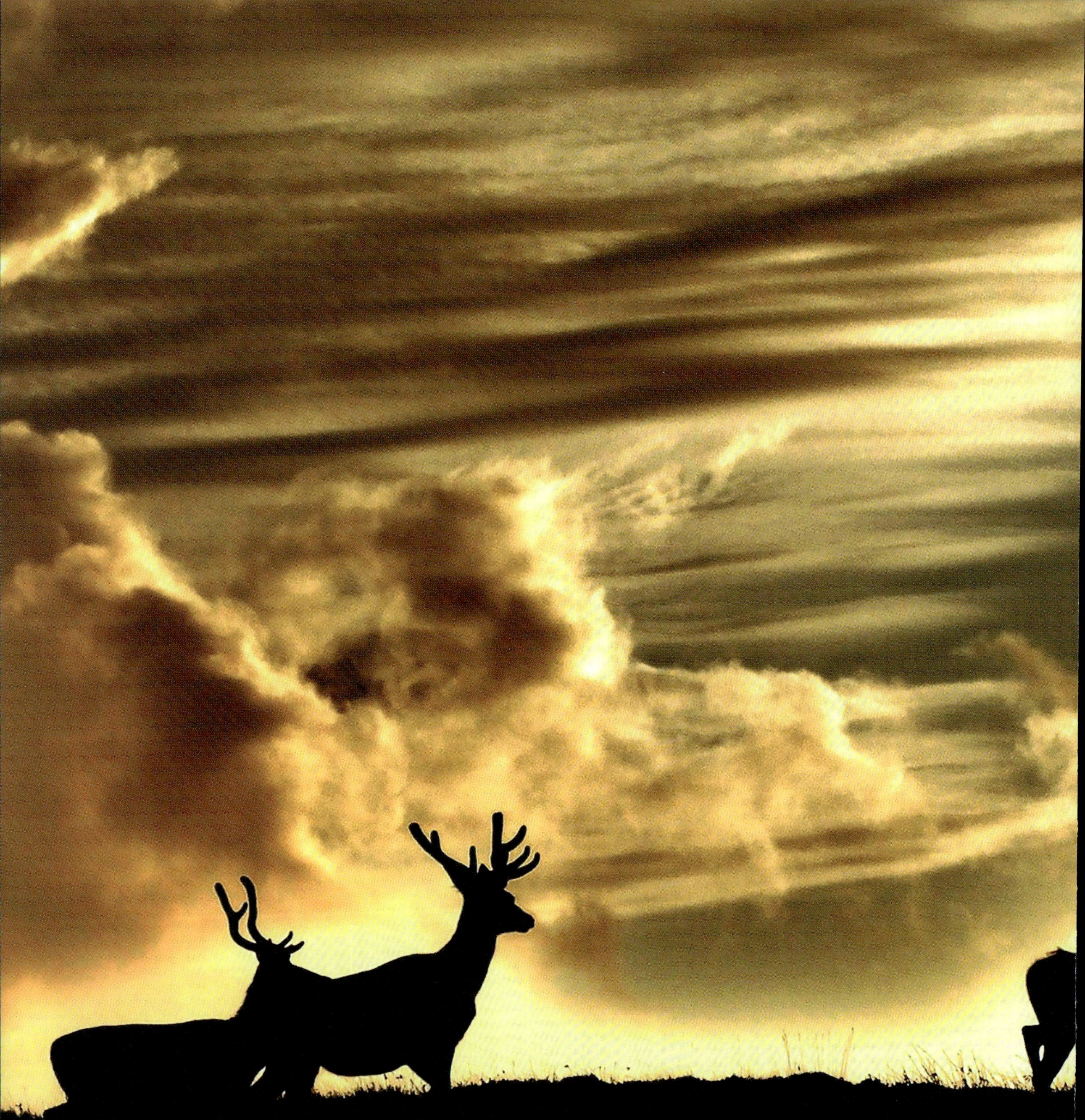

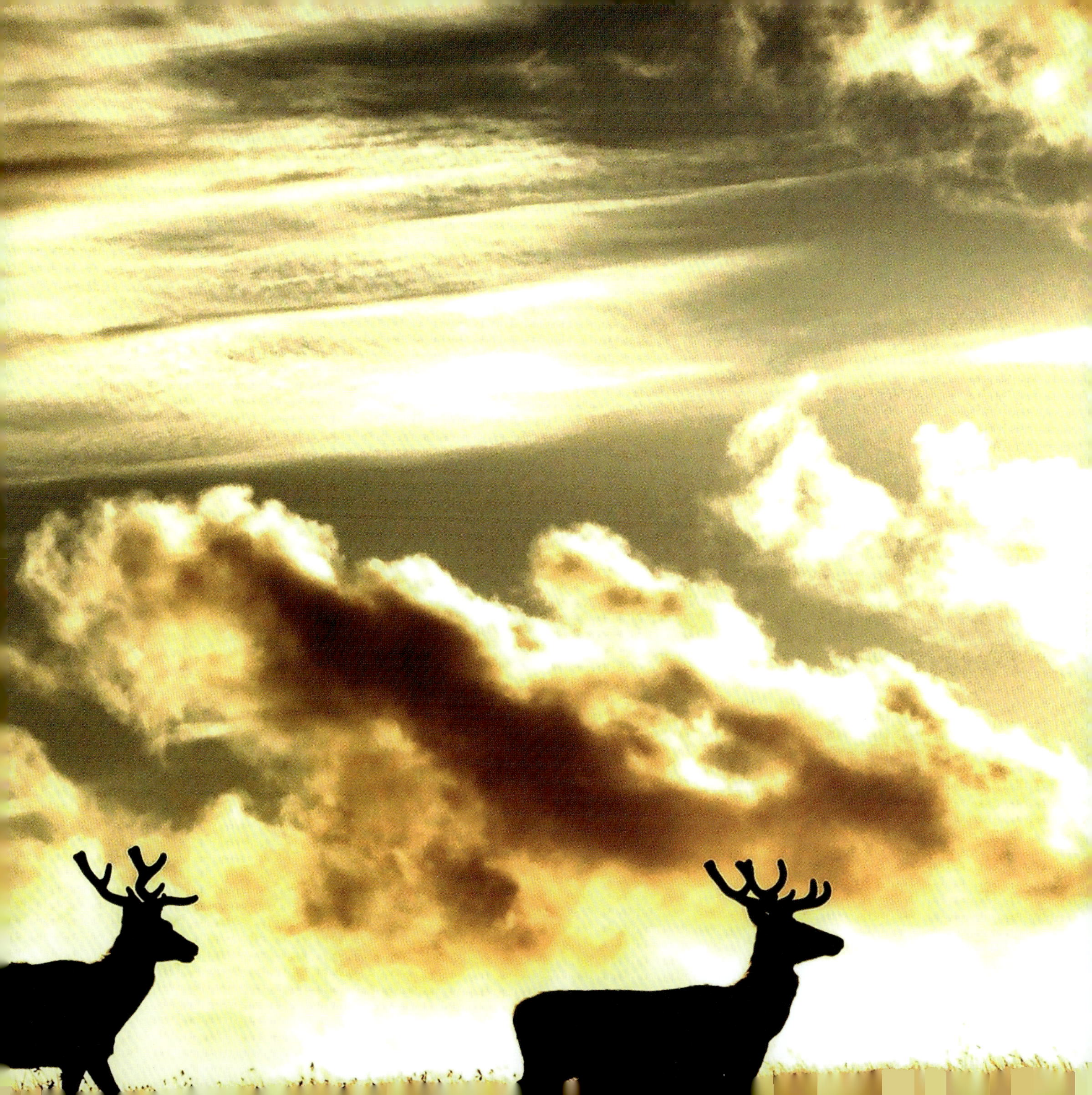

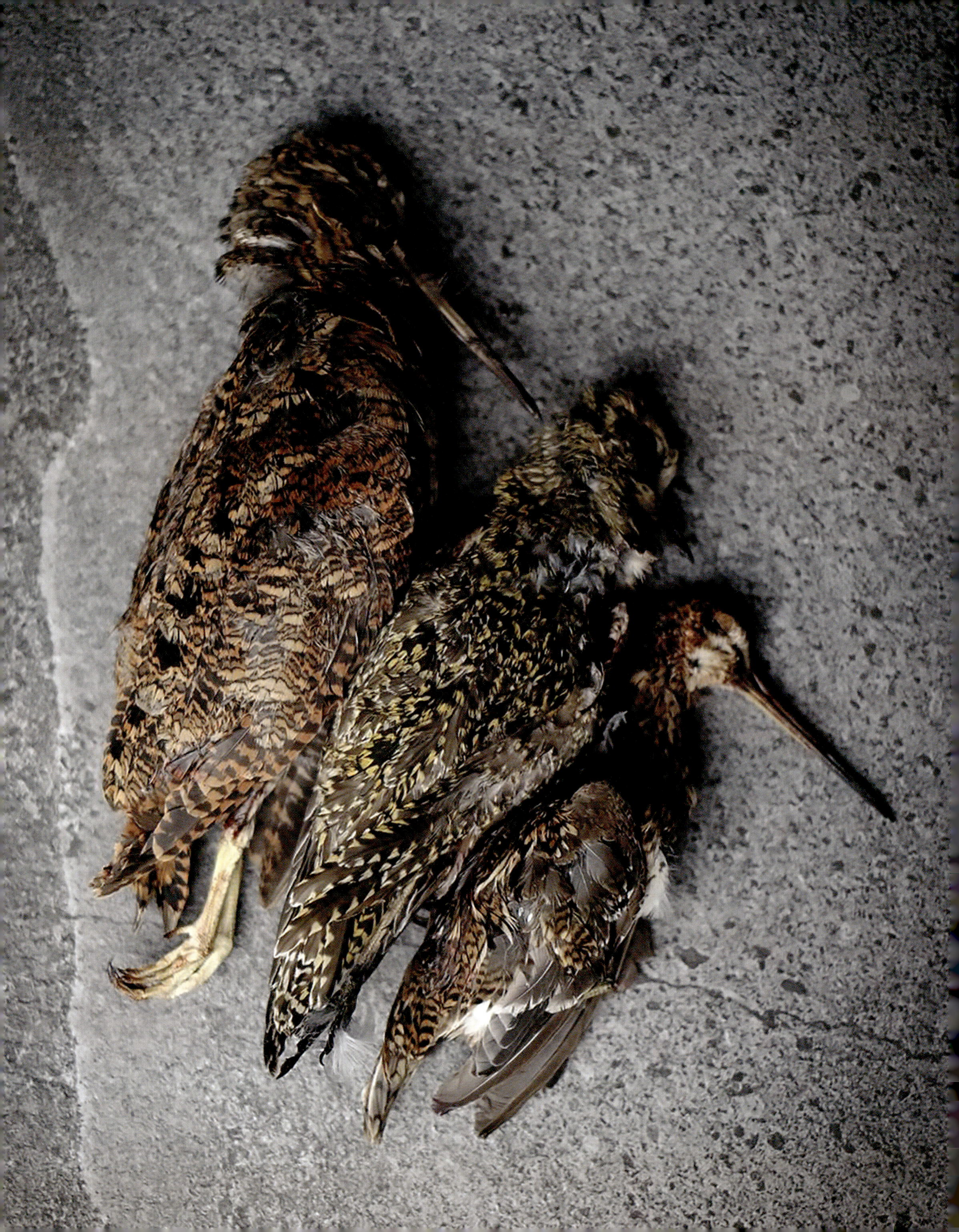

Wildfowl and Game
Eòin Fhiadhaich is Ainmhidhean

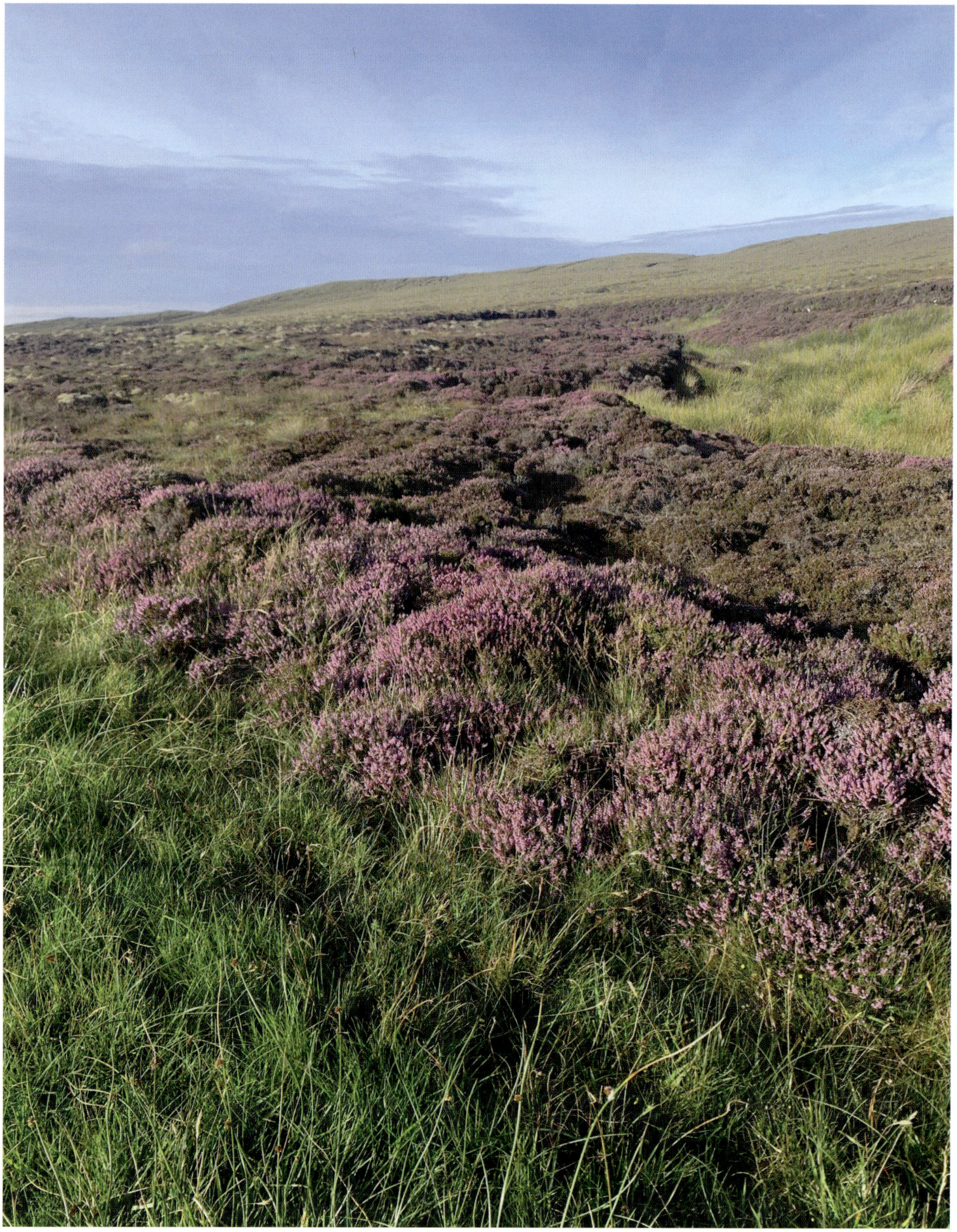

Pictured on page 106 are three birds that are very much on the quarry list for those who are into Hebridean wildfowl shooting; woodcock, golden plover and snipe. Angus is a gamekeeper and a friend who supplied me with the most amazing game over the years going back to my Sùlair days. He would even take me out to the moor now and again to shoot grouse and woodcock. The Hebrides have a bountiful supply of game birds and red deer. In Scotland the woodcock season runs from 1 September to 31 January.

Anns an dealbh air duilleag 106 tha trì eòin air a bheil sealgairean a tha dèidheil air sealg eòin fhiadhaich ann an eileanan Innse-Gall measail – coileach-coille, feadag bhuidhe agus naosg. Tha Aonghas na gheamair agus na charaid a tha air sitheann cho math 's a tha ri fhaighinn a chumail rium, a' dol air ais gu làithean Sùlair. An-dràsta 's a-rithist bheireadh e mi a-mach chun na mòintich a shealg cearcan-fraoich agus coilich-coille. Tha stòras de dh'èoin-seilge agus de dh'fhèidh anns na h-eileanan. Ann an Alba faodar coilich-coille a shealg eadar a' chiad latha den t-Sultain agus an latha mu dheireadh den Fhaoilleach.

GROUSE ROASTED OVER HEATHER — CRISPY KALE — A SAUCE MADE FROM GAMESTOCK, HEATHER AND WILD MOORBERRIES

The grouse should be hung for at least 2-3 days. This helps the meat to relax after shooting and for the gamey flavour which the grouse is famous for to develop.

CEARC-FHRAOICH AIR A RÒSTADH THAIRIS AIR FRAOCH — CÀL BRISG — SABHS DÈANTE LE STOC SITHINN, FRAOCH AGUS BRAOILEAGAN

Bu chòir don chearc-fhraoich a bhith crochte fad co-dhiù 2-3 làithean. Tha seo a' cuideachadh na feòla a shocrachadh an dèidh dhan urchair a dhol innte agus tha e a' leigeil le blas ainmeil nan cearcan-fraoich leasachadh.

Grouse
1 whole grouse

Remove the head, legs and wings, checking that all feathers have been removed. Wash the grouse making sure you get rid of any blood left in the cavity. Dry with a towel. Pre-heat oven to 180°C. Place your heather in the bottom of a lidded roasting pan with a rack sat on top. Brown the grouse in a pan over high heat until the skin is golden brown. Carefully light the heather until it starts smoking, placing the grouse on the rack and the lid on. Cook for 10 minutes. If the grouse needs longer, smoke the heather again before returning to the oven. To check that the grouse is cooked, squeeze the thickest part of the breast and it should have a nice spring to it. Rest for 10-15 minutes. Remove the breasts and keep the bones for the sauce.

Grouse Legs
200g salt
heather

Mix salt and heather together in bowl. In a container spread a generous layer of the salt mixture and place the grouse legs on top and cover with the rest of the salt. Cover and refrigerate for three hours. Rinse the salt from the legs and let them sit in clean water for 20 minutes changing the water after 10 minutes. While the grouse legs are soaking warm some duck fat up to 90°C. Remove the grouse legs after 20 minutes, dry and place in duck fat for about 3-4 hours but checking after two. The legs are ready when the meat comes away from the bone easily. Pan fry for a nice golden crispy skin.

Game Sauce
chicken stock
1 onion
1 celery
1 carrot
game bones
heather
moorberries

Pre-heat oven to 180°C. Place the bones in a roasting tray and cook until the bones are nicely golden all over. You don't want to over roast them or they will become bitter. Peel onion, carrot and wash celery. Chop into rough dice and roast in a pot, colouring all the vegetables. Set aside in bowl to cool. To the same pot add the bones and chicken stock. You want to get every bit of flavour from both bones and vegetables. Add enough stock to cover the bones and simmer for 1½ hours, add the roasted vegetables and cook a further 1½ hours or until you are happy with the flavour. Pass the stock through a sieve and reduce until you have a nice sauce consistency. Take off the heat and infuse with heather, checking after 10 minutes. If you can't taste heather leave for a further 10 minutes. Pass through a fine sieve or muslin and gently warm through, adding your moorberries just before serving.

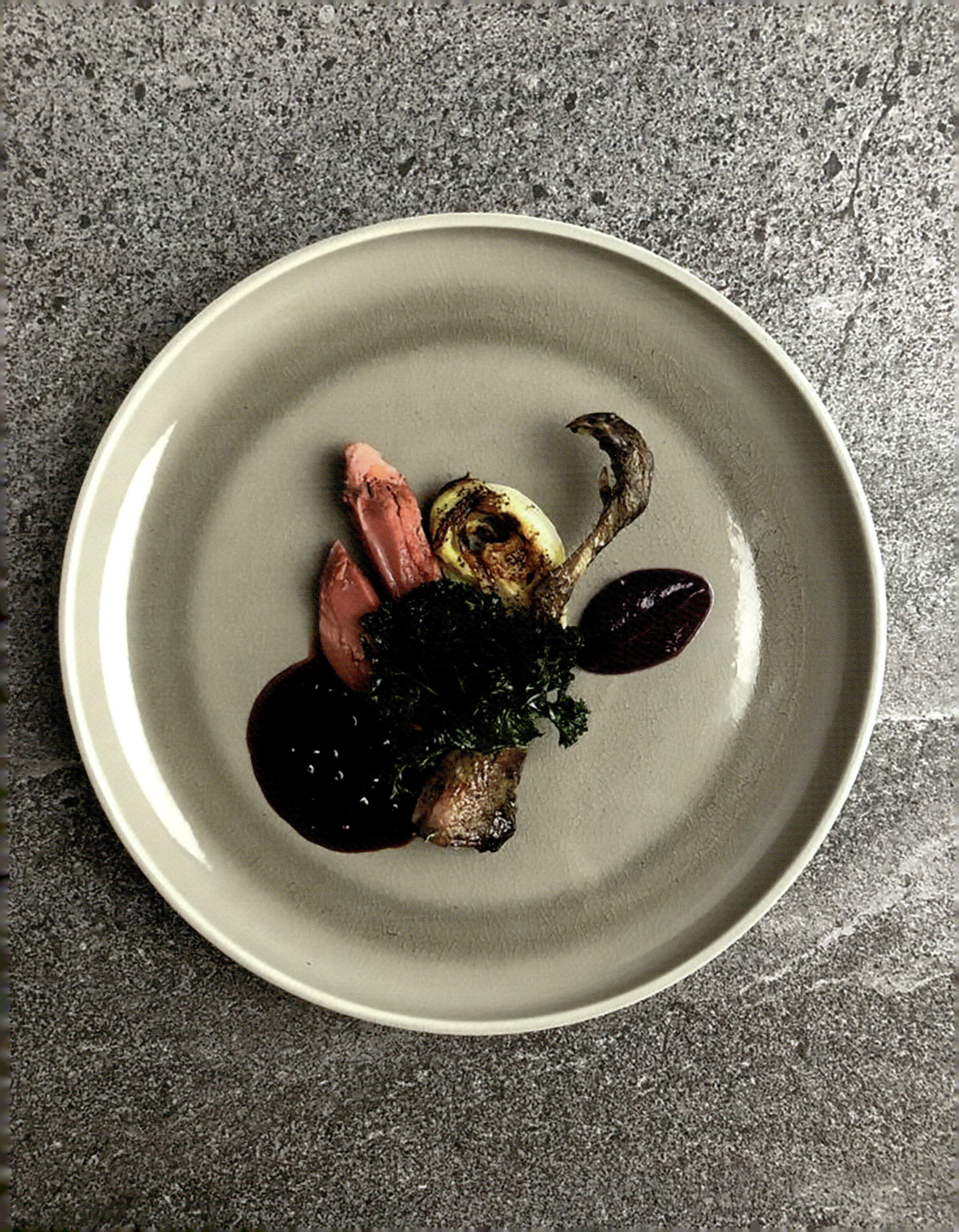

SLOW COOKED GREYLAG GOOSE LEG — SMOKED PUMPKIN — KALE — HONEY ROASTED PUMPKIN SEEDS — COLONSAY BEER AND HONEY GRAVY

Goose
goose legs
salt
thyme

Mix the salt and thyme together.
Spread a layer of salt and thyme mix on a tray, place the goose legs on top covering with another layer of salt. Cover and refrigerate overnight. Rinse the salt from the legs, leaving them to soak in clean water. Dry the goose legs and place in a deep tray or pot. Melt the goose fat and pour over the goose legs. Cook at 80°C until the meat is falling off the bone.

Smoked Pumpkin
½ pumpkin

Scoop the seeds from the pumpkin, season inside and place on a roasting tray flesh side down. Roast at 180°C for about 20 minutes. Check that it pierces easily with a knife. Using a smoking tray, place wood chips at the bottom, placing the scooped out pumpkin flesh on the perforated tray. Light the wood chips with small blow torch, cover with a lid and leave for 10 minutes. Remove the lid and relight wood chips for a further 10 minutes. Repeat depending on how smoky you like it. Mash the pumpkin.
You want to keep some texture of the pumpkin rather than having it smooth.

Kale
100g kale
pumpkin seed oil

Blanch kale in simmering water for about 30 seconds and refresh in iced water.
Dry and place on baking tray in oven at 140°C for about an hour.
Season and coat in pumpkin seed oil.

Pumpkin Seeds
seeds from ½ pumpkin
Colonsay honey

Warm up honey and in a bowl mix with pumpkin seeds coating them in the honey.
On a baking sheet, spread the seed mix and bake at 160°C for about eight minutes or until nice and golden.

Colonsay Beer and Honey Gravy
20g butter
70g shallots
3l chicken stock
1l veal stock
300ml Colonsay beer
275ml apple cider vinegar
goose bones

Sweat the onions in butter until golden, add the honey and caramelise.
Add the beer and vinegar and reduce to almost nothing. Add stocks, roasted bones and simmer for two hours. Pass through a sieve or muslin cloth and reduce until you have a delicious, rich, glossy sauce.

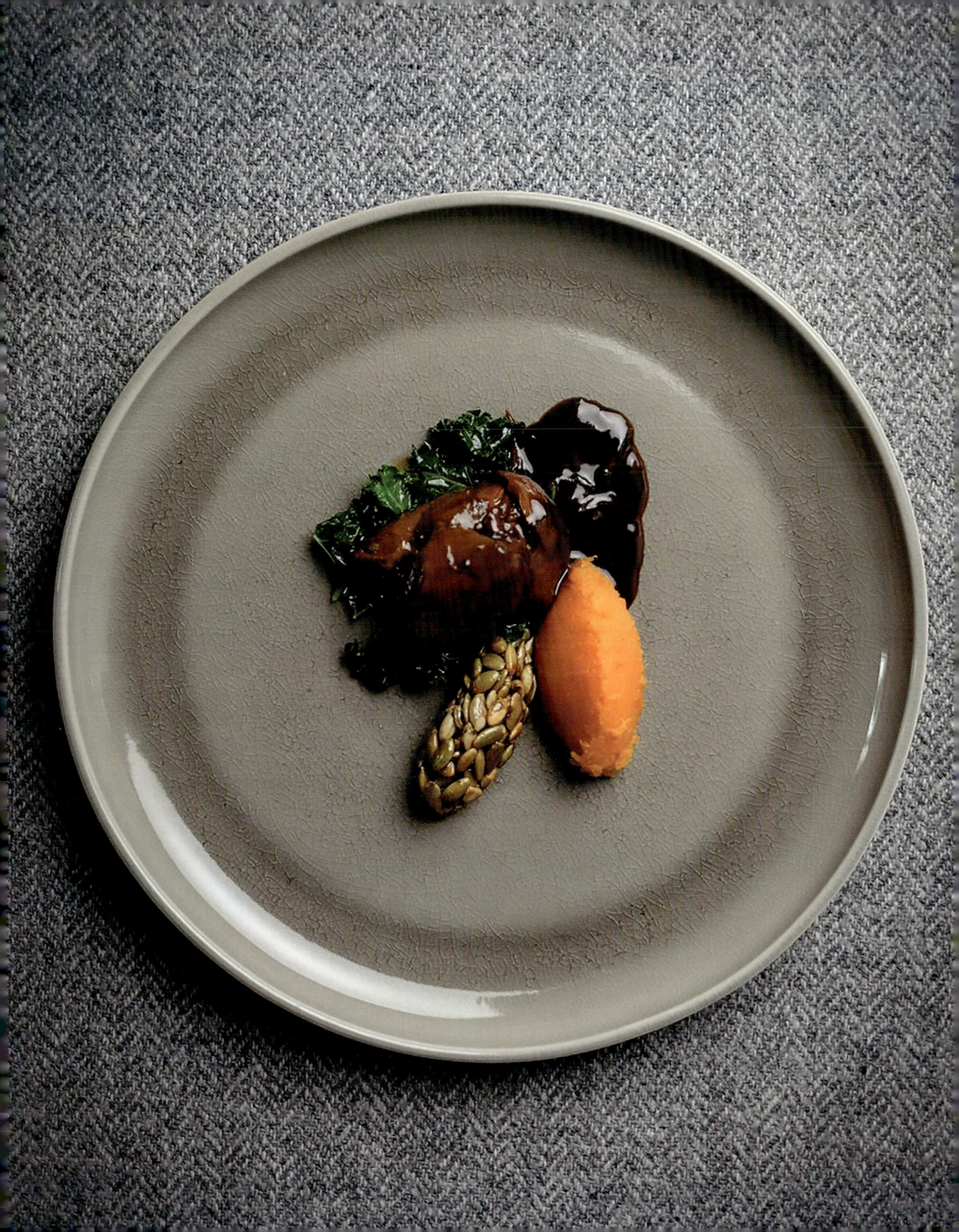

ROAST WOODCOCK — GREISEAGAN — PARSLEY ROOT, ELDERBERRY AND LIVER SAUCE

Woodcock has to be my favourite game bird to eat. It has a special, distinct flavour especially when cooked with its entrails intact. When you cook woodcock you can roast the bird whole, without having to remove any of the entrails because they empty their bowels when they take off. Traditionally the entrails would then be mashed and served on a piece of toast along with the roast bird. Here I have added the entrails to an old Hebridean dish called *greiseagan*. *Greiseagan* is similar to skirlie but instead of onions you use leeks that have been cooked in animal fat before adding oatmeal and then finishing with a handful of fresh moorberries, the little berries you find hidden away in the heather (bilberries or blaeberries).

Woodcock
2 whole woodcock
50g softened butter
salt and pepper

Pluck the feathers from the body and legs, remove the wings, leaving its legs and feathered head on, and prepare it for roasting by stuffing its beak through its thighs to hold it tight. Rub the birds with softened butter and season.
Roast in a very hot pre-heated oven (225°C) for 12-15 minutes. Giving an exact time is difficult as cooking game birds is very much about feel. Leave to rest.
Remove the entrails and add the *greiseagan* and the livers for the sauce.

Greiseagan
100g medium oatmeal
50g animal fat
white of 1 leek
60ml game stock
50g moorberries
cooked woodcock entrails

Melt the dripping in a heavy based pan and sweat the leeks off until softened.
Add the oatmeal to the leeks and continue to fry for about 10 minutes, stirring from time to time until the oatmeal is crisp and light brown.
Add the stock and berries and reduce.
Finish with the mashed entrails and season with salt and pepper to taste.

Parsley Root Purée
250g parsley root
120ml double cream
120ml whole milk

Peel and trim the parsley and cut into small pieces. Place into a small saucepan, pour over the milk and cream and place over a medium heat.
Bring to a gentle simmer and cook for around 25 minutes until soft and tender.
Blend until smooth to make it into a purée, adding salt to season.

Elderberry and Liver Sauce
roasted woodcock carcasses
cooked woodcock liver
1 small onion
1 carrot
bay leaf
100ml elderberry wine
500ml chicken stock
500ml game stock
elderberry jam and berries

Sweat off one small onion, one carrot and a bay leaf. Add some roasted carcasses (we keep the carcasses from the night before and roast them in the following day's sauce). De-glaze the pan with 100ml of elderberry wine, reduce, add 500ml chicken stock and 500ml of game stock. Reduce until the sauce is nice and glossy. Pass through a sieve with ½ tsp of elderberry jam and the cooked liver. Finish with a few elderberries.

COILEACH-COILLE RÒSTA — GREISEAGAN — SABHS LE FREUMH PEIRSILL, CAORA-DROMAIN AGUS ADHA

'S e coileach-coille an t-eun fiadhaich as fheàrr leam airson ithe. Tha blas sònraichte eadar-dhealaichte aige, gu h-àraid nuair a tha e air a chòcaireachd le mhionach air fhàgail na bhroinn. Nuair a tha thu a' còcaireachd coileach-coille faodaidh tu a ròstadh slàn gun a bhroinn a ghlanadh oir bithidh iad a' falmhachadh an innidh nuair a bhios iad a' dol air iteig. Gu traidiseanta, bhiodh am mionach air a phronnadh agus air a chur air pìos tost còmhla ris an eun ròsta. An seo tha mi air am mionach a chur ri seann bhiadh Innse-Gallach air a bheil greiseagan. Tha greiseagan coltach ri *skirlie* ach an àite uinneanan chleachdadh tu creamh-gàrraidh a chaidh a chòcaireachd ann an geir mus cuireadh tu ann a' mhin-choirce agus mu dheireadh làn cròig de bhraoileagan no corra-mhitheagan, na dearcan beaga a gheibh thu air falach san fhraoch.

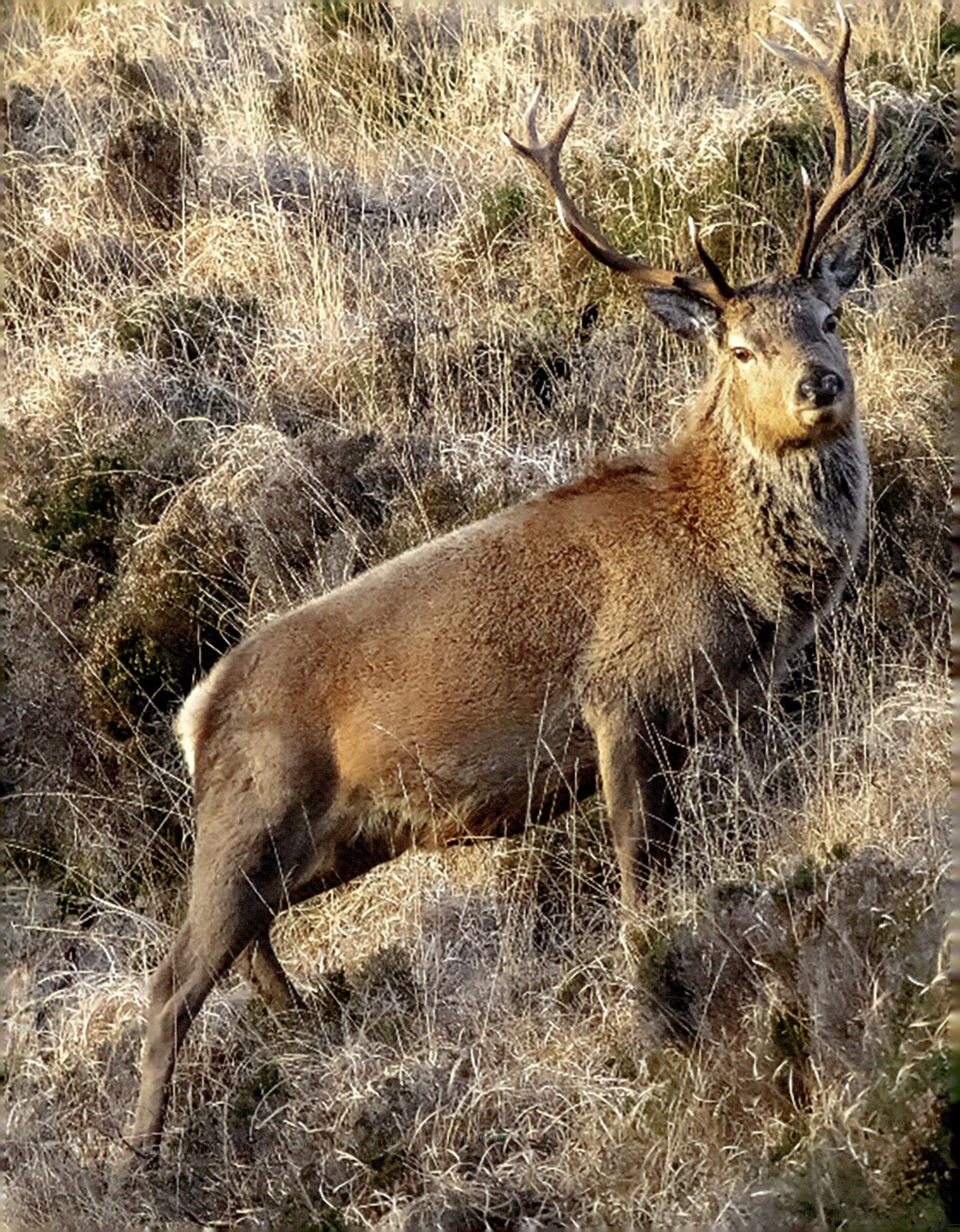

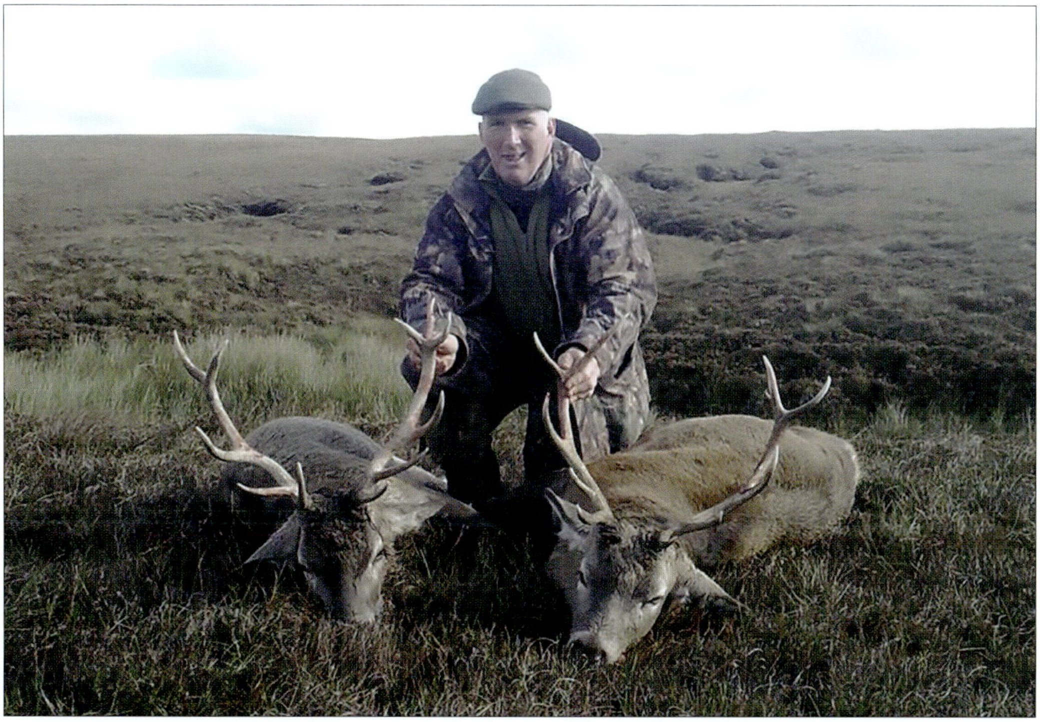

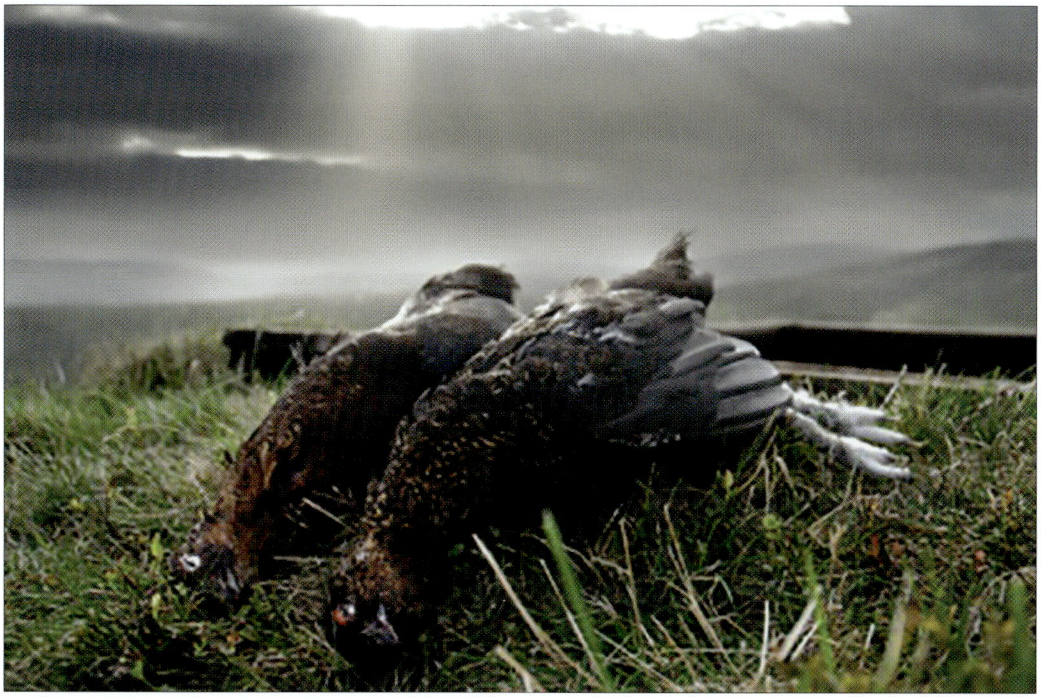

WILD GOOSE AND STORNOWAY BLACK PUDDING SCOTCH PIE — SMOKED TOMATO CHUTNEY

Wild Greylag geese are a pest throughout the Hebrides, causing untold damage to crofts. They need to be controlled by being shot and are available for the table if you know who to ask! This pie is definitely one of my favourite goose recipes. The wild goose breasts are minced with Sweeny's pork belly and Stornoway black pudding. It is mixed with game gravy, elderberry jelly, salt, pepper, sage and spices. It's baked in a water pastry with the rendered down pork fat.

PÀIDH DE GHÈADH FIADHAICH AGUS MARAG DHUBH STEÒRNABHAIGH — CHATNAIDH DE THOMÀTOTHAN SMOCTE

Air feadh eileanan Innse-Gall's e plàigh a th'anns na gèoidh ghlasa a tha a' dèanamh mòran millidh air croitean. Feumar smachd a chumail orra le bhith gan sealg le gunna agus gheibhear iad airson an ithe ma tha fhios agad cò dha a dh'fhaighnicheas tu! 'S e am pàidh seo aon de na reasabaidhean le gèadh as fheàrr leam. Tha broillich geòidh fhiadhaich air am mion-ghearradh le brù muicfheòil bho Sweeny agus marag dhubh Steòrnabhaigh. Tha e air a mheasgachadh le grèibhidh sithinn, silidh caora-dhromain, salainn, piobair, slàn-lus agus spìosraidhean. Tha e air a chòcaireachd ann an cèis de phastraidh uisge le geir muicfheòil air a leaghadh 's a ghlanadh.

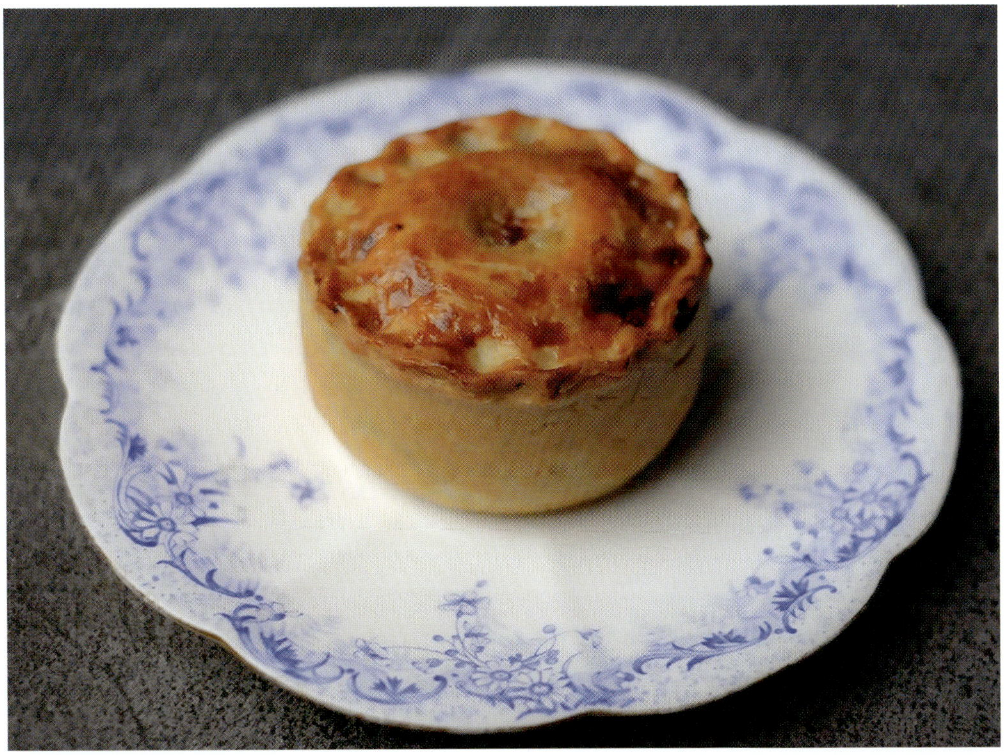

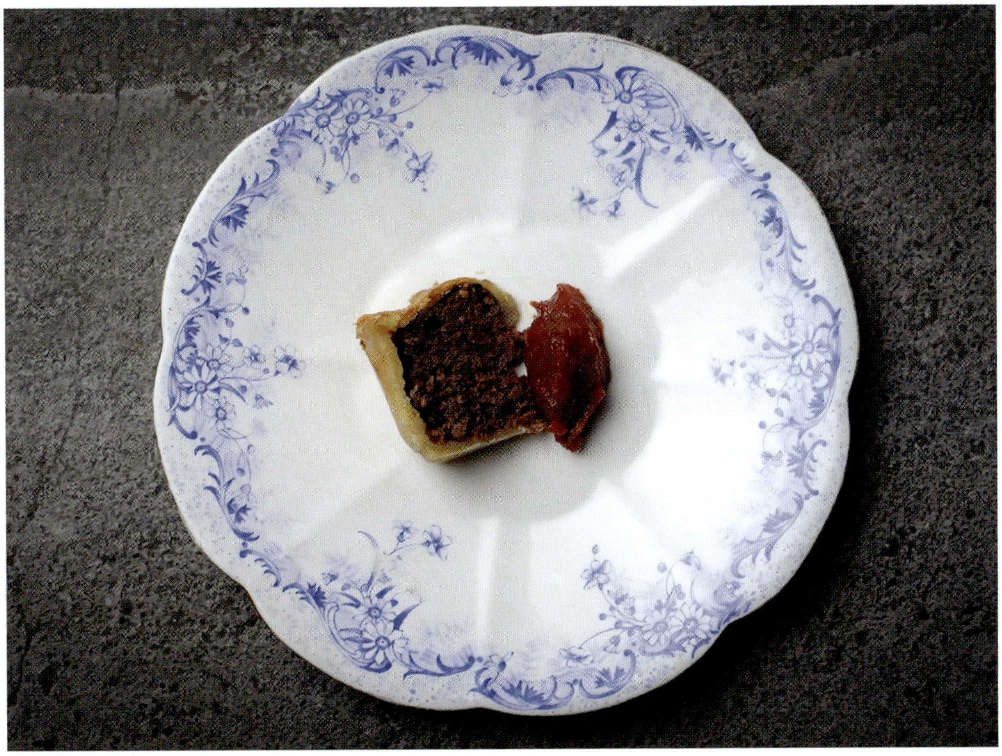

EISHKEN ESTATE RED DEER — BRUSSELS SPROUTS — GREISEAGAN — BRAMBLES

SITHEANN FÈIDH BHO OIGHREACHD ÈISGEIN — CÀL BEAG — GREISEAGAN — SMEURAN

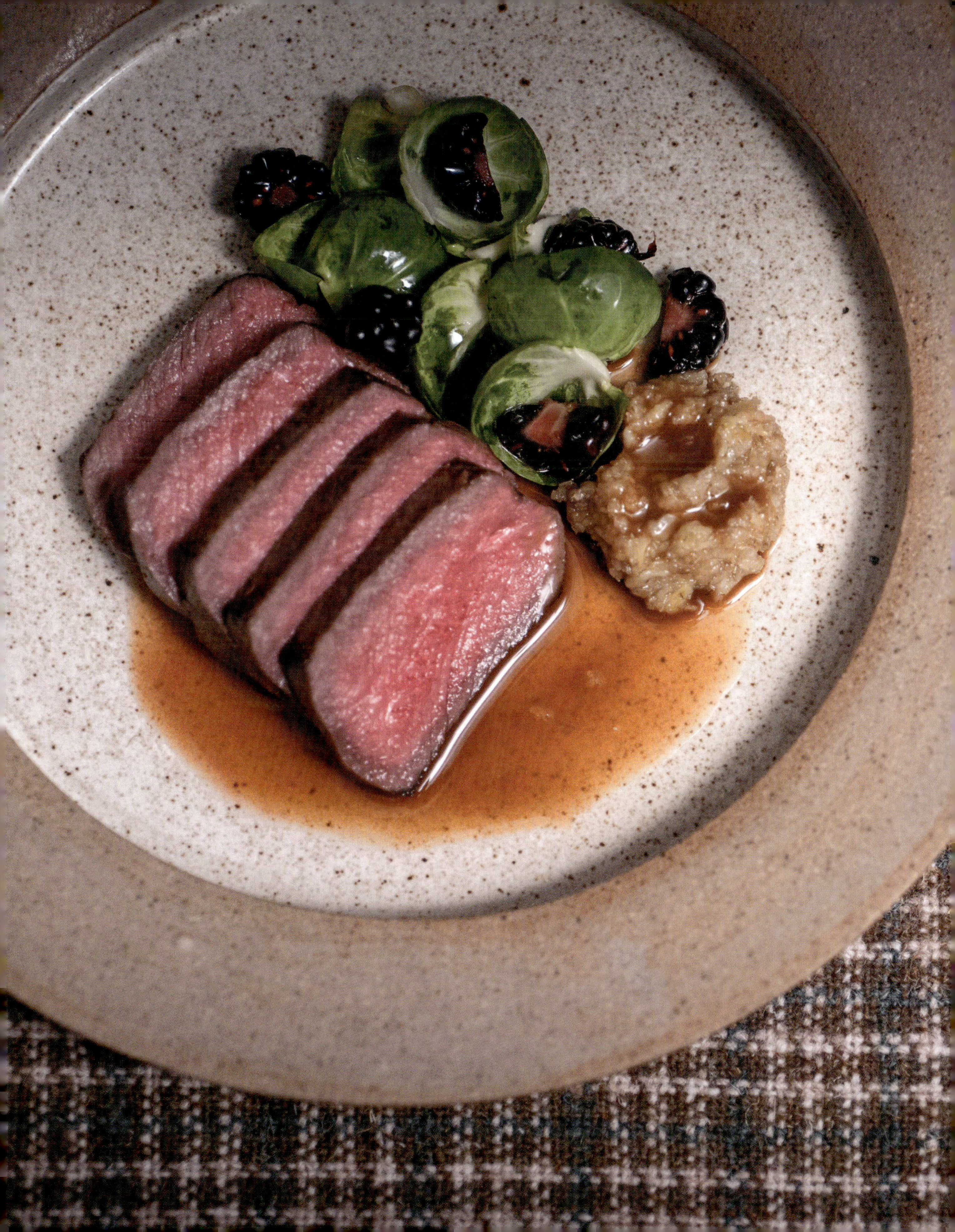

RAW BARVAS MOOR DEER — PEAT SMOKED GOLDEN BEETROOT — EWE'S MILK CROWDIE — ELDERBERRY AND BEETROOT KETCHUP

Venison lends itself well to being served raw. This is a lovely venison tartare with peat smoked beetroot seasoned with peat smoked oil, Skye sea salt, elderberry and caper vinegar, red onion and black pepper. As a foil to the venison there is a beetroot and elderberry ketchup, some freshly made ewe's milk crowdie cheese and some pumpkin seeds roasted in the smoked oil.

SITHEANN FÈIDH AMH BHO MÒINTEACH BHARABHAIS — BIOTAIS ÒR SMOCTE ANN AN CEÒ NA MÒNACH — GRUTH BAINNE CHAORACH — CEITSEAP CAORA-DHROMAIN AGUS BIOTAIS

Tha sitheann fèidh math amh. 'S e tartare sithinn a tha seo le biotais agus ola a chaidh a smocadh ann an ceò na mònach, salainn an Eilein Sgitheanaich, fìon geur caora-dhromain agus caparan, uinnean dearg agus piobar dubh a' cur ris a' bhlas. Airson blas na feòla a thogail tha ceitseap caora-dhromain agus biotais, gruth bainne chaorach air ùr dhèanamh agus sìol peapaig air an ròstadh san ola smocte.

PINE CURED RABBIT LOIN — SALT BAKED TURNIP — PINE NUTS — PRUNE AND PINE VINEGAR

This is a dish where we cure rabbit loins from a ¾ size young buck in a pine salt. We then coat the cured loins in pine oil and flash them in a hot pan to seal them and give them a sweet caramelised flavour. Once cooled we cut them into small pieces and dress them with a light pine oil and pine salt. The dish is then accompanied by slightly warmed salt baked turnip, toasted pine nuts, a prune and pine vinegar gel and some pickled young spruce shoots.

BLIAN COINEANAICH LE CIÙRADH GIUTHAIS — SNÈAP RÒSTA ANN AN SALAINN — CNOTHAN-GIUTHAIS — FÌON GEUR PRÙIN AGUS GIUTHAIS

Bidh sinn a' ciùradh blèin coineanaich bho bhoc trì-cairteal a mheud ann an salainn giuthais. Bidh sinn an uair sin gan còmhdach le ola giuthais agus gan cur ann am pana teth airson an fheòil a dhùnadh agus blas milis carra-mheillte a thoirt orra. Aon uair 's gu bheil iad air fuarachadh bidh sinn gan gearradh nam pìosan beaga agus a' cur craiteachan de dh'ola giuthais agus salainn giuthais orra. Còmhla riutha bidh snèap meadh-bhlàth a chaidh a ròstadh ann an craiceann salainn, silidh air a dhèanamh le fìon geur prùin agus giuthais agus buinnein picilte giuthais Lochlannach.

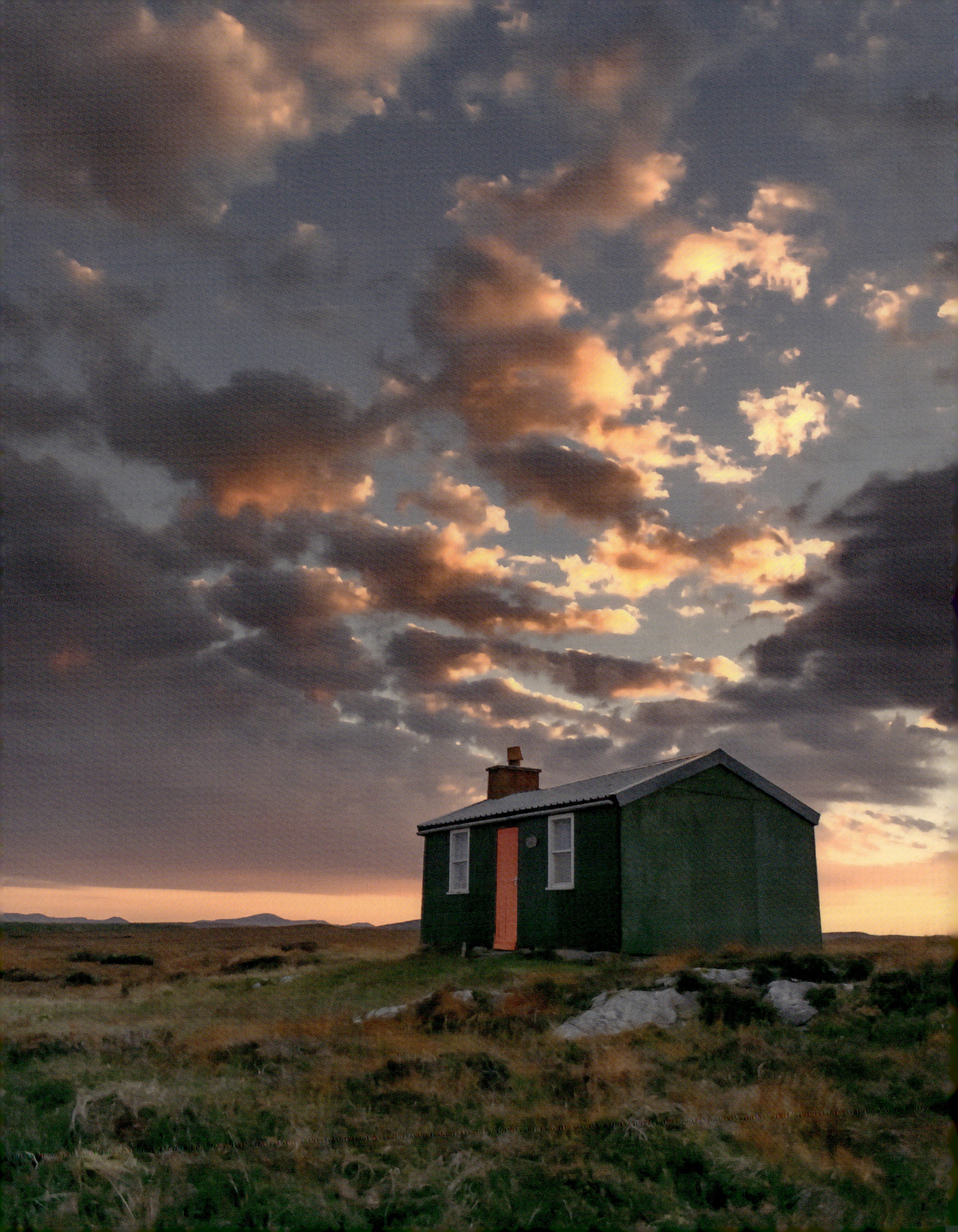

Sheiling
Àirigh

One of my favourite places in the world is out on the Skigersta moor at the *àirigh*. The atmosphere out at the *àirigh* on a beautiful Hebridean summer's day is special, the smell of peat smoke and heather filling the air, along with the sounds of the river flowing and the birds singing. The *àirighean* or sheilings were small thatched dwellings or huts situated out on the moor at Cuidhsiadar. In the summer months around May time, once the peats had been cut, locals would move their cattle from their winter quarters, giving the grass a rest and ensuring sufficient food for the cattle during autumn and winter. The sheiling huts were made from stone and turf, with a simple interior with a peat fire which would be used for all the cooking. Seating was made from a plank resting on two flat stones; the beds were made of heather and dried grass. The folk of Ness use their *àirigh* as a place of holiday and rest. I have such fond memories of summers spent out on the moor with my grandparents.

Am measg nan àitichean as fheàrr leam air an t-saoghal tha an àirigh a-muigh air mòinteach Sgiogarstaigh. Tha an àile air an àirigh air latha brèagha samhraidh cho sònraichte, le fàileadh ceò na mònach agus fàileadh an fhraoich gad chuairteachadh, 's gun fuaim ri chluinntinn ach crònan an uillt agus ceilearadh nan eun. B' e taighean beaga tughaidh no bothain a bh'anns na h-àirighean a bha a-muigh air a' mhòintich ann an Cuidhsiadar. Ann am mìosan an t-samhraidh bho thoiseach a' Chèitein, aon uair 's gun robh a' mhòine air a buain, bhiodh muinntir an àite a' gluasad a' chruidh bhon àite geamhrachaidh, a' toirt cothrom fàs dhan fheur is a' dèanamh cinnteach gum biodh biadh a' chruidh aca an ath fhoghar is geamhradh. Bha bothagan na h-àirigh air an dèanamh le clachan agus sgrathan, sìmplidh nam broinn, le teine mònach air am biodh a' chòcaireachd ga dhèanamh. Cha robh san àite-suidhe ach dèile fiodh air a chàradh air dà chlach rèidh. Bha na leapannan air an dèanamh le fraoch agus feur tioram. Bhiodh muinntir Nis a' cleachdadh an àirigh mar àite airson làithean-saora agus fois. Tha cuimhne cho blàth agam air samhraidhean air a' mhòintich còmhla ri mo sheanair 's mo sheanmhair.

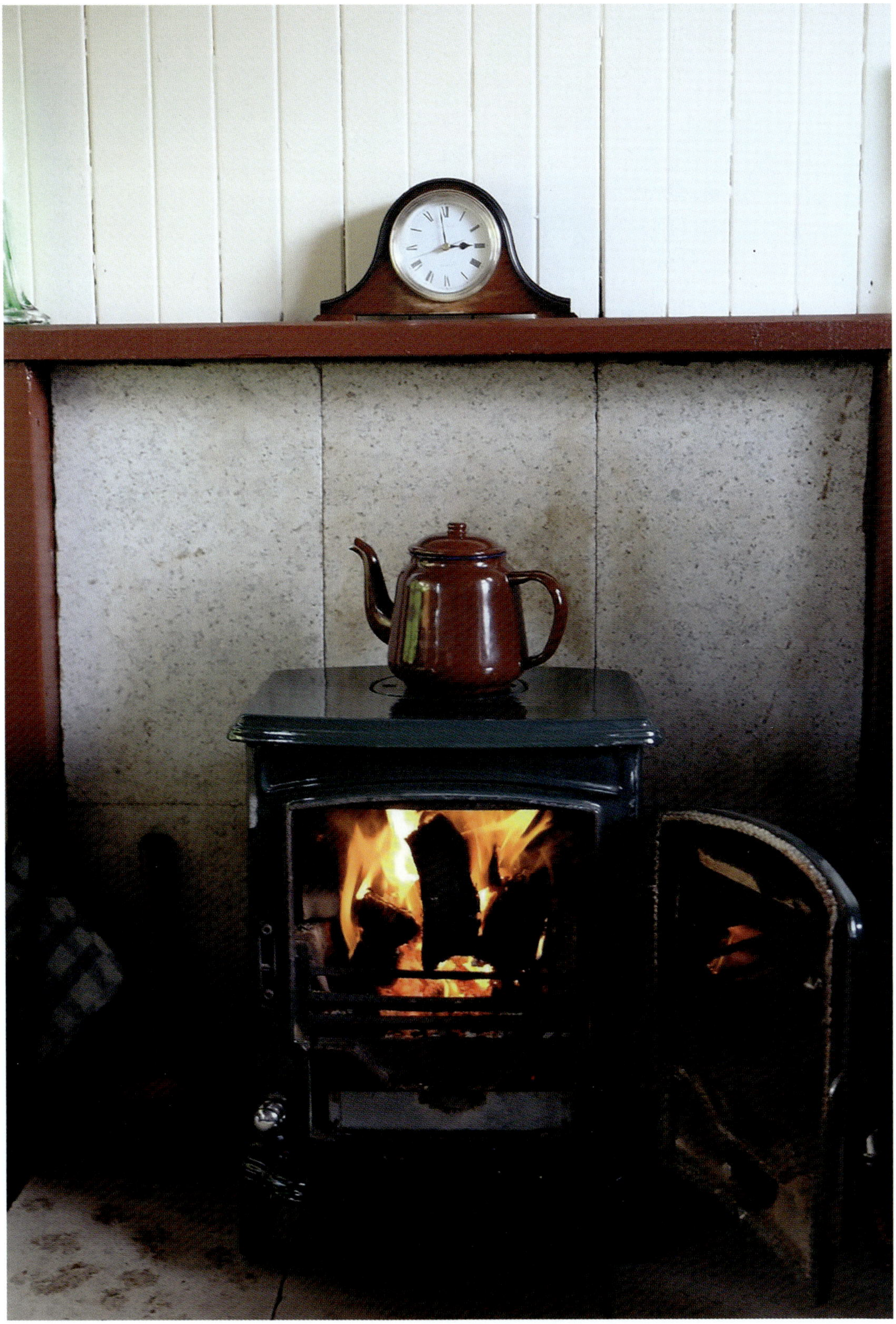

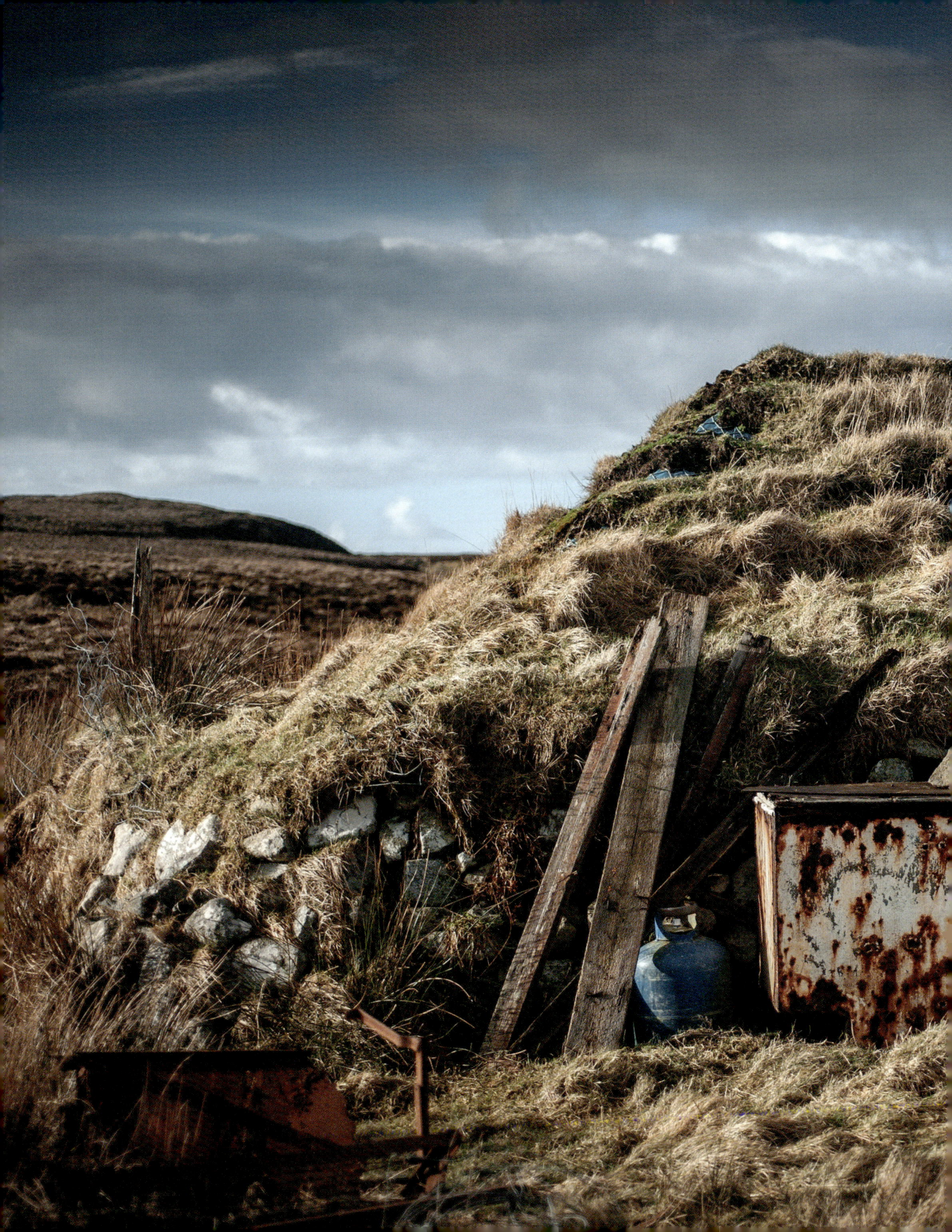

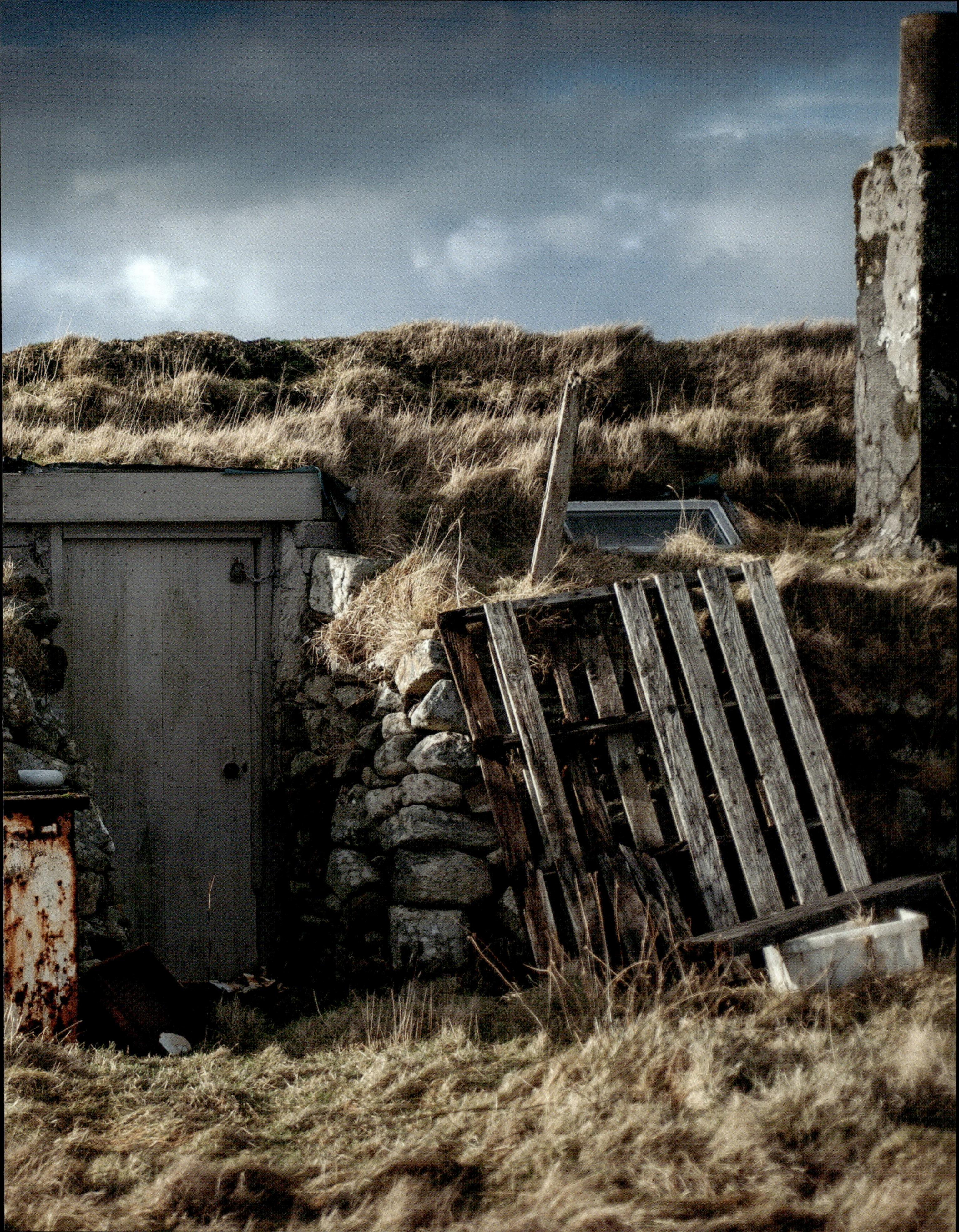

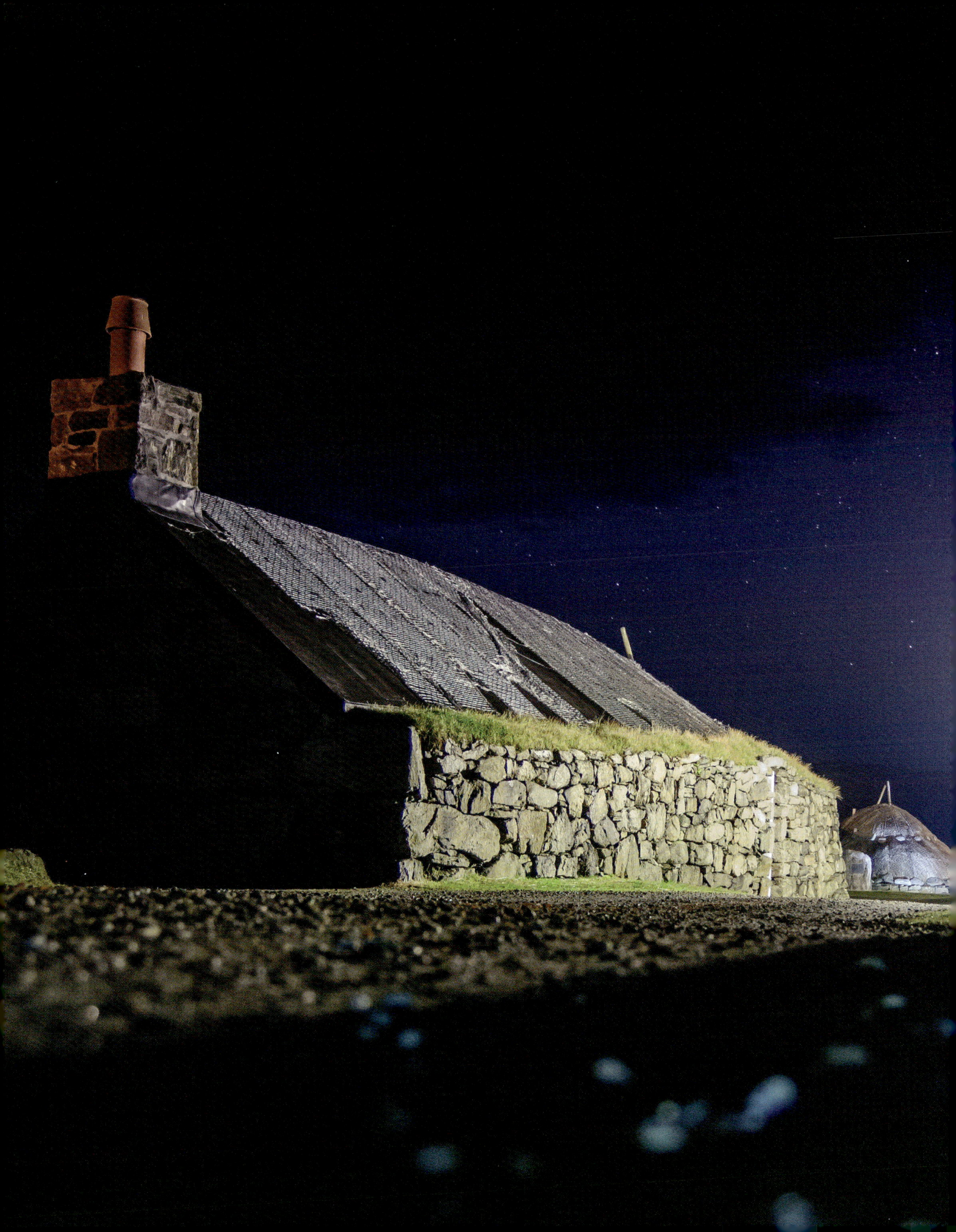

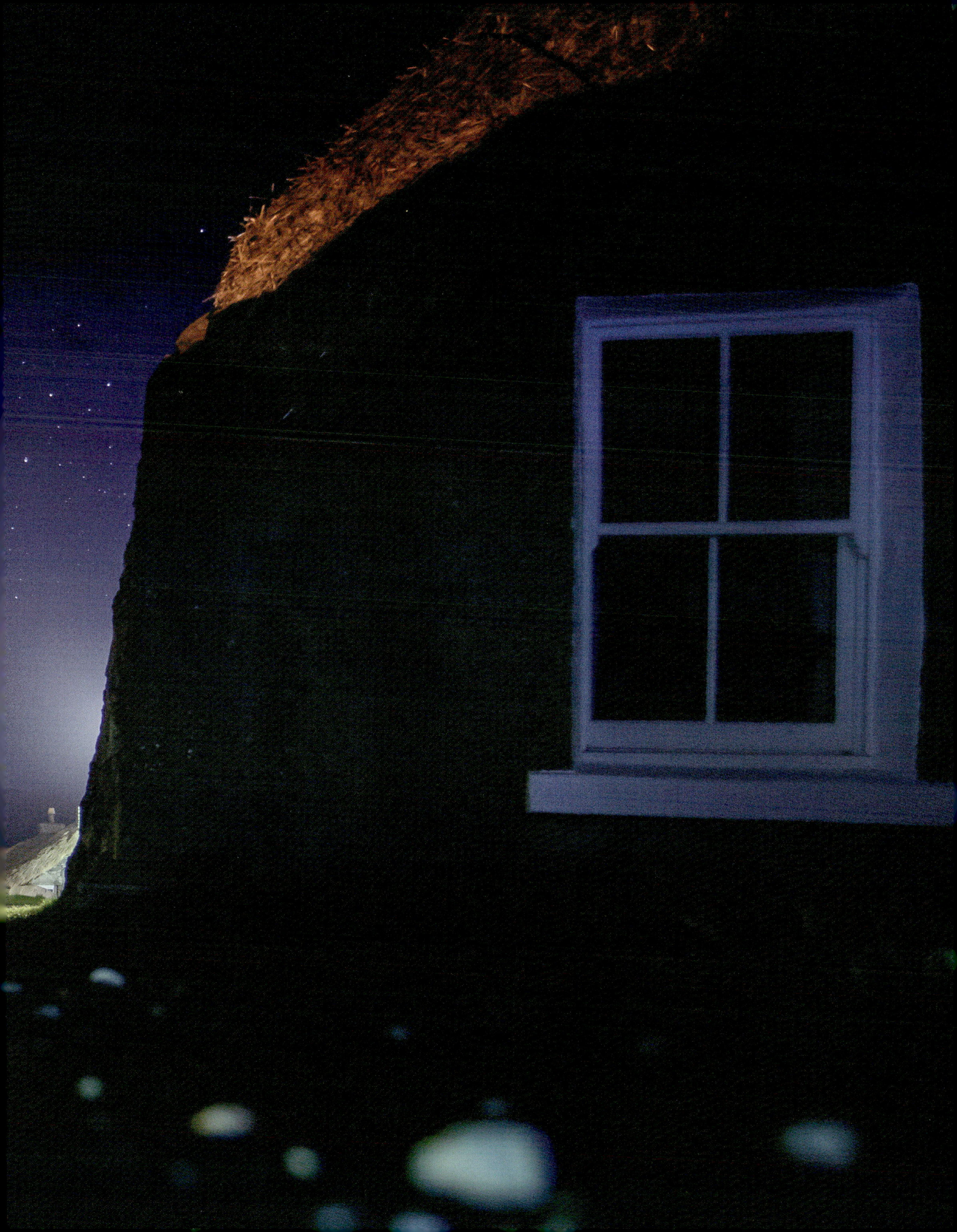

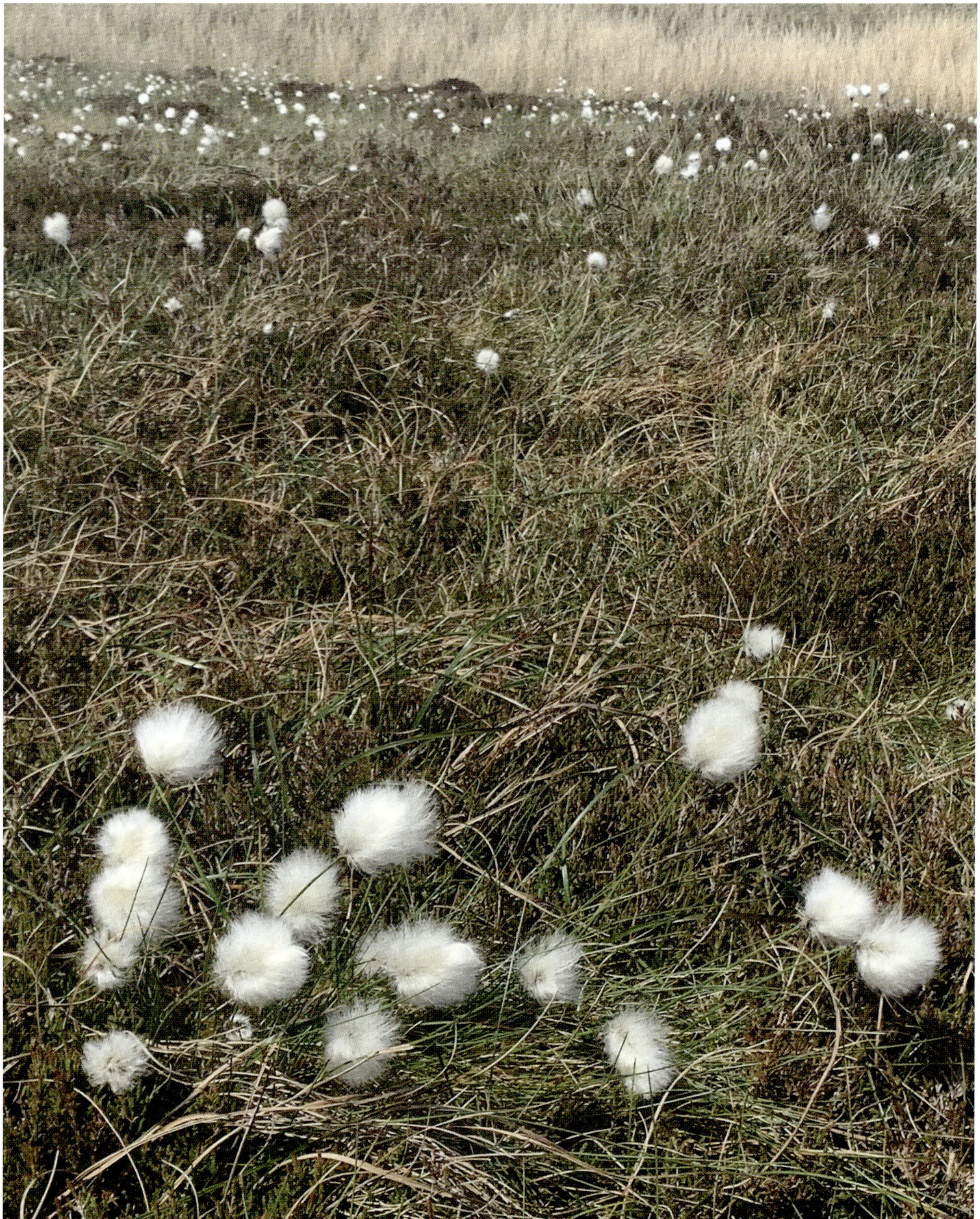

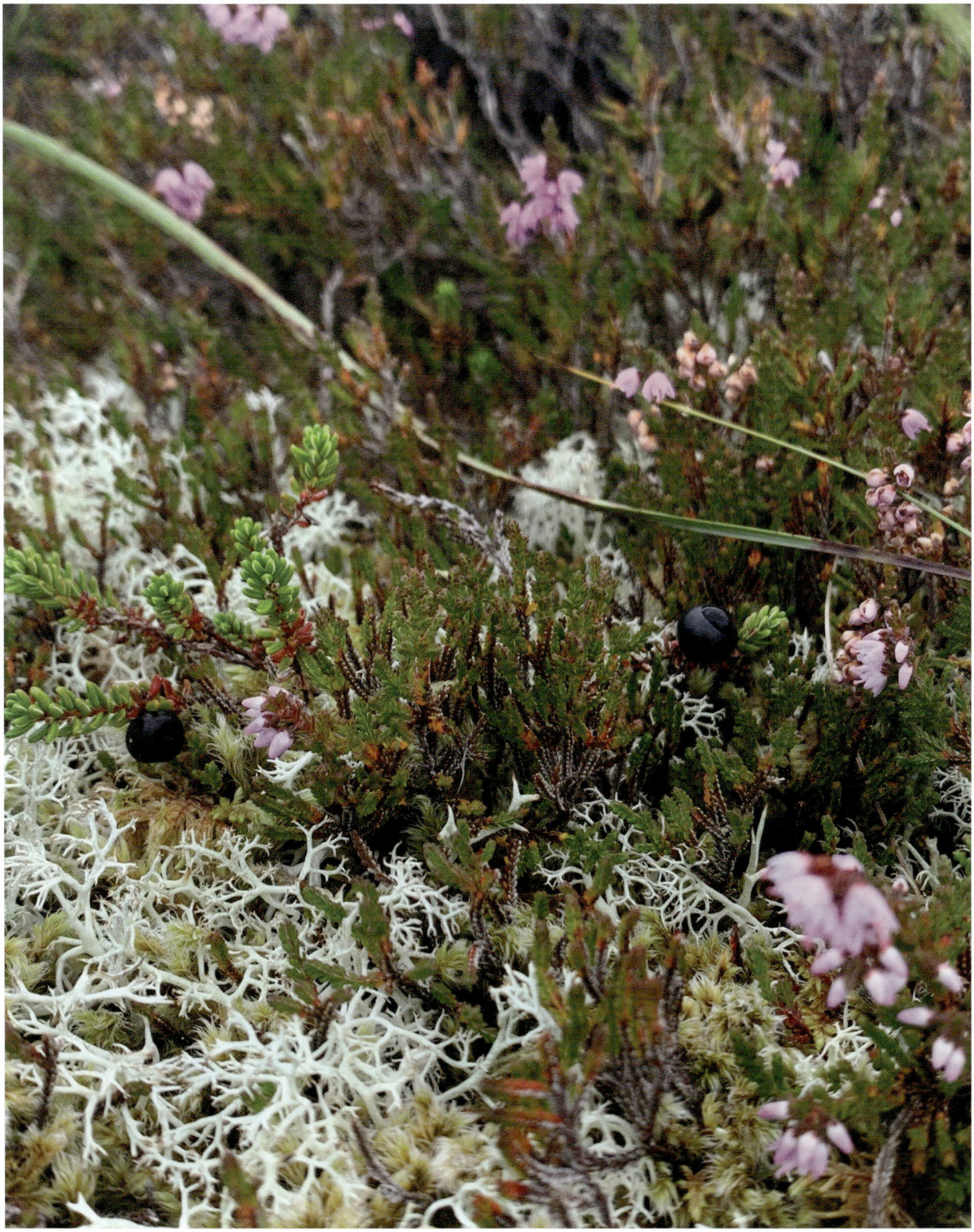

WILD ARCTIC HARE — FRUIT PUDDING — FERMENTED CELERIAC — APPLE AND ROSEHIP SAUCE

The Arctic hare is found on the moors of Lewis and has a distinctive white fur during the winter months. They are absolutely delicious, although many folk in the north of the island would not eat them because of superstition. They were thought to be witches in disguise and a bad omen to anyone who crossed the path of one!

Here I have paired it with fermented celeriac and rosemary purée, a tart apple and rosehip sauce and a slice of *marag mhilis* (fruit pudding), my take on the traditional Hebridean fruit pudding, made with oats that have been soaked in buttermilk, beef fat, barley flour, barley malt, onions, chopped prunes, rosemary and some spices. The dish is finished with a sauce made with the bones of the hare.

GEÀRR-GHEAL FHIADHAICH — MARAG MHILIS — SEILEARAG TÒIRNICHTE — SABHS ÙBHLAN AGUS MUCAGAN

Tha a' gheàrr-gheal ri lorg air mòintichean Leòdhais agus tha a còta sònraichte geal tro mhìosan a' gheamhraidh. Tha iad air leth blasta ged a tha mòran an ceann a tuath an eilein nach itheadh iad air adhbharan saobh-chràbhach. Bha cuid dhen bheachd gur e bana-bhuidsichean ann am breug-riochd a bh' annta agus gur e droch mhanadh a bh' ann dha neach a thigeadh tarsainn air tè.

An seo tha mi air a feòil a chur còmhla ri purée de sheilearag tòirnichte agus ròs-Màiri, sabhs geur ùbhlan agus mucagan agus sliseag de mharag mhilis, mo thionndadh-sa de mharag mhilis thraidiseanta, air a dèanamh le min-choirce a bha air a bhogadh ann am blàthach, geir mairtfheòil, flùr eòrna, braich eòrna, uinneanan, prùnaichean air an gearradh beag, lus-Màiri agus spìosraidhean. Tha e air a chriochnachadh le sabhs air a dhèanamh le cnàimhean a' gheàrr.

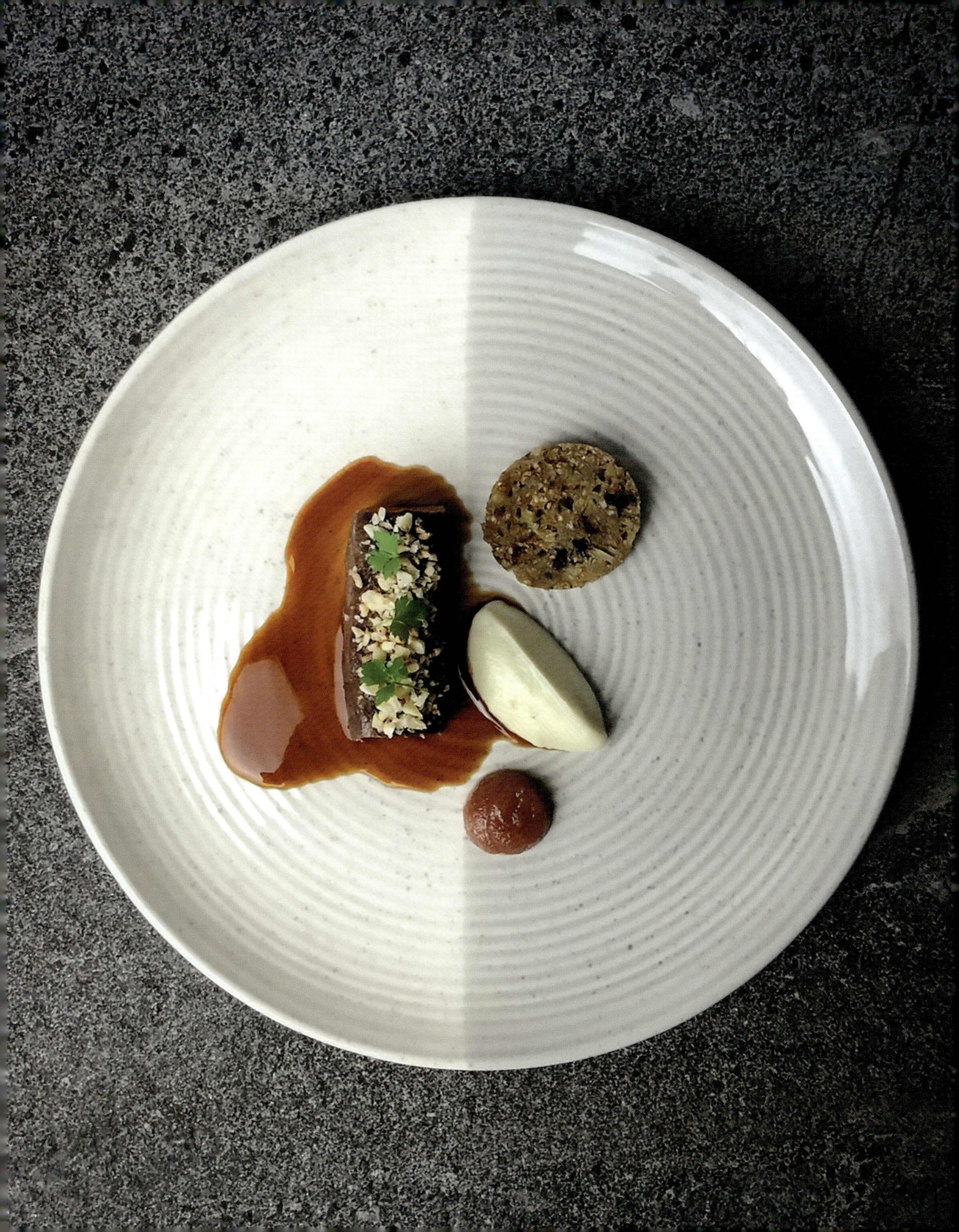

ROAST SNIPE — BLOOD AND BUCKWHEAT PORRIDGE —
MINT — DRIED MOORBERRIES

NAOSG RÒSTA — BROCHAN CRUITHNEACHD-BUIDHE AGUS FUIL —
MEANNT — BRAOILEAGAN TIORAM

WILD TEAL — BLACK PUDDING — WHITE SPROUTING BROCCOLI —
SALT BAKED CANDY BEETS AND BRAMBLES

CRANN-LACH FIADHAICH — MARAG DHUBH — CÀL-BROILEIN GEAL GUCAGACH —
BIOTAIS MILIS AIR AN RÒSTADH ANN AN SALAINN AGUS SMEURAN

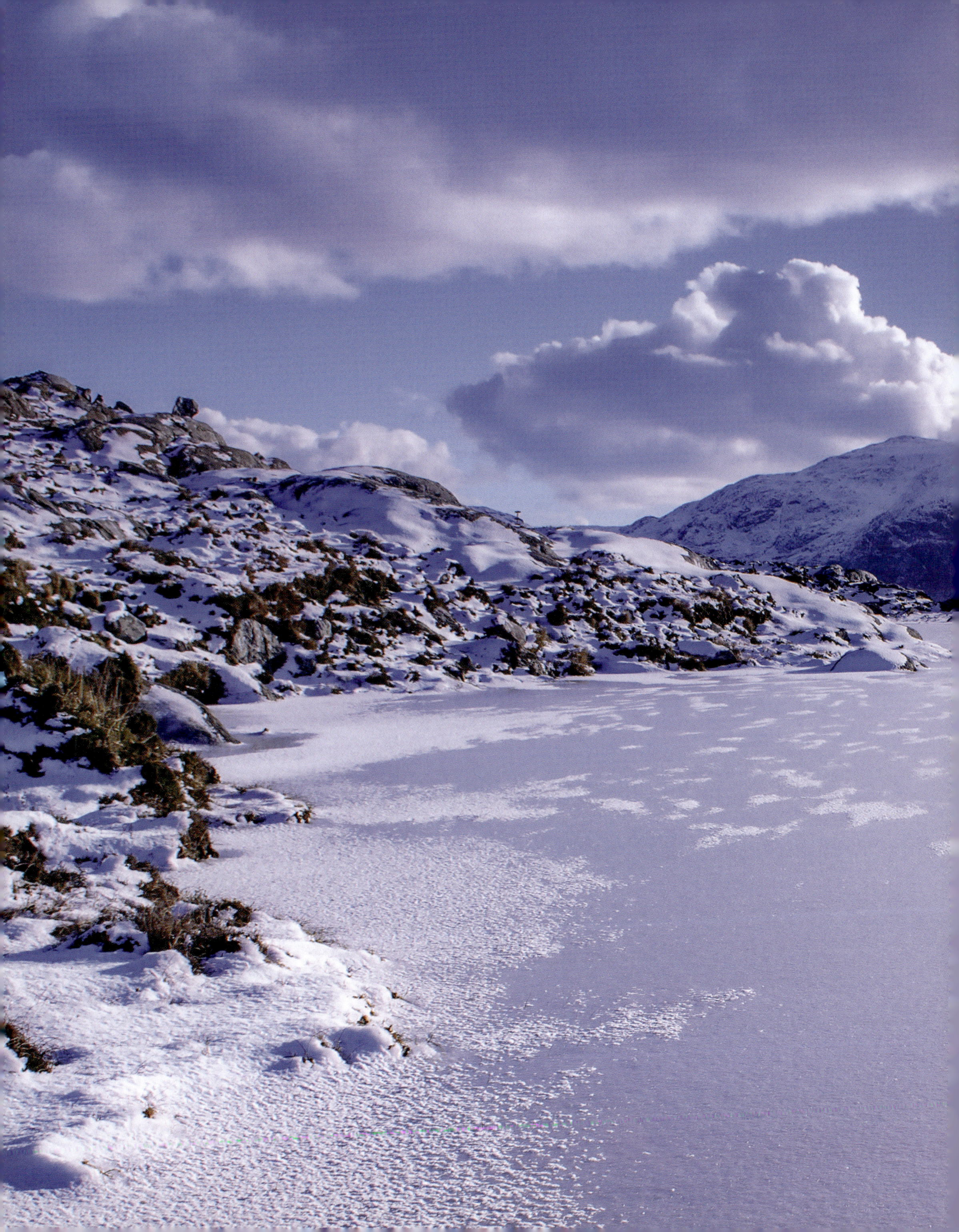

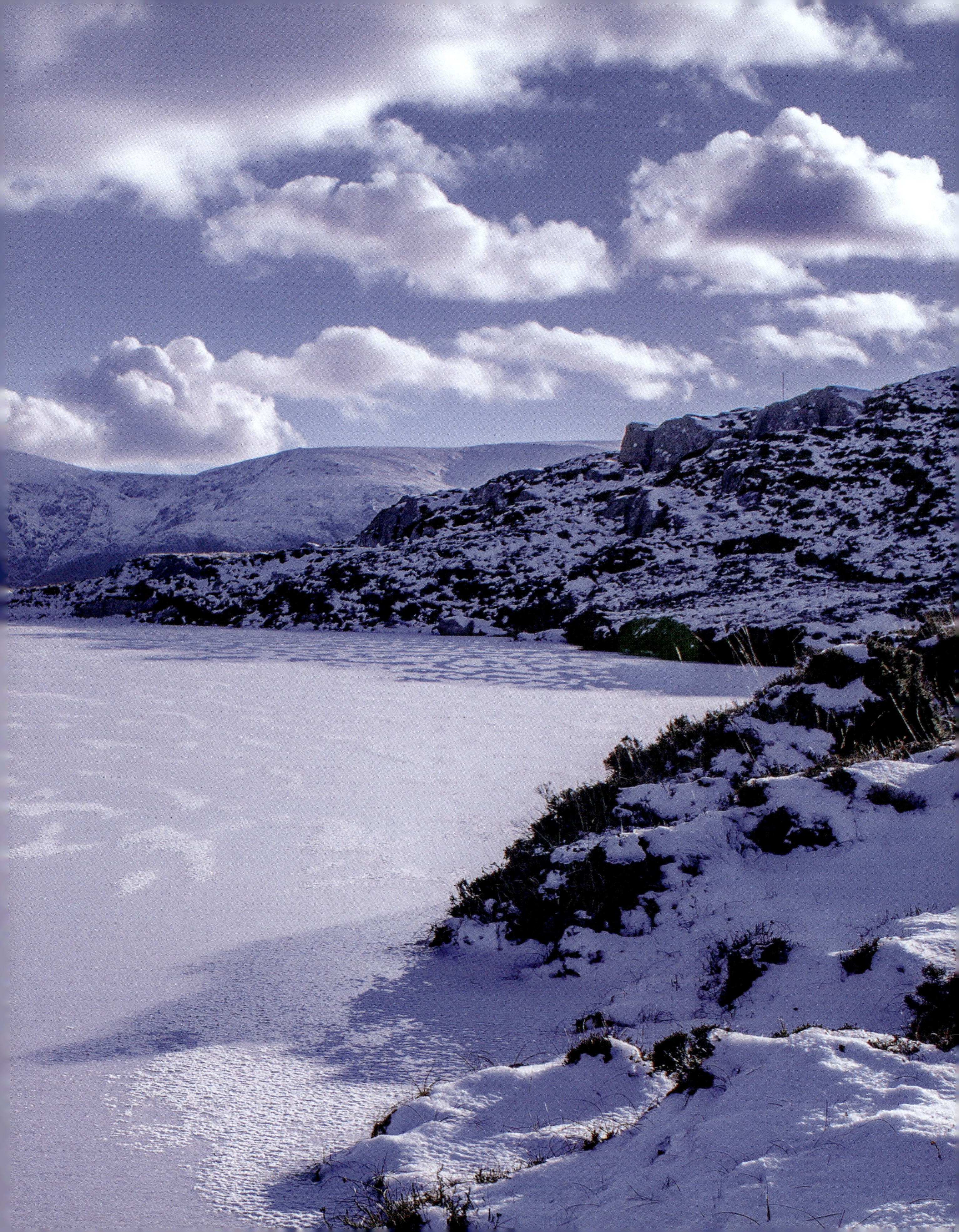

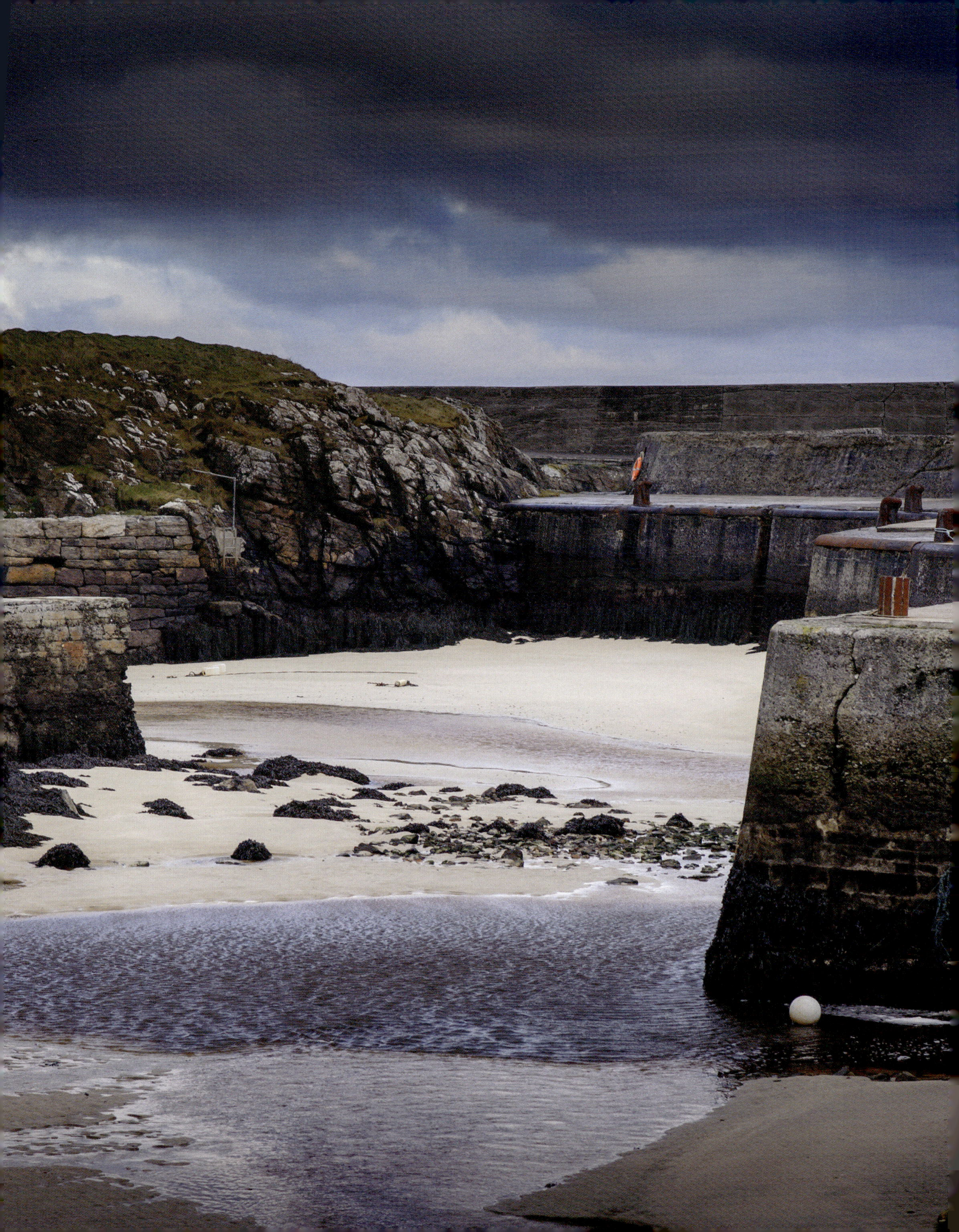

Sea and River
Muir is Abhainn

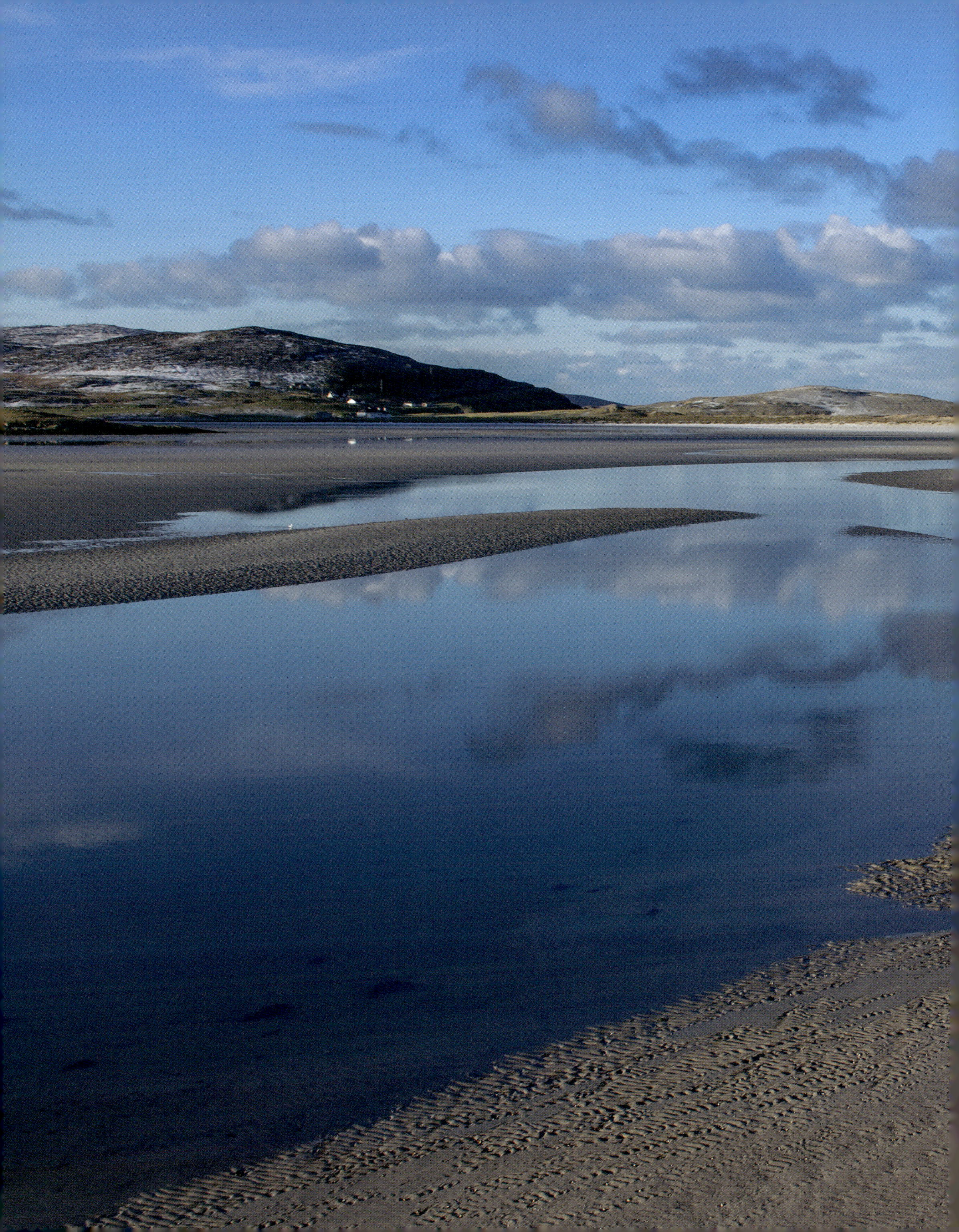

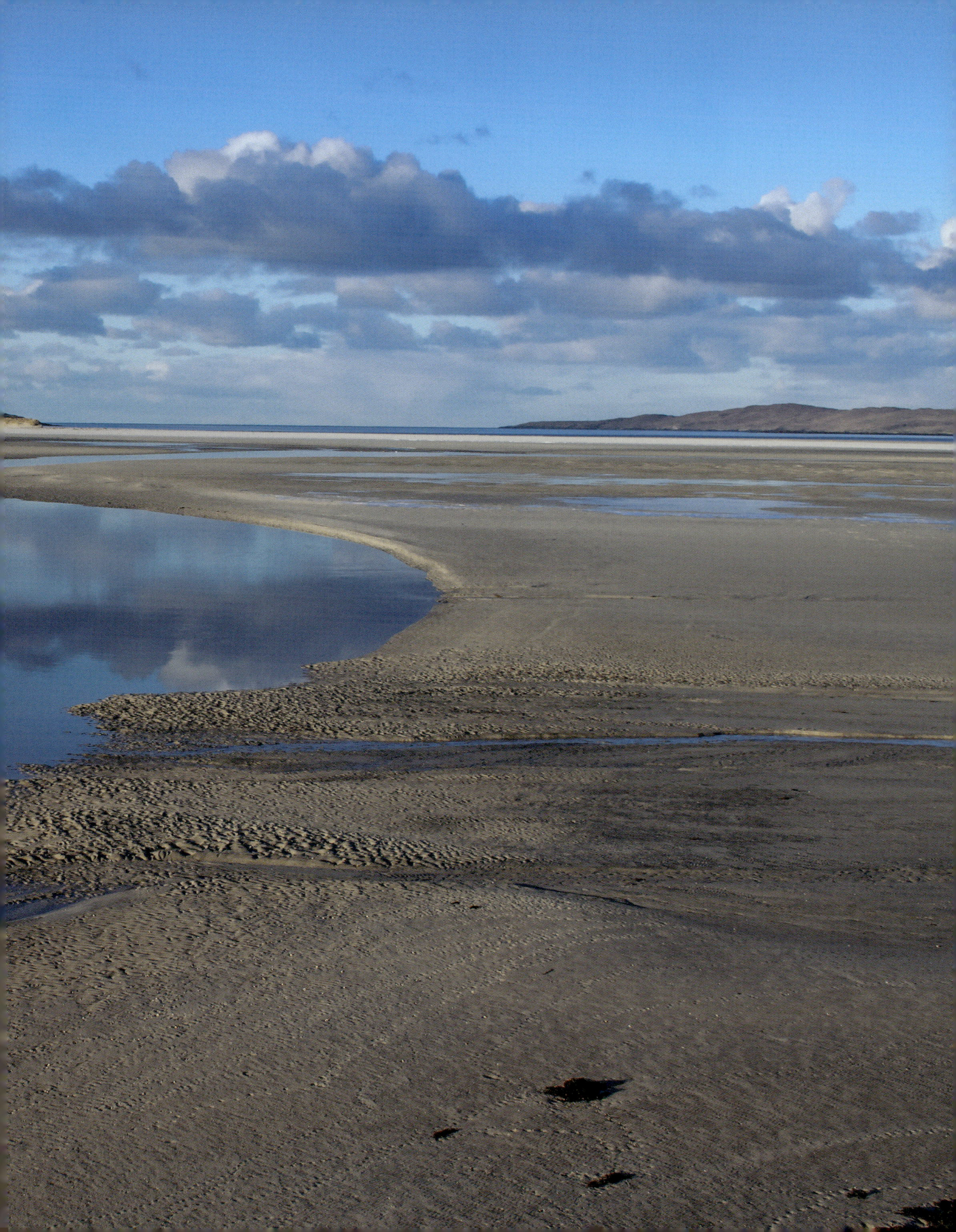

LIGHTLY PEAT SMOKED HADDOCK — CRISPY CHICKEN SKIN — CROFT LEEKS — PEAS AND MINT — SAUCE MADE FROM BONES — CULTURED CREAM — MINT VINEGAR

ADAG SMOCTE ANN AN CEÒ NA MÒNACH — CRAICEANN CIRCE BRISG — CREAMH-GÀRRAIDH NA CROIT — PEASAIREAN AGUS MEANNT — SABHS BHO NA CNÀIMHEAN — UACHDAR TÒIRNICHTE — FÌON GEUR MEANNT

Haddock
100g haddock fillet

Pre-heat the oven to 130°C. Remove skin and bones from the fillet and season with Skye sea salt. In a smoking tray place peat along with wood chip, place the haddock fillet on the perforated tray that sits on top, making sure to oil it to stop the fish from sticking. Light the peat and wood chips, cover with lid and place in oven for 10 minutes. Remove from the oven and relight the peat, returning it for a further 10 minutes. Repeat the process one more time returning it to the oven for 10 more minutes or until the fish is cooked.

Crispy Chicken Skin
chicken skin
Skye sea salt

Pre-heat oven to 190°C. Lay the chicken skins skin side down and scrape off any excess meat and fat. Line a tray with greaseproof paper and lay the chicken skins stretched out skin side up, season with a sprinkling of Skye sea salt and bake for about 15-20 minutes until golden and crispy.

Croft Leeks
1 large croft leek
100ml white wine
200ml chicken stock
butter

Chop the leek and sweat it off in butter and oil. Add the wine and reduce to almost nothing, add stock and cook until the leeks are soft and tender, reducing the liquid until it has evaporated. Add butter and season.

Sauce made from Bones
750g fish bones
40g diced shallots
100ml Noilly Prat vermouth
1 thyme sprig
60g butter
2 tbsp cultured cream

Rinse the fish bones and place in a pot and cover with water, simmer for two hours, skim and pass through sieve.
Sweat the shallots in butter and oil, add the vermouth and reduce to almost nothing. Add stock and thyme and reduce to sauce consistency. Pass through a sieve or muslin. Return to low heat, whisking in cultured cream and chilled butter.

Cultured Butter
500ml cream
3 tbsp whey or buttermilk

Place the cream and the whey in a jar leaving an inch at the top. Place the lid on the jar and leave up to 24 hours at 22-25°C to culture. The cream will thicken from the top down. Store in a fridge for up to three weeks.

Mint Vinegar
500ml white wine vinegar
250g mint leaves

Bring the vinegar to the boil and pour over mint leaves. Leave at room temperature for a week. Pour vinegar through muslin into a jar or bottle and seal with an airtight lid.

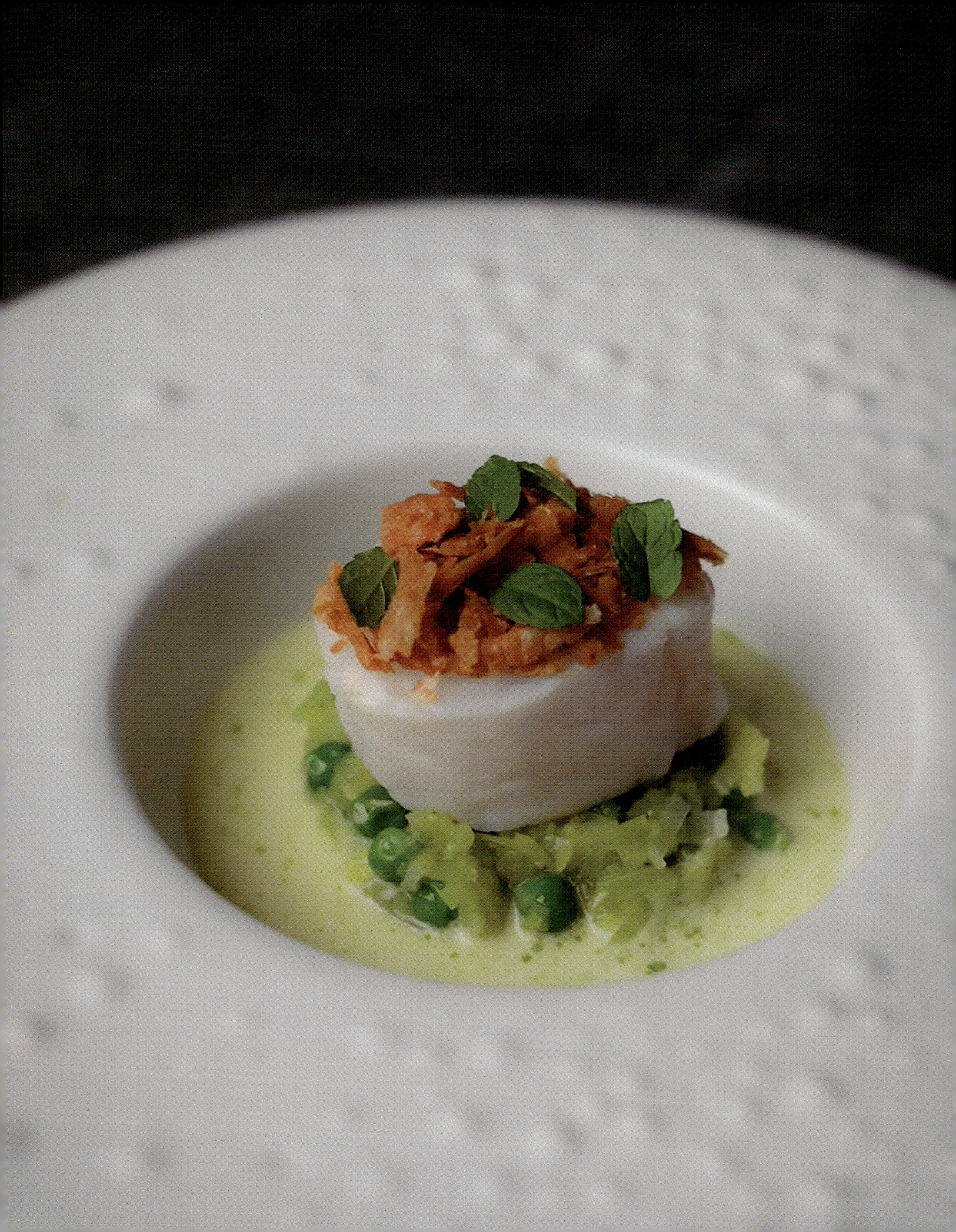

WILD LINE CAUGHT SEA TROUT — PORT OF NESS CRAB — CRUSHED CROFT NEW POTATOES — HAZELNUT — A SAUCE MADE FROM BUTTERMILK, CRAB STOCK AND SORREL

BÀNAG GLACTE LE SLAT — CRÙBAG PORT NIS — BUNTÀTA ÙR PRONN NA CROIT — CNÒ-CALLTAINN — SABHS DÈANTE LE BLÀTHACH, STOC CRÙBAIG AGUS SEALBHAG

Trout
80-100g trout fillet

Score the skin of the trout and season with Skye sea salt.
Heat oil in a warm pan and place the trout skin side down, pressing down the fish to stop it from curling. Baste the flesh with the oil from the pan. Once the fish has been cooked three quarters of the way, turn the fish over. Add a knob of butter and baste a couple of times. Finish with a squeeze of lemon juice.

Crab
1 whole fresh crab
(weighing about 1kg)

Bring a large pan of salted water to the boil, lower the crab into the boiling water and cook for about 8-10 minutes. Once cooked, remove and leave to cool. Once cooled remove the white crab meat, keeping the shells for the stock. The white crab meat is gently mixed through the crushed potatoes.

Crab Stock
2 carrots
2 onions
celery stick
1 leek
small fennel bulb
300ml dry white wine
thyme
parsley
lemon juice

Pre-heat the oven to 200°C.
Place the crab shells in a roasting dish. Roast for about 10 minutes.
In a large pan place the roasted shells along with the roughly chopped vegetables, herbs and wine, add around three litres of water, bring to the boil and simmer for about an hour. Strain the stock through a muslin cloth, return to the pan and reduce to half.

Croft New Potatoes
200g croft potatoes, washed and scrubbed
Cullisse Highland rapeseed oil

Simply boil the potatoes in salted boiling water for about 10-15 minutes. Drain, gently crush and coat with rapeseed oil. Season with Skye sea salt.

Sauce
200ml buttermilk
100g sorrel
crab stock

Blend the buttermilk and sorrel together. Heat gently in a pan adding some of the reduced crab stock to taste. Pass through a muslin cloth and return to the pan adding a couple of knobs of butter. Foam the sauce with a stick blender.

Hazelnut
handful of whole hazelnuts

Place hazelnuts on a baking tray and toast for about 8-10 minutes at 180°C. Once cooled, finely chop, mixing a small amount through the crab and potato. Garnish the fish with a small scattering of the hazelnuts.

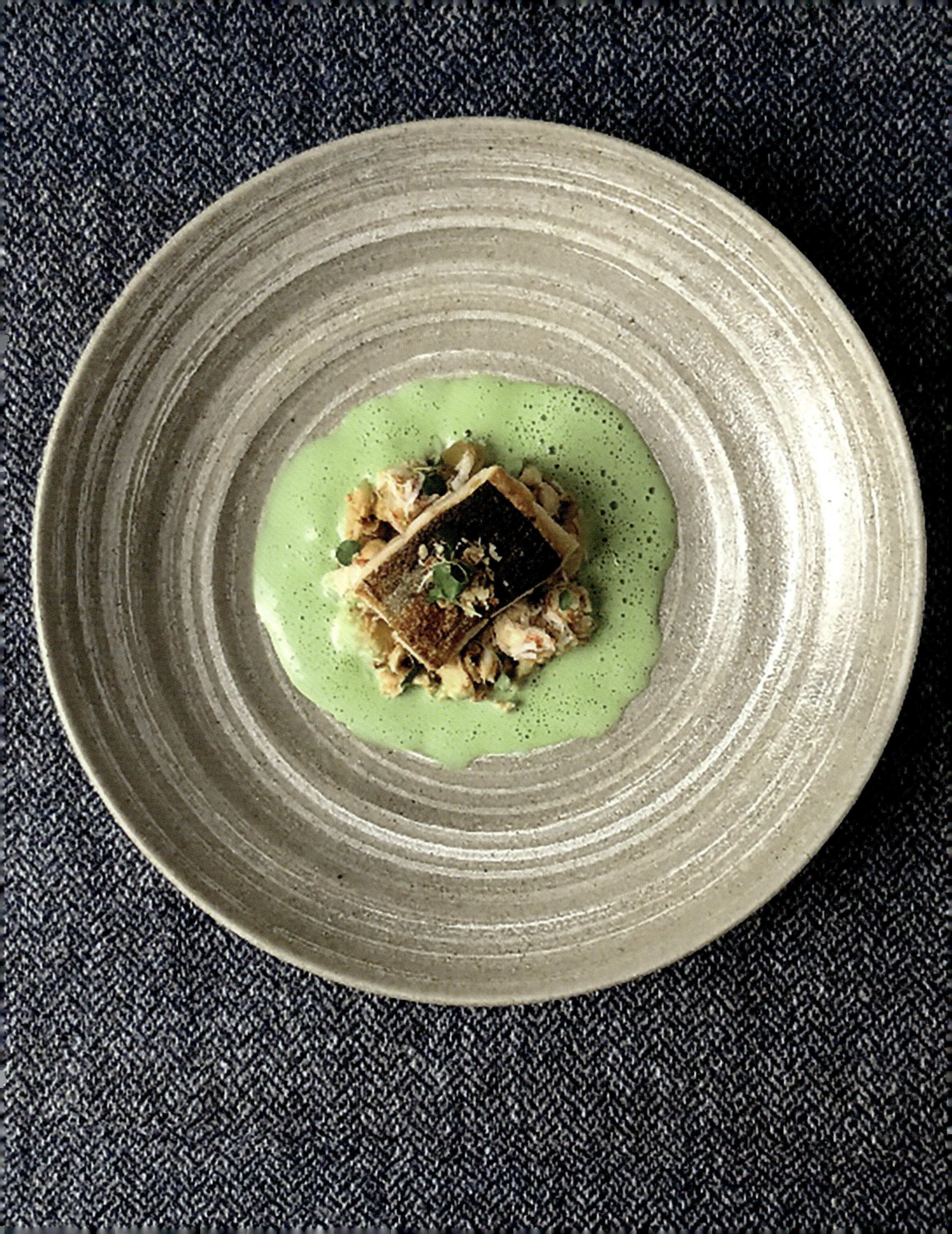

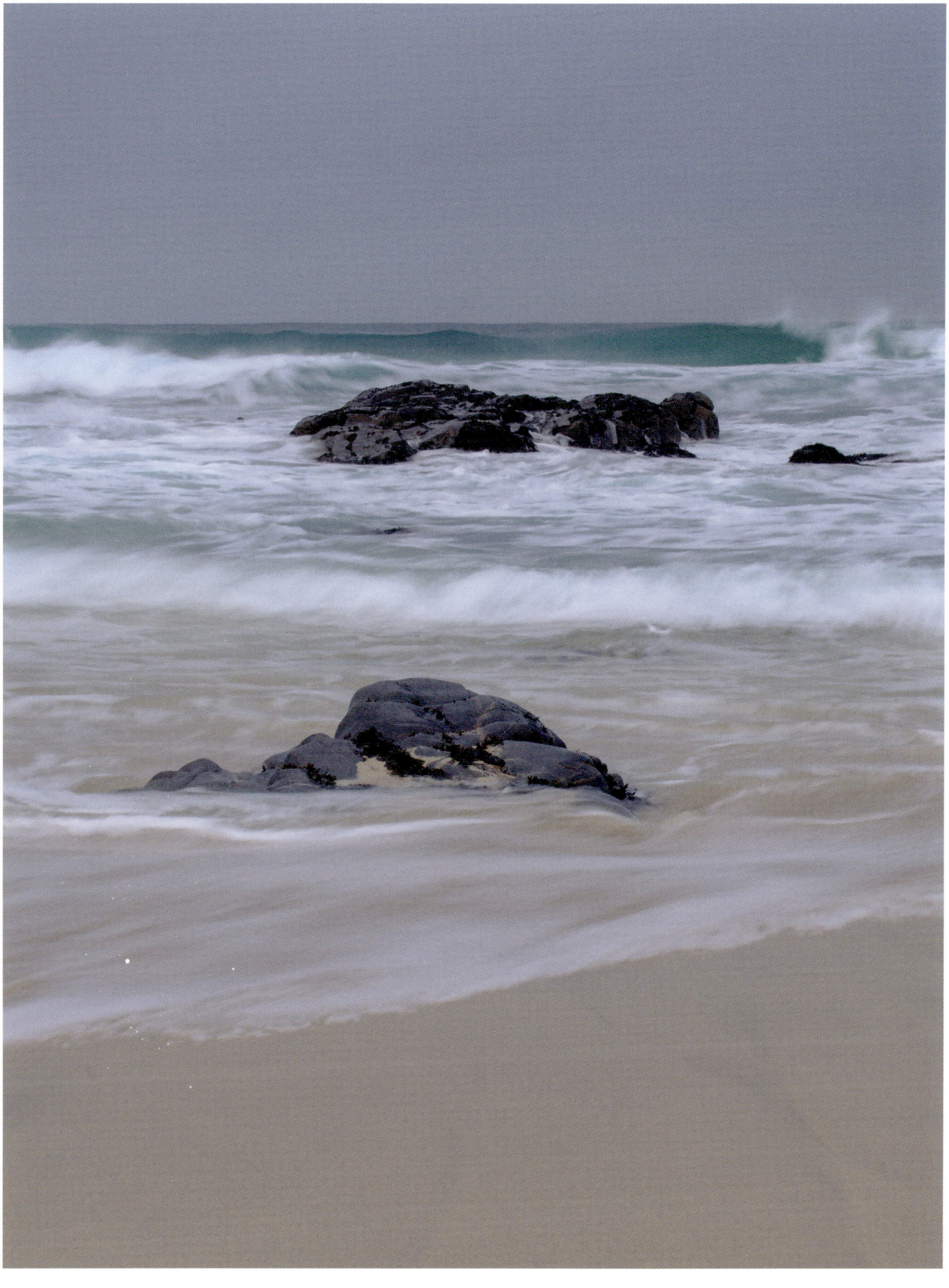

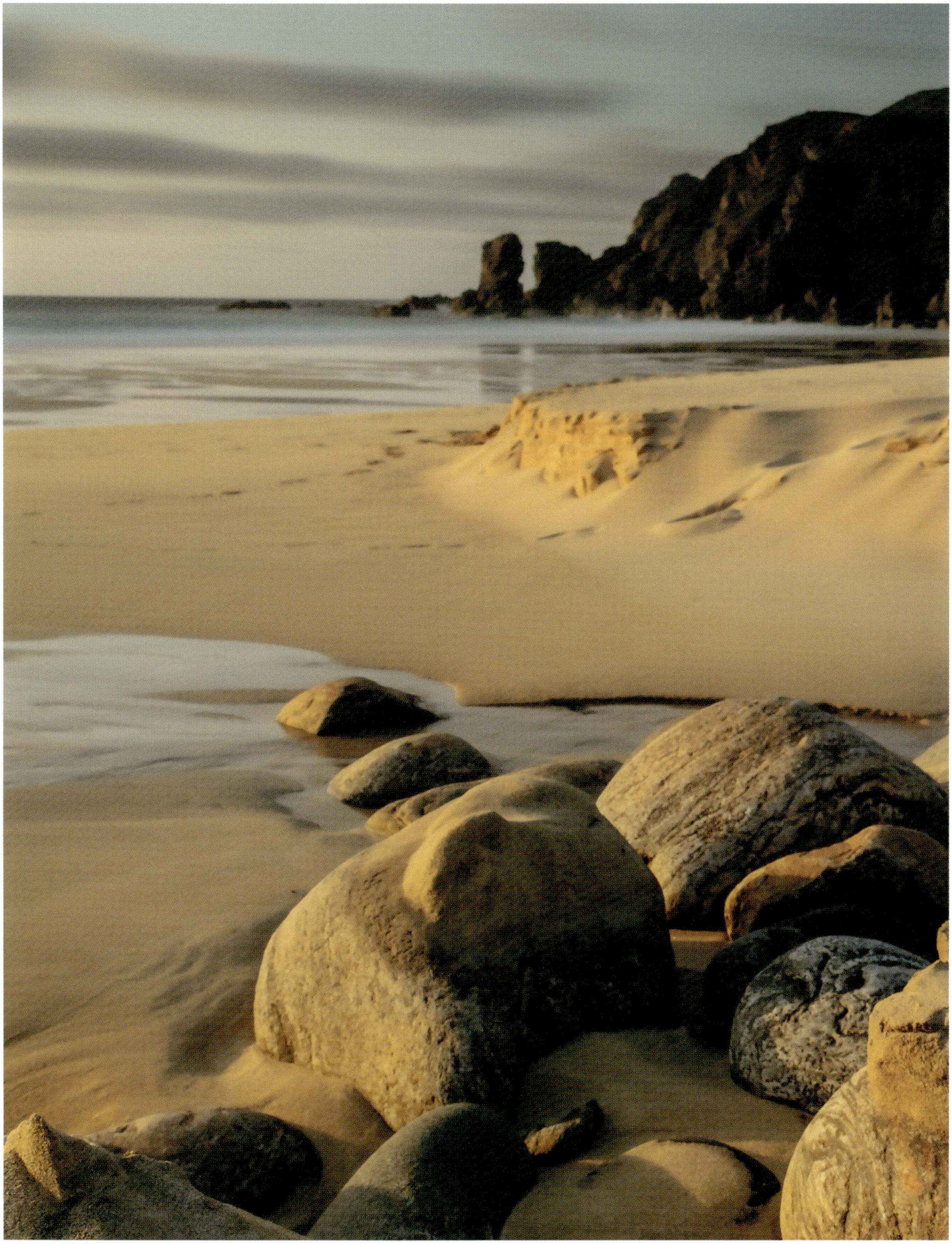

DIVER CAUGHT SCALLOP 'COCK A LEEKIE' — CHARRED LEEK EMULSION — PUFFED WILD RICE — CRISPY CHICKEN SKIN

This was a favourite at the HAAR pop-ups and the first of the fish dishes, consisting of a beautiful hand dived Uig scallop, caramelised and served with puffed black rice, leek ash emulsion and finished with crispy chicken skin.

'COCK A LEEKIE' DE CHREACHAIN GLACTE LE DÀIBHEAR — CO-MHEASGACHADH DE CHREAMH-GÀRRAIDH GUALAICHTE — RUS FIADHAICH BÒCTE — CRAICEANN CIRCE BRISG

Bha seo a' còrdadh gu mòr ri aoighean aig gach HAAR sealach agus b' e a' chiad bhlasad aca air iasg – creachan àlainn glacte le dàibhear ann an Ùig, carra-mheillte agus còmhla ris rus dubh bòcte, le co-mheasgachadh de chreamh-gàrraidh gualaichte agus craiceann circe brisg.

Leek Ash Emulsion
2 soft boiled eggs
1 large leek; burnt outer leaves
100g cashew nuts, soaked overnight and puréed
200ml grape seed oil
200ml hazelnut oil
juice from 2 lemons
salt and pepper
squid ink

With a hand blender, whisk all the ingredients except for the oils in a deep narrow container.
Slowly add the mixed oils until everything is smoothly emulsified into a black mayonnaise.
Adjust seasoning.

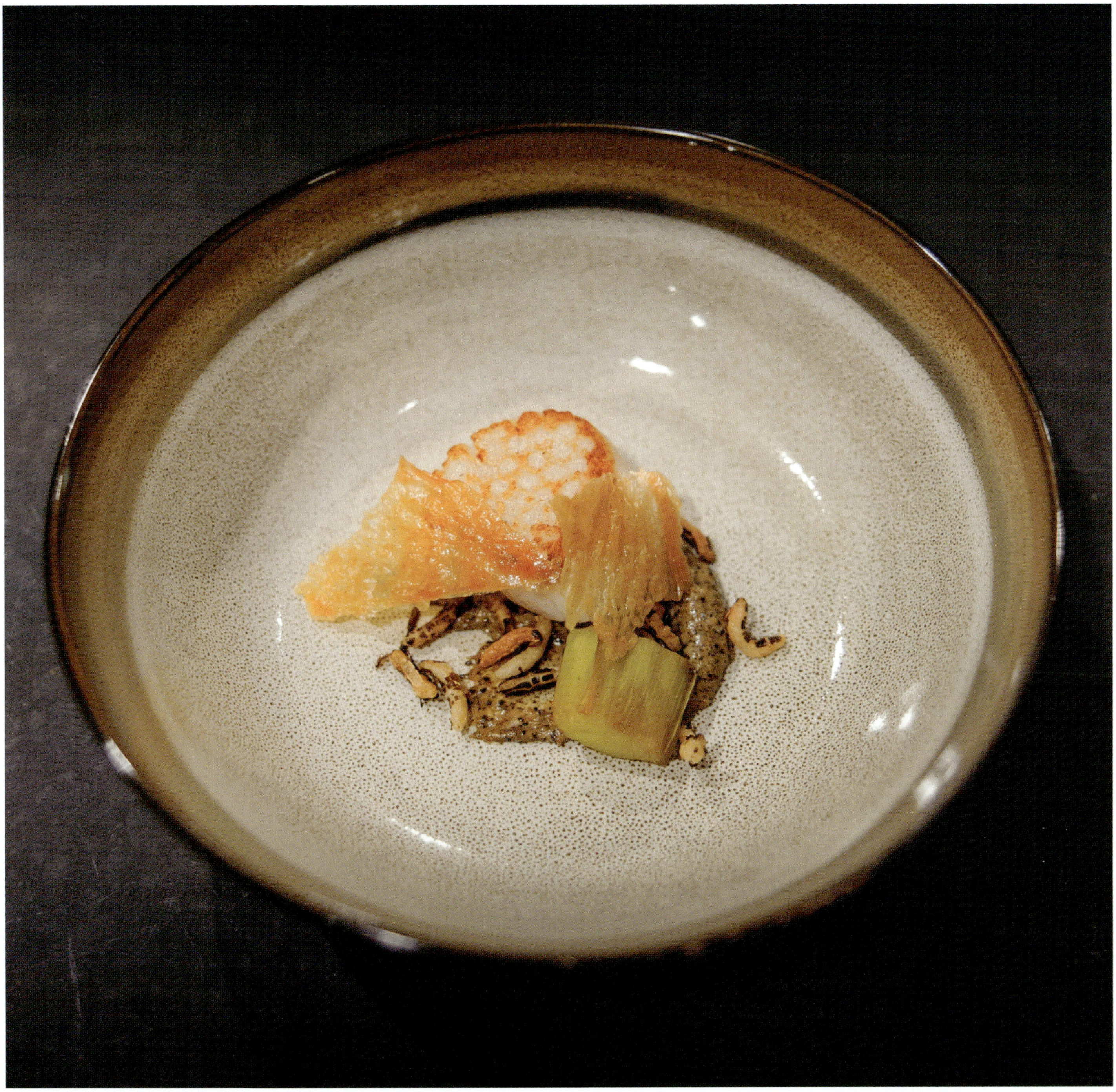

UIG DIVER CAUGHT SCALLOPS — PORK CRUMB — SALT BAKED TURNIP — SOUSED PEAR

CREACHAIN À ÙIG — CRIOMAGAN MUICFHEÒIL — SNÈAP AIR A RÒSTADH ANN AN SALAINN — PEUR PICILTE

Pan Roasted Scallops
hand dived scallops
olive oil
Skye sea salt

Remove skirts, muscles and corals from the scallops. Gently wash in cold salted water. Lay on a cloth and pat dry. Heat a non-stick frying pan with olive oil. You do not want too much oil, just enough to thinly coat the pan. The pan needs to be nice and hot.
Season the scallops with Skye sea salt and fry for about a minute on each side. You want a lovely caramelised colour on the scallop, which needs to reach 40°C.

Salt Baked Turnip
1 medium turnip
150g fine salt
150g plain flour
100ml water
10ml rapeseed oil

Pre-heat oven to 170°C.
Mix all ingredients together to form a dough. Cover the turnip and place on a baking tray. Bake until you have a core temperature of 95°C.

Pork Crumb
1lb pig skin

Boil the pig skin just covered with water, uncovered for two hours until tender. Leave to sit for 45 minutes.
Scrape excess hair off with a razor blade. Cut into playing card size pieces and put in an airtight container for 1½ hours. Dehydrate for 12 hours at 64°C. Fry for 30 seconds. Sprinkle with salt. Blitz into crumbs.

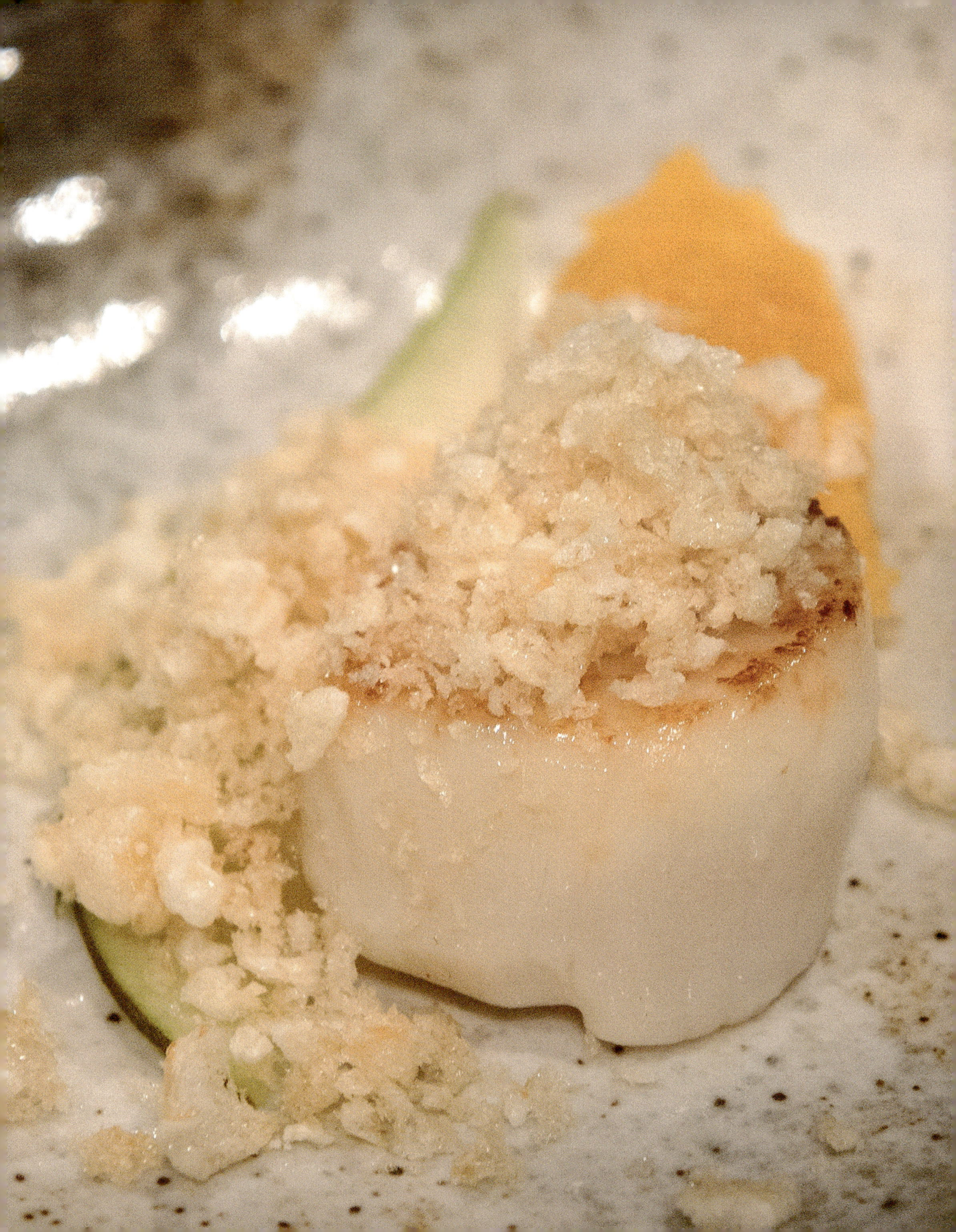

UIG SCALLOP ROASTED OVER HOT COALS AND GLAZED
IN SEAWEED VINEGAR AND SCALLOP ROE BUTTER —
FINELY CHOPPED LEEKS COOKED IN A SCALLOP STOCK —
CRISPY FRIED LEEKS

CREACHAN À ÙIG AIR A RÒSTADH AIR ÈIBHLEAGAN,
GLAINNICHTE LE FÌON GEUR FEAMAINN AGUS ÌM LE IUCHAIR CREACHAIN —
CREAMH-GÀRRAIDH AIR A GHEARRADH MÌN AIR A CHÒCAIREACHD
ANN AN STOC CREACHAIN —
CREAMH-GÀRRAIDH AIR A FHRAIDHIGEADH BRISG

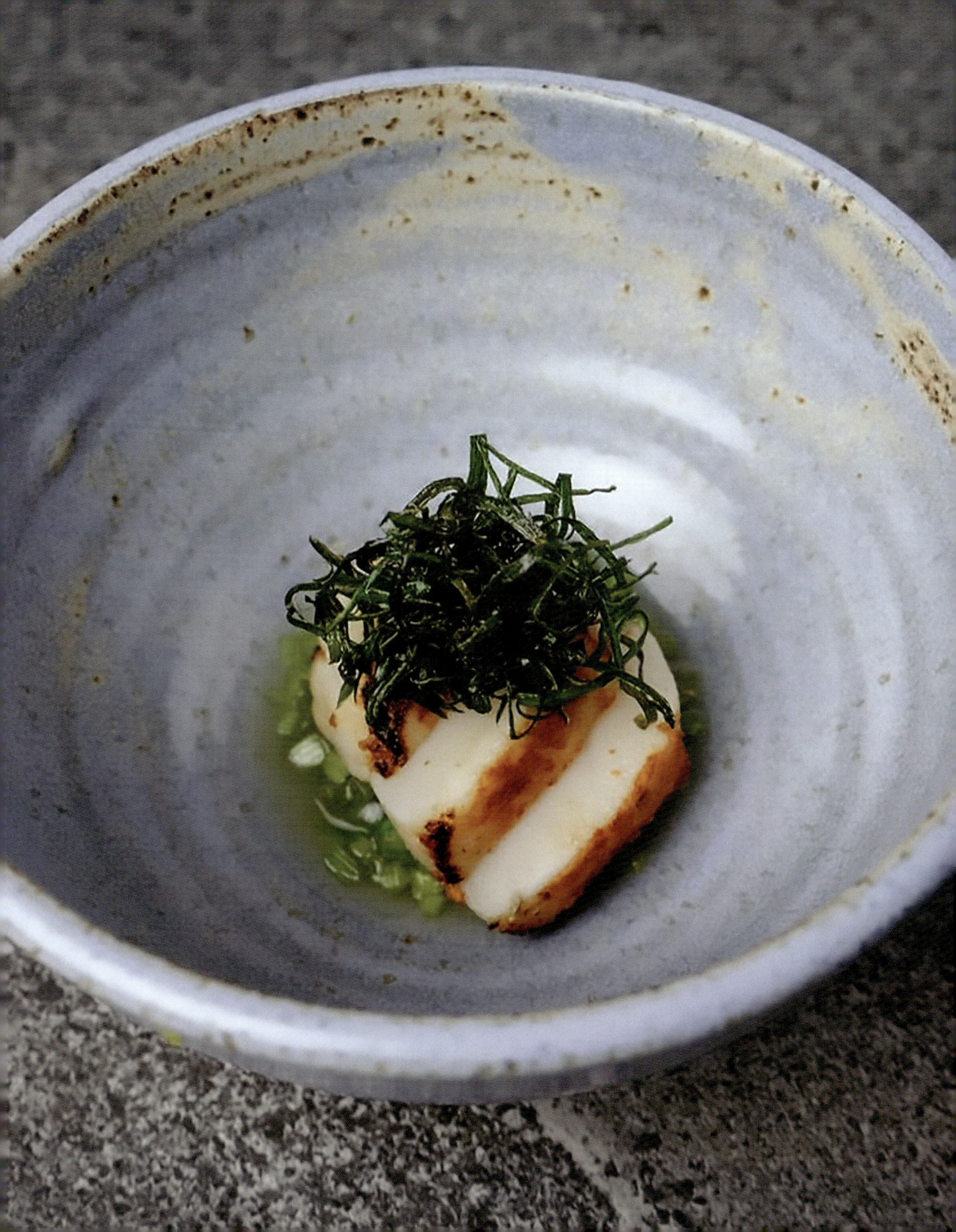

SQUID — PEAS — FRESH CROWDIE —
CURED AND DRIED HALIBUT ROE

GIOBARNACH — PEASRAICHEAN — GRUTH ÙR —
IUCHAIR BRADAIN-LEATHANN AIR A CHIÙRADH 'S AIR A THIORMACHADH

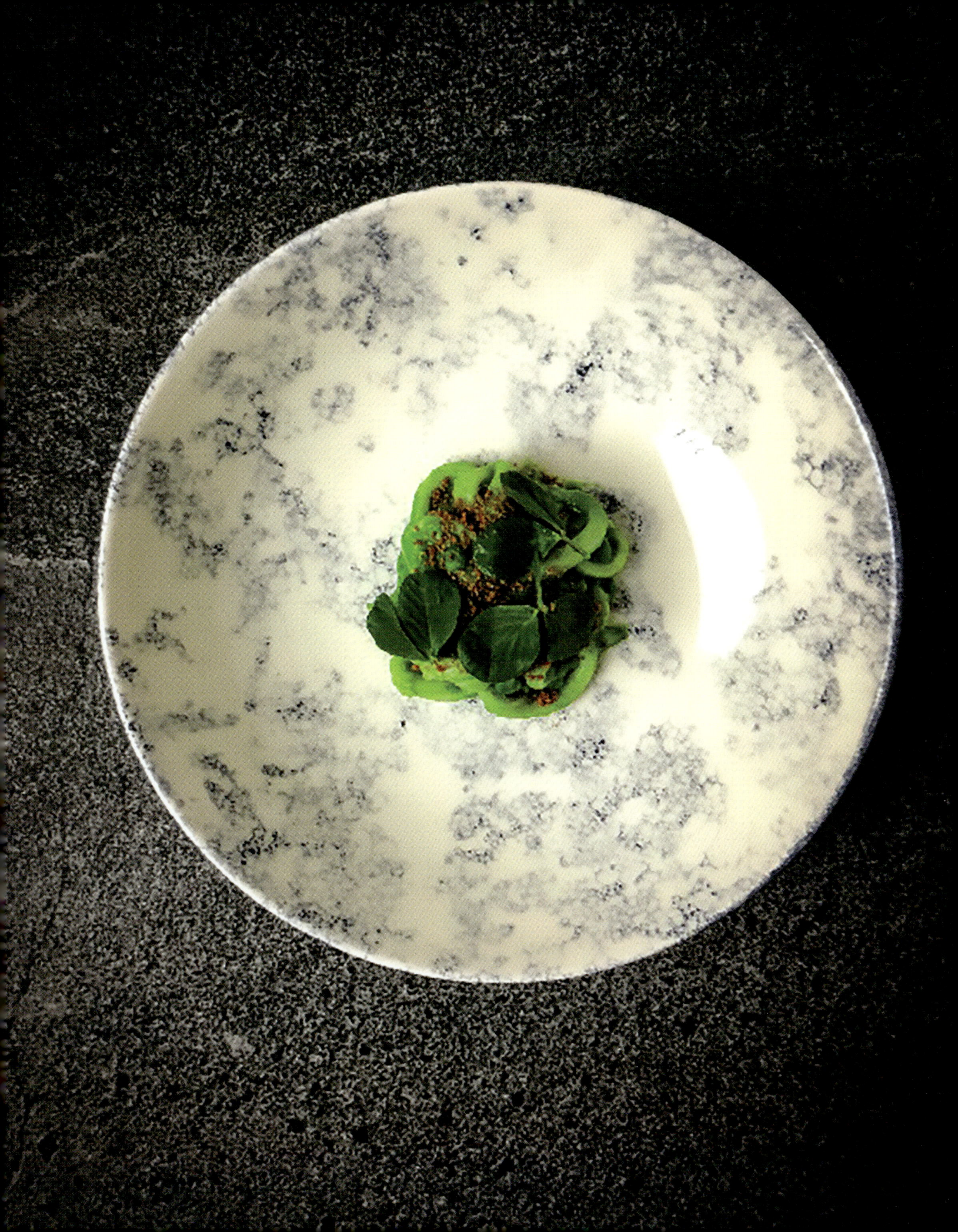

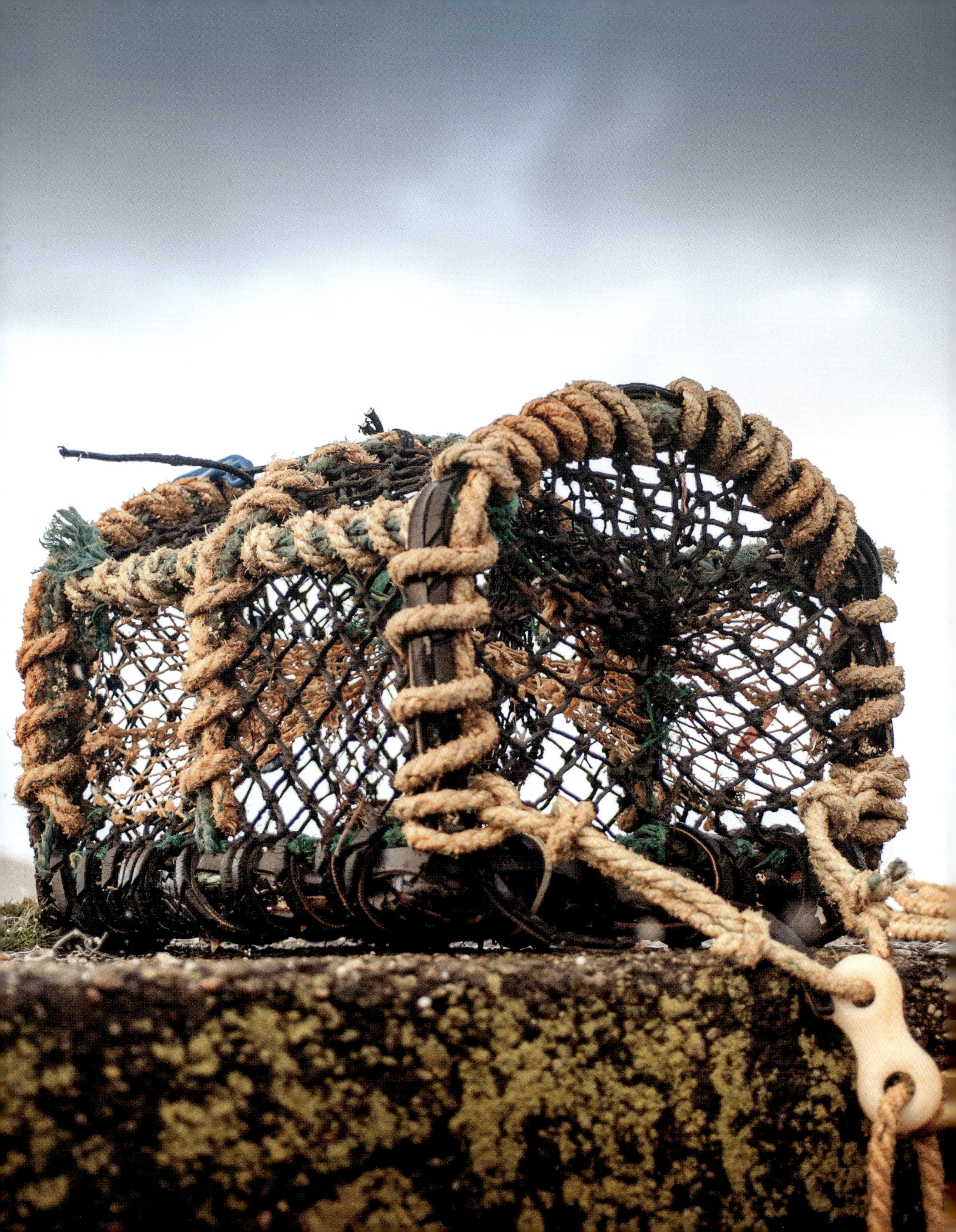

Creel Fishermen
Iasgairean Chlèibh

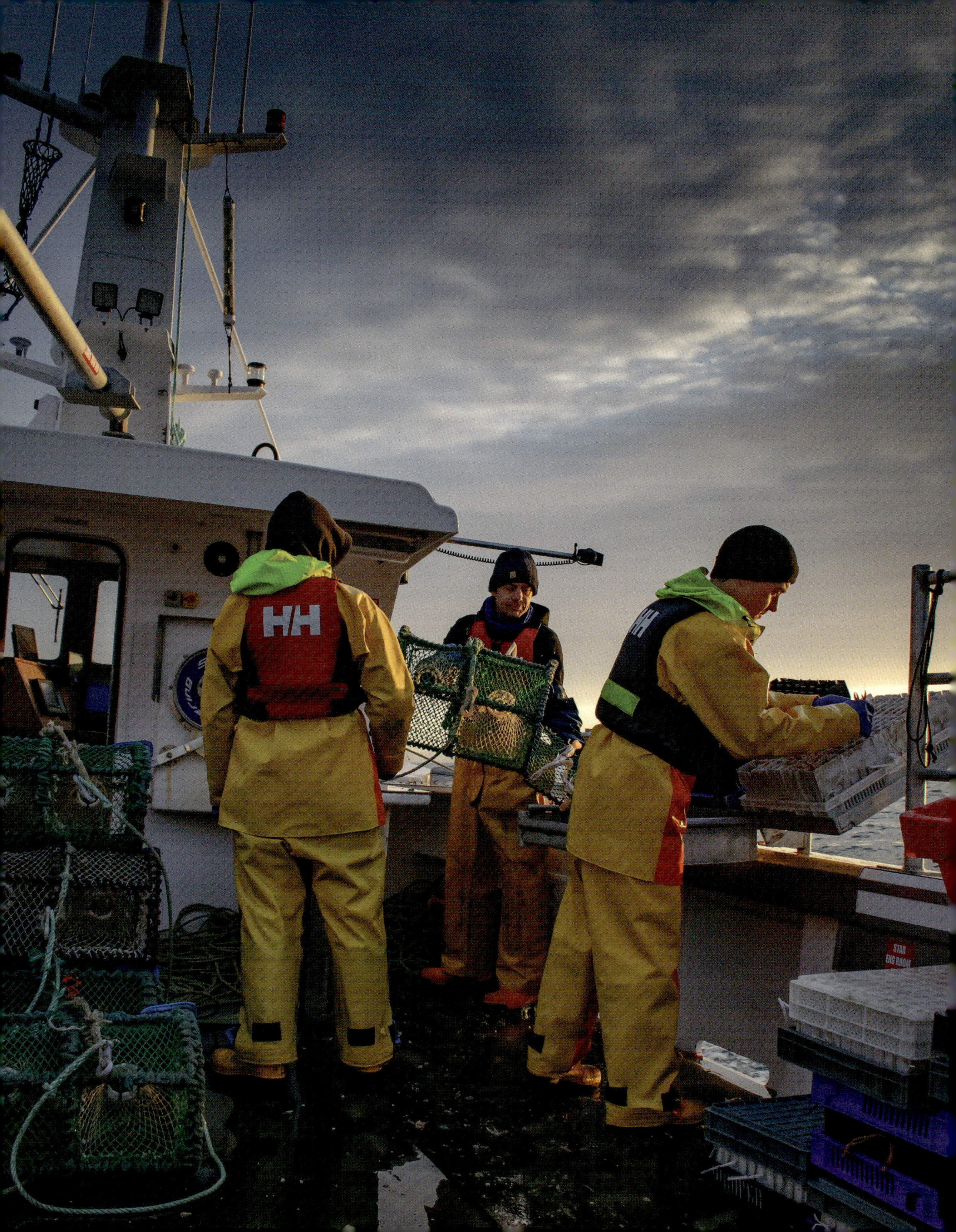
HH
HH
STAR

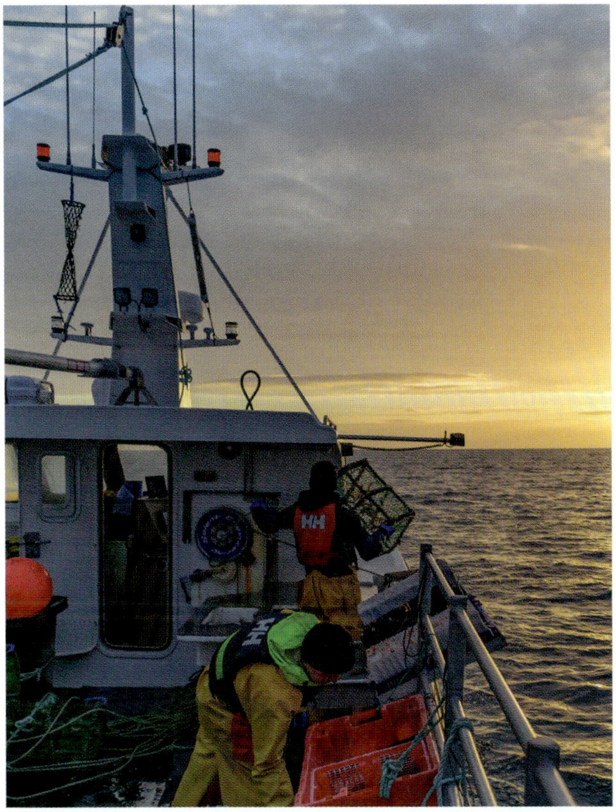

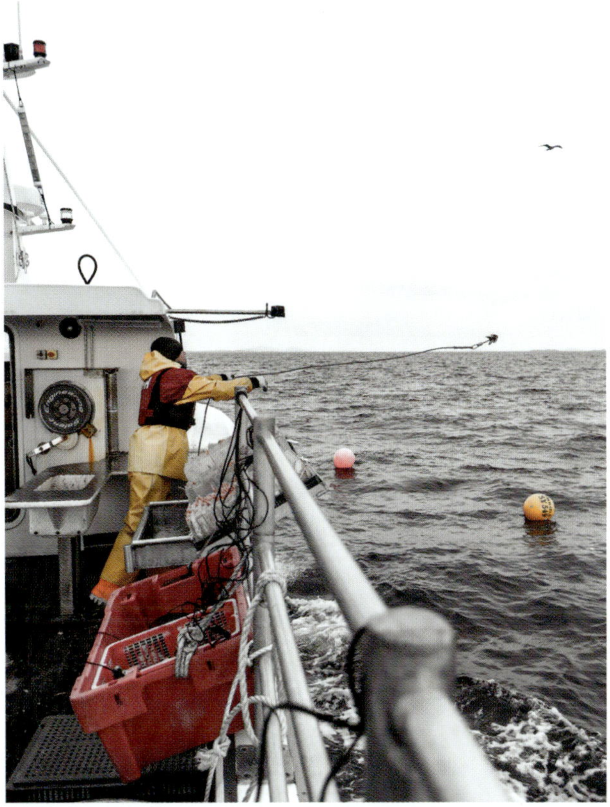

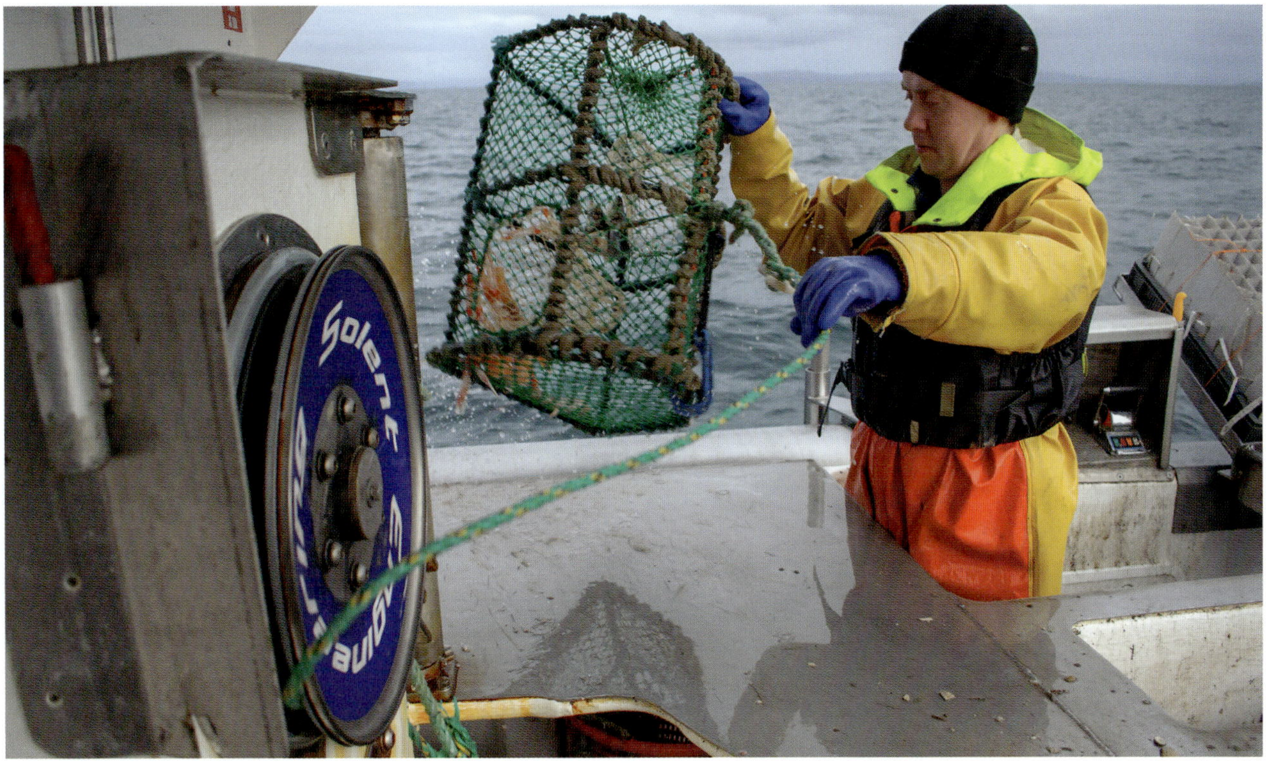
Solent

LOBSTER COOKED OVER HOT COALS — PEA AND MARJORAM CUSTARD

GIOMACH AIR A RÒSTADH AIR ÈIBHLEAGAN — UGHAGAN PEASAIR AGUS LUS-MARSAILIDH

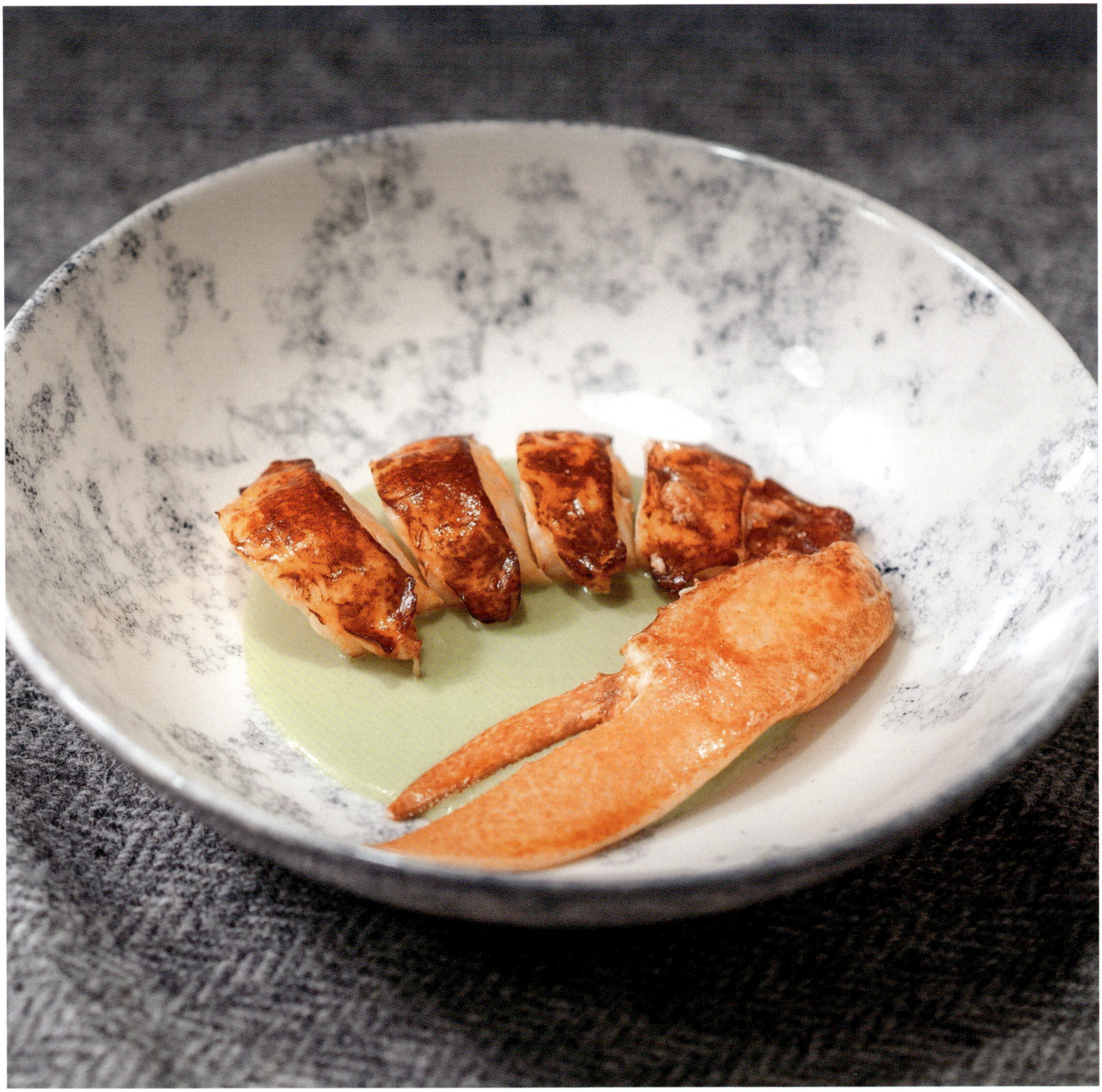

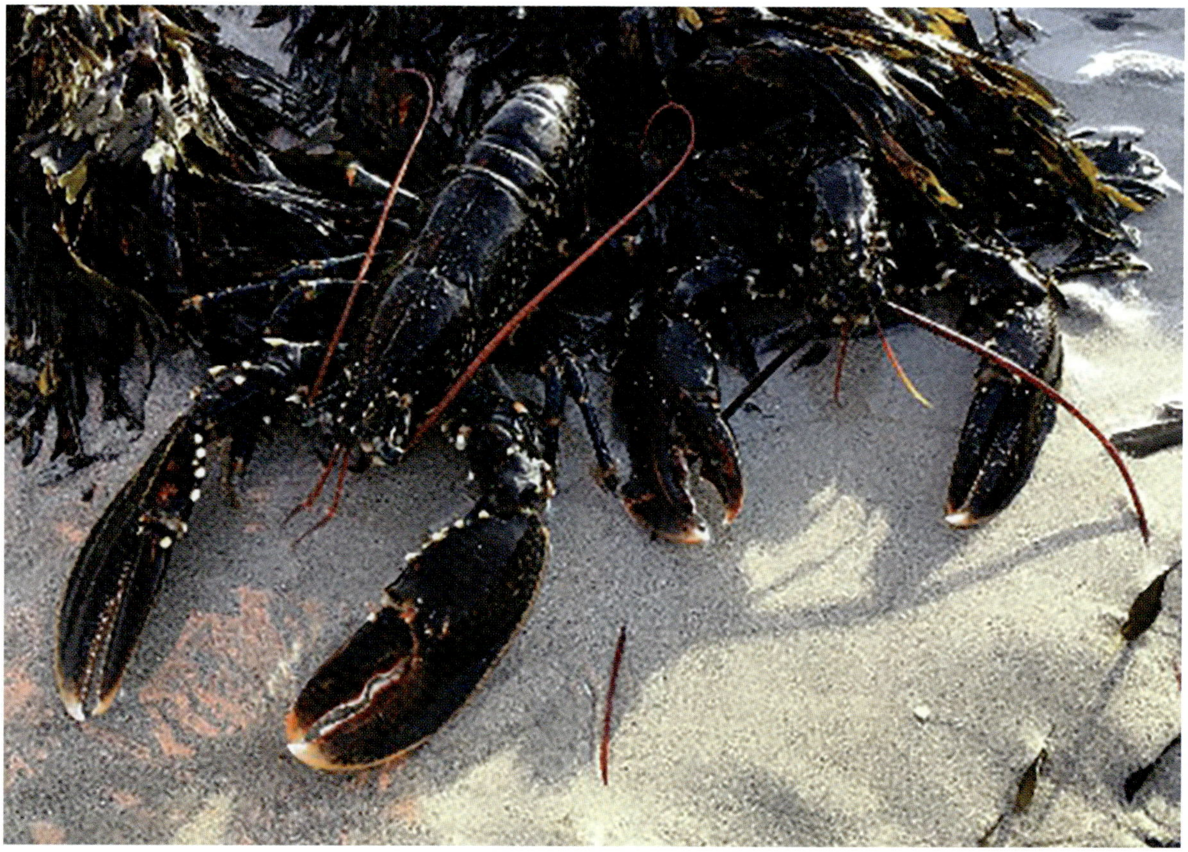

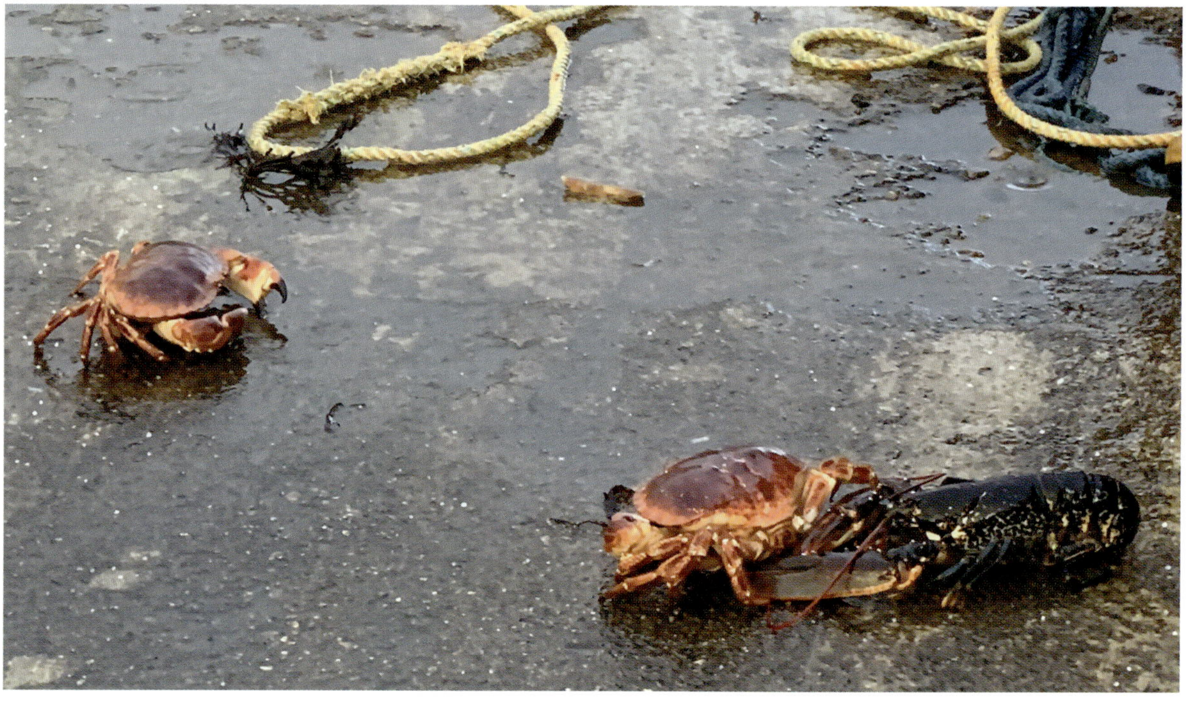

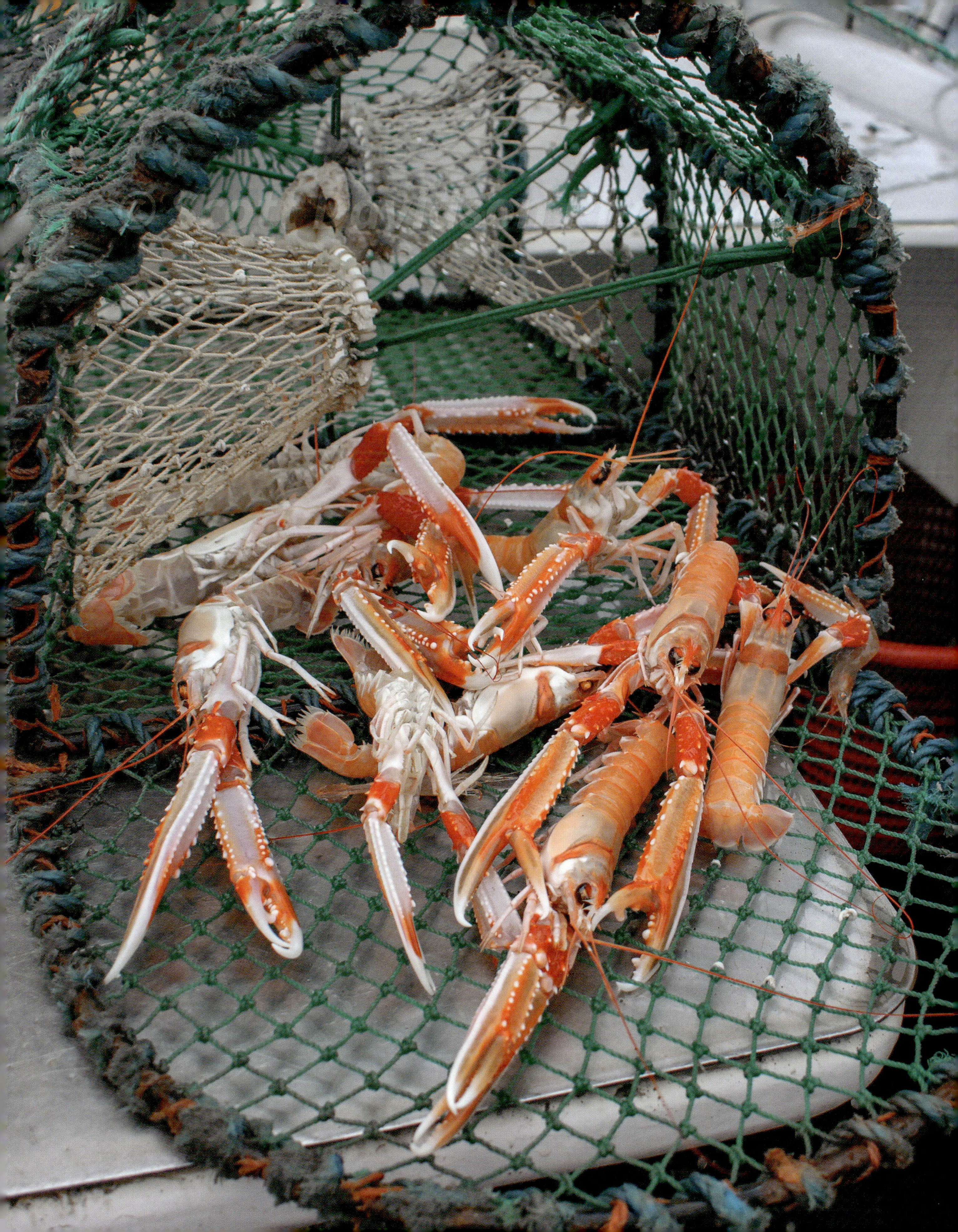

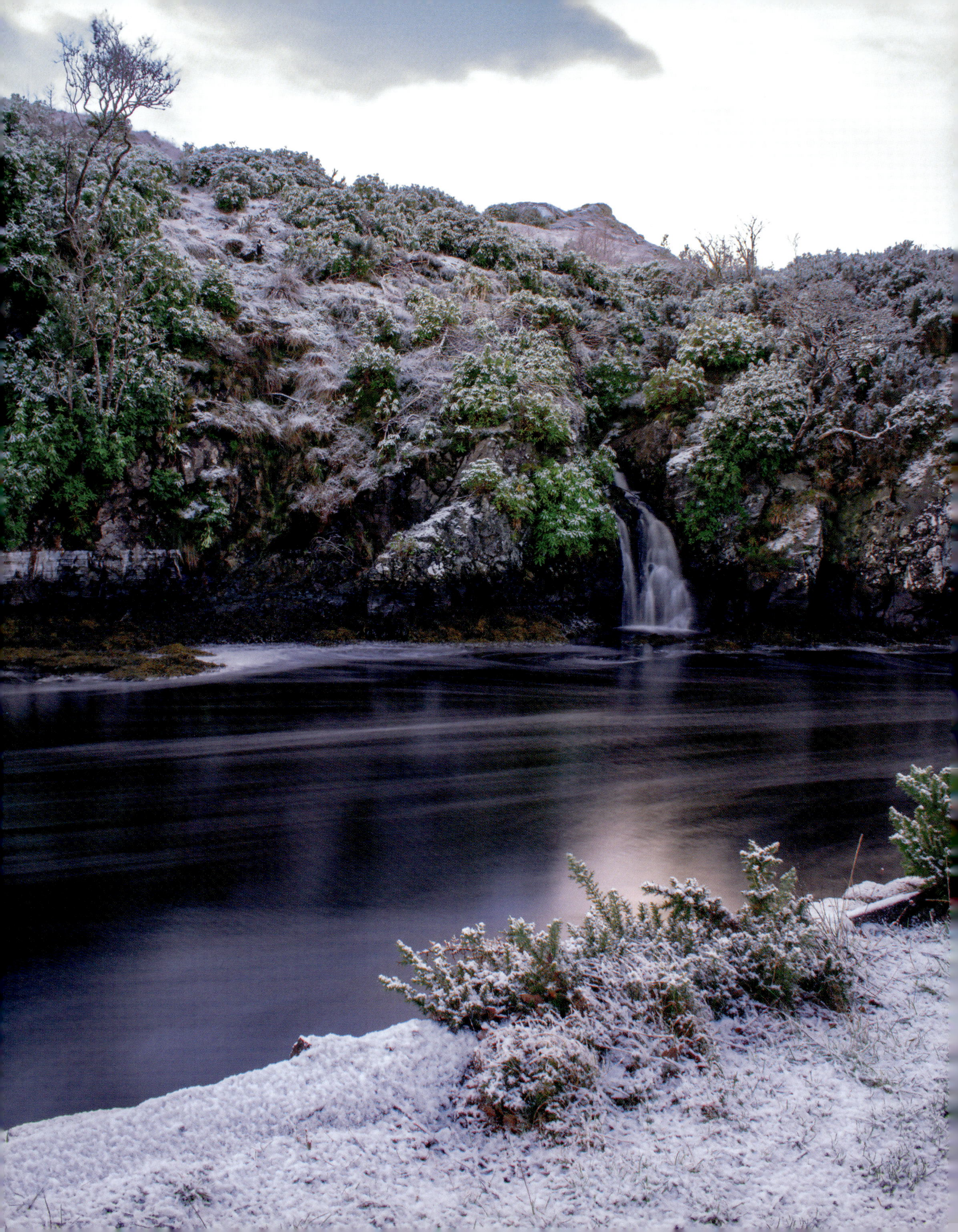

Hebridean Salmon Rivers
Aibhnichean Bhradan nan Eilean

The Hebrides are an angler's delight, with fishing for trout and salmon the main sporting activity on numerous lochs and rivers. On Lewis the river Grimersta coming out of Loch Langavat, although less than two miles long, is reported to be one of the best salmon rivers in Europe.

Tha eileanan Innse-Gall nan adhbhar tlachd dha iasgairean, le iasgach bhreac is bhradan na phrìomh spòrs air mòran lochan is aibhnichean. Ann an Leòdhas tha cliù aig abhainn Ghrìomarsta a' tighinn a-mach à Loch Langabhat, nas lugha na dà mhìle de dh'fhaid, mar aon de na h-aibhnichean bhradan as fheàrr san Roinn-Eòrpa.

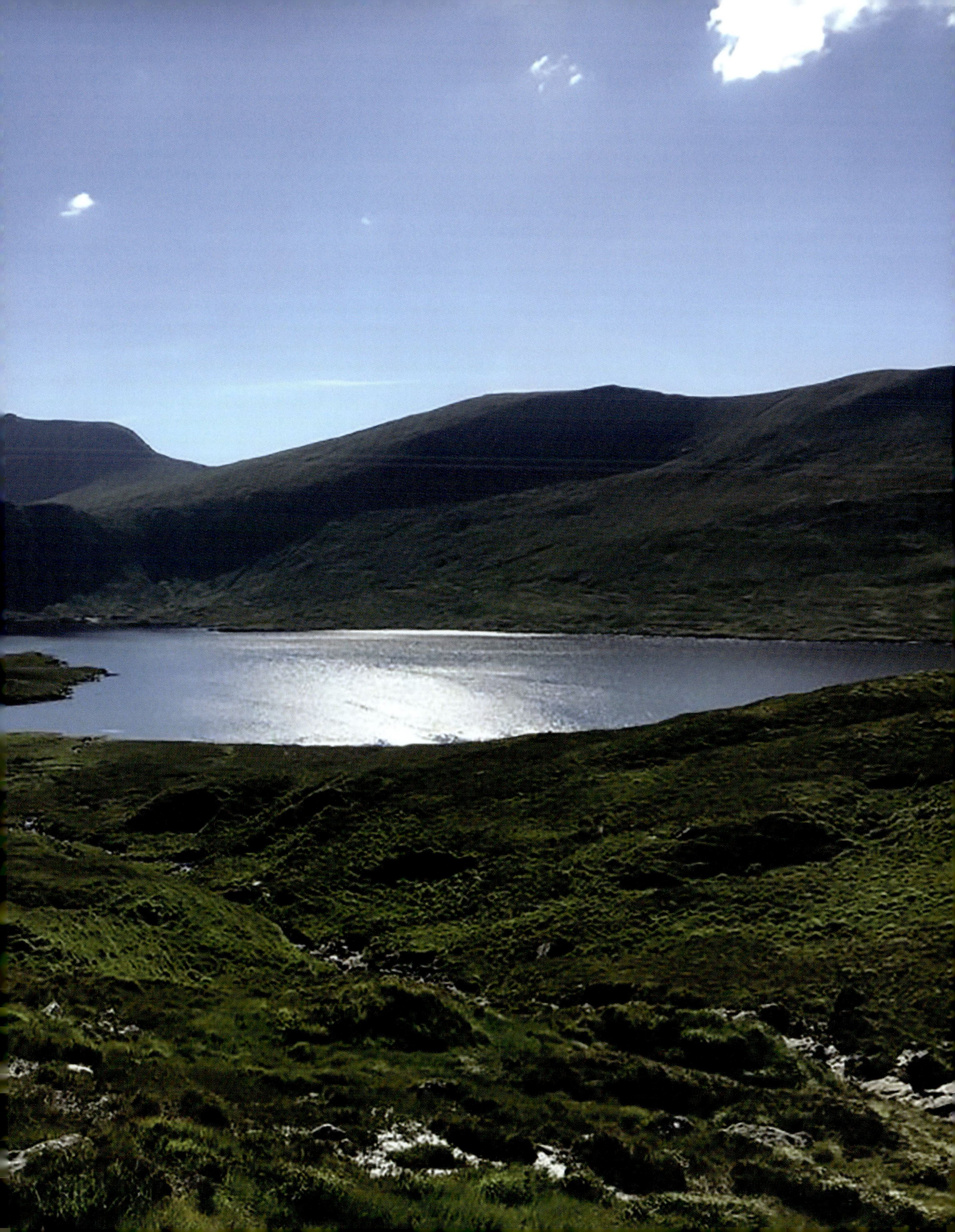

TOBERMORY SMOKED TROUT — FERMENTED RHUBARB — CELERY JAM — FROZEN BUTTERMILK — GORSE FLOWERS

Another great Hebridean product – the Tobermory Fish Co. smoked trout. We introduced this to our menu whilst having the privilege to cook at the iconic Duart Castle on the Isle of Mull. The smoked trout is served with fermented summer rhubarb, celery jam, frozen buttermilk, garnished with gorse flowers. A delightful light dish.

BREAC SMOCTE THOBAR MHOIRE — RUADH-BHÀRR TÒIRNICHTE — SILIDH SOILIRE — BLÀTHACH REÒTHTE — FLÙRAICHEAN CONAISG

'S e toradh sgoinneil Innse-Gallach eile a tha anns a' bhreac smocte aig Companaidh Èisg Thobar Mhoire. Chuir sinne seo air a' chlàr-bìdh againn nuair a fhuair sinn cothrom iongantach còcaireachd ann an Caisteal suaicheanta Dhubh Àird air Eilean Mhuile. Còmhla ris a' bhreac smocte tha ruadh-bhàrr samhraidh tòirnichte, silidh soilire agus blàthach reòthte, uile air an sgeadachadh le flùraichean conaisg.

ISLE OF HARRIS GIN AND SUGAR KELP CURED SEA TROUT — FERMENTED RHUBARB — APPLE — FRESH YOGHURT — MUSTARD SHOOTS

Isle of Harris Gin with the addition of sugar kelp, Isle of Skye sea salt, juniper and sugar makes a lovely delicate cure for the wild sea trout that are found in the rivers and bays of the Hebrides during summer. Paired with fermented rhubarb, rhubarb and apple purée, diced apple, fresh sugar kelp yoghurt, chives and some mustard shoots, it makes a great summer starter.

BÀNAG AIR A CIÙRADH LE SINEUBHAR NA HEARADH AGUS MILEARACH — RUADH-BHÀRR TÒIRNICHTE — UBHAL — IOGART ÙR — BUINNEIN SGEALLAIN

Tha sineubhar na Hearadh le milearach, salainn an Eilein Sgitheanaich, aiteann agus siùcar na cheann a' dèanamh ciùr aotrom, àlainn airson nam bànagan fiadhaich a gheibhear ann an aibhnichean agus ann am bàigh nan eilean as t-samhradh. Còmhla ri ruadh-bhàrr tòirnichte, purée de dh'ubhal agus ruadh-bhàrr, ubhal air a ghearradh mìn, iogart ùr le blas milearaich, feurain agus buinnein sgeallain, nì e deagh thoiseach-tòiseachaidh air biadh samhraidh.

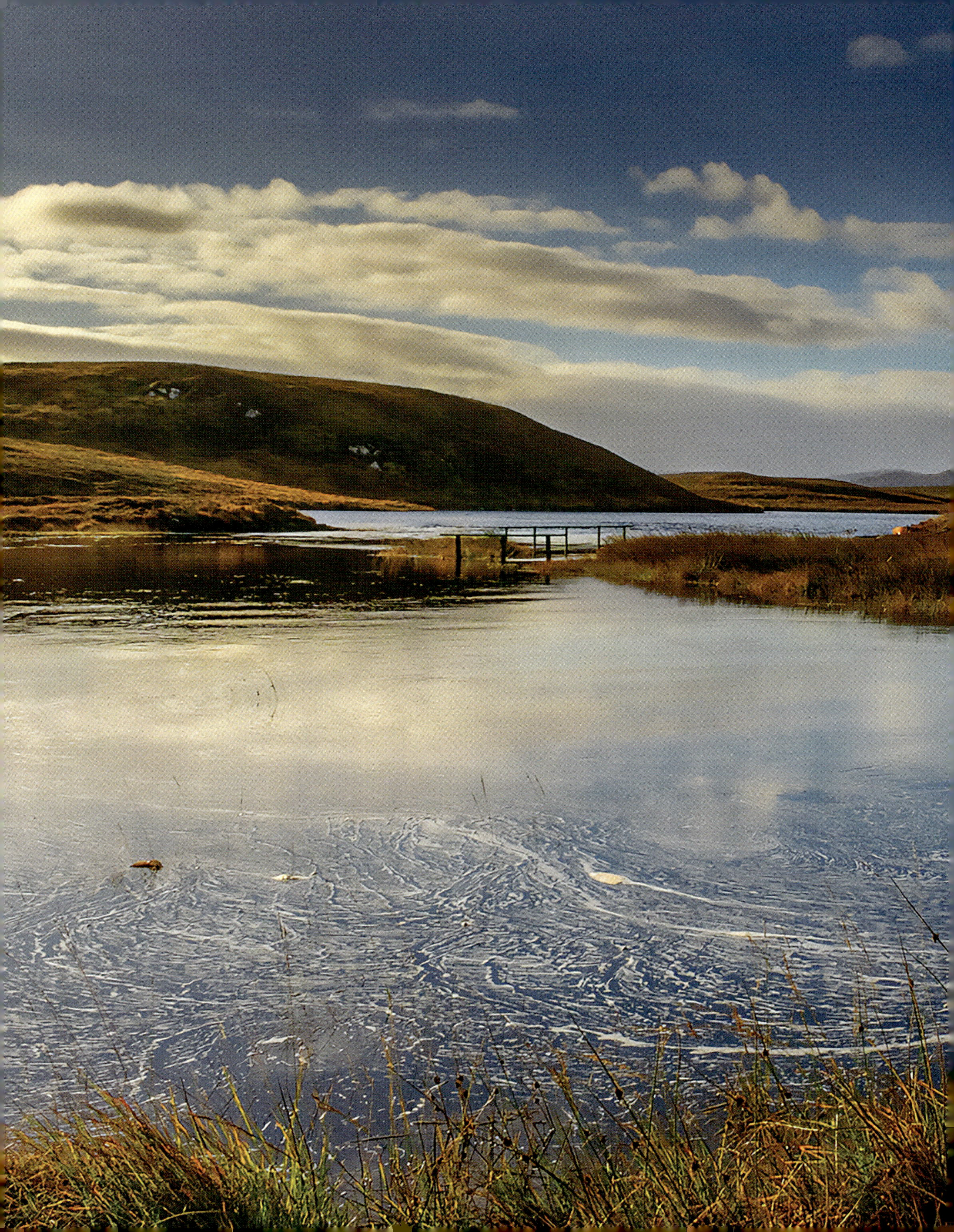

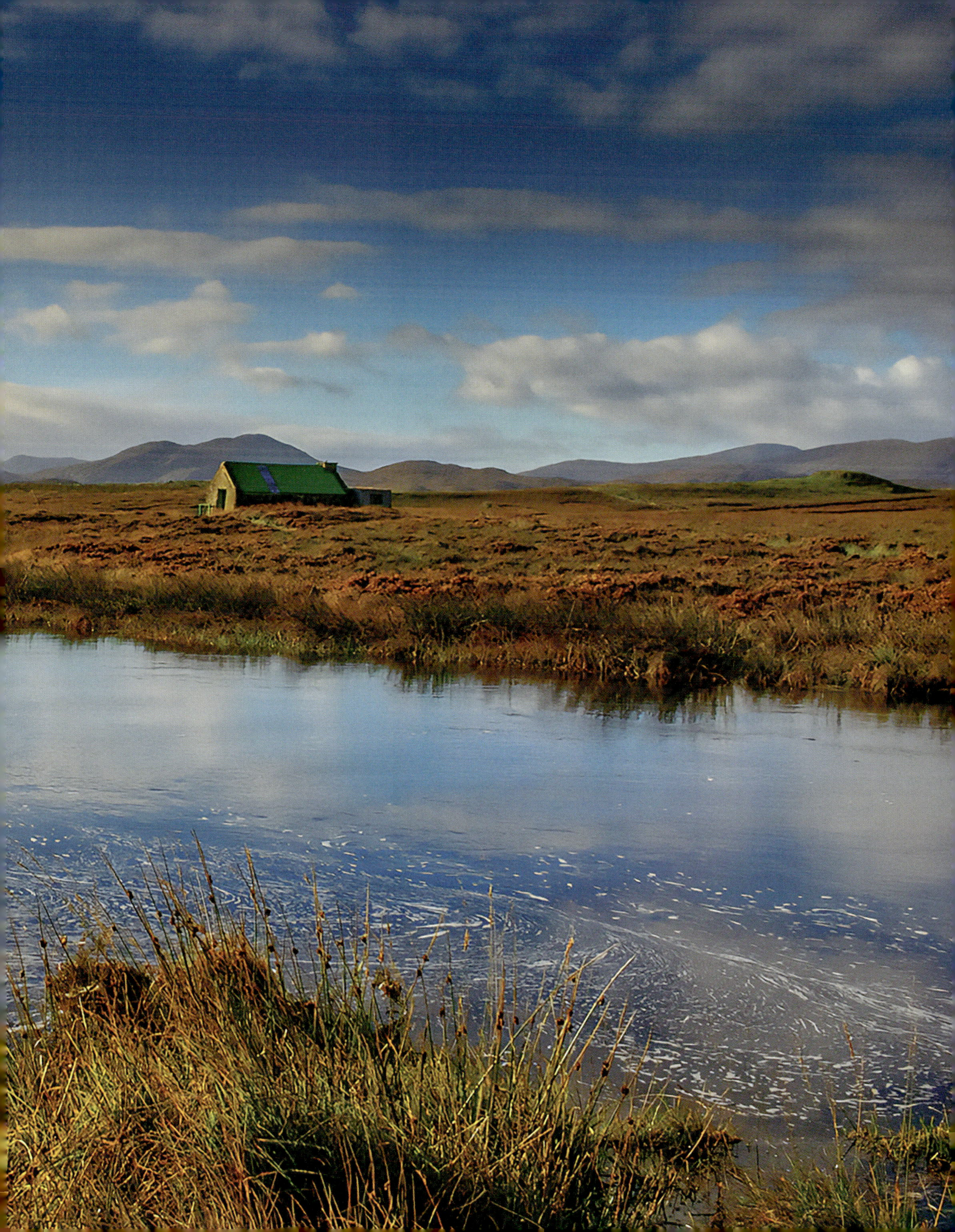

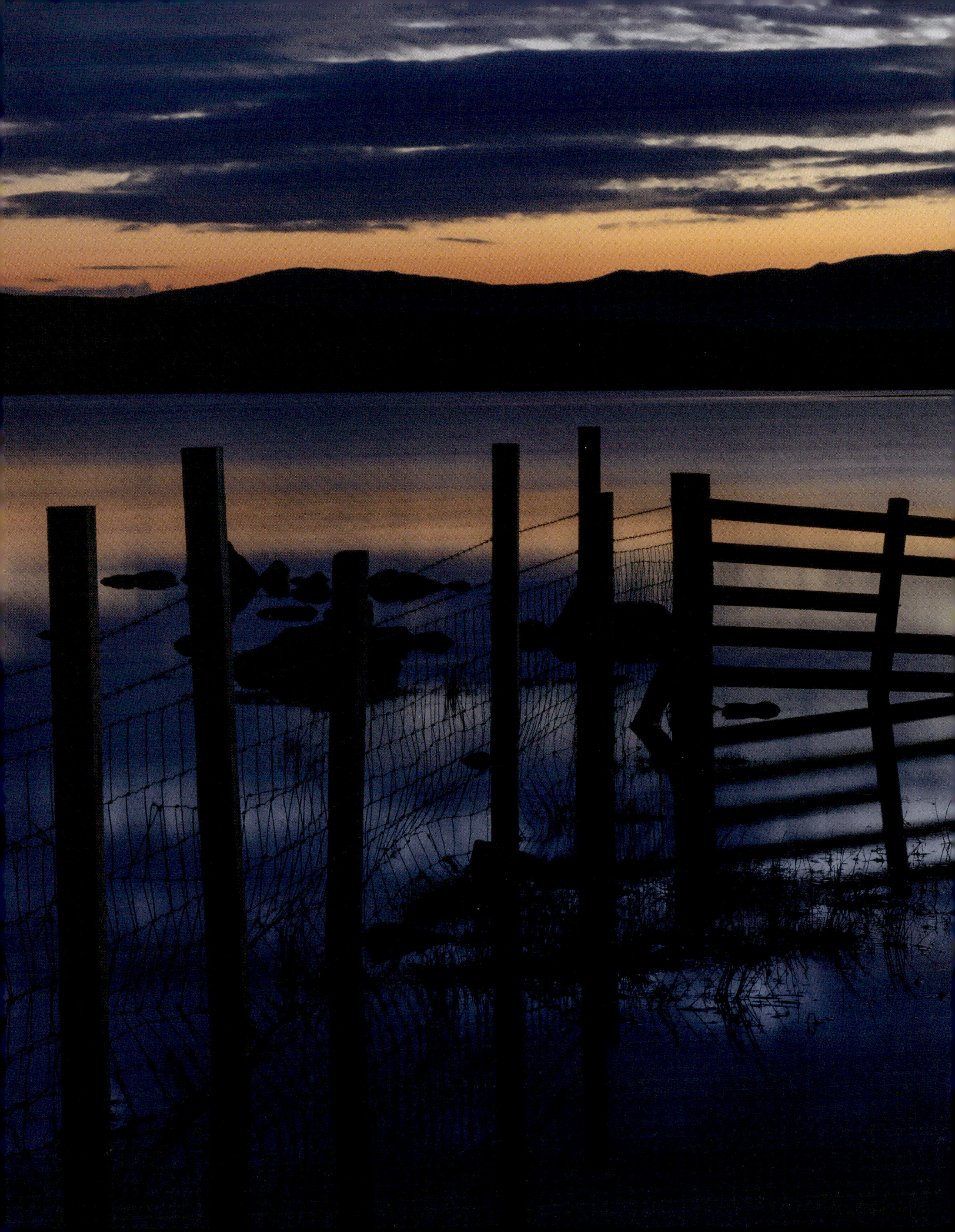

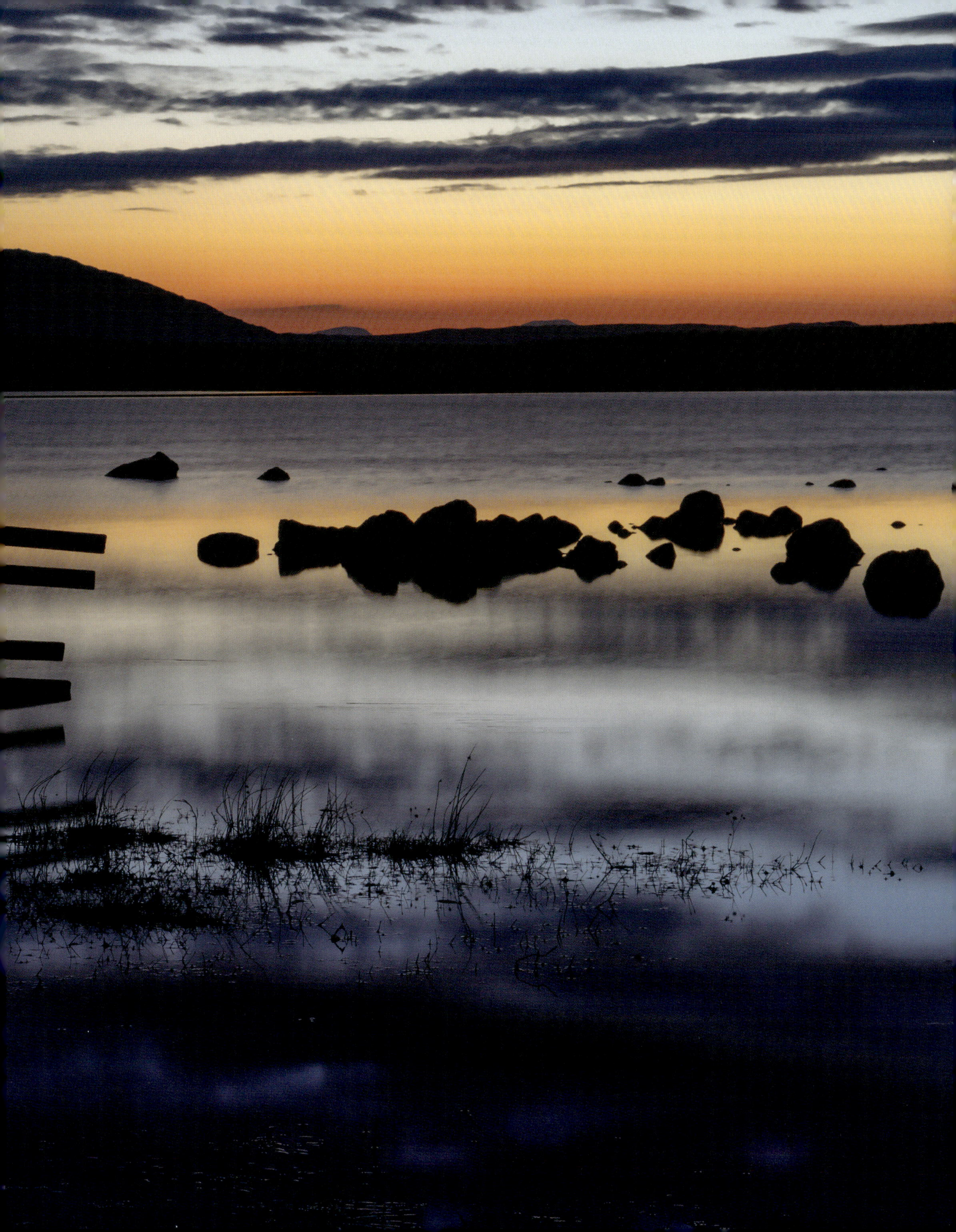

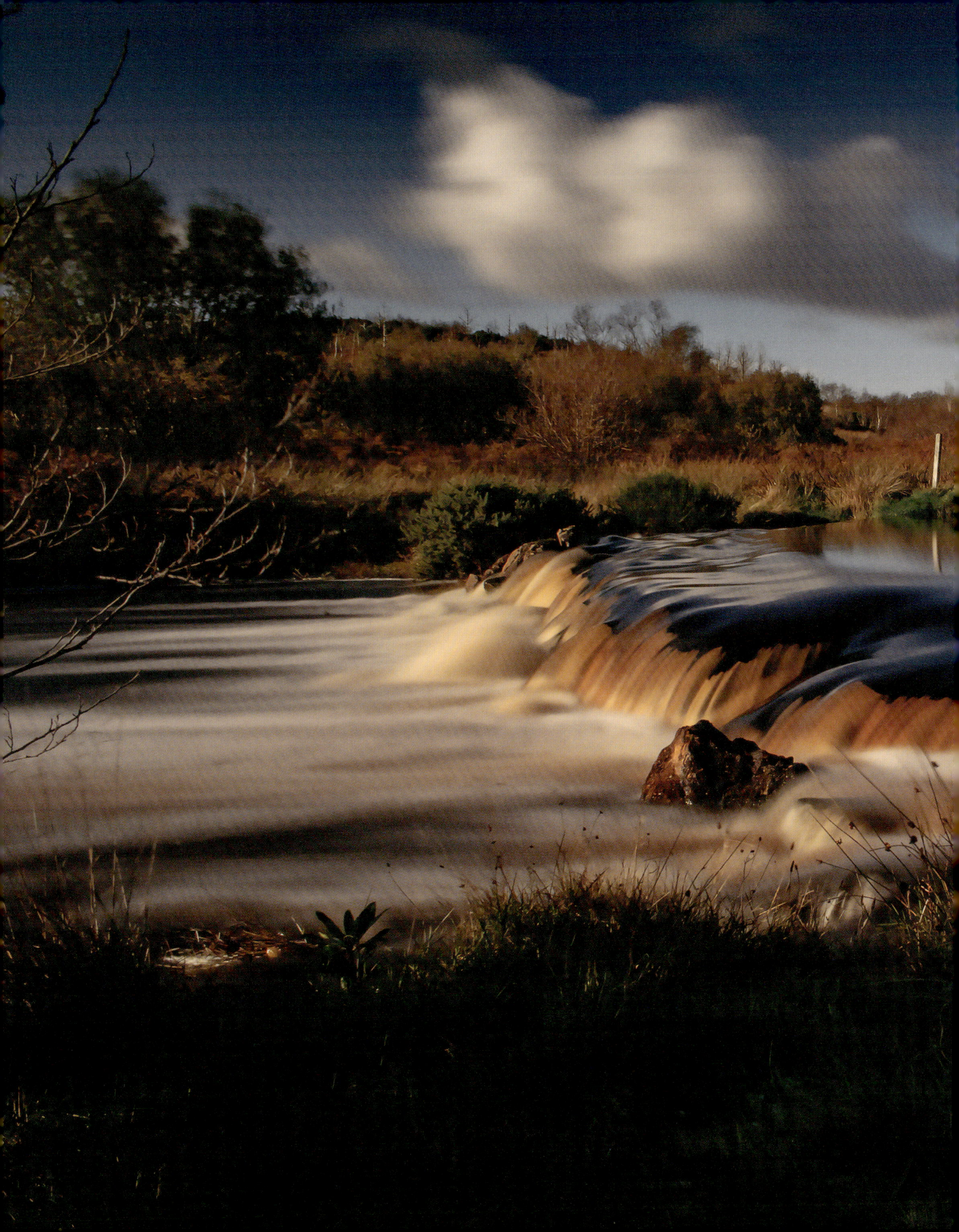

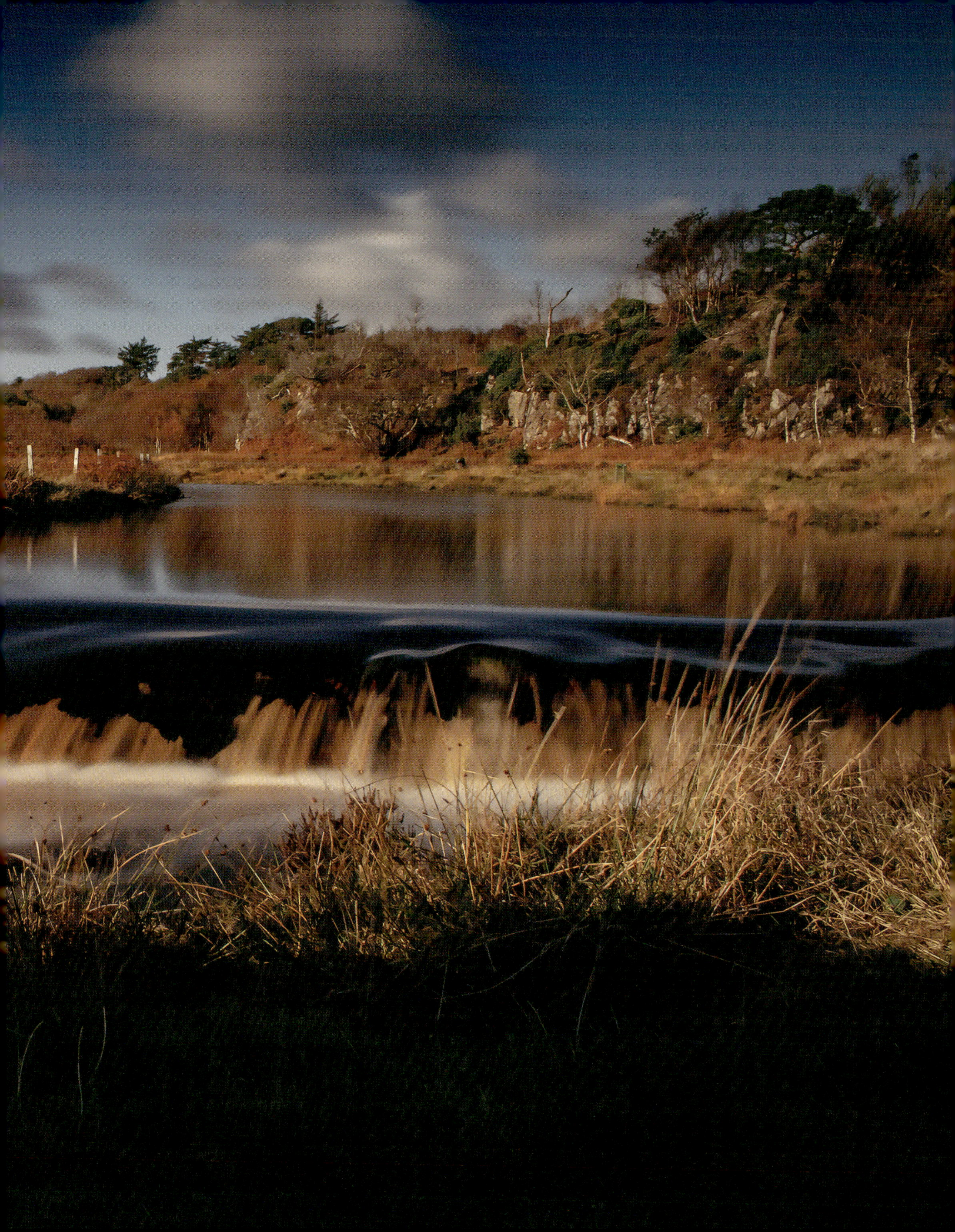

WILD SALMON COOKED IN RAPESEED OIL — BLACK PUDDING — PEAS — BROAD BEANS — SWEET MARJORAM — PEA AND BUTTERMILK CREAM

BRADAN FIADHAICH AIR A BHRUICH ANN AN OLA LUS-OLA — MARAG DHUBH — PEASRAICHEAN — PÒNAIREAN-LEATHANN — LUS-MHARSAILIDH MILIS — BÀRR LE PEASRAICHEAN IS BLÀTHACH

Wild Salmon
100/150g wild salmon fillet
Cullisse Highland rapeseed oil

Remove fillet from fridge 30 minutes before cooking to bring up to room temperature. Carefully remove the skin and set aside. Half fill a pan with the oil and bring the temperature to 43°C. Place the salmon in the oil and gently cook for about 8-10 minutes, checking that the oil stays at 43°C throughout cooking.

Salmon Skin
skin from fillet
oil for frying
Skye sea salt

Carefully scrape off as much of the fat and flesh as you can. Bring a pan of water to simmering and blanch the skin until you can break it by rubbing between your fingers. Chill in a bowl of iced water and pat dry. Place the skins evenly on a non-stick tray and dehydrate at 60°C overnight. Put enough neutral oil into a pan to be able to fry the skin. The skin will puff up and double in size so take this into consideration when choosing your pan.
Bring the oil up to 180°C and drop your skin in. If you have kitchen tweezers, you can use these to pull and shape the skin. The skin will start to puff up in seconds. Remove and place on a tray lined with paper towel. Season with Skye sea salt.

Black Pudding
150g Stornoway black pudding

Crumble the black pudding in a bowl and gently warm enough to be able to mix together. Roll the pudding out between two pieces of baking paper to a thickness of 1cm. Refrigerate for 30 minutes.
Once chilled, cut into rounds, cut the disks in half and place on a lined tray. Grill until cooked.

Pea Purée and Broad Beans
300g peas
handful of broad beans

Remove peas and beans from pods. The pods can be kept to flavour vegetable stocks. Blanch the beans in boiling water for 30 seconds and chill straight away in iced water. Remove the outer skin of the beans. This is tough and not pleasant to eat. Blanch the peas in the same water until just cooked and blend straight away (keeping a few peas back), using a bit of the water to get a smooth consistency. Chill in a bowl set up over iced water. This keeps the lovely green vibrant colour of the peas. Chill until cold.
To serve, gently heat the peas and beans in a knob of butter and just enough water to coat them. Add the purée to warm through, check the seasoning, finish with a touch of lemon juice and buttermilk.
Garnish with fresh marjoram leaves.

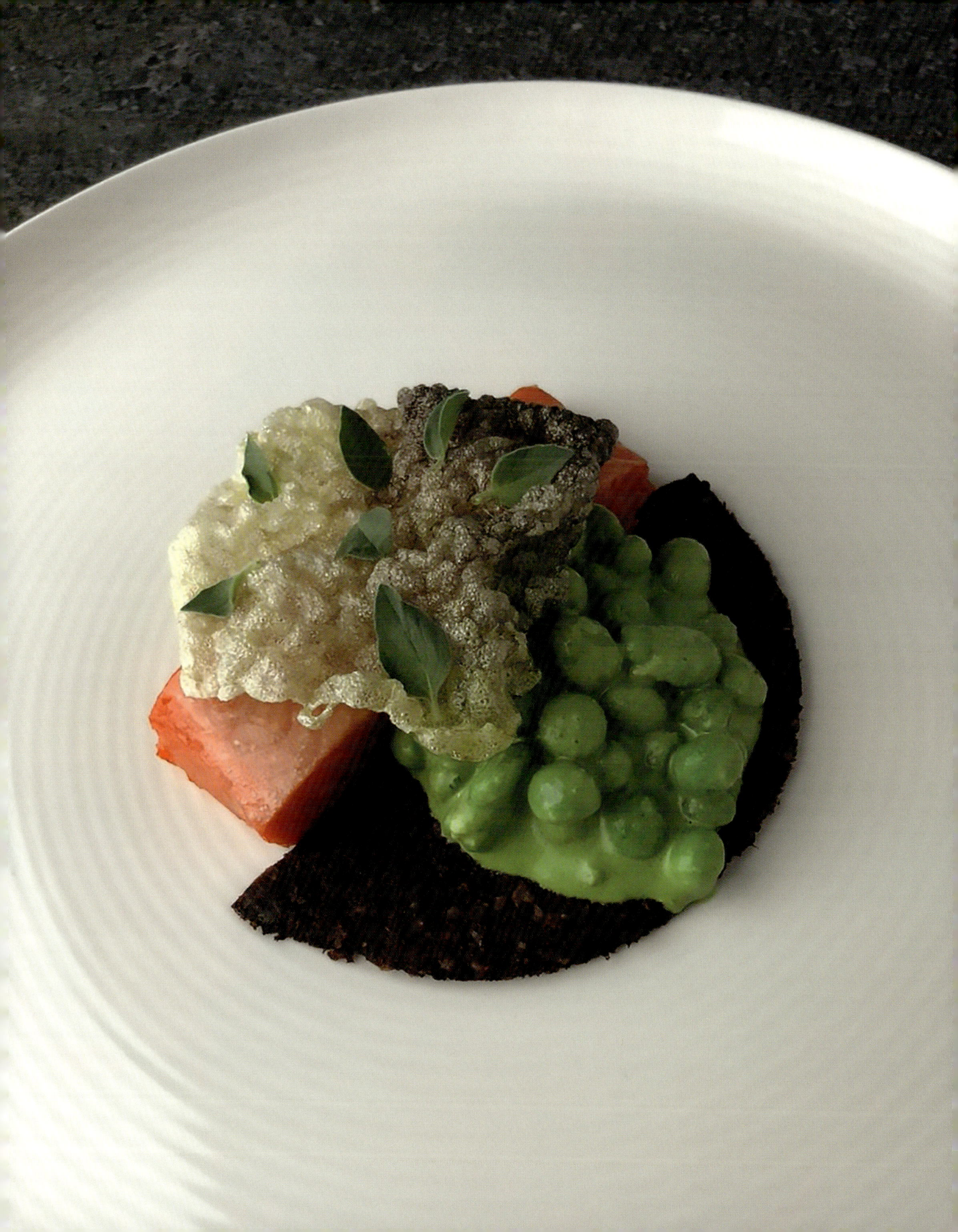

BROWN TROUT SMOKED OVER HEATHER — CHIVE BUTTERMILK — CHIVES — CRISPY FRIED POTATO PEELINGS — HEATHER OIL

As a child, I spent much of my time fishing the many moor lochs that are to be found on the Isle of Lewis. I loved to cook any trout that I caught right there and then by the lochsides. I would gather some heather and tightly pack it around the fish and set the heather alight and cook the beautiful, delicate trout. The blackened crispy skin was delicious and the heather added a lovely smoky, earthy flavour to the fish, which was fleshy pink and moist on the inside. These are the memories which inspire this dish. The crispy potato peelings add a lovely textural contrast. What can be more Hebridean than fish and potatoes? The slightly tart buttermilk and chive sauce helps to balance the dish along with the heather oil and fresh chives.

BREAC AIR A SMOCADH THAIRIS AIR FRAOCH — BLÀTHACH FEURAIN — FEURAIN — RÙSGAN BUNTÀTA AIR AM FRAIDHIGEADH BRISG — OLA FRAOICH

Nam leanabh chuir mi tòrr dhem ùine seachad ag iasgach nan iomadh loch a tha air mòintichean Leòdhais. Bha e a' còrdadh rium breac sam bith a ghlacainn a chòcaireachd dìreach far an robh mi, air bruaichean nan loch. Bhuaininn geugan fraoich agus chuirinn iad teann mun cuairt air a' bhreac is chuirinn teine ris an fhraoch airson am breac àlainn a ròstadh. Bhiodh an craiceann brisg, loisgte cho blasta agus bha am fraoch a' toirt blas ceòthach, talmhaidh dhan iasg a bha cho pinc agus cho tais na bhroinn. Sin na cuimhneachain a tha air cùl an reasabaidh seo. Tha rùsgan buntàta brisg cho eadar-dhealaichte ris a' chòrr. Dè tha nas eileanach na iasg is buntàta? Tha an sabhs blàthaich le feurain rud beag geur agus tha sin, còmhla ri ola fraoich agus feurain ùra, a' cothromachadh nam blasan.

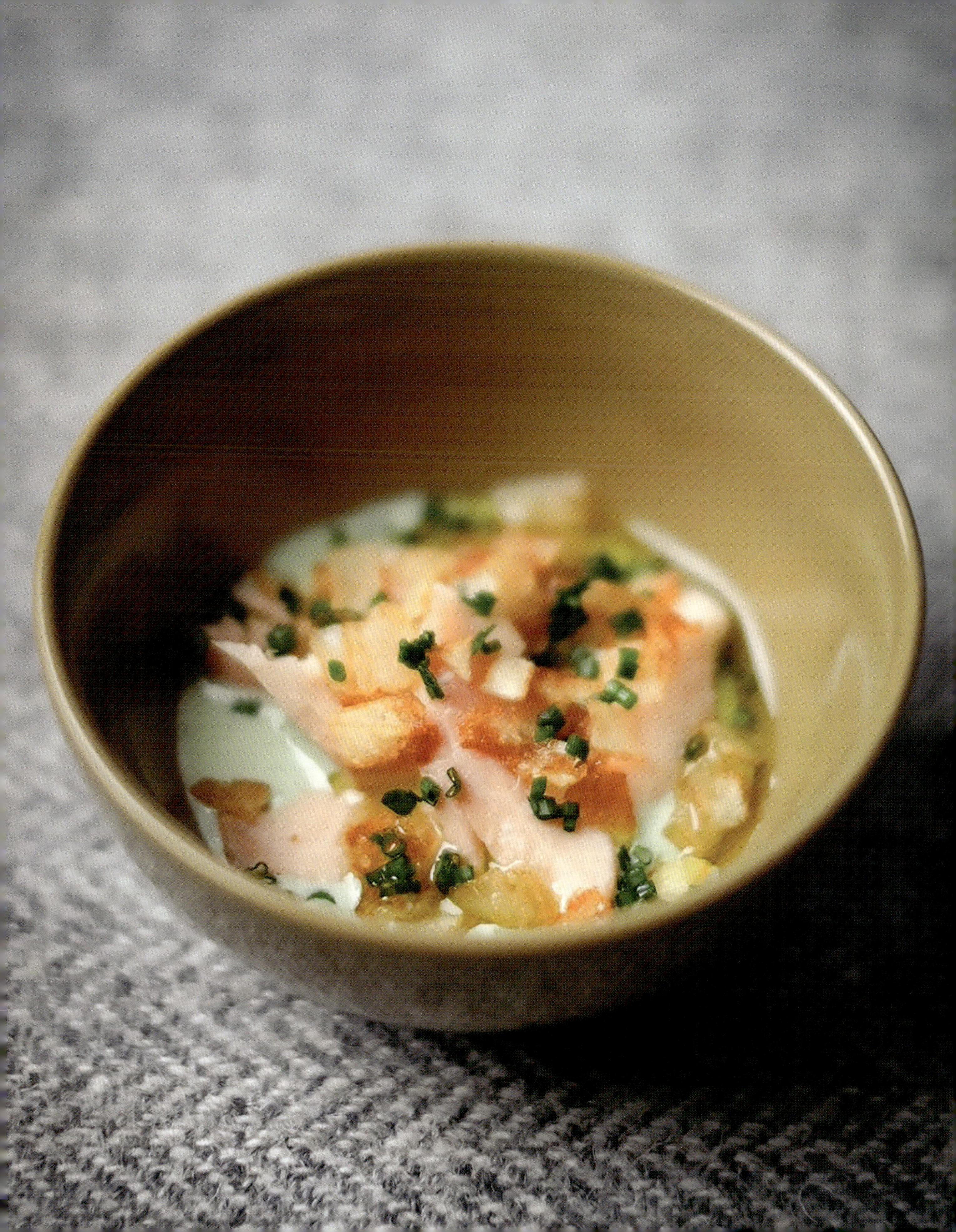

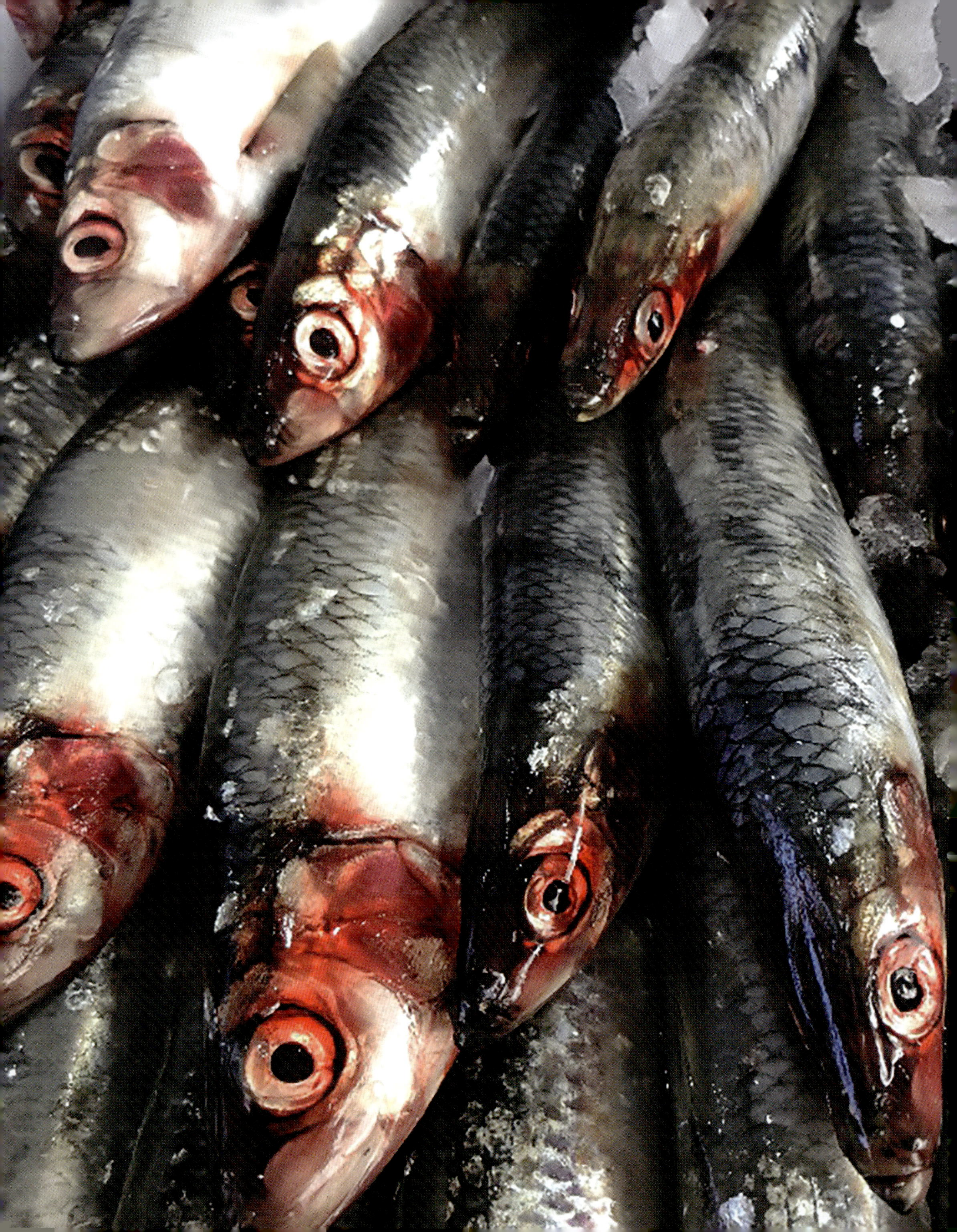

A Good Catch
Deagh Iasgach

Hebridean herring were of the finest quality in Europe and Stornoway developed into a main centre of the Scottish herring industry. In 1912 Stornoway had a population of 4000 and a fleet of a thousand sailing boats. Beautiful fresh herring, known as silver darlings, once a staple of the Hebridean diet, are such an underated fish today. A beautiful, plump, silver eye-catching fish, the herring is not just a basic food but to islanders, the food of kings. It is best served fresh off the boat and fried in oatmeal. The glut of leftover herring would be salted and no Island crofter would face a winter without a barrel of salt herring. Salt herring would be served with potatoes but tasted just as good with oatcakes, scones or *aran-eòrna* (barley bread) and of course a cup of tea stewed in the pot!

To Salt Herring
fresh herring
coarse salt

Gut the herring, leaving the heads on. In a large plastic bucket or small wooden barrel, sprinkle a thick layer of salt in the base. Place the herring slightly on their sides with heads up. Put the next layer of salt with the herring lying in the opposite direction. Continue the layers until the barrel is full. Cover and store in a cool place for up to a year.

Bha sgadan Innse-Gallach cho math ri sgadan sam bith san Roinn-Eòrpa agus bha Steòrnabhagh am measg nam prìomh bhailtean-puirt ann an Alba airson iasgach an sgadain. Ann an 1912 bha 4000 neach sa bhaile agus bha mu mhìle bàta-siùil ag iasgach a-mach às. Chan eil daoine a' cur mòran sùim an-diugh ann an sgadan àlainn ùr, "silver darlings" mar a chante riutha, a bha uair cho cudromach mar bhiadh eileanach. Chan e dìreach biadh àbhaisteach dha eileanaich a tha ann an sgadan reamhar, àlainn, airgeadach is tarraingeach, ach biadh nan uaislean. 'S e an dòigh as fheàrr air sgadan ùr ithe fhaighinn dìreach a-mach às a' bhàta air a fhraidhigeadh ann am min-choirce. Bhiodh an sgadan nach ithte ùr air a shailleadh agus cha smaoinicheadh croitear eileanach air aghaidh a chur air a' gheamhradh gun bharaille sgadan saillt. Bhiodh e air ithe le buntàta ach bha e a cheart cho math le aran-coirce, sgonaichean no aran-eòrna agus cupa tì a bha air deagh ghoil fhaighinn sa phoit!

A' Sailleadh Sgadan
sgadan ùr
salainn garbh

Sgoilt agus glan an sgadan ach fàg na cinn orra. Cuir tiughad de shalainn garbh air bonn pucaid phlastaig no baraille beag fiodh. Cuir an sgadan beagan air an cliathaich le an cinn suas. Cuir tiughad eile de shalainn air an uachdair agus an uair sin sgadain eile len cinn ceart aghaidh a' chiad fheadhainn. Cùm a' dol mar seo gus a bheil am baraille làn. Cuir mullach air agus cùm e ann an àite fionnar airson suas ri bliadhna.

Salt Herring
salt herring fillets
unpeeled tatties

Remove the heads from the herring, wash and leave in cold water overnight, changing the water at least three times. Scrub the potatoes, cover with water in a saucepan and bring to the boil. Once the potatoes are half cooked, place the herring over the potatoes, cover and cook in the steam until ready – about 10-15 minutes. Lift the herring onto a hot plate. Steam the potatoes until dry. Delicious!

PICKLED HERRING — CUCUMBER — BARLEY BREAD

A simple but tasty dish, served just with cucumber strands and fresh barley bread.

SGADAN PICILTE — CULARAN — ARAN-EÒRNA

Biadh sìmplidh ach blasta, sgadan le dìreach duail chularain agus aran-eòrna ùr.

Pickled Herring
6 fresh herring
65g salt
900ml water

Pickling Liquor
300ml water
480ml vinegar
50g sugar
3 bay leaves
1 sliced onion
1 sliced carrot
1½ tbsp mustard seeds
2 tbsp allspice
20g fresh dill

Clean and fillet the herring. Bring to the boil the salt and 900ml water and cool. Arrange fillets in a container and pour on the saline mix. Cover and refrigerate for 24 hours. Drain the herring and rinse well in cold water.

Simmer the rest of the ingredients for two minutes and cool. Place the herring in the pickle and refrigerate for one week before using. Keep for up to one month.

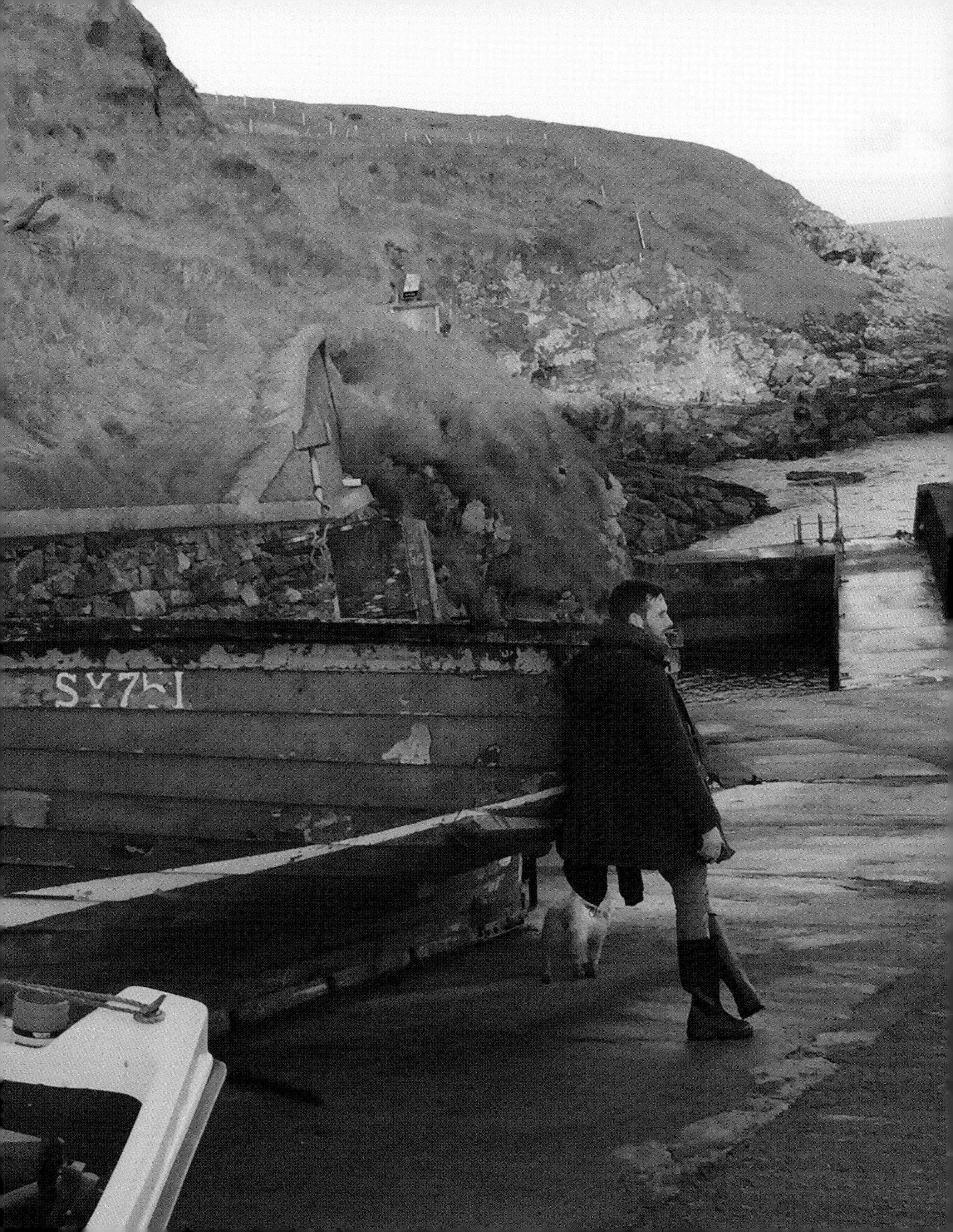

BBQ, SWEET CURED AND FRIED HERRING — PICKLED HERRING SALAD CREAM — BARLEY BANNOCK — APPLE — RED CLOVER

This is a lovely delicate dish of barbequed, sweet cured and crispy fried herring, served with a pickled herring salad cream, apple compressed in dill vinegar, sweet pickled onions and barley bannock, garnished with fresh red clover petals and fresh dill.

SGADAN AIR BBQ, LE CIÙR MILIS AGUS AIR A FHRAIDHIGEADH — UACHDAR SAILEAD SGADAN PICILTE — ARAN-EÒRNA — UBHAL — SEAMRAG DHEARG

'S e biadh aotrom a tha seo de sgadan air BBQ, sgadan le ciùr milis, agus sgadan air a fhraidhigeadh brisg. Còmhla ris tha uachdar sailead sgadan picilte, ubhal brùthte ann am fìon geur dile, uinneanan milis picilte agus aran-eòrna, air a sgeadachadh le flùr-bhileagan seamraig dheirg agus dile ùr.

Pickled Herring Salad Cream
2 pickled herring fillets
2 tbsp plain flour
8 tbsp sugar
2 tbsp mustard powder
pinch of salt
4 eggs
200ml white wine vinegar
300ml double cream
squeeze of lemon juice

Whisk the flour, sugar, mustard powder, salt and eggs in a bowl over simmering water until pale and thickened.
Remove pan from heat and stir in vinegar, cream and lemon juice. Set aside to cool. Add pickled herring and blitz. Transfer into a squeezy bottle.

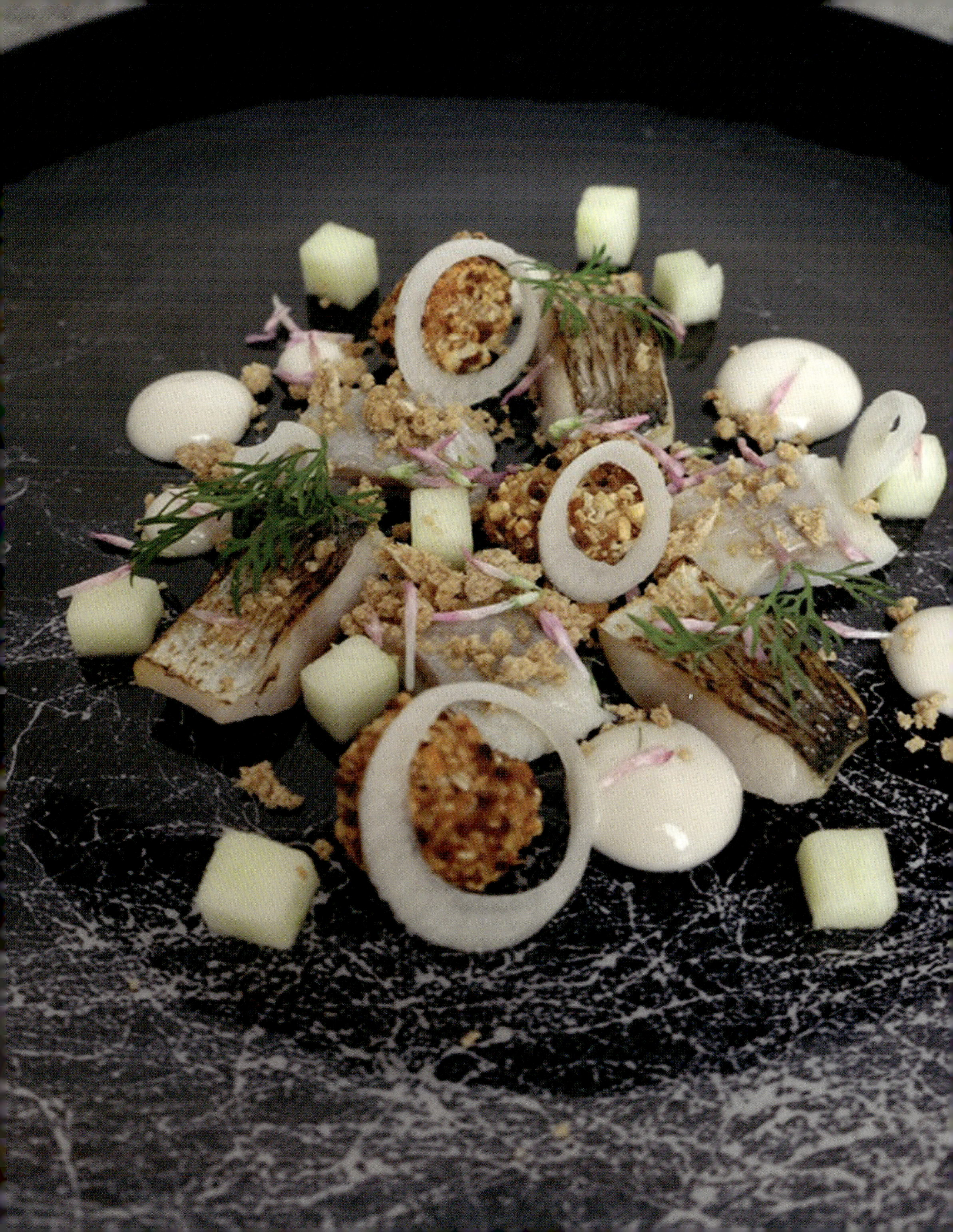

ROASTED SKATE WINGS — BARRA COCKLES — CREAMED PARSNIP — SYBOES — GREEN ELDERBERRY CAPERS — COCKLE AND BUTTER BROTH

SGIATHAN SGAIT RÒSTA — COILLEAGAN BARRACH — CURRAIN-GHEALA UACHDARAICHTE — UINNEANAN-EARRAICH — CAPAIREAN CAORAN-DHROMAIN UAINE — BROT CHOILLEAGAN IS ÌM

Skate
1 large skate wing, cut in half

Warm up pan with oil, once hot add the skate wing. Once the fish starts to caramelise turn, add butter and baste. Remove fish from the bone.

Cockles
handful of fresh cockles
100ml dry white wine
1 shallot
sprig of thyme
rapeseed oil

Rinse the cockles to clean any dirt from them. In a pan cook the finely chopped shallot in a little rapeseed oil, cooking until soft. Add the wine and thyme along with the cockles and cover the pan with a lid and cook for a couple of minutes until the shells open. Remove from the shells, reserving the liquid for the broth.

Creamed Parsnips
2 parsnips
1 tbsp double cream

In a pan of slightly salted boiling water add the peeled and chopped parsnips, cooking until the parsnips are tender. Once cooked, drain the parsnips and mash adding the cream and seasoning.

Syboes
2 syboes trimmed and cut in half

Gently warm up a small amount of broth, adding syboes and a knob of butter.

Green Elderberry Capers
100g green elderberries
salt
75ml cider vinegar
1 tbsp caster sugar

Pick the berries from the stalk and rinse. Place in a container and cover with salt, leaving for a few days. Once cured, rinse off the salt and place in a kilner jar. In a pan simmer the vinegar, sugar and a splash of water until the sugar is dissolved. Pour over the capers completely covering them and leave in the fridge for three weeks. Use as garnish, giving the dish lovely little bursts of salty tangy flavour.

Cockle and Butter Broth

Heat up the reserved broth, adding emulsified butter. Check the seasoning, adding a squeeze of lemon juice. Garnish with sea aster.

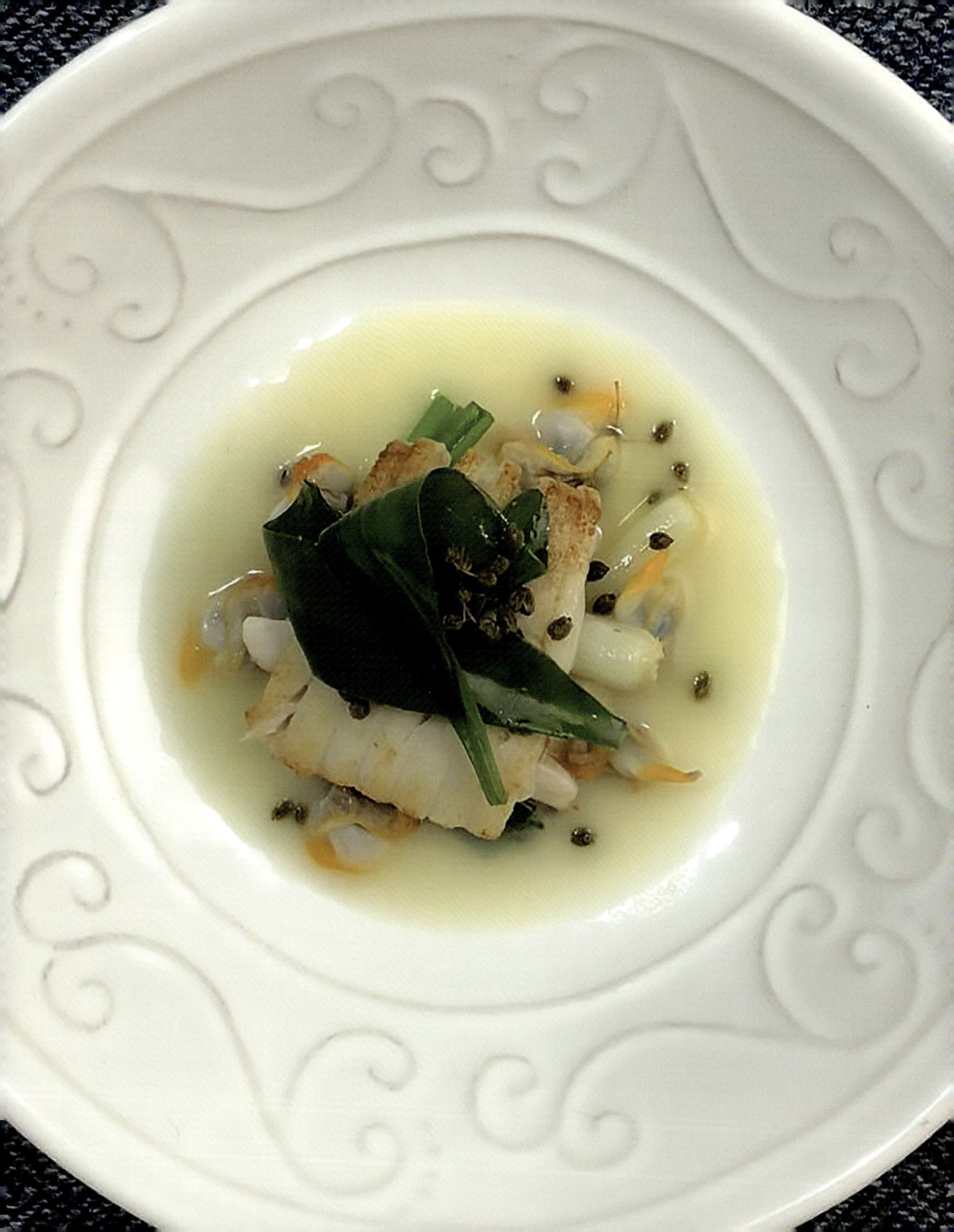

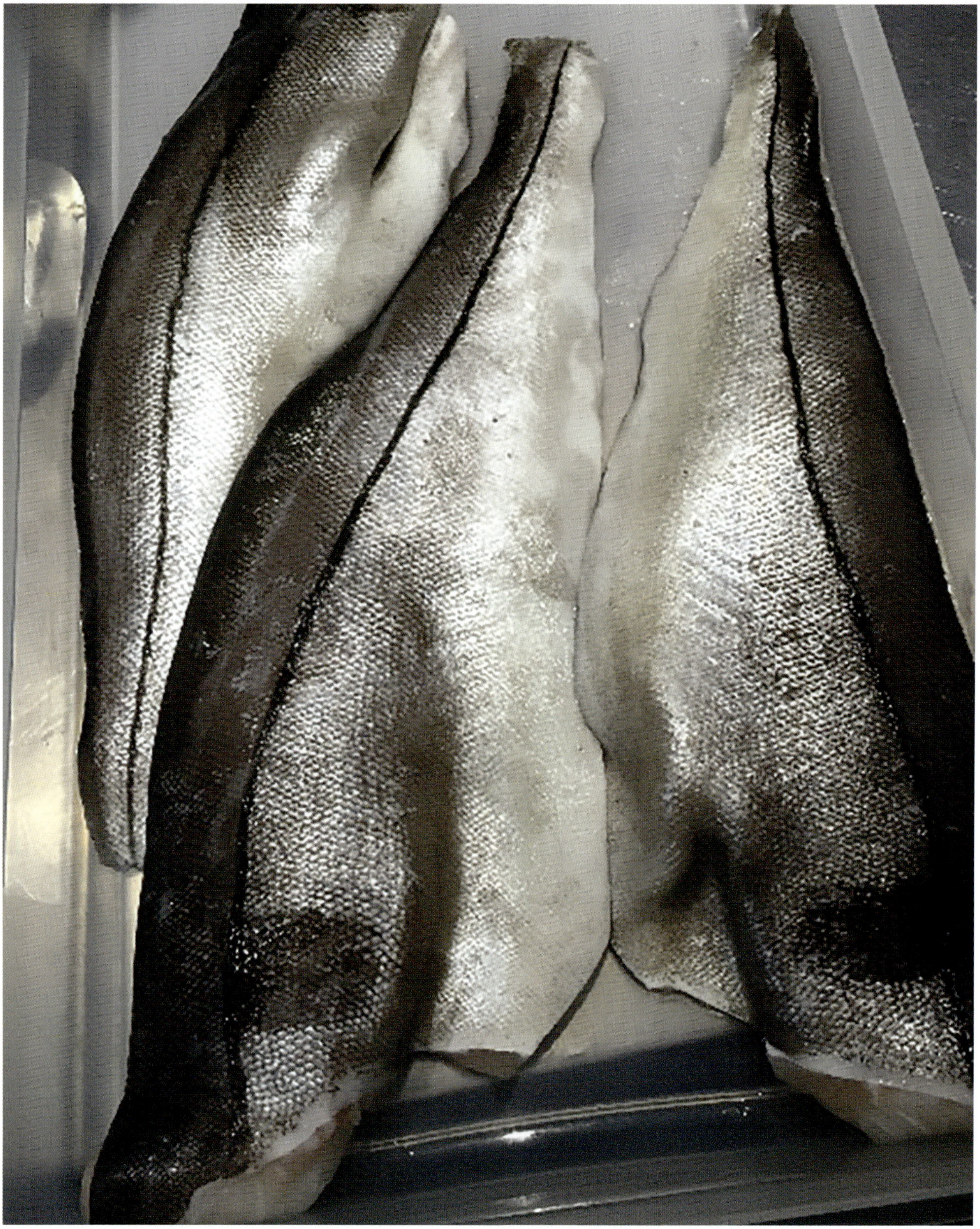

AIR
INTAKES
KEEP
CLEAR
SHUT
IN EVENT
OF FIRE

DNG
AIR
INTAKES
KEEP
CLEAR

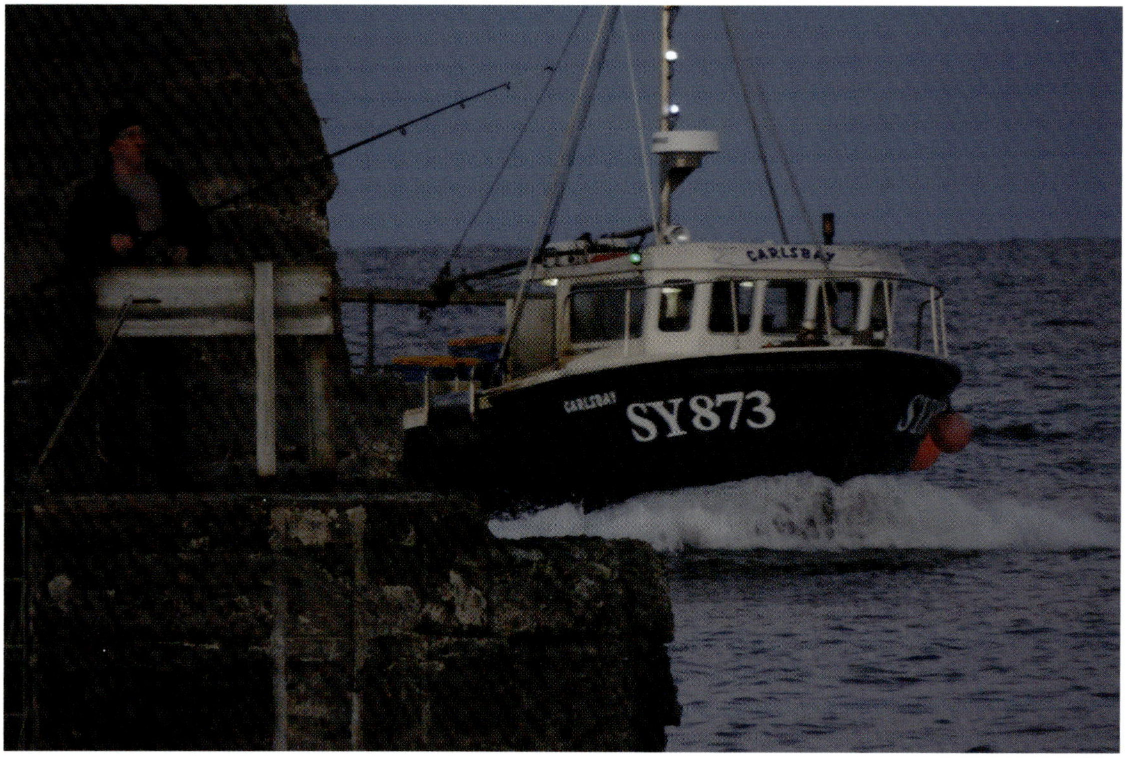
CARLSBAY
CARLSBAY
SY873

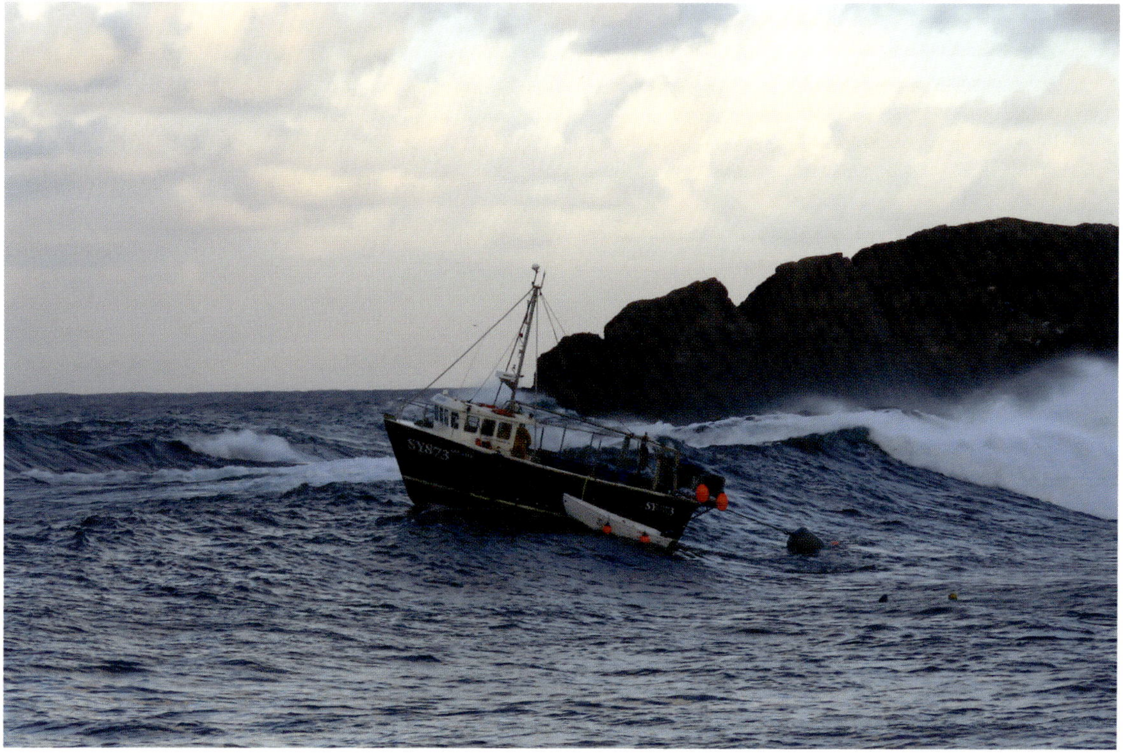
SY873

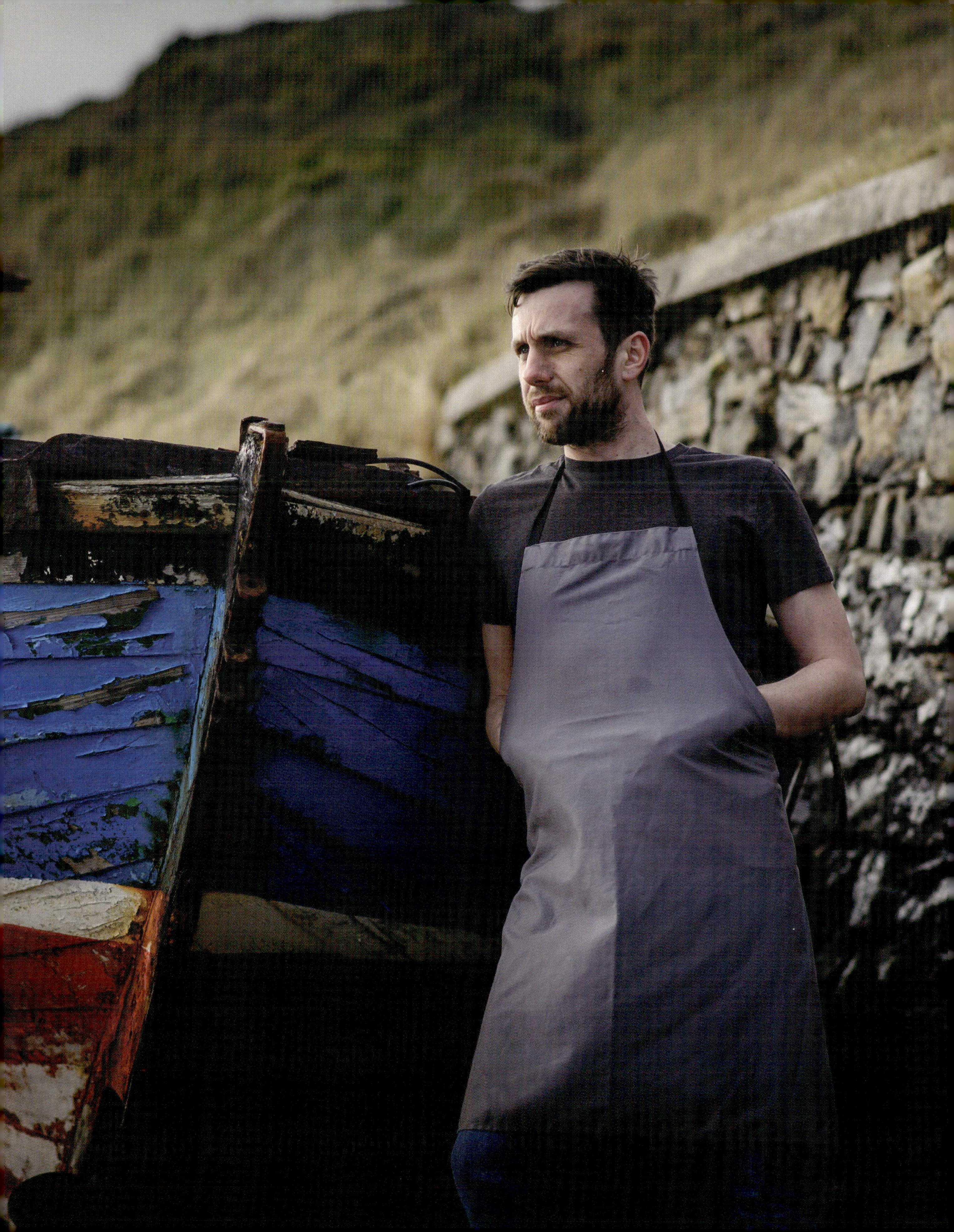

LING CURING AT PORT OF NESS

Ness was a thriving curing district in the 19th century. The ling having been washed and cleaned would be placed in large, rectangular, timber salting vats – *acaraiche amaraichean* – and left in the brine for around 24 hours. When the salting process was completed the ling would be removed from the vats and sub-contracted out in lots of 1000 to households who would take responsibility for drying the fish. The ling caught were laid out on the shingle beach to dry. Unlike Skigersta, which had a shingle shoreline on which the processed fish could be dried, the beach at Port of Ness was sand and therefore, the fish had to be carried over to Beirgh where they would be laid out on rocky ledges. There the sun and coastal breeze would ready the fish for market.

CIÙRADH LANGA ANN AM PORT NIS

Anns an naoidheamh linn deug bha sgìre Nis na àite trang airson ciùradh èisg. An dèidh an nighe agus an glanadh bhiodh an langa air a chur ann an amair mhòra, cheart-cheàrnach fhiodha agus air am fàgail sa phicil timcheall air ceithir uairean fichead. Nuair a bha an sailleadh dèante dheigheadh an langa a thoirt às na h-amair agus bhiodh iad air an roinn a-mach, le mìle langa a' dol gu gach teaghlach a ghabhadh uallach airson an t-iasg a thiormachadh. Bha na langannan air an càradh air a' mhol airson an tiormachadh. Eu-coltach ri Sgiogarstaigh aig a bheil cladach muil air an gabhadh an t-iasg a thiormachadh, b' e gainmheach a bha air tràigh a' Phuirt agus mar sin dh'fheumte an t-iasg a thoirt a-null gu Beirgh far am biodh iad air an càradh air pallachan creagach. An sin dheasaicheadh a' ghrian agus gaoth na mara an t-iasg airson margaid.

A fascinating fishing report detailing the fish caught by Port of Ness boats in 1898. This was when the ling curing industry was at its height in Port of Ness, Lewis. Over 17,000 ling were caught during the month of March!

Iomradh inntinneach ag innse na chaidh de dh'iasg a ghlacadh le eathraichean Port Nis ann an 1898. Bha seo nuair a bha obair giullachd langa aig àirde anns a' Phort. Chaidh còrr air 17,000 langa a ghlacadh anns a' Mhàrt.

1893

Fishing Statistic

			cwt	
March	17384 Ling	9 to the cwt	1970	8/-
	Cod		499	5/-
	Haddock		128	5/-
	Halibut		310	25/-
	Skate		1000	1/6
April	8000 Ling		888	1/6
	Cod		173	5/6
	Haddocks		89	5/-
	Turbot		10	18/6
	Halibut		190	7/-
	Skate		539	1/8
May 31	13000 Ling		1444	7/-
	Cod		300	5/-
	Haddocks		60	5/-
	Turbot		30	11/-
	Halibut		300	6/6
	Skate		300	1/6
	Eel		30	5/-
June 30	30000 Ling		3000	6/6
	Cod		300	5/-
	Haddocks		50	5/-
	Halibut		150	
	Turbot		12	5/-
	Skate		476	
	Eel		40	1/6

KELP CURED LING

Curing fish is a technique that goes back hundreds of years. While methods vary, the basic technique is the same; using salt to draw out water from the fish. In times gone by when salt was expensive and scarce, ashes of seaweed were often used as a preservative. Curing the ling with kelp provides it with a fresh and lively taste of the sea. Rehydrate the kelp at room temperature in water, just until it becomes soft. Drain the kelp and place on cling film. Place the ling on top of the kelp and put another piece of kelp on top of the fish. Wrap in cling film and refrigerate overnight.

LANGA AIR A CIÙRADH LE CEILP

Tha dòighean ciùraidh èisg a' dol air ais ceudan bhliadhnaichean. Ged a tha dòighean eadar-dhealaichte ann, tha dòigh bunaiteach aca uile, a' cleachdadh salainn airson uisge a tharraing às an iasg. Sna làithean a dh'fhalbh, nuair a bha salainn daor agus tearc, bha luath feamainn tric air a chleachdadh airson grèidheadh. Tha ciùradh langa le ceilp a' toirt dha blas ùr, beothail na mara. Cuir a' cheilp am bogadh ann an uisge aig teothachd an t-seòmair dìreach gus am fàs e bog. Traogh a' cheilp agus cuir e air pìos film-còmhdachaidh. Cuir an langa air uachdar na ceilp agus cuir an tuilleadh ceilp air uachdar na langa. Còmhdaich gu teann e le film-còmhdachaidh agus fàg e oidhche san fhuaradair.

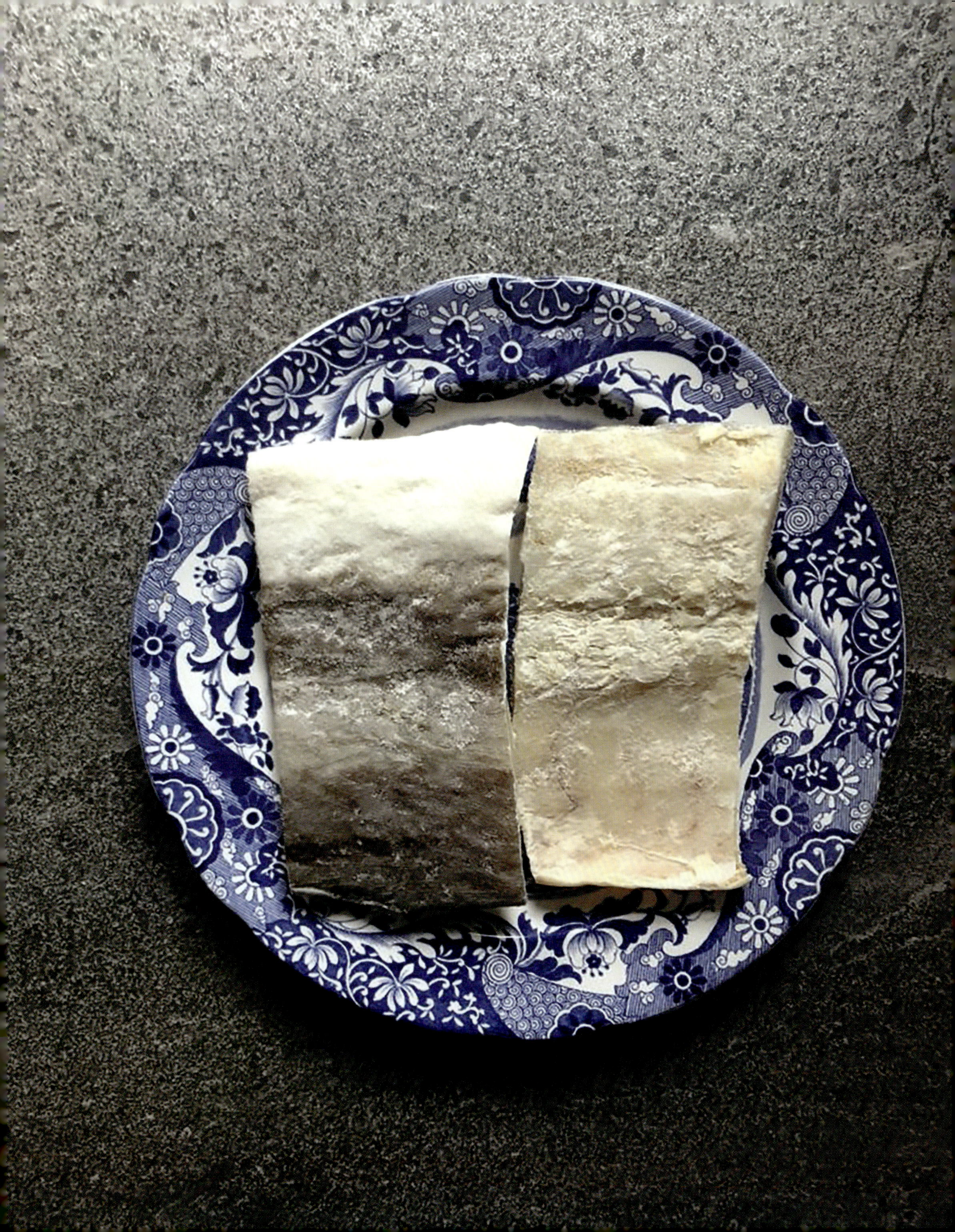

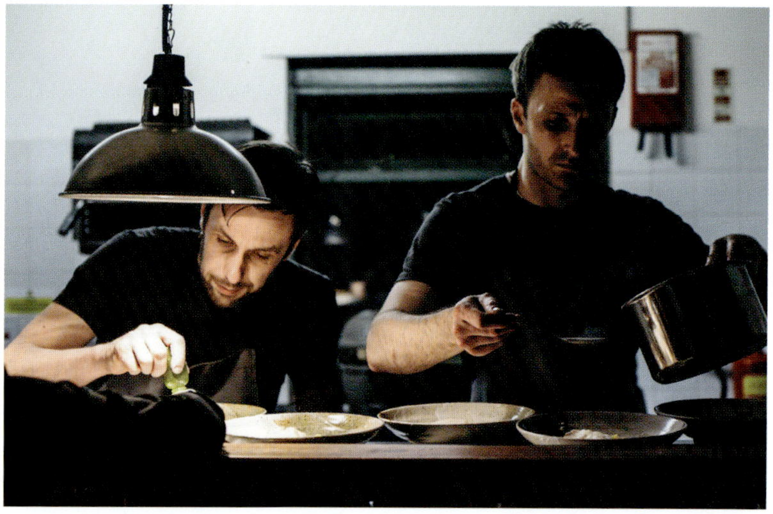
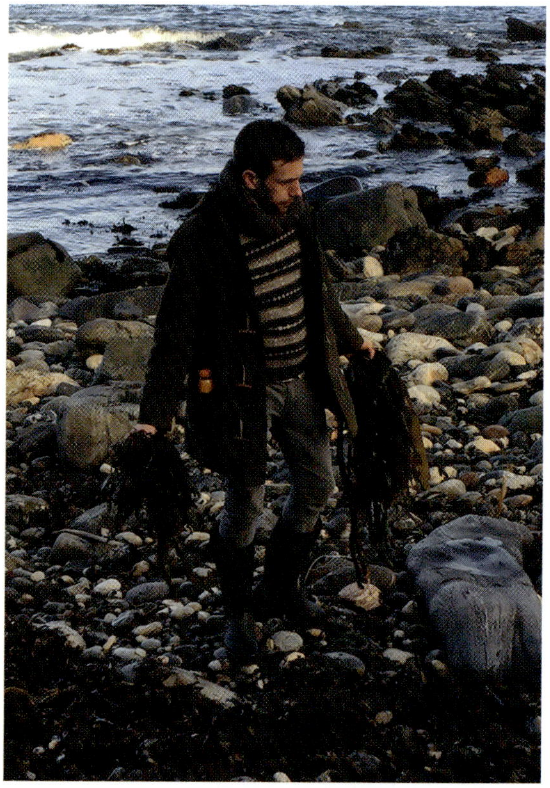
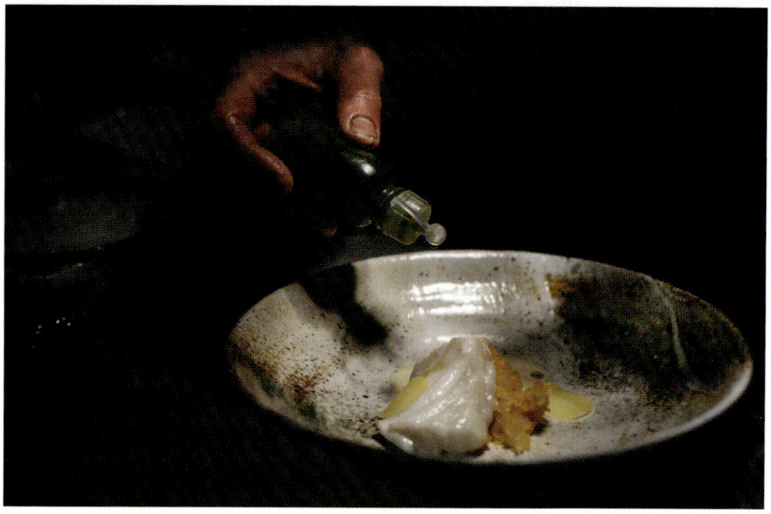
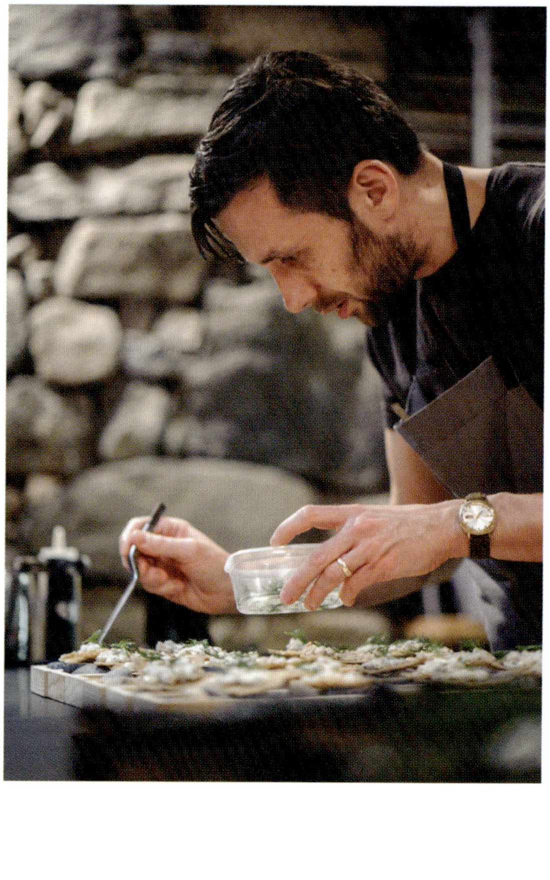
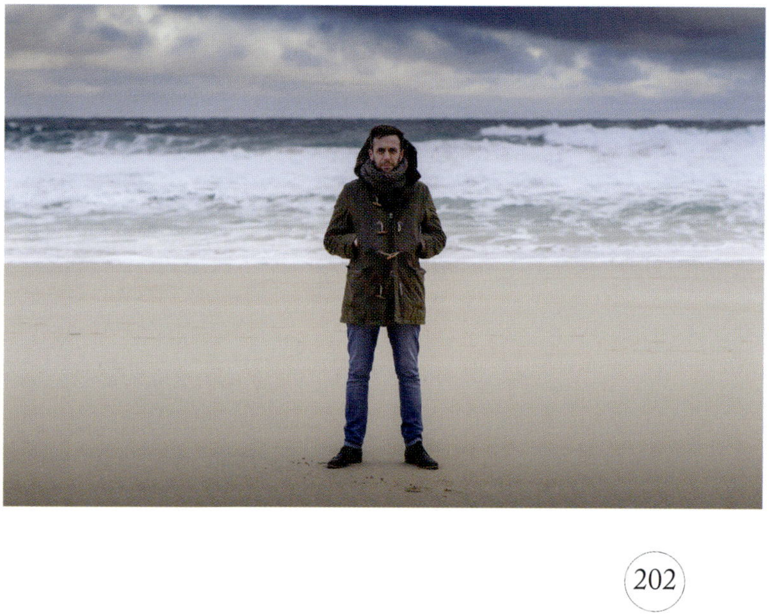

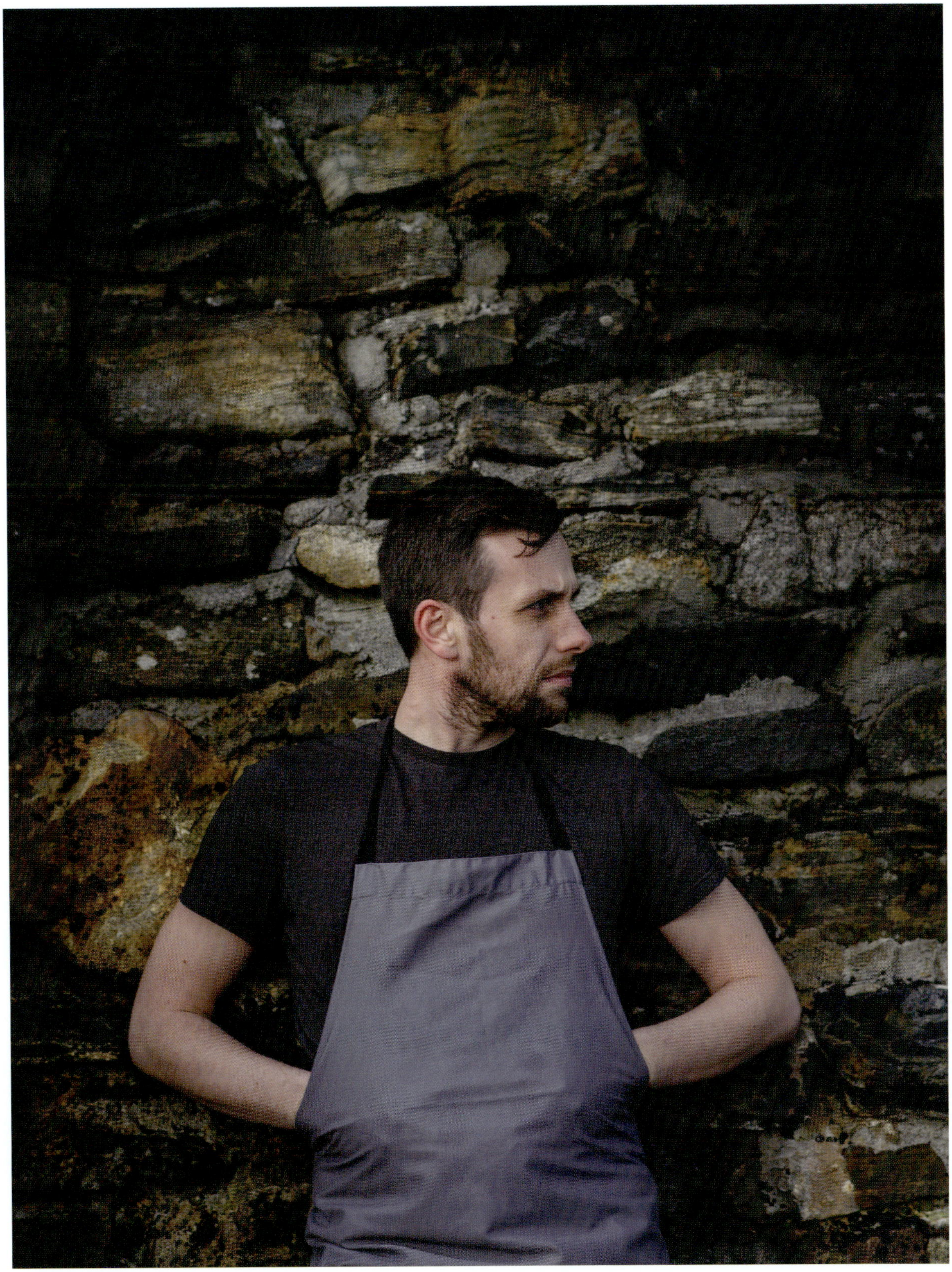

KELP CURED LING — WHEY — FERMENTED GOOSEBERRY — HAZELNUT

LANGA AIR A CIÙRADH LE CEILP — MEANG — GRÒSAID TÒIRNICHTE — CNÒ-CALLTAINN

HALIBUT — LEEKS — PRUNE — CHICKEN SAUCE

BRADAN-LEATHANN — CNEAMH-GÀRRAIDH — PRÙN — SABHS CIRCE

UNCLE JOHN'S SMOKED MACKEREL — SALT BAKED CROFT BEETROOT — SWEET PICKLE CUCUMBER — APACHE POTATOES — SEA BEETS — HORSERADISH YOGHURT

A classic but delicious Hebridean dish of smoked mackerel, beetroot and potatoes. My uncle John produces amazing smoked fish particularly his whole smoked mackerel. He doesn't sell it commercially so it is only available to family and friends, but believe me it is special. The contrast of the sweet pickled cucumber and the horseradish sheep's yoghurt makes this a perfectly balanced dish.

RIONNACH SMOCTE M' UNCAIL IAIN — BIOTAIS CROITE RÒSTA ANN AN SALAINN — CULARAN PICILTE MILIS — BUNTÀTA APACHE — BIOTAIS NA MARA — IOGURT RÀCADAIL

Biadh Innse-Gallach, clasaigeach ach air leth blasta, de rionnach, biotais agus buntàta. Bidh m' uncail Iain a' dèanamh iasg smocte a tha barraichte, gu h-àraid rionnach slàn smocte. Cha bhi e ga reic gu coimearsalta 's le sin chan fhaigh ach teaghlach agus caraidean grèim air. Feumaidh sibh m' fhacal a ghabhail a thaobh cho sònraichte 's a tha e. Còmhla ris airson eadar-dhealachadh blas tha cularan picilte milis a rinneadh aig an taigh agus iogurt chaorach le ràcadal.

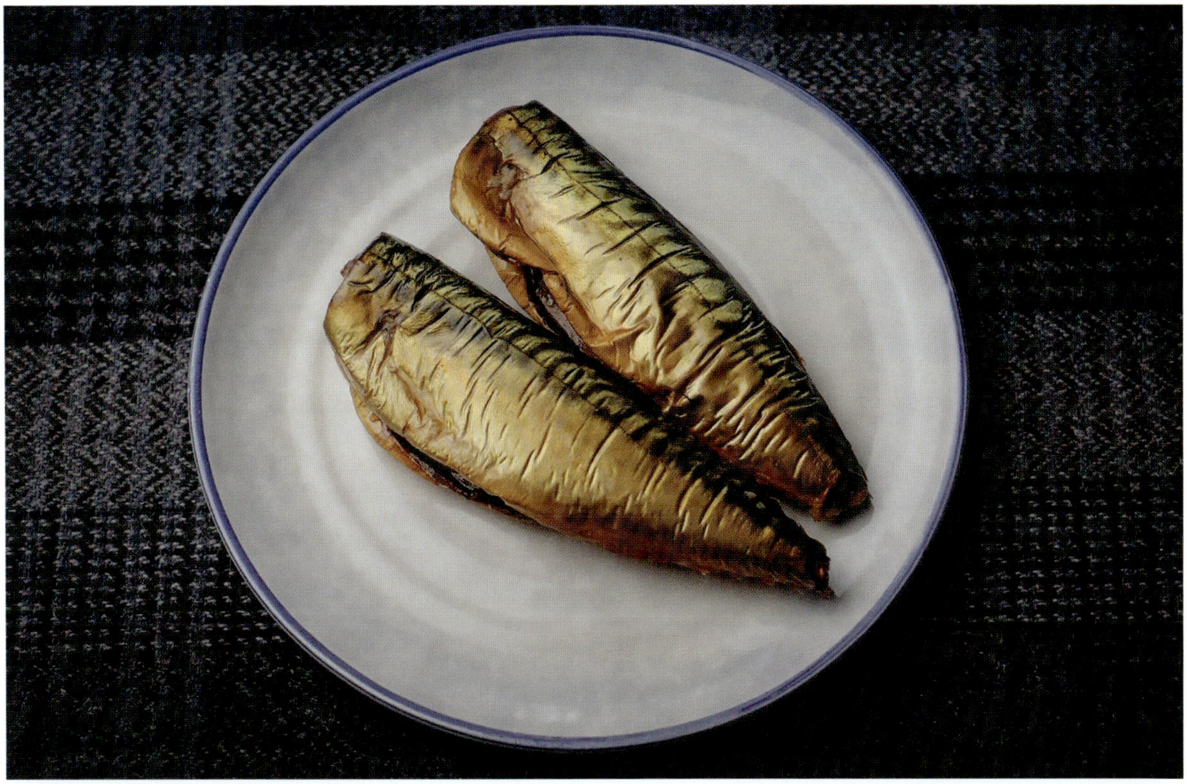

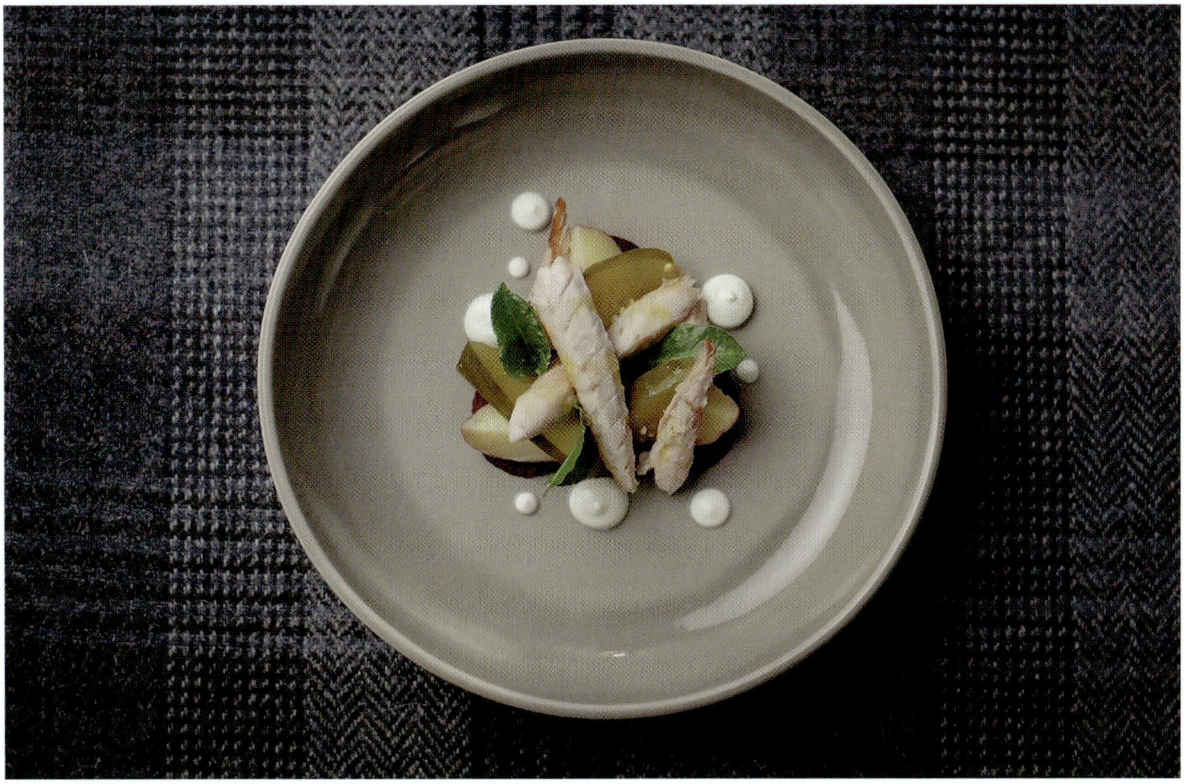

BRINED AND GRILLED MACKEREL —
FERMENTED GREEN STRAWBERRIES — SWEET AND SOUR GOOSEBERRIES —
CREAMED KHOLRABI AND BUTTERMILK — MINT OIL

Mackerel is one of the tastiest fish in the sea and very much underrated. Traditional recipes serve mackerel with acidic fruits or sauces such as gooseberries or rhubarb as I have done here. The mackerel has been salted flesh side down for an hour and pickled in a brine of water, sherry vinegar and rice wine vinegar for a further hour. The mackerel is gently torched and served with fermented green strawberries and gooseberries, creamed kholrabi and mint oil.

RIONNACH MEIREALTE AGUS GRÌOSAICHTE —
SÙIBH-LÀIR UAINE TÒIRNICHTE — GRÒSAIDEAN MILIS AGUS GEUR —
KHOLRABI AGUS BLÀTHACH UACHDARAICHTE — OLA MEANNT

Tha rionnach air iasg cho blasta 's a th' anns a' mhuir agus chan eil àite gu leòr air a thoirt dha. Tha reasabaidhean traidiseanta a' cur measan geura no sabhsan mar gròsaidean no bàrr ruadh ris mar a tha mise air a dhèanamh an seo. Tha an rionnach air a bhith air a shailleadh fad uair a thìde le taobh na feòla sìos agus air a bhith ann am meireal de dh'uisge, fìon geur searaidh agus fìon geur fìon ruis fad uair a thìde eile. Tha e air a losgadh gu socair agus air ithe le sùibh-làir uaine tòirnichte agus gròsaidean milis agus geur, kholrabi air uachdarachadh agus ola meannt.

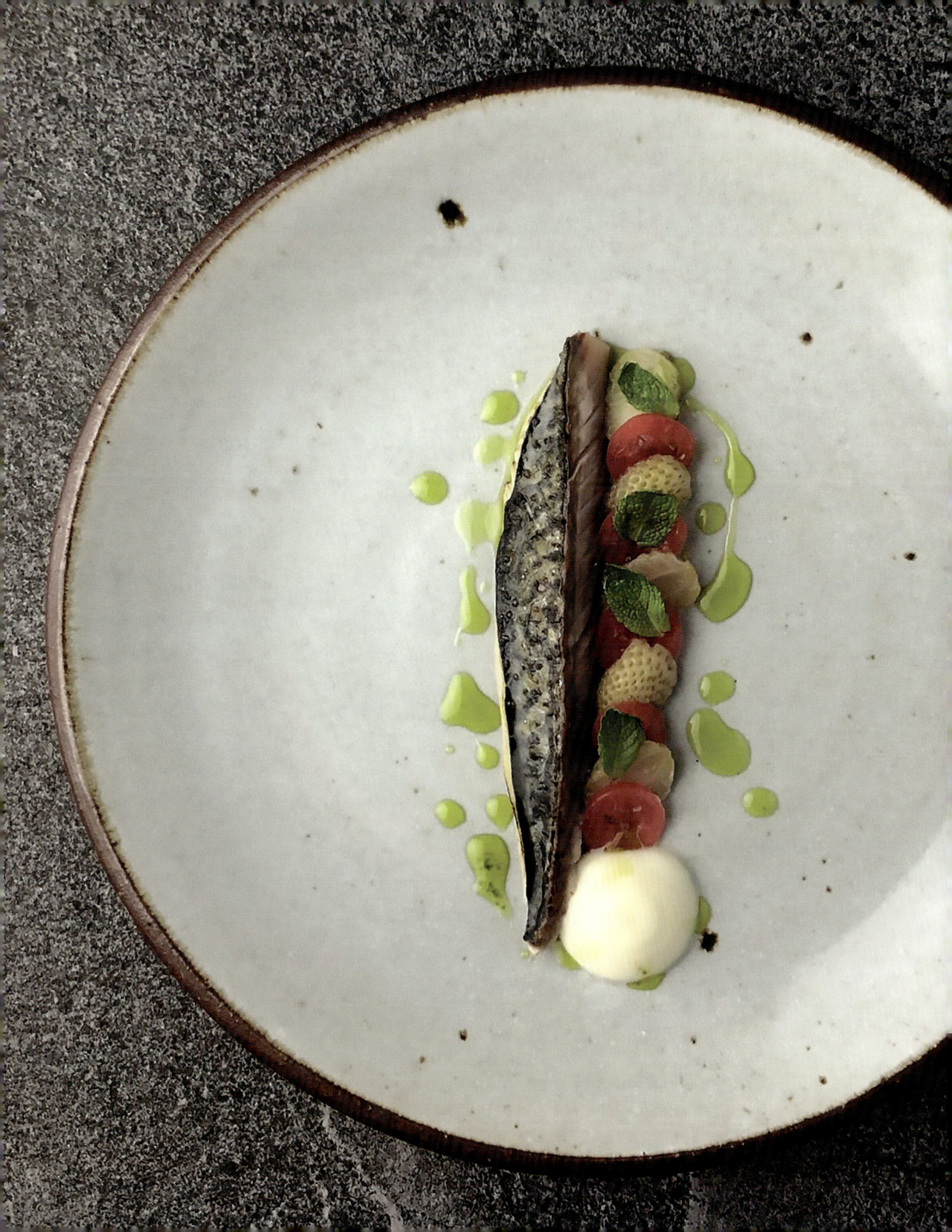

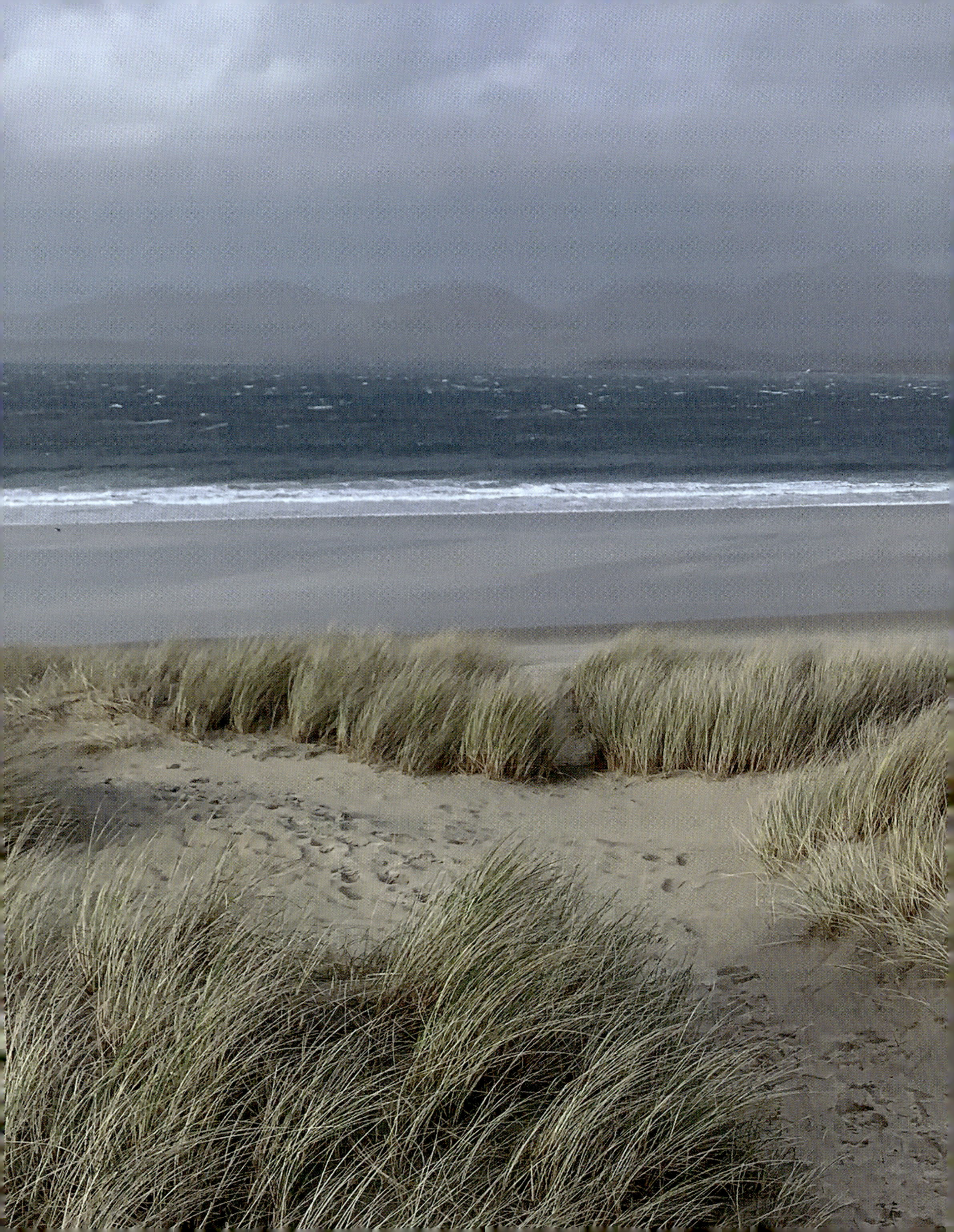

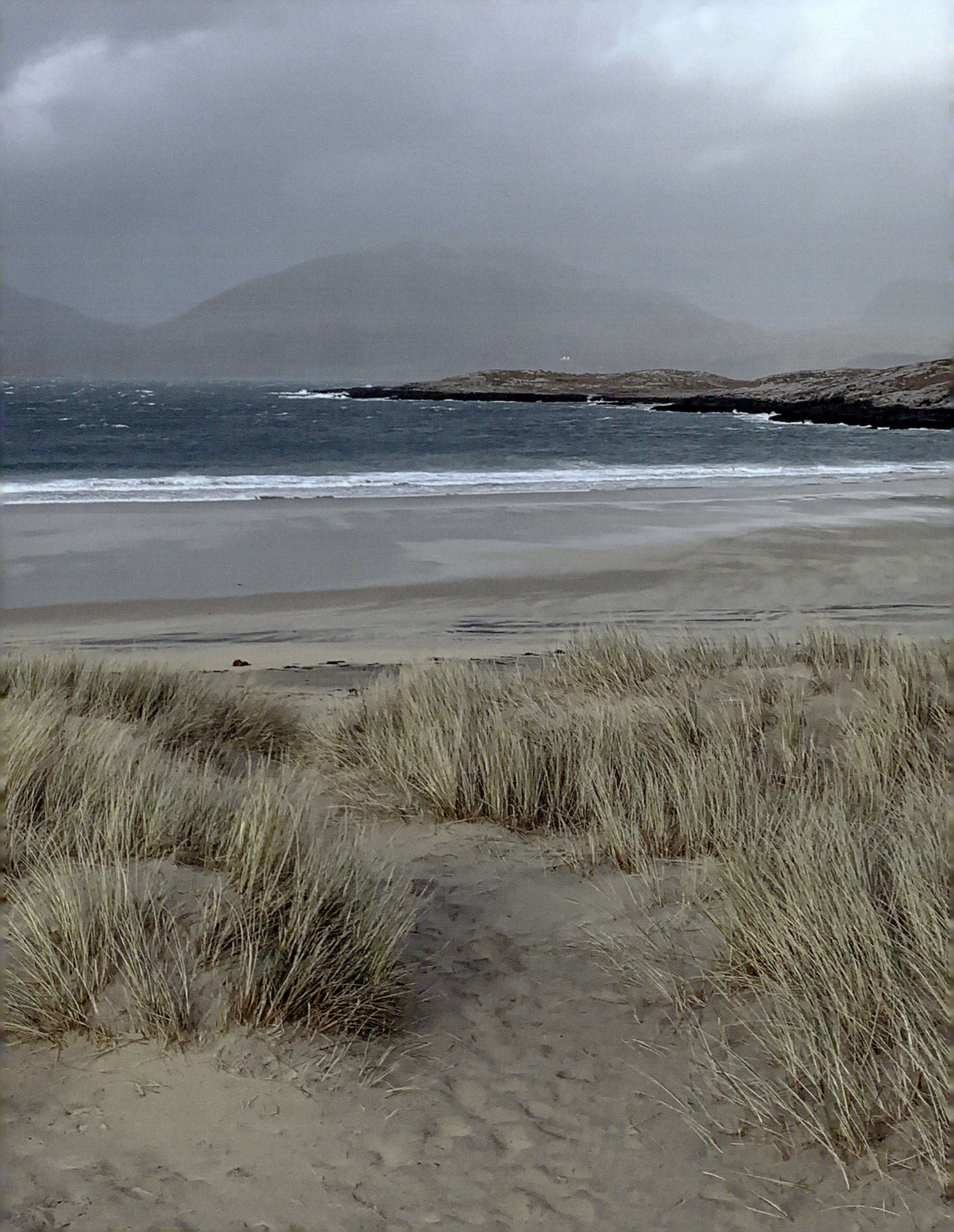

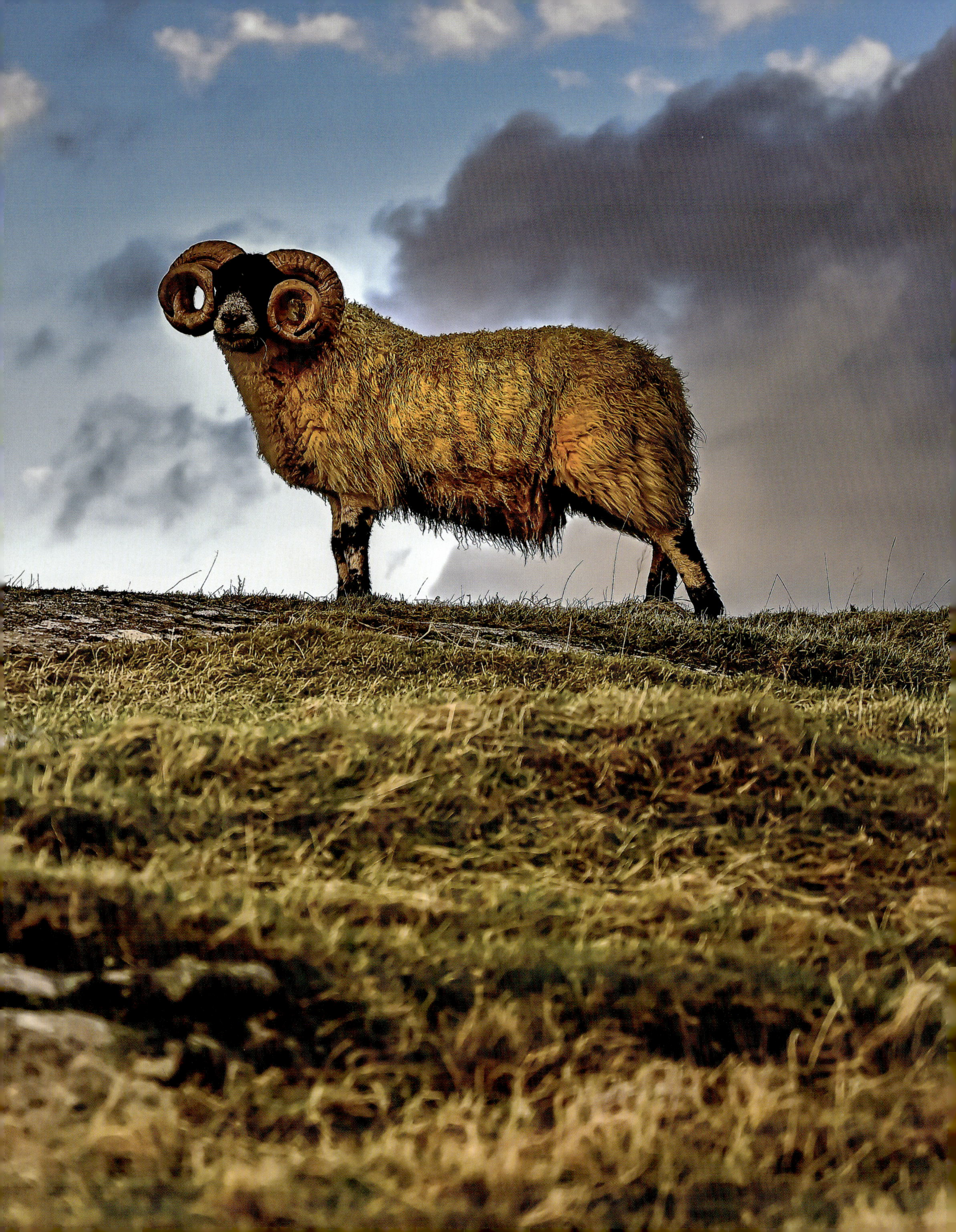

From the Croft
Bhon Lot

CHICKEN COOKED IN ITS OWN FAT — SMOKED LEEKS — GIROLLE MUSHROOMS — PRUNES COOKED IN ELDERBERRY JUICE

CEARC AIR A CÒCAIREACHD NA GEIR FHÈIN — CREAMH-GÀRRAIDH SMOCTE — BALGAIN-BUACHAIR GIROLLE — PRÙNAICHEAN AIR AM BRUICH ANN AN SÙGH CAORAN-DHROMAIN

Chicken
1 chicken breast
200g chicken fat

Remove the breast from the fridge half an hour before to bring up to room temperature. In a pan heat the chicken fat to 65°C, place the breast into the oil for 55 minutes.

Smoked Leeks
1 large leek
knob of butter

Split the leek in half and using the smoking tray, place the wood chips in the bottom of the tray and the leeks on the perforated tray on top.
Light the wood chips with a blow torch and place the lid on, leave for 10 minutes. Re-light the wood chips and leave for a further 5-10 minutes. Slice the leek and sweat in a pan with some Highland rapeseed oil and season with salt. Once the leeks are translucent add a knob of butter.

Girolle Mushrooms
300g girolle mushrooms
Cullisse Highland rapeseed oil
double cream
butter

Once the mushrooms have been cleaned and prepared, cut in half. In a pan heat up the oil, add the mushrooms and roast until you have some caramelisation. Finish with a knob of butter and some double cream.
Blend until smooth, adding more cream if needed.
Pass through a sieve.

Prunes
75g dried prunes
300ml elderberry juice

Warm the elderberry juice in a pan, adding the prunes until nice and soft. Blend the prunes with enough of the liquid to give a silky smooth purée.

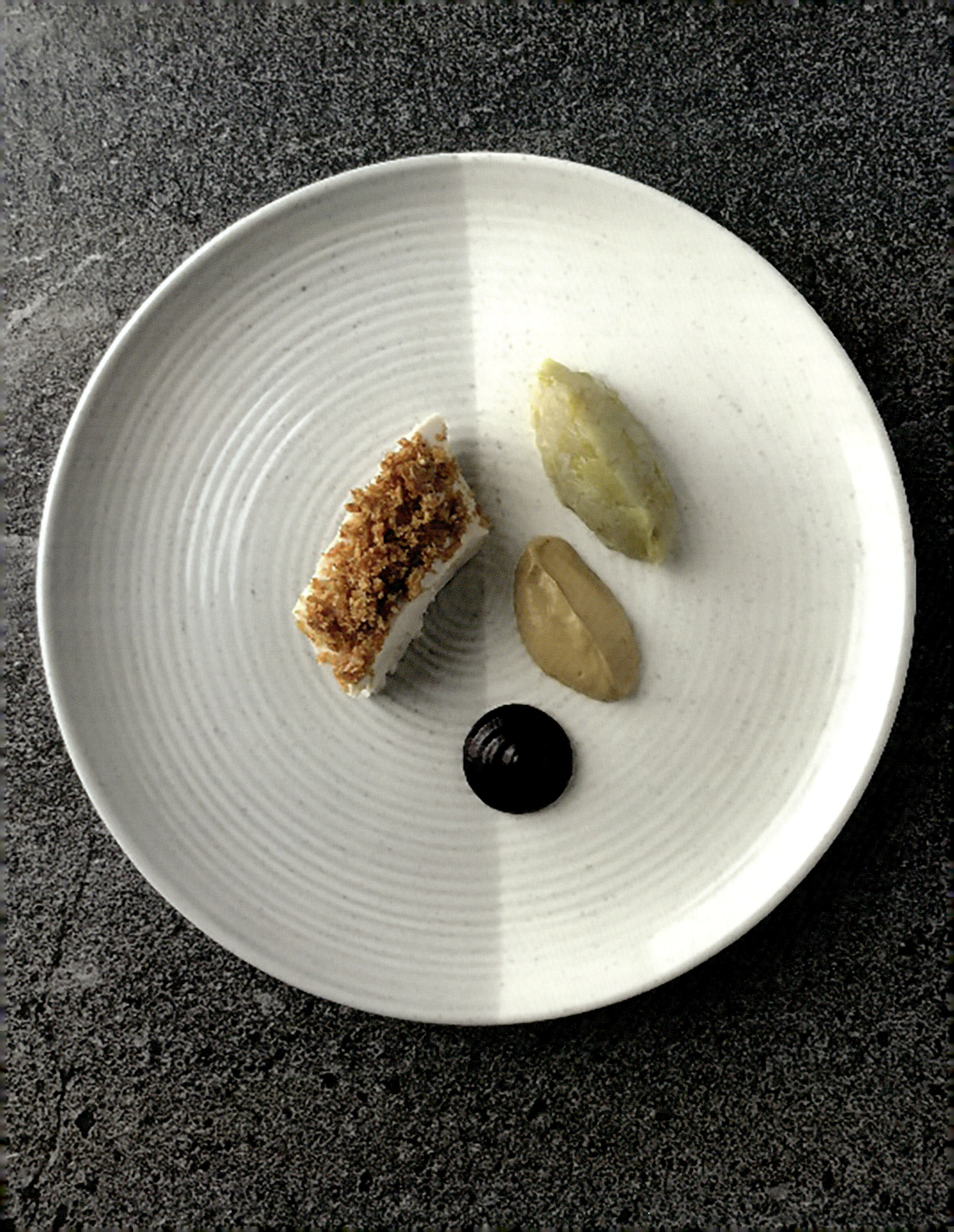

**HEBRIDEAN MUTTON CHOP — BEETROOT AND BARLEY PORRIDGE —
GOLDEN BEETROOT COOKED IN MUTTON FAT —
FERMENTED WHITE BEETROOT PURÉE — BUTTERED SEA BEETS —
FRESH SHEEP'S CHEESE — DRIED ROSEHIP**

**SGINEACH MUILTFHEÒIL INNSE-GALLACH — BROCHAN EÒRNA AGUS BIOTAIS —
BIOTAIS ÒR-BHUIDHE AIR AM BRUICH ANN AN GEIR MUILTFHEÒIL —
PURÉE DE BHIOTAIS GEAL TÒIRNICHTE — BIOTAIS-MARA LE ÌM —
CÀIS CAORACH ÙR — MUCAGAN AIR AN TIORMACHADH**

Hebridean Mutton Chop
1 large mutton chop

Heat oven to 180°C. Brush the mutton chop with oil and season. Heat a non-stick oven proof pan over a medium heat. Render down the fat until crisp and seal the meat on all sides, then place in oven for 3-5 minutes. The thickest part of the chop should be between 45-50°C.

Beetroot and Barley Porridge
1 large beetroot
250g barley
1 onion finely diced
1.25l lamb stock
50g lamb fat
15ml barley vinegar

Pre-heat oven to 200°C. Place beetroot on a tray lined with foil, season and add a small amount of water. Cover with more foil making sure to seal round the edges and cook for 1-1½ hours until tender. Once the beetroot has cooled enough for you to handle, rub off the skin. Chop and blend until smooth. Season with Skye sea salt. Cook the barley while the beetroot is in the oven. Gently sweat the onion in half of the lamb fat for eight minutes, add the barley and stir for one minute, deglaze with the barley vinegar, add stock, season and gently simmer for 40-50 minutes until tender. Add the beetroot purée and the remaining lamb fat. Check the seasoning.

Golden Beetroot
small cooked golden beetroot
lamb fat

Heat a pan with the lamb fat, add the beetroot and caramelise. Season with Skye sea salt.

Fermented White Beetroot Purée
1kg small white beetroot
20g Skye sea salt
2l water

Trim, wash and peel the beetroot and cut into large pieces. Place in a sterilised Kilner jar along with water and salt. Leave for a week in a dark place, checking every couple of days. Remove from the brine and blend until you have a smooth consistency.
Season with Skye sea salt.

Buttered Sea Beets
handful of sea beet leaves
knob of butter

In a non-stick frying pan, wilt the sea beets in butter and a splash of water. Season with Skye sea salt.

Serve with fresh sheep's cheese and a sprinkling of dried rosehip.

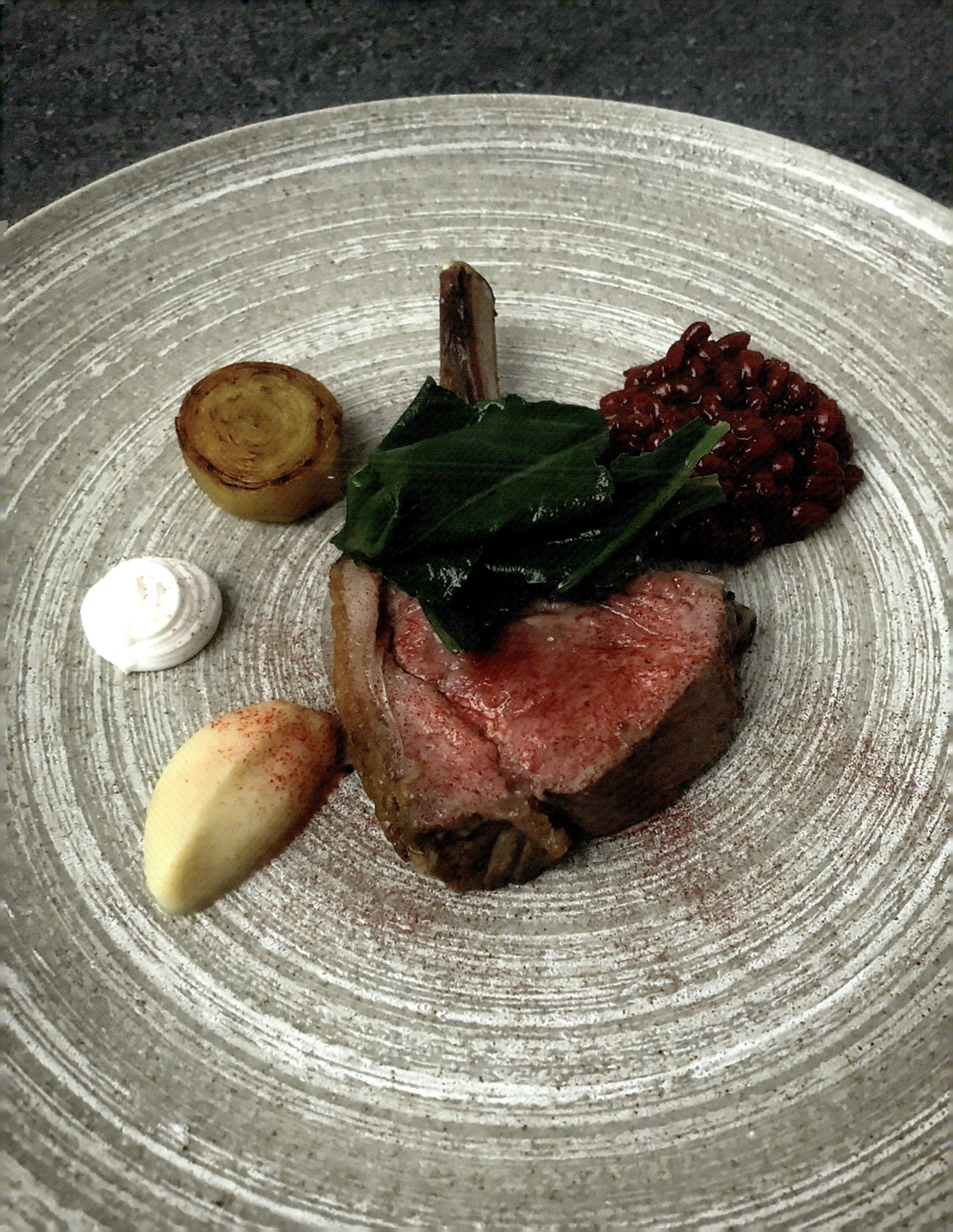

BRAISED HOGGET NECK — LIMPETS —
CARAMELISED SUMMER CABBAGE — LAMB AND DULSE BROTH

AMHAICH UAIN REITHE AIR A BHREUSADH — BÀIRNICH —
CÀL SAMHRAIDH CARRA-MHEILLTE — BROT UAIN AGUS DUILEASG

STEAMED HEBRIDEAN MUTTON — BARLEY AND TURNIP PUDDING —
COLONSAY BEER AND SEAWEED GRAVY

MUILTFHEÒIL EILEANACH CEÒ-THEASAICHTE — MARAG EÒRNA AGUS SNÈAP —
GRÈIBHIDH LE LEANN COLBHASACH AGUS FEAMAINN

LOIN OF BLACK FACE LAMB — MINT, BARLEY AND LAMB FAT PORRIDGE — BRAISED CROFT ONIONS — MINT OIL

The Scottish blackface sheep are widely found across the Hebrides and the outstanding qualities of the breed are survivability, adaptability and versatility, with the ability to fit into any farming situation. They are one of the hardiest sheep breeds in the country and are the backbone of the Scottish sheep industry.

BLIAN UAN DUBH-CHEANNACH — LIT LE MEANNT, EÒRNA AGUS GEIR UAIN — UINNEANAN CROITE AIR AM BREUSADH — OLA MEANNT

Tha dubh-cheannaich bheag Alba rim faighinn air feadh Innse-Gall. Am measg nam feartan barraichte aca tha maireannachd agus fàsaidh iad suas ri iomadh seòrsa suidheachadh air iomadh seòrsa tuathanas. Tha iad am measg nan caorach as tapaidh san dùthaich agus 's iad cnàimh-droma gnìomhachas chaorach na h-Alba.

Lamb Loin
400g trimmed lamb loin
40g rendered lamb fat

Place the prepared loins in a sous-vide bag along with the lamb fat. Place in a water bath at 60.5°C for 35 minutes, remove from the bag, season and just before serving finish over hot coals to achieve a nice colouration and smoky flavour.

Barley and Mint Porridge
250g pearl barley
1 onion finely diced
50g lamb fat
1.25l lamb stock
100g blanched spinach
100g blanched mint
15ml barley vinegar
50g sheep's cheese

Gently sweat the onion in 25g of the lamb fat for eight minutes, add the barley and stir for one minute, deglaze with the barley vinegar, add the stock, season and gently simmer for 40-50 minutes until tender.
Purée the blanched spinach and mint for six minutes and add to the porridge along with the remaining lamb fat and sheep's cheese. Check seasoning and season with Skye sea salt and freshly ground white pepper to your taste.

Braised Onions
12 baby onions
200g water
100g barley vinegar
100g sugar
5 white peppercorns
10 mustard seeds
sprig of mint

At HAAR we would cook the onions sous-vide in roasted onion stock at 85°C for 35 minutes before cutting in half and caramelising on a plancha or frying pan. However, you can just wrap the onions in a foil parcel with a little onion stock and roast at 120°C in the oven for around an hour until the onions are tender.
Peel the onions, cut in half and caramelise the cut side until they are deep golden. Heat up the ingredients for the pickle then drop the caramelised onions into the pickle for 12-15 minutes.
Remove from the pickle and separate the onion leaves and keep them warm until serving.

Mint Oil
50g blanched baby spinach
50g blanched mint
100ml Highland rapeseed oil
4g salt

For the mint oil blend all the ingredients together for 6-7 minutes then strain through some muslin and store in a small plastic bottle.

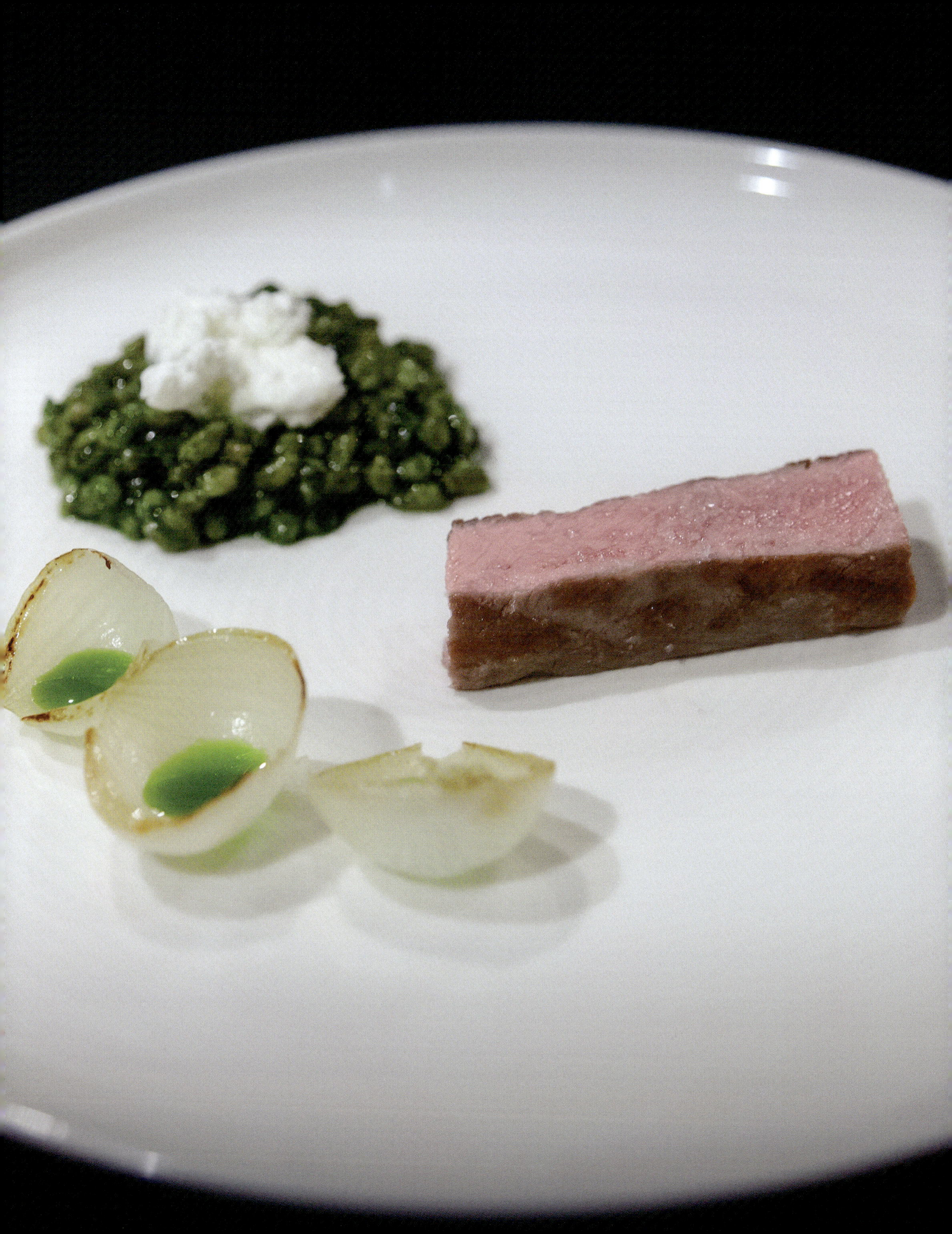

TURNIP COOKED IN RENDERED MUTTON FAT — SHEEP'S HEAD AND SEAWEED BROTH — FRESH SHEEP'S CHEESE

Sheep's heads were always used on the Hebrides to make a hearty soup. Traditionally they would be soaked for a day, split and then cooked with barley and vegetables from the croft, served with floury potatoes. Here I have made a broth from the head and some kelp seaweed. The sticky meat is then picked off and glazed in some of the reduced cooking liquor and placed in the bottom of the bowl. On top of that are balls of turnip that have been cooked in rendered mutton fat, fresh sheep's cheese and some dried seaweed. The broth is then poured into the bowl to finish the dish off.

SNÈAP ANN AN GEIR GHLAN CHAORACH — BROT CEANN CAORACH IS FEAMAINN — CÀIS CAORACH ÙR

Bha cinn chaorach air an cleachdadh sna h-Eileanan Siar airson brot susbainteach a dhèanamh. Gu h-àbhaisteach bhiodh an ceann am bogadh ann an uisge fad latha, air a sgoltadh agus an uair sin air a bhruich le eòrna agus lusan bhon lot agus air ithe le buntàta tioram. An seo tha mi air brot a dhèanamh leis a' cheann agus beagan ceilp. Tha an fheòil steigeach air a toirt dheth agus air a glainneachadh ann am beagan den t-sùgh lùghdaichte agus air a cur ann am bonn a' bhobhla. Air a mhullach tha bàlaichean den t-snèap a chaidh a bhruich ann an geir ghlan chaorach, càis caorach ùr, agus feamainn thioram. Tha am brot an uair sin air a dhòrtadh dhan bhobhla.

POTATO COOKED AND SMOKED ON THE ASHES OF A PEAT FIRE — POTATO SKIN GRAVY — POTATO CRISP — SMOKED HERRING ROE

BUNTÀTA AIR A BHRUICH AGUS AIR A SMOCADH ANN AN LUATH TEINE MÒNACH — GRÈIBHIDH RÙSG BUNTÀTA — BUNTÀTA BRISG — IUCHAIR SGADAIN SMOCTE

This really was a HAAR signature dish. The baby potatoes are smoked over a peat fire, removed from their skins and made into a buttery, silky smooth mash. Half the skins are used to make a potato and chicken gravy and the other half are dehydrated into crisps. The dish is then filled with peat smoke using a smoking gun.

B' e seo grèim bìdh cho suaicheanta 's a bh' aig HAAR. Bha am buntàta beag ùr air an smocadh thairis air teine mònach agus an rùsg air a thoirt dhiubh. Bha iad air am pronnadh le ìm gu robh iad air leth mìn. Bha leth nan rùsgan air an cleachdadh airson grèibhidh circe agus buntàta a dhèanamh agus bha an leth eile air an tiormachadh gus an robh iad brisg. Bha an truinnsear an uair sin air a lìonadh le ceò na mònach, a' cleachdadh gunna smocaidh.

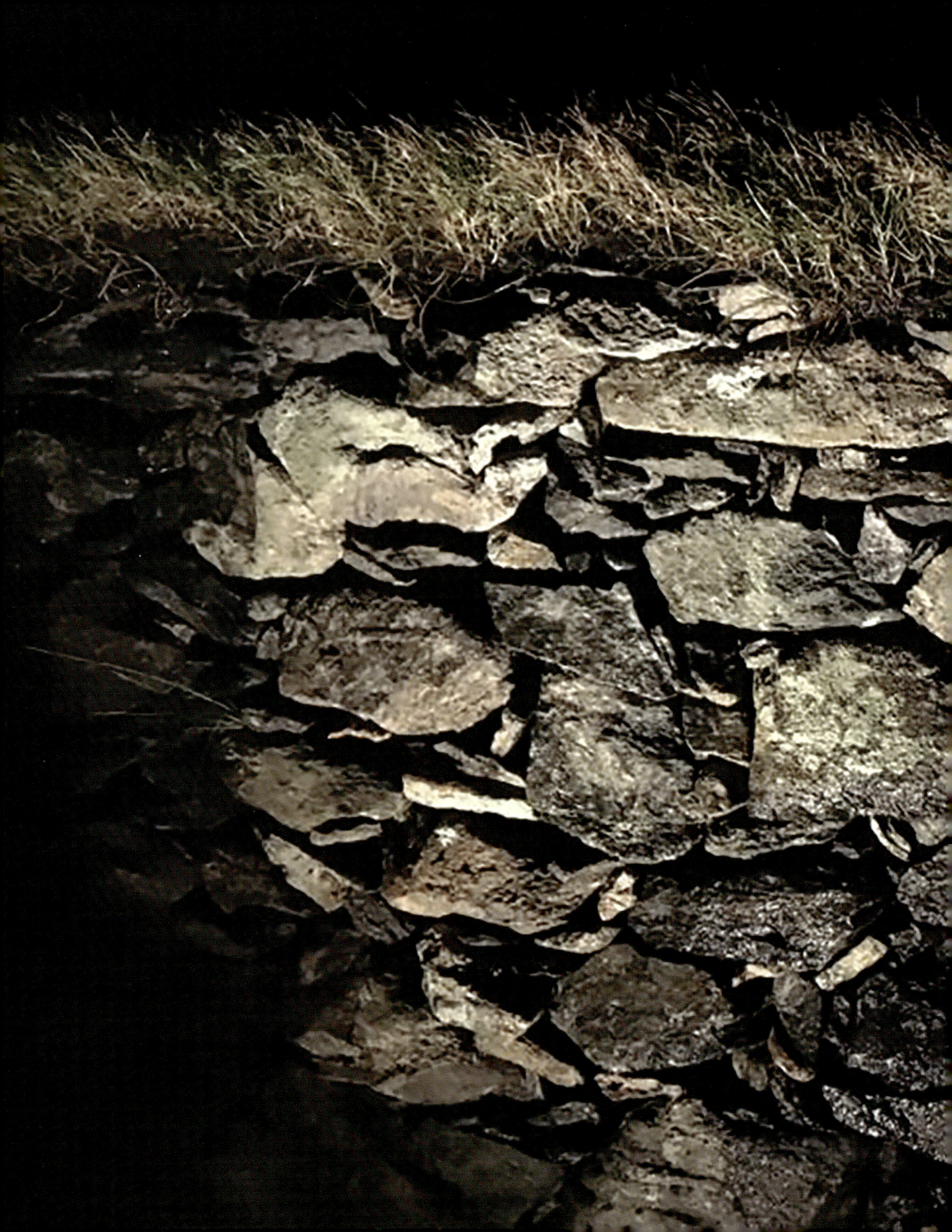

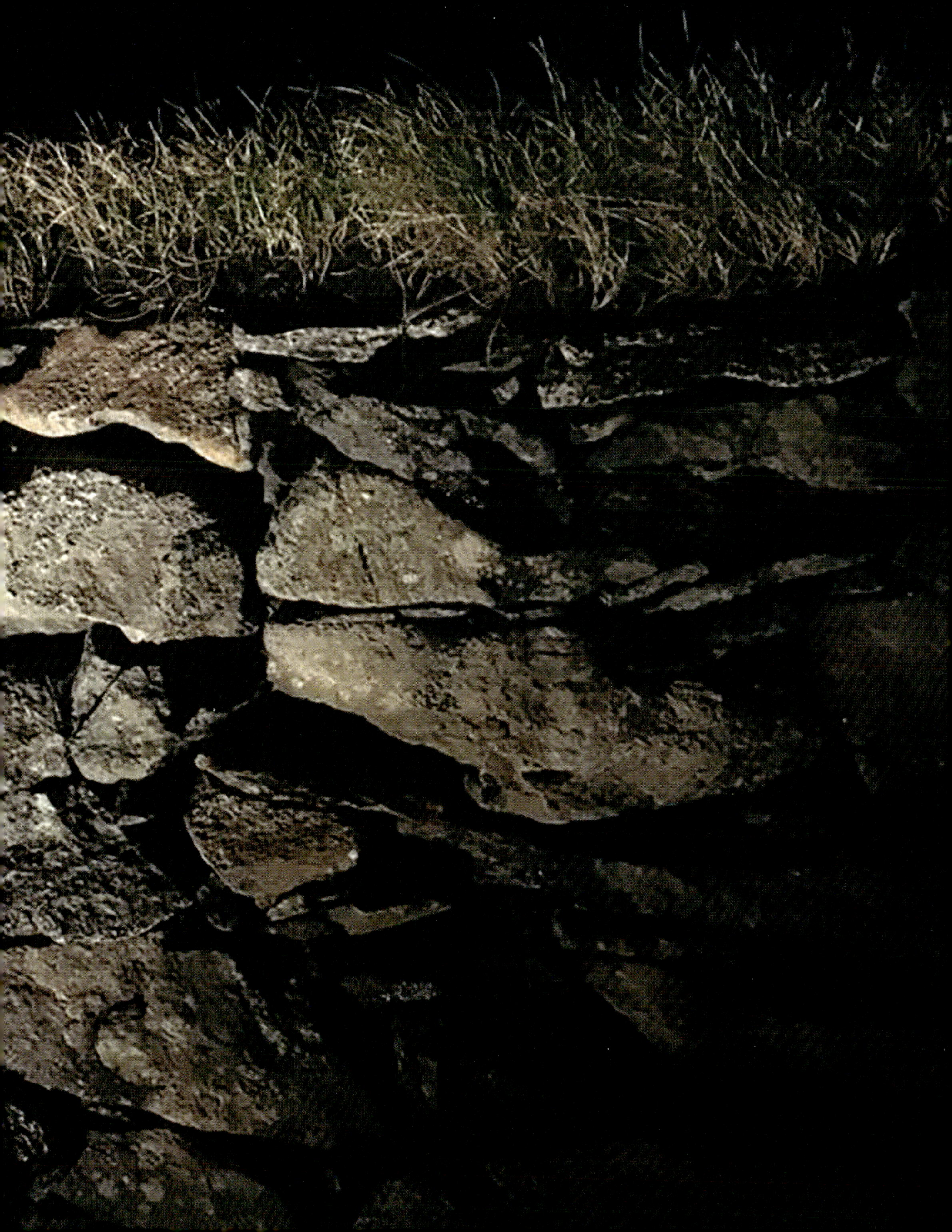

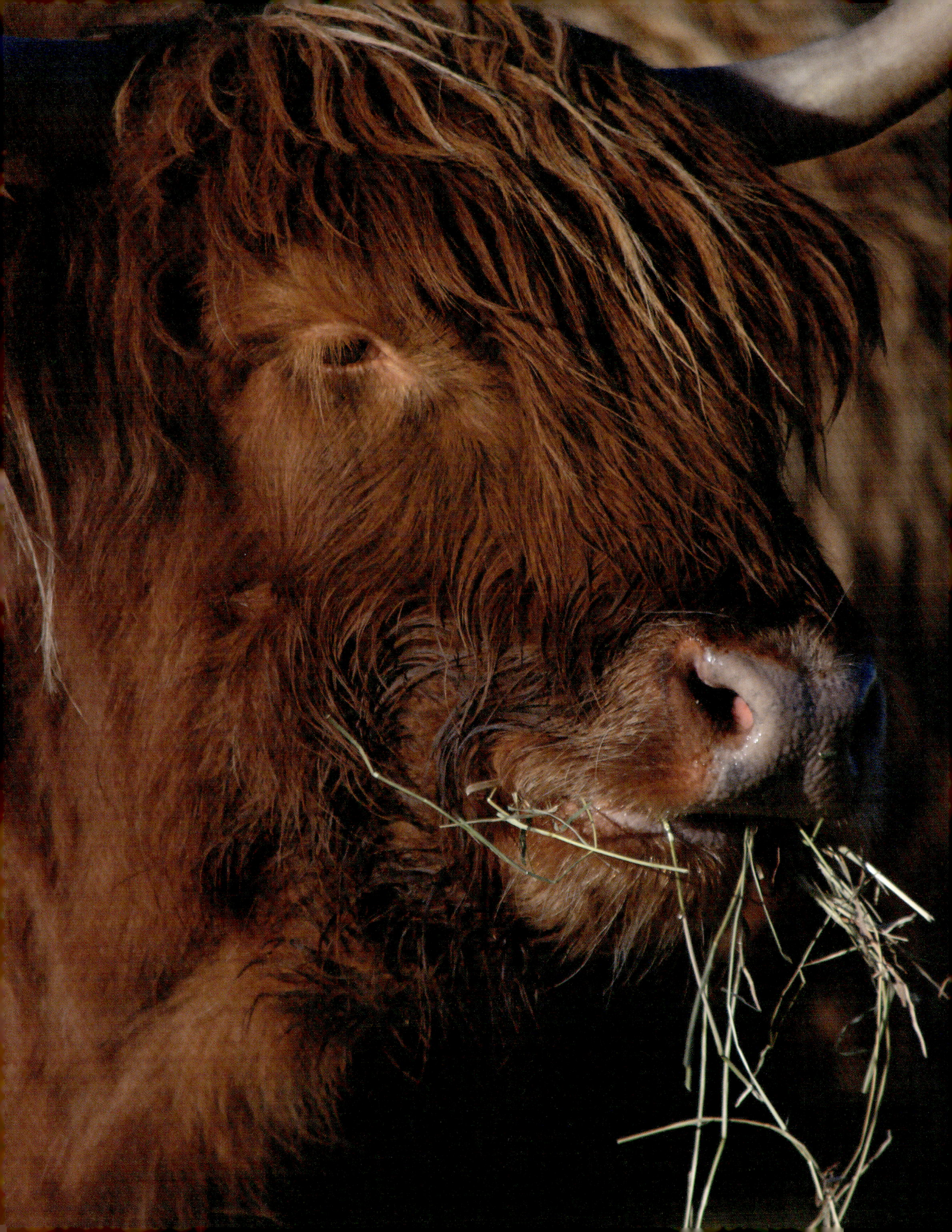

Highlander Beef
Mairtfheòil Crodh Gàidhealach

AGED BRUE HIGHLANDER BEEF — FERMENTED PUFFED BARLEY — CARAMELISED CROFT ONIONS — MALT GLAZED CARROT — A SAUCE MADE FROM BEEF BONES, MALT EXTRACT AND BARLEY VINEGAR

Highland beef really is the best quality meat. It has less fat and is lower in cholesterol than other varieties. The flavour from the beef really is wonderful. The beef in this dish has been slowly braised and served with a caramelised onion purée, baby carrot glazed in malted barley extract and butter, finished with moorberry sauce using the beef bones, garnished with puffed barley and barley vinegar.

MAIRTFHEÒIL AOISEIL CRODH GÀIDHEALACH BHRÙ — EÒRNA TÒCTE TÒIRNICHTE — UINNEANAN NA LOT CARRA-MHEILLTE — CURRAN GLAINICHTE LE BRAICHE — SABHS AIR A DHÈANAMH LE CNÀIMHEAN MAIRT, BRÌGH BRAICHE AGUS FÌON GEUR EÒRNA

Chan eil feòil ann nas fheàrr na mairtfheòil crodh Gàidhealach. Chan eil uiread de gheir ann agus tha e nas ìsle a thaobh coileastarail na seòrsaichean eile. Tha an fheòil anabarrach blasta. An seo tha an fheòil air a bhith air a breusadh gu socair agus tha i air a h-ithe le purée uinneanan carra-mheillte, currain bheag ùr air an glainneachadh le ìm agus brìgh braiche, crìochnaichte le sabhs braoileagan air a dhèanamh a' cleachdadh cnàimhean mairt, sgeadaichte le eòrna tòcte agus fìon geur eòrna.

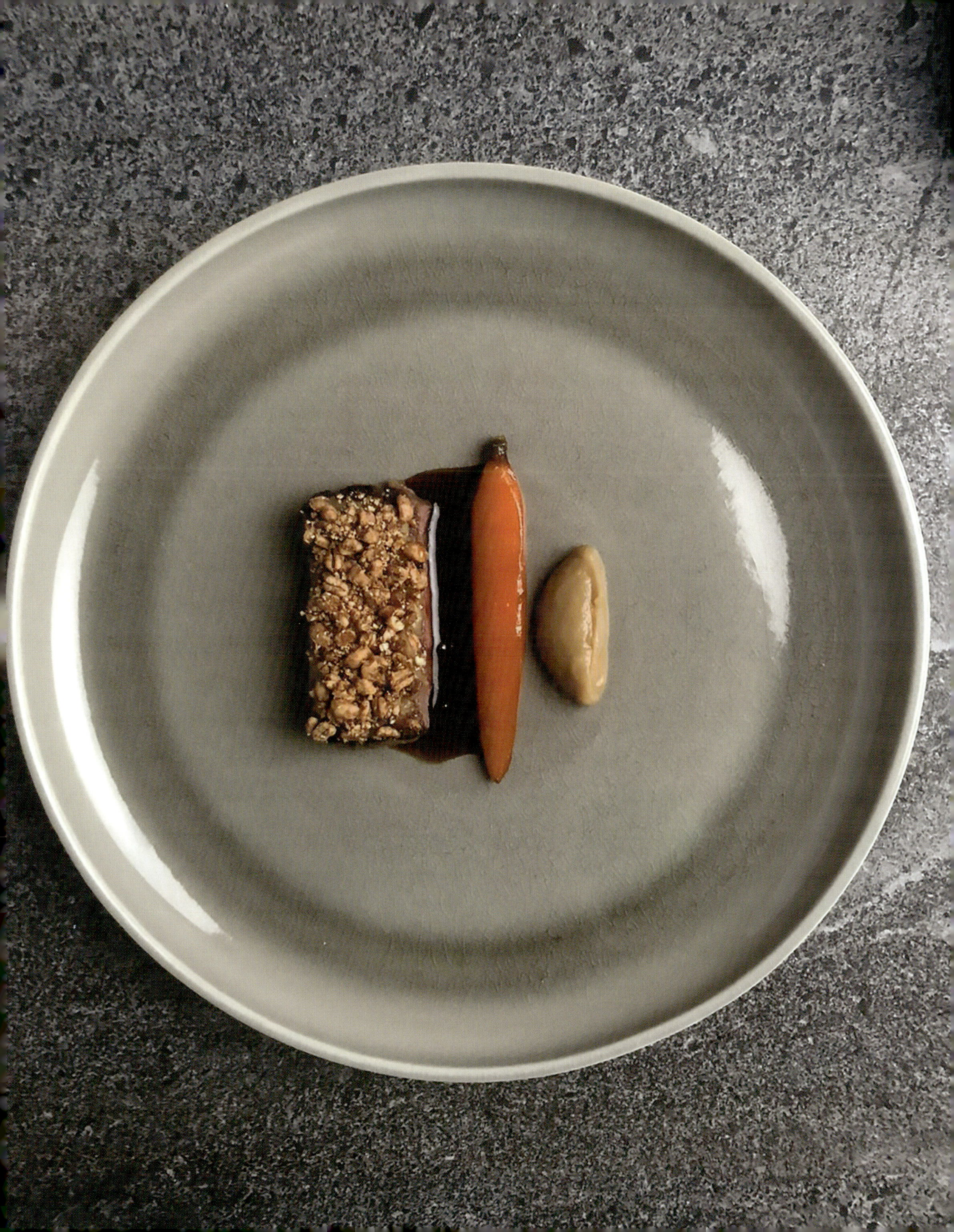

TREACLE GLAZED BRUE HIGHLAND BEEF BRISKET — ROASTED BABY GEM — SOUSED RADISHES AND ELDERBERRY CAPERS — OYSTER SAUCE

BROILLEACH MAIRTFHEÒIL CRODH GÀIDHEALACH BHRÙ GLAINNICHTE LE TRÈICIL — BABY GEM RÒSTA — MEACAN-RUADH PICILTE AGUS CAPAIREAN CAORAN-DHROMAIN — SABHS EISIREAN

Treacle Glazed Brue Highland Brisket
1kg Brue Highland brisket
2 onions cut in half
2 carrots cut in half
thyme
200ml water
treacle

Preheat the oven to 120°C. Heat oil in a non-stick frying pan over a medium heat. Seal the brisket on each side until brown. In a roasting tray, place the onions, carrots, thyme and water and place the brisket on top. Cover with foil. Cook for about 6-8 hours, turning the meat after three hours, cooking it until really tender. Once the brisket has rested, slice and glaze with treacle, place on a baking tray and flash under a hot grill until glazed. Brush again with a mix of treacle and juices from the roasting dish. Garnish with elderberry capers and micro leaves.

Roasted Baby Gem
1 baby gem cut in quarters
1 tbsp Cullisse Highland rapeseed oil
Skye sea salt

Heat oil in a non-stick frying pan, add the baby gem and cook until caramelised. Season with Skye sea salt.

Soused Radishes
sliced radishes
100g sugar
100ml white wine vinegar
100ml water
1 tsp salt

In a pan gently heat up water and vinegar, adding salt and sugar until dissolved. Once cooled, transfer to a container and add the sliced radishes. Leave in pickling liquor overnight.

Oyster Sauce
50g fresh oysters plus juice
150ml Cullisse Highland rapeseed oil
juice of half a lemon

Blend the oysters with the lemon juice, adding the oil in a steady flow to create an emulsion. Use the oyster juice to create the right consistency. Check seasoning and place in a squeezy bottle.

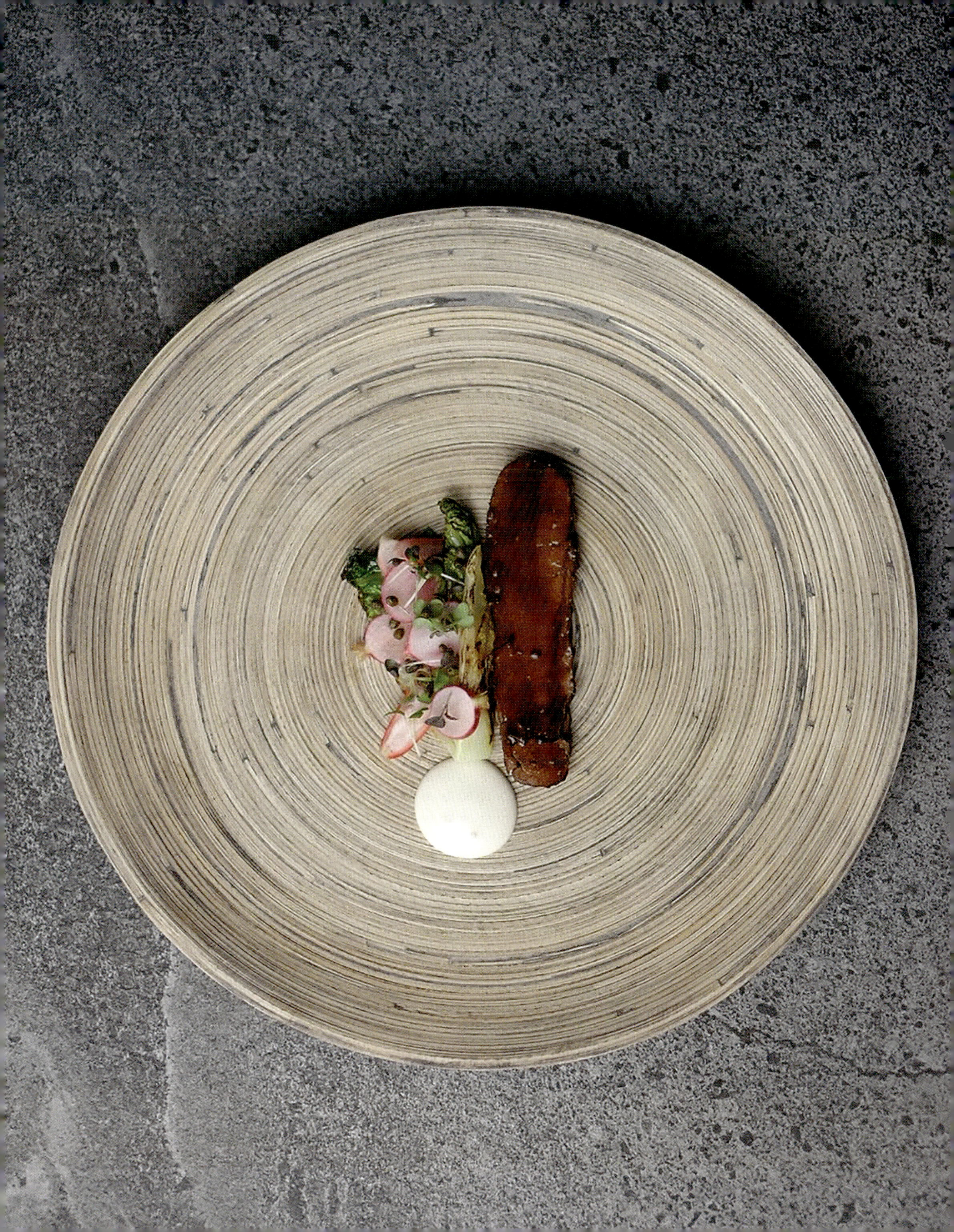

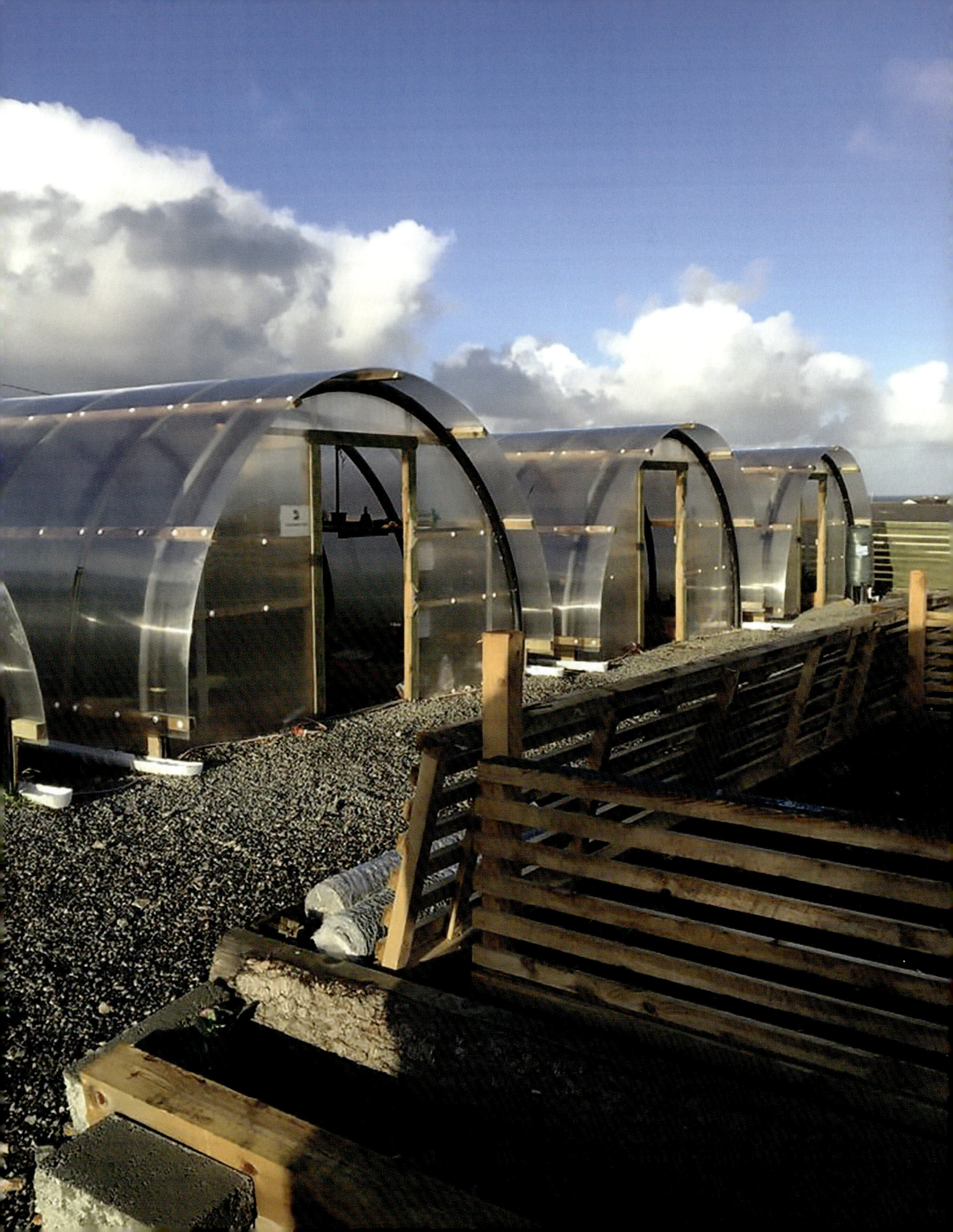

Polycrubs
Tunailean-fàis

234

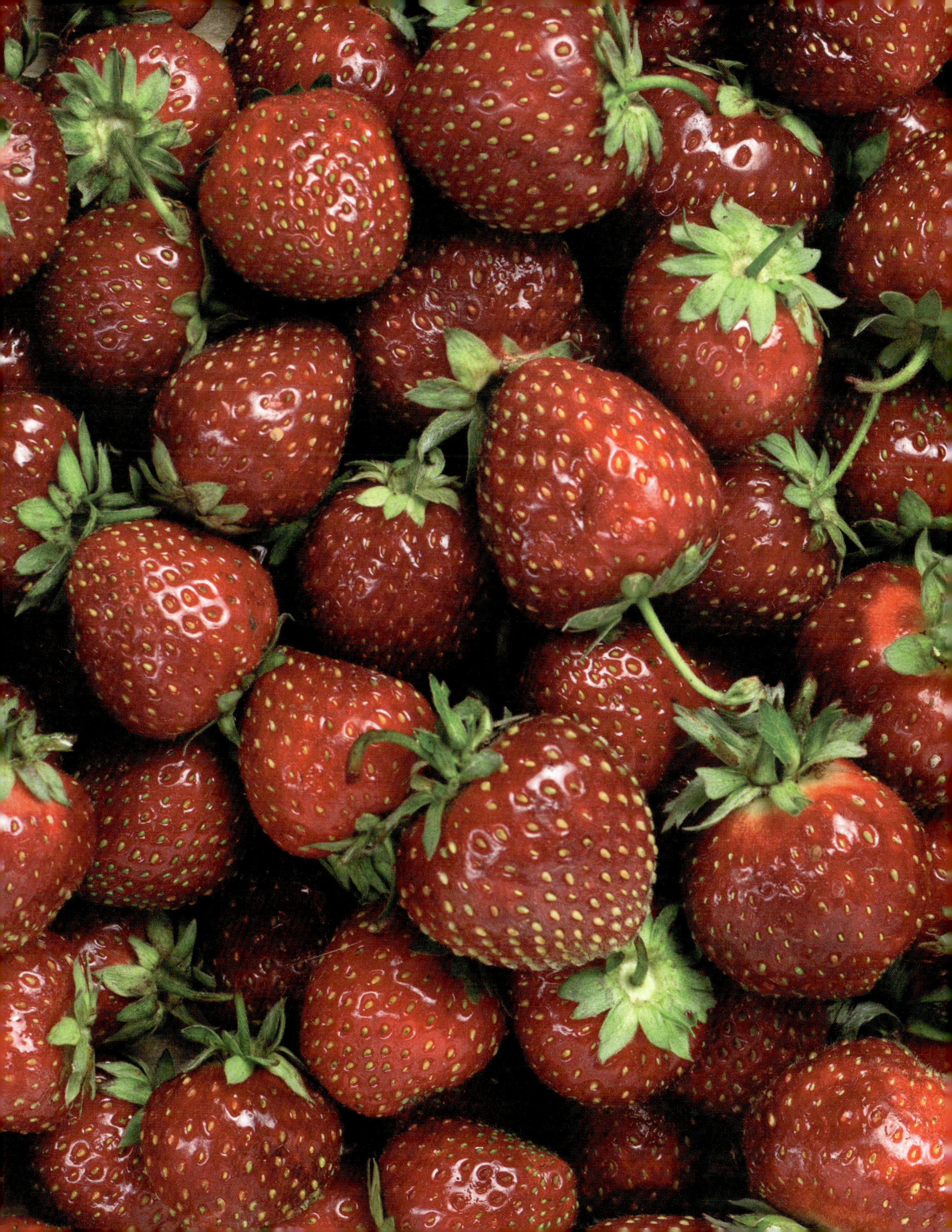

CELERIAC COOKED IN ITS SKIN ON A PEAT FIRE — HAZELNUTS — APPLE — BUTTERMILK AND SORREL SAUCE

Place a small celeriac in the embers of the peat fire, checking every 10 minutes and turning it until the skin is nicely charred all over. If it needs longer finish the cooking in the oven until a knife pierces it easily. Slice off a piece and season.

Blend 200ml buttermilk with 50g chopped sorrel. Gently warm the sauce in a pan. Check seasoning. Pour some of the sauce into a small bowl, place the slice of celeriac on top, adding diced apple, toasted hazelnuts and finishing with a squeeze of lemon juice, a drizzle of rapeseed oil and micro herbs.

SEILEARAG AIR A RÒSTADH NA RÙSG AIR TEINE MÒNACH — CNOTHAN-CALLTAINN — UBHAL — SABHS LE BLÀTHACH AGUS SEALBHAG

Cuir seilearag beag ann an èibhlean teine mònach, a' cumail sùil air gach deich mionaidean agus ga thionndadh gus a bheil an rùsg air a dheagh losgadh. Ma dh'fheumas e nas fhaide cuir crìoch air a' chòcaireachd san àmhainn gus an tèid sgian troimhe gu furasta. Geàrr slis dheth agus cuir blas ris le salainn agus piobar.

Coimeasgaich 200ml blàthach le 50g duilleagan sealbhaig air an geàrradh mìn. Blàthaich an sabhs gu socair ann am poit agus cuir blas ris ma tha e feumach air. Dòirt beagan sabhs ann am bobhla beag. Cuir an t-slis seilearag air uachdar. An uair sin sgaoil beagan ubhal air a ghearradh mìn agus cnothan-calltainn air an ròstadh air uachdar agus crìochnaich e le drùdhag bheag sùgh liomaid, beagan ola lus-ola agus craiteachan meanbh luibhean.

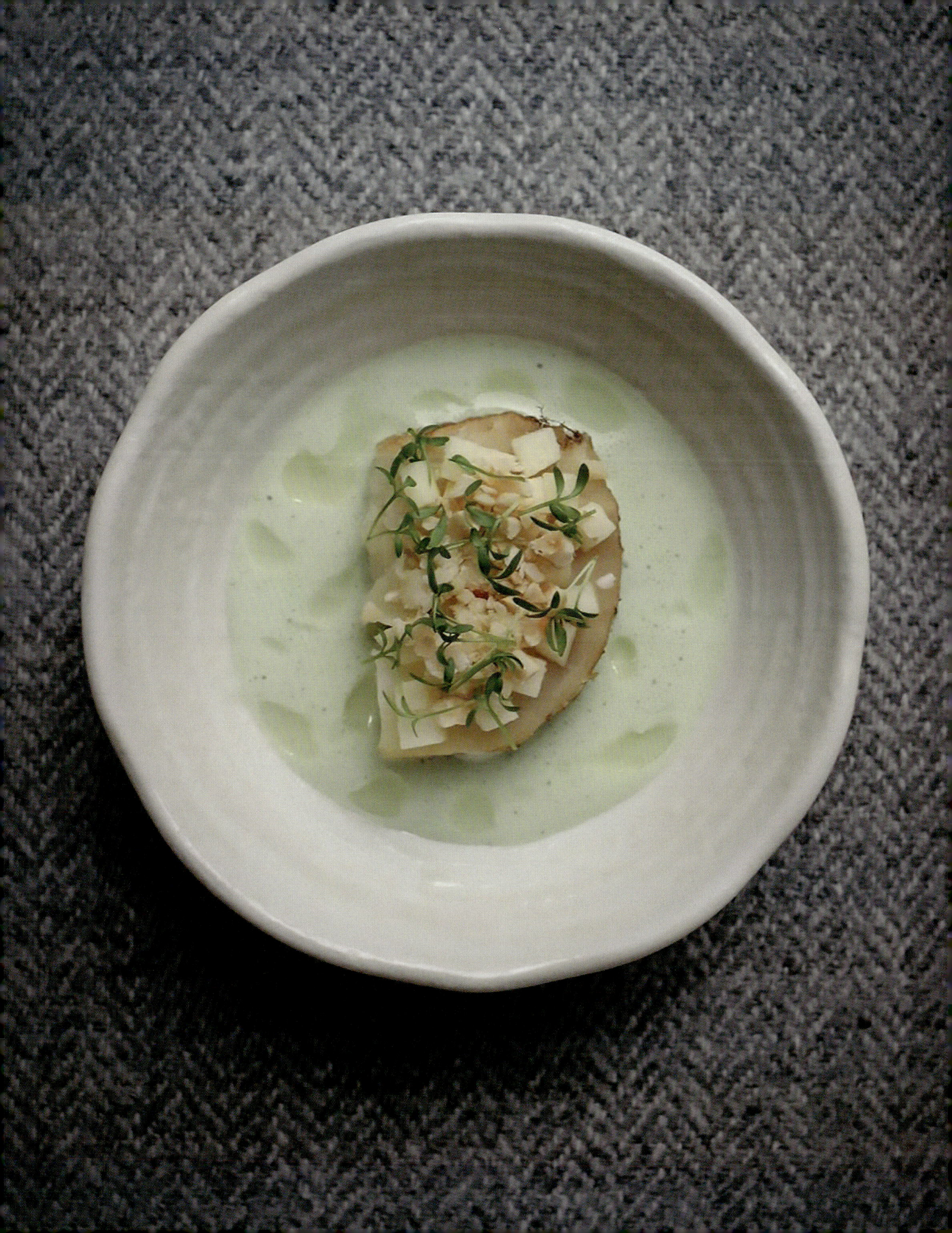

PEAT SMOKED GOLDEN AND CANDY CROFT BEETROOT — EGG YOLK GENTLY COOKED IN HIGHLAND RAPESEED OIL — SHEEP'S YOGHURT — LAND CRESS

BIOTAIS ÒR AGUS CANDAIDH NA CROITE SMOCTE LE CEÒ NA MÒNACH — BUIDHEAGAN UGH AIR A CHÒCAIREACHD GU SOCAIR ANN AN OLA LUS-OLA GÀIDHEALACH — IOGART BAINNE CHAORACH — BIOLAIR-FRAING

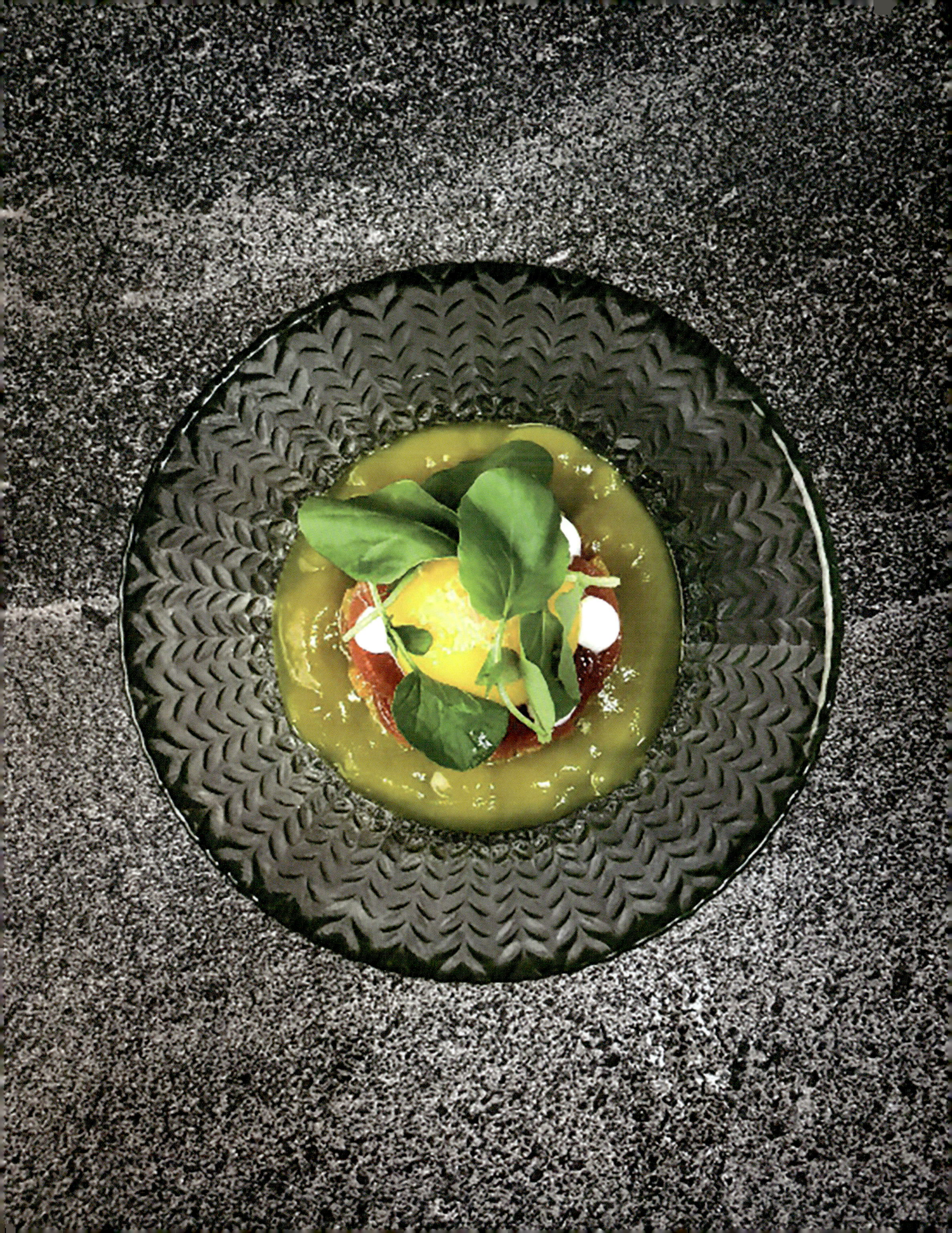

OLD CROFT HEN, KALE AND BARLEY BROTH — CHICKEN FAT AND ROSEMARY DUMPLINGS

BROT SEANN CHEARC CROITE, CÀL-GREANNACH AGUS EÒRNA — TURRAISG GEIR CIRCE AGUS RÒS-MÀIRI

Broth
1 plump croft hen
3l water
2 onions, finely chopped
3 large carrots, finely chopped
200g kale, chopped
50g pearl barley salt and pepper
bay leaf/parsley stalks/sprigs of thyme (tied together)

In a deep pot, add the water and the bird. Bring slowly to the boil, skim (keeping fat for dumplings) and reduce to a simmer. Add the herbs, onions and seasoning. Cook gently for two hours until the bird is tender.
After one hour add the barley and carrots. Once cooked remove the bird and cool slightly. Add the kale and cook for a further 10 minutes. Chop up part of the meat and return to the broth. Remove the herbs and check the seasoning.

Rosemary Dumplings
125g self-raising flour
50g chicken fat
1 tsp baking powder
2 tbsp finely chopped rosemary
salt and pepper
cold water

Mix all the ingredients with cold water to form an elastic dough. Roll into balls and place on top of the simmering broth and cook for 20 minutes.

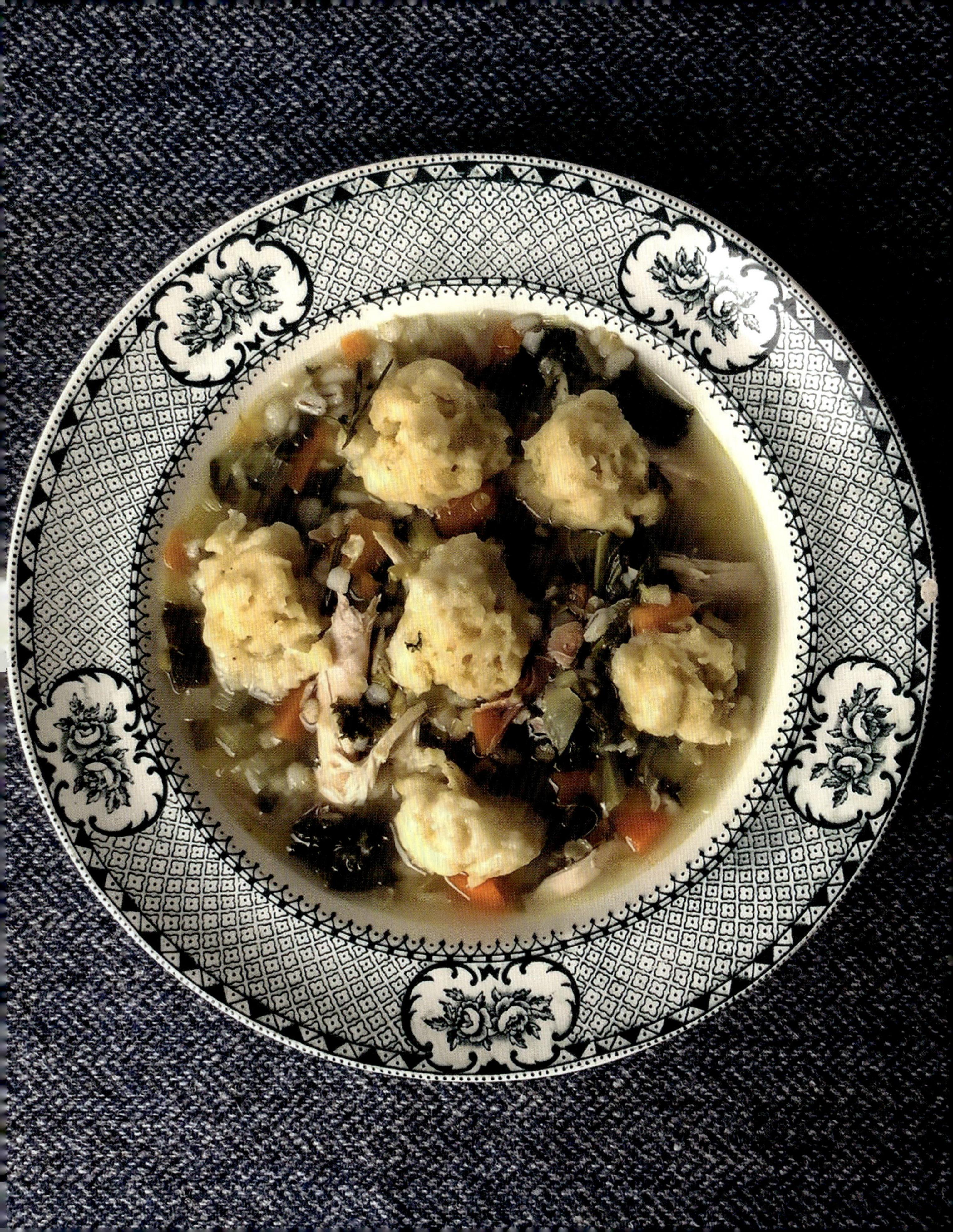

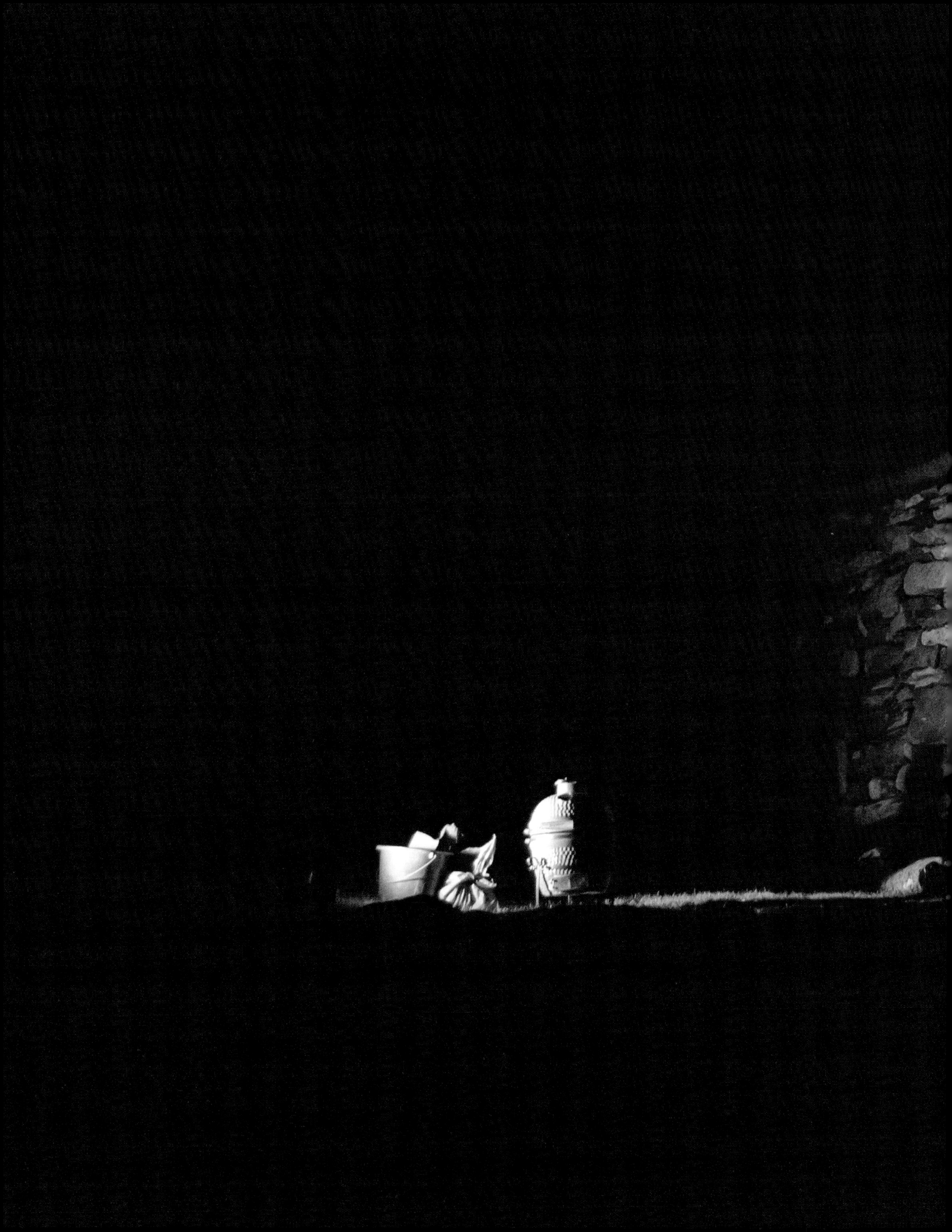

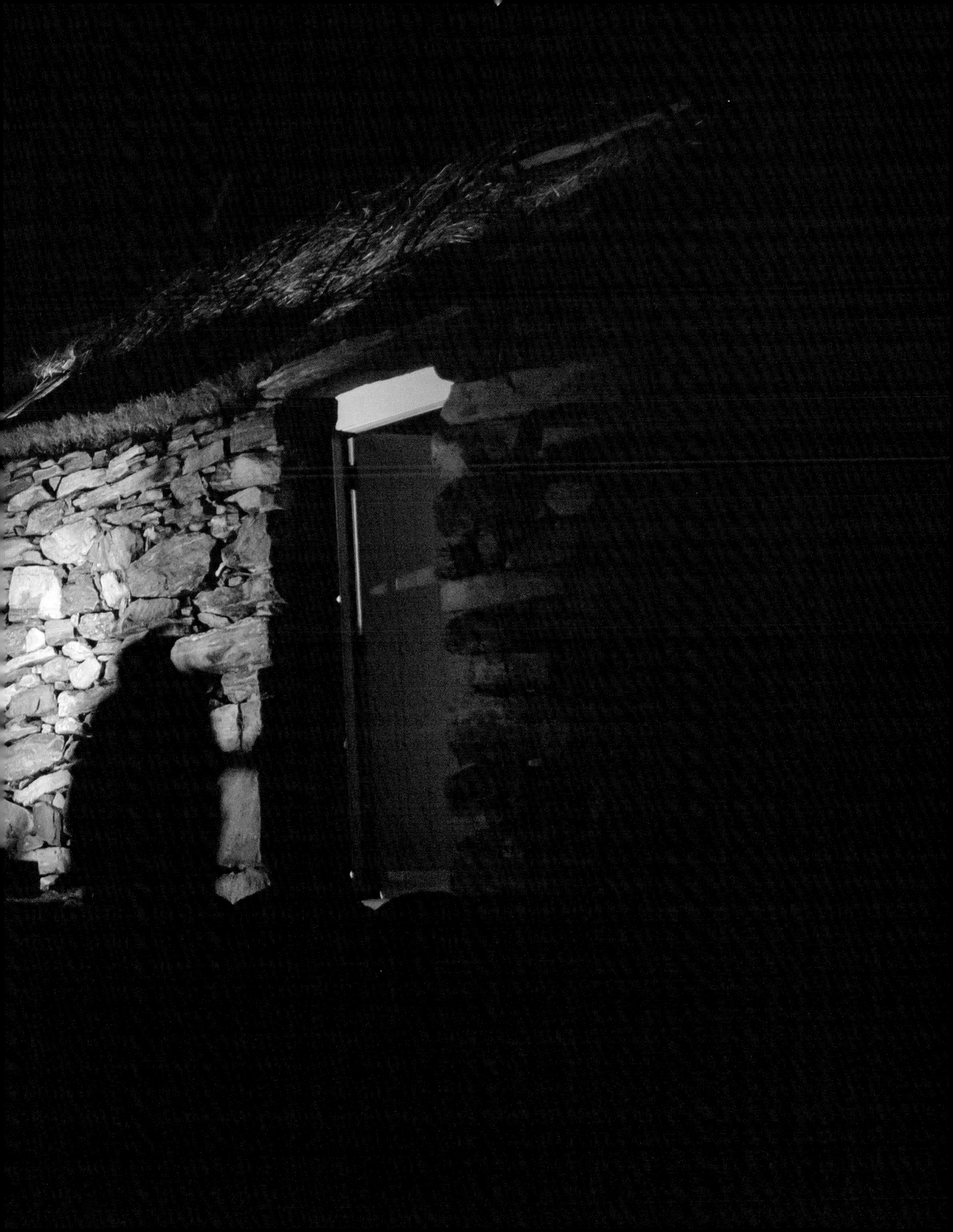

BLACK PUDDING — FRESH PEAS — SHEEP'S CHEESE — ELDERFLOWER — RAPESEED OIL

This is a beautiful light summer dish incorporating sweet and tender young fresh peas and the first of the summer's elderflowers. A warm black pudding, apple and elderflower mousse is piped onto the plate which is then topped with raw young peas, fresh sheep's cheese, some crispy black pudding and finally some fresh elderflowers. Table side, we pour onto the plate a juice made of the pea pods, fresh apple and some elderflowers. A little Highland rapeseed oil and baby gem shoots finish off this delightfully fresh dish.

MARAG DHUBH — PEASRAICHEAN ÙRA — CÀIS CHAORACH — DROMAIN — OLA LUS-OLA

'S e biadh àlainn, aotrom, samhraidh a tha seo le peasraichean milis, maoth, ùr agus ciad caoran-dhromain an t-samhraidh. Tha mousse blàth de mharag dhubh, ubhal agus caoran-dhromain air a chur air an truinnsear. Air uachdar bidh peasraichean ùra amh, càis chaorach ùr, beagan marag dhubh brisg agus mu dheireadh dha na thrì fhlùraichean-dhromain. Aig a' bhòrd, dhòrtadh sinn sùgh de rùsgan nam peasraichean, ubhal ùr agus caoran-dhromain air an truinnsear. Tha drùdhag bheag de dh'ola lus-ola Gàidhealach agus buinein Baby Gem a' cur crìoch air a' bhiadh ùrail, thaitneach seo.

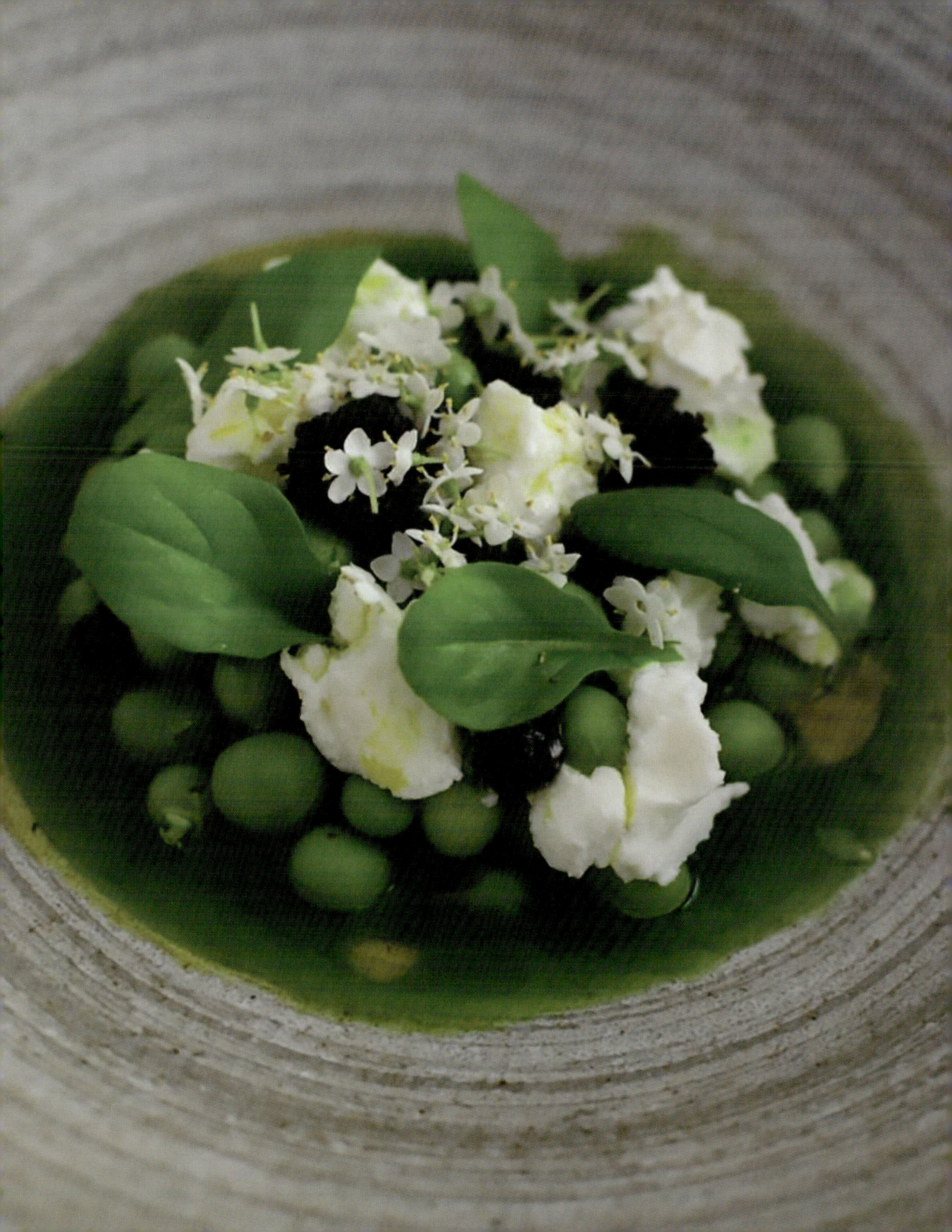

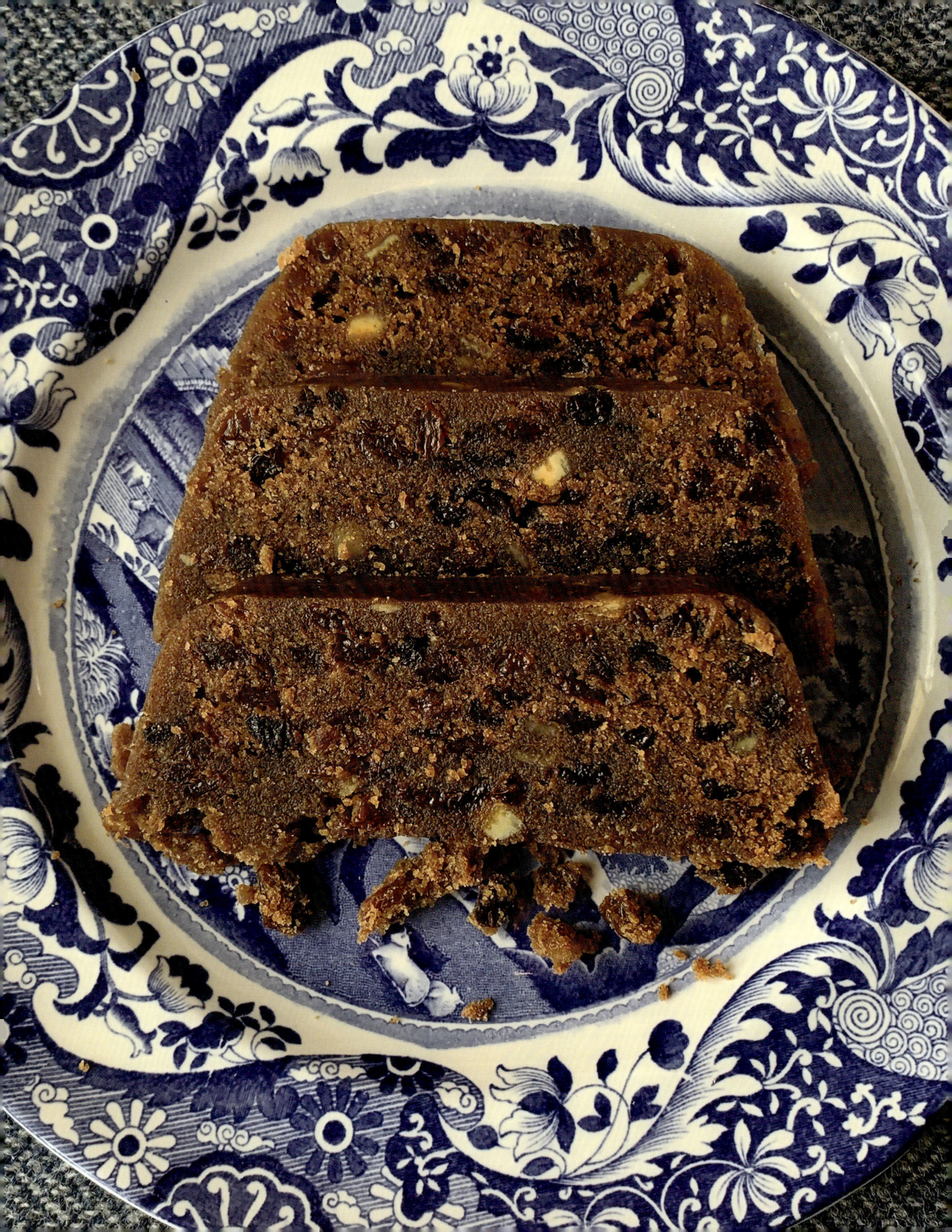

Baking and Desserts
Bèicearachd agus Mìlsean

ROSEHIP PETTICOAT TAILS

This shortbread was the perfect way to finish off our winter 2016 HAAR menu.

ARAN-MILIS NAM MUCAG

Bha an t-aran-milis seo a' toirt clàr-bidh HAAR 2016 gu crìch choileanta.

150g plain flour
150g self-raising flour
250g butter
125g icing sugar
pinch of salt
lemon zest
dried rosehip

Pre-heat oven to 130°C. Sift dry ingredients into a bowl. Add the butter and rub until the mixture resembles fine breadcrumbs. Add lemon zest and turn the mixture out on to a board and knead together into a firm dough. Roll out into saucer size rounds about ½cm thick. Crimp the edges and prick all over with a fork. Bake for 45 minutes then reduce the heat to 100°C for a further 15 minutes. Cut into triangles and dust with dried rosehip.

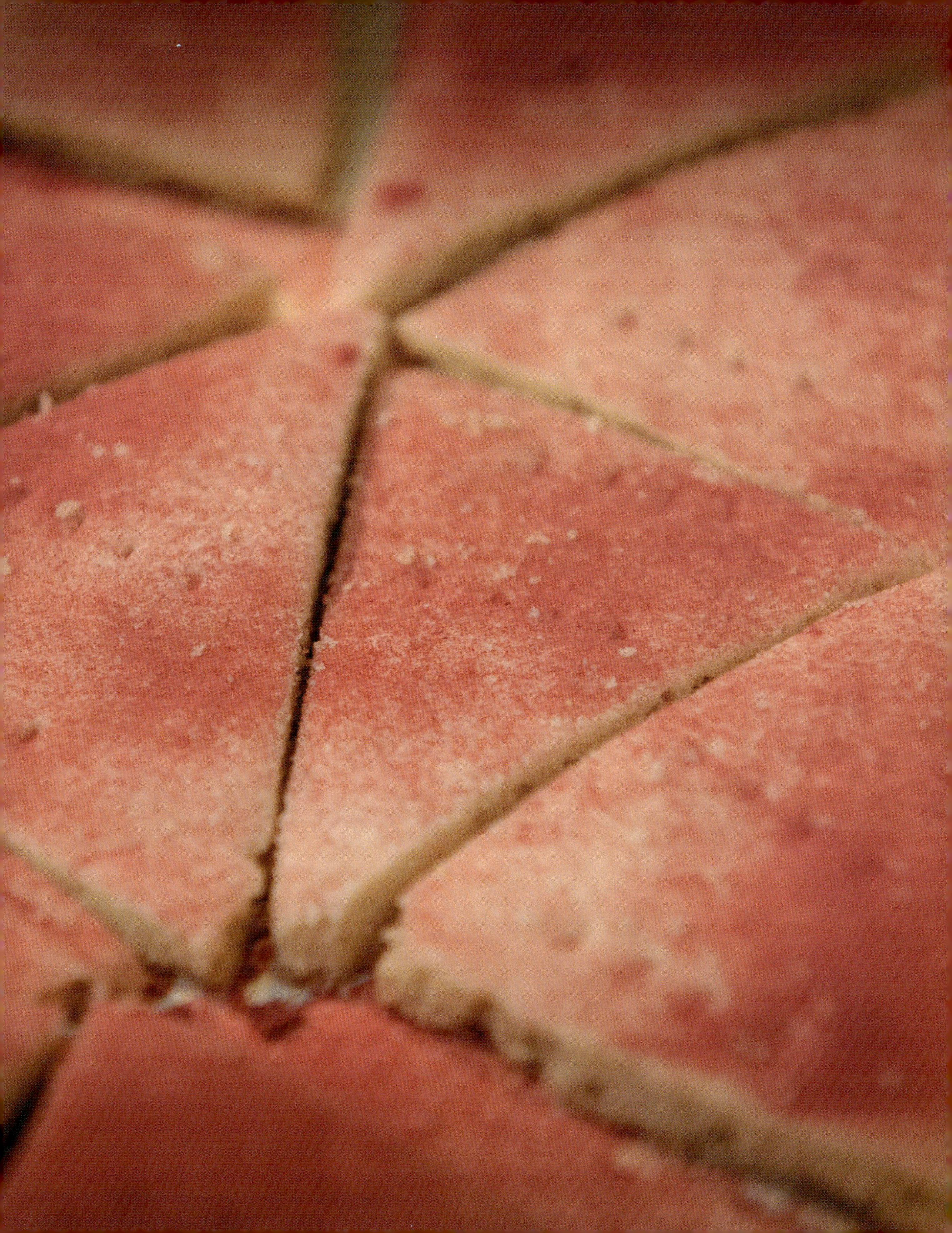

DUFF

Duff (clootie dumpling) is a traditional Hebridean pudding. It would be made for special occasions like Christmas, Communions or at times of peat cutting. The recipes are varied and seldom written down, therefore no two duffs are the same. Essentially the ingredients would be the same; flour, suet, sugar, dried fruit, cinnamon and eggs. The cloth is dipped into boiling water, dusted with flour and the mix put into it and boiled for 2-3 hours. Duff is delicious eaten hot or cold. At HAAR we served it hot with Colonsay honey ice cream. The HAAR duff recipe remains a closely guarded secret though!

DUF

Tha duf na mìlseag dhualchasach anns na h-eileanan. Bhiodh i air a dèanamh airson amannan sònraichte mar an Nollaig, na h-Òrduighean, no àm buain na mònach. Tha gach reasabaidh eadar-dhealaichte, ainneamh air an sgrìobhadh sìos, agus le sin chan eil dà dhuf ann coltach ri chèile. Gu bunaiteach, 's e na h-aon ghrìtheidean a bha a' dol annta – flùr, geir, siùcar, measan tioram, cainneal agus uighean. Tha an clobhd air a bhogadh ann an uisge goileach, craiteachan flùr air a chur air, am measgachadh air a chur ann agus air a bhruich airson 2-3 uairean a thìde. Tha duf anabarrach blasta teth no fuar. Aig HAAR bhiodh sinn ga riarachadh teth le reòiteag air a dhèanamh le mil à Colbhasa. Ach 's e fìor rùn-dìomhair a th' ann an reasabaidh duf HAAR!

DUFF PANCAKES — MALTED BARLEY ICE CREAM — CARROT GOLDEN SYRUP

For those who don't like duff in its original form then I'm quite sure you will love this! The classic duff is made in a cloth. Once cooked, it is sliced and dehydrated for 30 hours and then blitzed into a powder. To make the pancakes the duff powder is used along with barley flour, buttermilk, eggs, golden syrup, treacle, cinnamon, butter and raising agents. For the ice cream, toast the pearl barley and infuse it with vanilla and malt extract in your custard mix before churning in an ice-cream machine. The syrup is made by juicing fresh carrots and reducing the liquor right down to a couple of tablespoons, before mixing it with golden syrup.

FOILEAGAN DUF — REÒITEAG EÒRNA BRAICHTE — SIORAP ÒR CURRAIN

Mur a toigh leat duf àbhaisteach tha mi cinnteach gun còrd seo riut! Tha duf àbhaisteach air a dèanamh ann an clobhd. Aon uair's gu bheil i deiseil tha i air a slisneadh agus air a tiormachadh fad 30 uairean a thìde agus an uair sin air a pronnadh gu fùdar. Airson na foileagan a dhèanamh, tha fùdar duf air a chleachdadh còmhla ri min-eòrna, blàthach, uighean, siorap òr, treicil, cainneal, ìm agus stuthan-èirigh. Airson an reòiteag a dhèanamh, tost an eòrna neamhnaide agus drùidh e le faoineag agus brìgh braiche nad mheasgachadh ughagain, mus cuir thu e ann an inneal reòiteig. Tha an siorap air a dhèanamh le bhith a' toirt an t-sùgh à currain ùra agus ga lùghdachadh gu dha na thrì làn spàinnean-mòra, mus tèid a mheasgachadh le siorap òr.

STICKY TREACLE AND PARSNIP PUDDING — CARAMELISED WHEY SAUCE — PARSNIP ICE CREAM — CANDIED PARSNIPS

MÌLSEAG STEIGEACH TREICIL AGUS CURRAN-GEAL — SABHS TOFAIDH MEANG CARRA-MHEILLTE — REÒITEAG CURRAN-GEAL — CURRAN-GEAL SIÙCAR-CANDAIDH

Sticky Treacle and Parsnip Pudding
125g unsalted butter
150g pitted dates
(soaked in boiling water for 10 minutes)
½ tsp bicarbonate of soda
150g muscovado sugar
200g self-raising flour
2 tbsp treacle
250g parsnip, peeled and grated
3 eggs
milk to loosen

Pre-heat oven to 150°C and grease a 23cm square tin. Drain the dates and blitz into a paste. Cream butter and sugar and gradually add eggs. Add all the other ingredients along with a pinch of salt. Bake for 30 minutes.

Caramelised Whey and Toffee Sauce
250g whey
50g sugar
200g unsalted butter

Boil the whey, sugar and butter until thickened.

Parsnip Ice-cream
450g parsnips
300ml milk
5 egg yolks
50g sugar
50g glucose
125g crème fraiche

Cook the parsnips in the milk until soft.
Remove the parsnips and purée with 125ml of the milk. Whisk the egg yolks, sugar and glucose, slowly adding the milk. Whisk in the parsnip purée and crème fraiche. Pass through a fine sieve. Churn in an ice-cream machine.

Candied Parsnip
2 parsnips
200ml water
200g sugar

Peel and finely slice parsnips. A vegetable peeler will be fine. In a pan bring the water and sugar to a simmer making sure the sugar is dissolved. Add the parsnips, coating them in the syrup and simmer until the parsnips are translucent and the syrup is thickened, about 10-15 minutes. Remove to a wire rack to drain and harden.

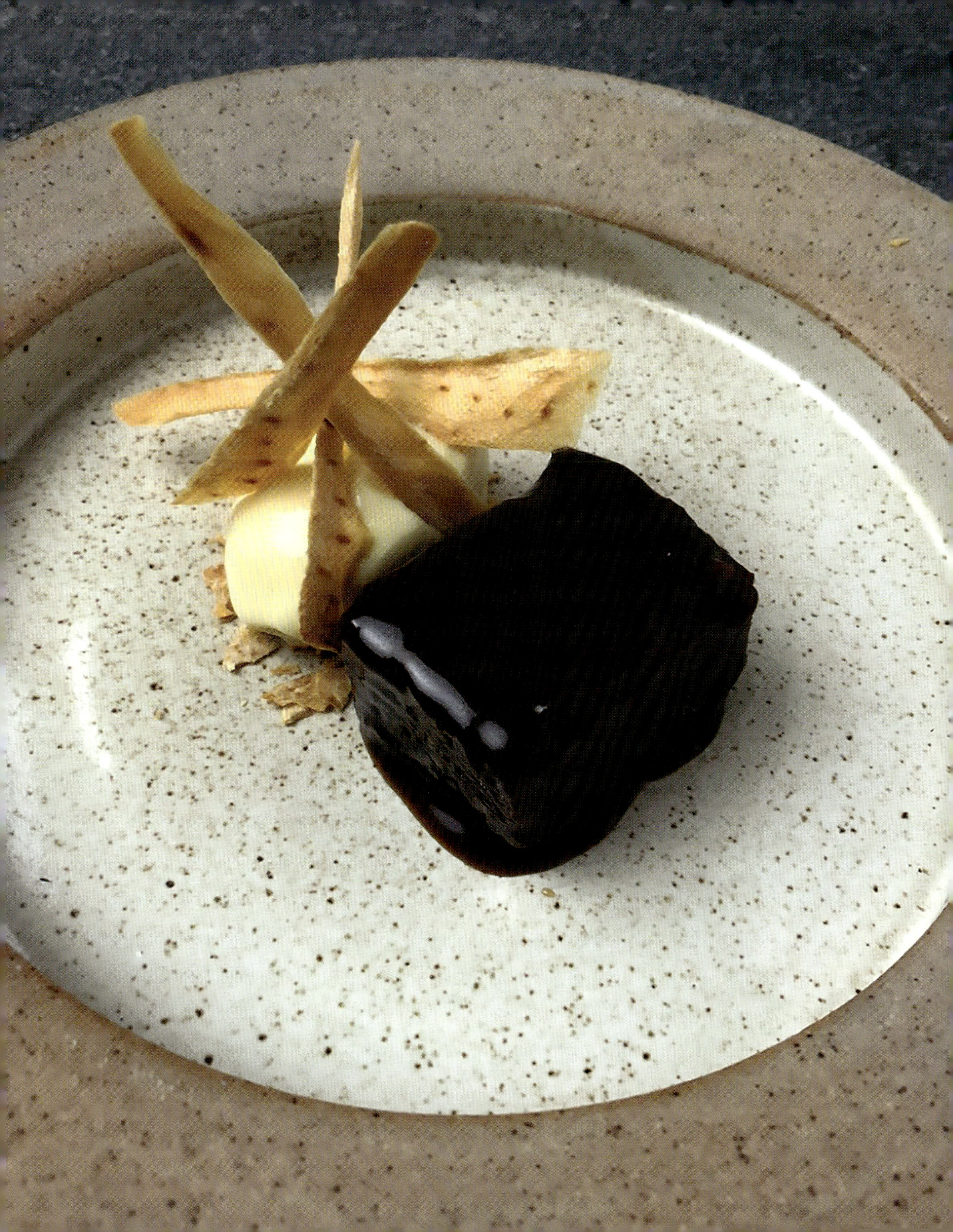

BONNACH IMEACH 'HEBRIDEAN OATCAKES'

Hebridean oatcakes are different from the thin crisp variety. They are thicker and less brittle. The Gaelic name translates 'cake with butter.' Delicious served with fresh crowdie or Isle of Mull cheddar.

BONNACH IMEACH 'ARAN-COIRCE EILEANACH'

Tha am bonnach imeach glè eadar-dhealaichte bhon aran-coirce tana, brisg. Tha e nas tighe agus chan eil e cho brisg. Tha e fìor mhath le gruth ùr no càis Cheddar à Muile.

350g medium oatmeal
15g butter
1 egg
100ml buttermilk
pinch of salt

Pre-heat the griddle (*greideal*). It should feel nicely warm if you hold your hand over it. Put the oatmeal into a bowl, add salt and rub in the butter. Make a well in the centre, add the egg and buttermilk. Mix to a fairly stiff dough. Roll out to a ½cm large round and cut into 12 triangles. Bake for about five minutes on both sides.

JESSIE'S OATCAKES

This oatcake is slightly sweeter with the addition of brown sugar. The texture is crumbly and melt-in-the-mouth. This is our friend's mum's recipe. She was known for her amazing oatcakes but sadly she is no longer with us. At HAAR we served them as a pre-dessert, crumbled and with the exceptionally tasty Isle of Mull blue cheese.

ARAN-COIRCE SHEASAIDH

Le siùcar donn ann tha aran-coirce Sheasaidh beagan nas mìlse. Faodaidh e a bhith beagan briste agus leaghaidh e nad bheul. 'S e seo an reasabaidh aig màthair ar banacharaid, a bha ainmeil airson a h-aran-coirce iongantach. Gu mì-fhortanach chan eil i còmhla rinn a-nis. Aig HAAR bhiodh sinn gan riarachadh ro na mìlsean, air am briseadh agus leis a' chàis Cheddar air leth blasta à Muile.

170g butter
60g light brown sugar
1 egg
285g oatmeal
170g self-raising flour
½ tsp salt
½ tsp bicarbonate of soda

Beat together the butter and sugar. Add flour, bicarb, salt and egg along with oatmeal. Roll out and cut into rounds. Place on a baking tray and top with oatmeal. Bake at 170°C for about 20 minutes.

GRIDDLE SCONES

There wouldn't have been a home in the Hebrides that did not have a cast iron griddle for cooking scones, oatcakes, barley bread and pancakes. Before the days of stoves and cookers, the griddle would have been suspended above the fire with a chain and hook known as a *slabhraidh*. The griddle below belonged to our grandmother, who produced exceptional scones served with rhubarb jam.

SGONAICHEAN GREIDEIL

Cha bhiodh dachaigh anns na h-Eileanan Siar anns nach robh greideal iarainn airson sgonaichean is aran-coirce, aran-eòrna agus foileagan a dhèanamh. Aig àm mus robh stòbhaichean is cucaran ann, bhiodh a' ghreideal air a crochadh os cionn an teine air sèine le dubhan air a ceann, ris an cante slabhraidh. B' ann le ar seanmhair a bha a' ghreideal san dealbh. Bhiodh i a' dèanamh sgonaichean a bha air leth math air an ithe le silidh ruadh-bhàrr.

450g self-raising flour
120g butter
1 tsp baking powder
2 tbsp syrup
whey/buttermilk
(to bring the mix together)
2 eggs whisked

Heat the griddle until it feels nicely warm when you hold your hand over it about an inch from the surface. Sift the flour and baking powder, rub in butter, add the eggs and syrup and stir in. Add the whey until it forms a softish sticky dough. It should be neither too soft nor too stiff. The dough should be light and soft. If it's too wet it will be doughy inside and if too dry it will be hard. Flour your work surface, handle the dough lightly and knead for about 10 seconds until smooth. Roll out to about 1½-2cm thick and shape into a large round and cut into quarters.
Cook slowly on the griddle for about 5-6 minutes on each side. Once cooked, wrap them in clean tea towel to keep them soft.

COLONSAY HONEY AND BUTTERMILK ICE-CREAM

This honey is unique with the taste and smell bringing you straight back to childhood memories of time spent on the machair. It is the fragrant nectars from the machair wildflowers that give it that special flavour.

MIL CHOLBHASA AGUS REÒITEAG BLÀTHAICH

Tha am mil seo air leth, le fhàileadh agus a bhlas gad thoirt dìreach air ais gu làithean d' òige is cuimhne air ùine air a chur seachad air a' mhachair. 'S e an t-sile chùbhraidh bho fhlùraichean na machrach a tha a' toirt am blas sònraichte dha.

grated zest of 1 lemon
25ml lemon juice
250ml milk
300g double cream
4 egg yolks
110g Colonsay honey
20g sugar
500ml buttermilk

Bring lemon zest and juice to the boil. Add milk and cream and return to the heat but do not boil.
Whisk honey, egg yolks and sugar. Slowly add the cream mixture. Finally whisk in the buttermilk. Leave overnight in the fridge for the flavour to mature. Churn and freeze.

TURNIP AND PINE CAKE — BROWNED BUTTER CULTURED CREAM AND CROWDIE FROSTING — SALTED HAZELNUTS

This is a deliciously moist cake made in a similar way to carrot cake. Instead of carrots I have used turnip and an oil flavoured with Douglas Fir pine needles.

CÈIC SNÈIP AGUS GIUTHAIS — CÒMHDACH DÈANTE LE GRUTH AGUS UACHDAR GEUR LE ÌM DONN — CNOTHAN CALLTAINN SAILLTE

Tha a' chèic seo blasta agus tais agus air a dèanamh san aon dòigh ri cèic churrain. An àite currain tha mi a' cleachdadh snèap agus ola air a bhlasachadh le giuthas MhicDhùghlais.

Turnip and Pine Cake
225g self-raising flour
225g light brown sugar
3 large eggs, beaten
225ml pine oil
300g grated turnip
1 tsp mixed spice
1 tsp cinnamon
1 tsp bicarbonate of soda
1 tsp vanilla
pinch of salt

Pre-heat oven to 150°C. Grease two 8 inch round tins.
Mix eggs, sugar and oil in bowl. Fold in dry ingredients and turnip. Bake for 1½ hours. Leave the cake to cool completely on a wire rack before icing.

Pine Oil
Douglas Fir pine needles
225ml Cullisse rapeseed oil

Blitz young pine needles in the oil for about eight minutes. Leave to infuse and pass through muslin.

Browned Butter, Cultured Cream and Crowdie Frosting
100g browned butter at room temp
100g cultured cream
100g crowdie
600g icing sugar

In a bowl, mix together the cream and crowdie adding the browned butter until smooth. Slowly add the icing sugar until fully combined and you have a nice consistency.

Salted Hazelnuts
2 tbsp pine oil
150g hazelnuts salt

Mix hazelnuts with oil and salt. Roast on baking sheet for 15 minutes at 170°C. Allow to cool.

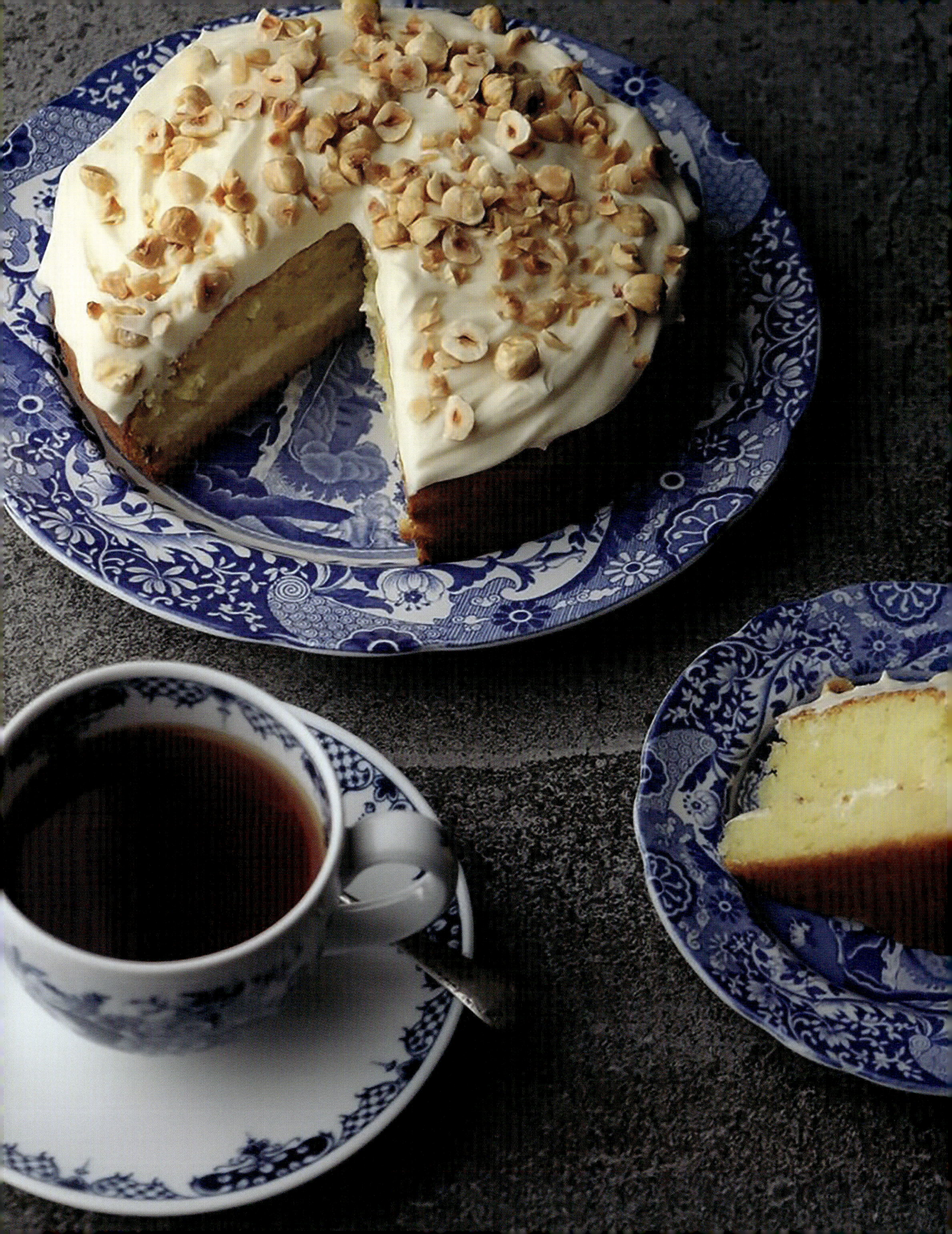

CROWDIE PANNA COTTA

A slightly different take on this classic, using our own home-made crowdie. Served with toasted oats, gooseberries fermented in Harris Gin and sugar kelp syrup.

PANNA COTTA GRUTH

Tionndadh beagan eadar-dhealaichte bhon àbhaist, a' cleachdadh gruth a rinn sinn fhìn. Bidh sinn ga riarachadh le min-choirce air a thostadh, gròsaidean tòirnichte ann an sineubhar na Hearadh agus siorap milearaich.

450g crowdie	Soak the gelatine leaves in cold water until soft.
225g double cream	Heat cream and sugar until the sugar dissolves. Cool to room temperature.
120g sugar	Blend crowdie and pass through sieve. Squeeze water out of the gelatine.
5g leaf gelatine	Heat a small amount of lemon juice and dissolve the gelatine. Stir it into the cream mixture. Add the cream mixture to the crowdie and pass through a sieve again. Pour into moulds and set in the fridge for at least an hour.

RED AND GREEN STRAWBERRIES — CULTURED CREAM — WILD THYME SHORTBREAD
SÙIBH-LÀIR DEARG IS UAINE — UACHDAR GEUR — ARAN-MILIS LUS AN RÌGH

Strawberry Soup
500g mix of red and green strawberries
20g sugar

Place the strawberries and sugar in a glass bowl cover with clingfilm and place over a pan of simmering water for one hour. Pass through muslin. Place halved small red strawberries in the soup with sliced green strawberries. Macerate overnight.

Cultured Cream
500ml cream
3 tbsp whey or buttermilk

Place in a jar, leaving an inch at the top. Place lid on jar. Leave up to 24 hours at 22-25°C to culture. The cream will thicken from the top down. Store in fridge for up to three weeks.

Garnish with wild thyme shortbread, (using our shortbread recipe on page 248) with the addition of thyme flowers and wild strawberry flowers. A lovely light summer dessert with the green strawberries adding a nice sour note to a sweet dish.

SWEET CROWDIE —
FRESH CROWDIE AND CULTURED CREAM SWEETENED WITH HEATHER HONEY — RASPBERRIES — APPLE AND DILL PURÉE — CRUNCHY PORRIDGE

Fresh crowdie sweetened with heather honey and mixed with cultured cream, fresh raspberries, apple and dill purée and garnished with crunchy porridge and some dill leaves.

GRUTH MILIS —
GRUTH ÙR AGUS UACHDAR GEUR AIR A MHÌLSEACHADH LE MIL FRAOICH — SÙBHAN-CRAOIBHE — PURÉE UBHAL AGUS DILE — LIT BRISG

Gruth ùr air a mhìlseachadh le mil fraoich agus air a mheasgachadh le uachdar geur, sùbhan-craoibhe, purée ubhal agus dile, air a sgeadachadh le lit brisg agus duilleagan dile.

Crunchy Porridge
50g pine nuts
100g pumpkin seeds
200g mixed nuts
200g oats
20g maple syrup
20g Colonsay honey
5g salt

Pre-heat oven to 170°C.
Bake dry ingredients for 10 minutes. Mix maple syrup and honey and bake for a further 10 minutes. Cool and chop.

Apple and Dill Purée
3 apples
fresh dill

Wash, peel and core apples, keeping the peel and cores for making into jam, jelly or apple butter or freeze them until needed.
Place the apples in a pan with a good splash of water, a pinch of salt and a knob of butter. Cover and steam for 10-15 minutes until the apples are soft. Remove the lid and cook until you have a firmer texture and the flavour is more concentrated. For a smooth consistency, blend adding a splash of apple vinegar to taste. Finely chop the dill and mix through the purée.

TRADITIONAL CROWDIE CRANACHAN

The Bruichladdich 'Classic Laddie' from the Island of Islay was the perfect Hebridean dram to end the night at HAAR - smooth, clean, fresh and lively with the oak and the Scottish grain in perfect harmony. Added to the cranachan along with Colonsay honey, it gives this simple dish a luxurious feel.

CRANNACHAN GRUTH TRAIDISEANTA

B' e 'Classic Laddie' bho thaigh-staile Bhruaich a' Chladaich ann an Ìle an drama a b' fheàrr airson crìoch a chur air oidhche aig HAAR. Tha i mìn, glan, ùrail agus beothail, leis an darach agus an gràn a' còrdadh gu mòr ri chèile. Air a cur ris a' chrannachan còmhla ri mil Cholbhasach, tha a' mhìlseag shìmplidh seo a' faireachdainn sòghail.

50g oatmeal
75ml Bruichladdich whisky
2 tbsp Colonsay honey
50g fresh crowdie
125g fresh raspberries
150ml double cream

Toast the oatmeal by spreading a layer on a baking sheet and heating up in the oven. Leave to cool.
Whisk the cream and fold into fresh crowdie along with the honey and whisky.
Fold in the toasted oatmeal. Top with fresh raspberries.

SHEEP'S MILK YOGHURT, BUTTERMILK AND SALTED WHEY CARAMEL MOUSSE — SHEEP'S MILK YOGHURT MERINGUES — FROZEN HARRIS GIN, TONIC, MINT

MOUSSE IOGART BAINNE CHAORACH, BLÀTHACH AGUS CARRA-MHEILLE MIÙG SAILLTE — MEIREANG IOGART BAINNE CHAORACH — SINEUBHAR NA HEARADH REÒITE, TONAIC, MEANNT

Whey Caramel
250ml whey
50g sugar
Skye sea salt

Boil ingredients until syrupy. Add salt.

Mousse
lemon juice
100ml whey caramel
10g gelatine leaves
400g sheep's yoghurt
200g buttermilk
400g double cream

Warm but do not boil yoghurt and buttermilk. Heat lemon juice and gelatine then add the whey caramel, buttermilk and yoghurt.
Whip cream to ribbon stage and fold into mix.
Pour into moulds and refrigerate until set.

Gin and Mint Ice
220g caster sugar
120ml water
170ml Harris Gin
500ml Macgregor's Tonic water
2 Bramley apples, peeled and grated
juice of 1 lemon
30g chopped mint

Bring water and sugar to boil. Once sugar has dissolved, remove from heat. Add gin, tonic, lemon, apple and mint. Set aside to cool completely. Blitz with a blender and pass through a sieve and freeze, whisking every 30 minutes, for about four hours.

Sheep's Yoghurt Meringue
2 egg whites
125g caster sugar
50g sheep's yoghurt

Whisk the egg whites until stiff, gradually adding the sugar a spoon at a time. Whisk until thick and glossy. Fold in the sheep's yoghurt until combined. Spread out smoothly on a tray lined with parchment paper, place in a dehydrator on a low temperature for about five hours. Alternatively dry out in the oven at 110°C.

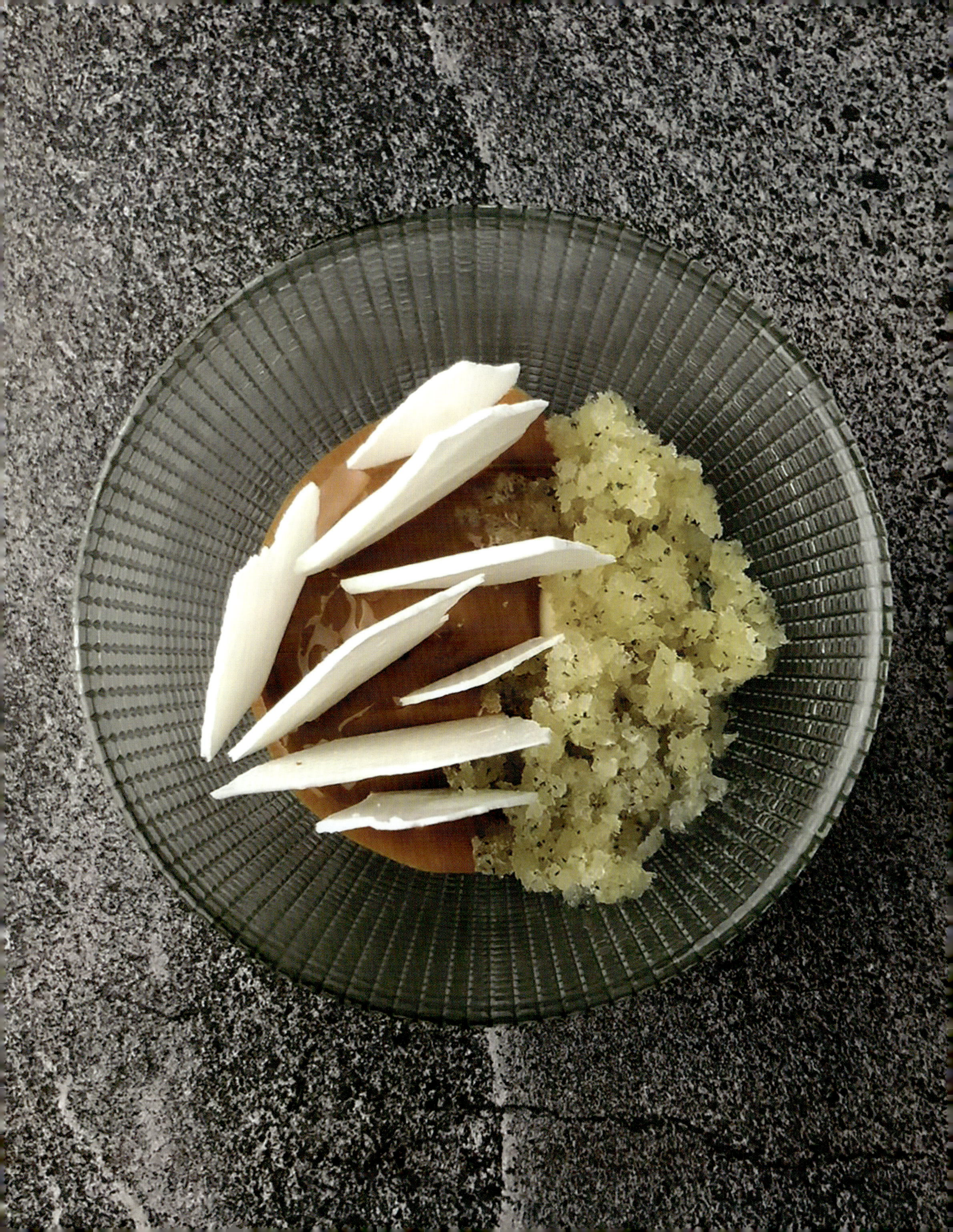

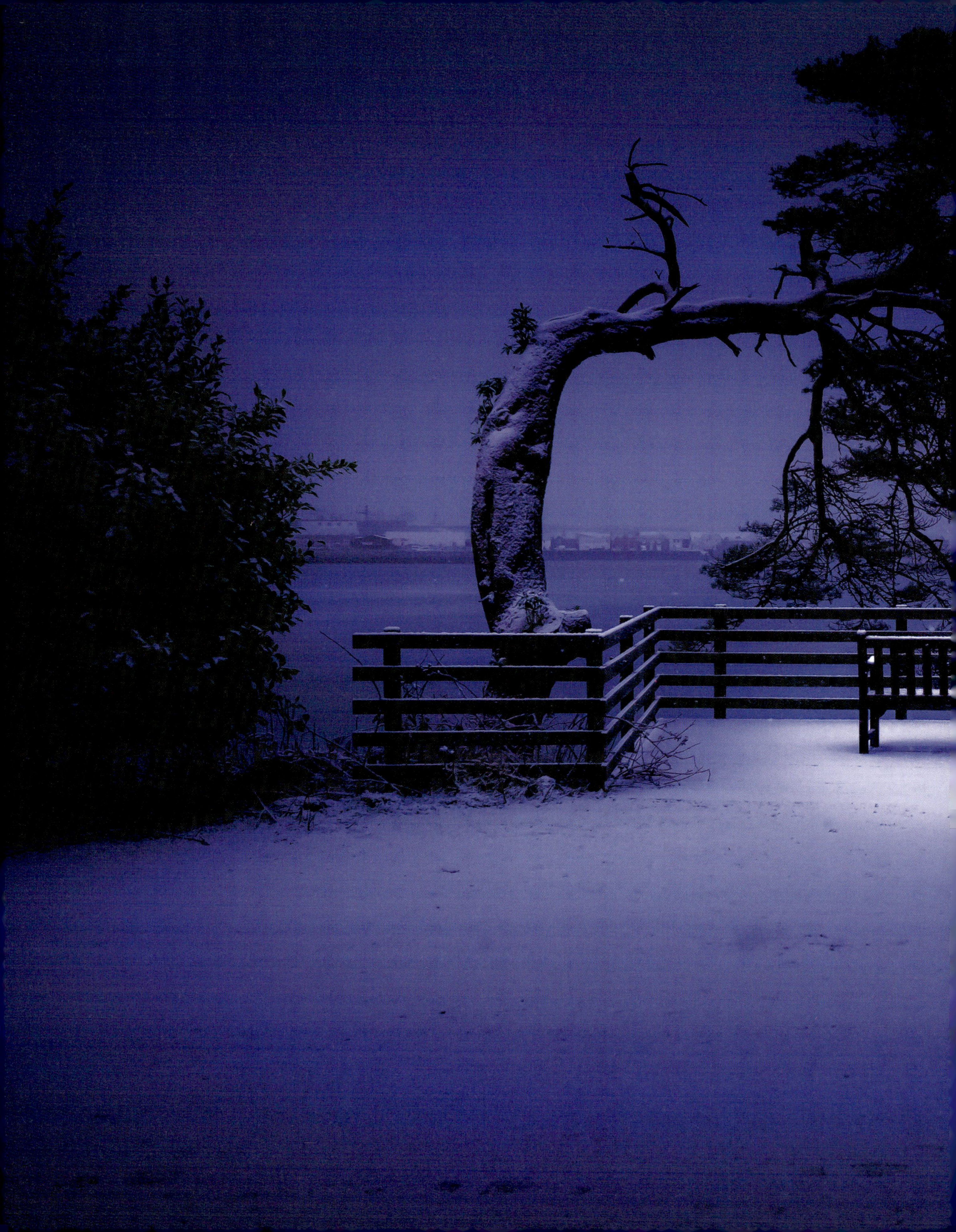

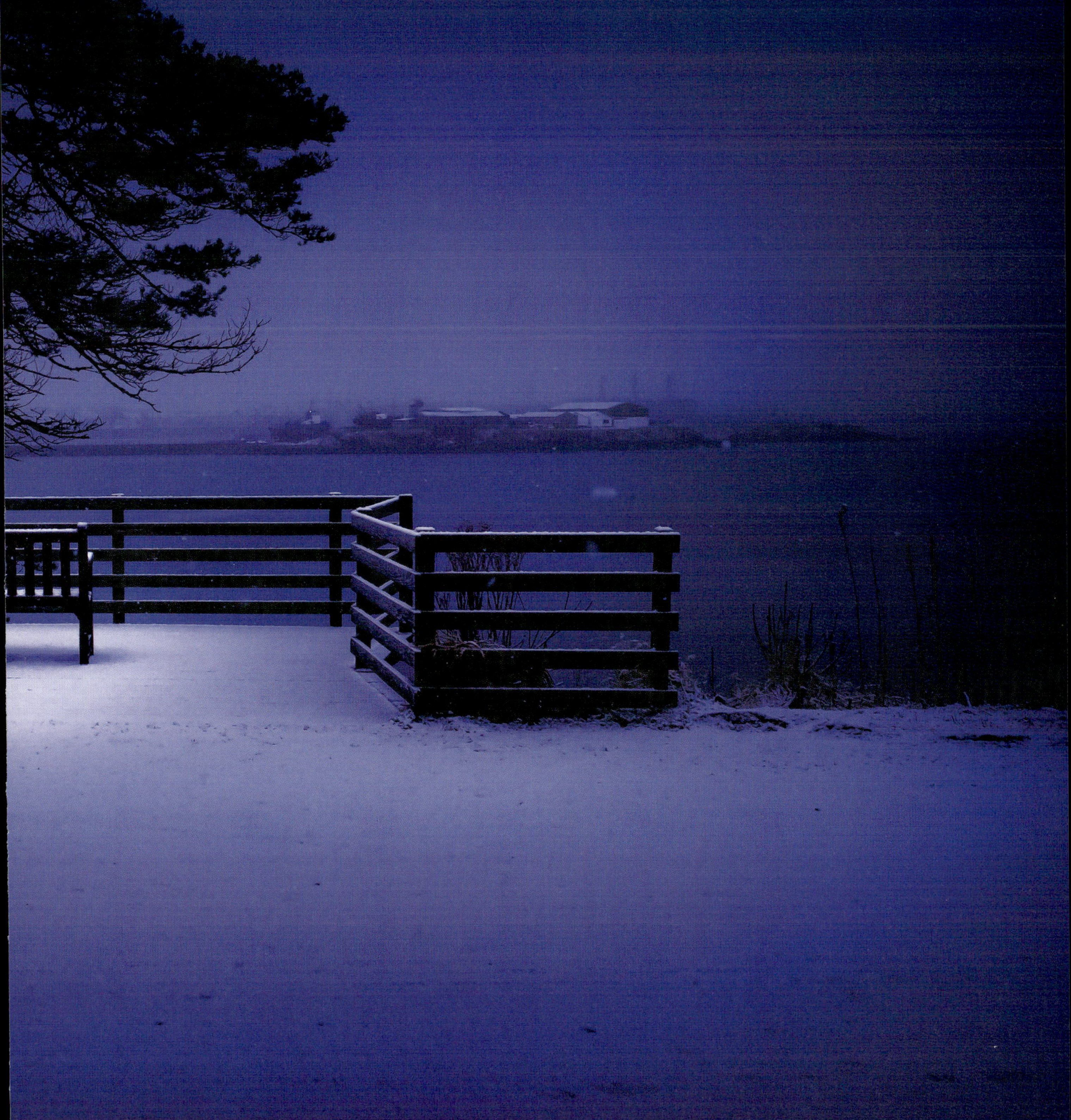

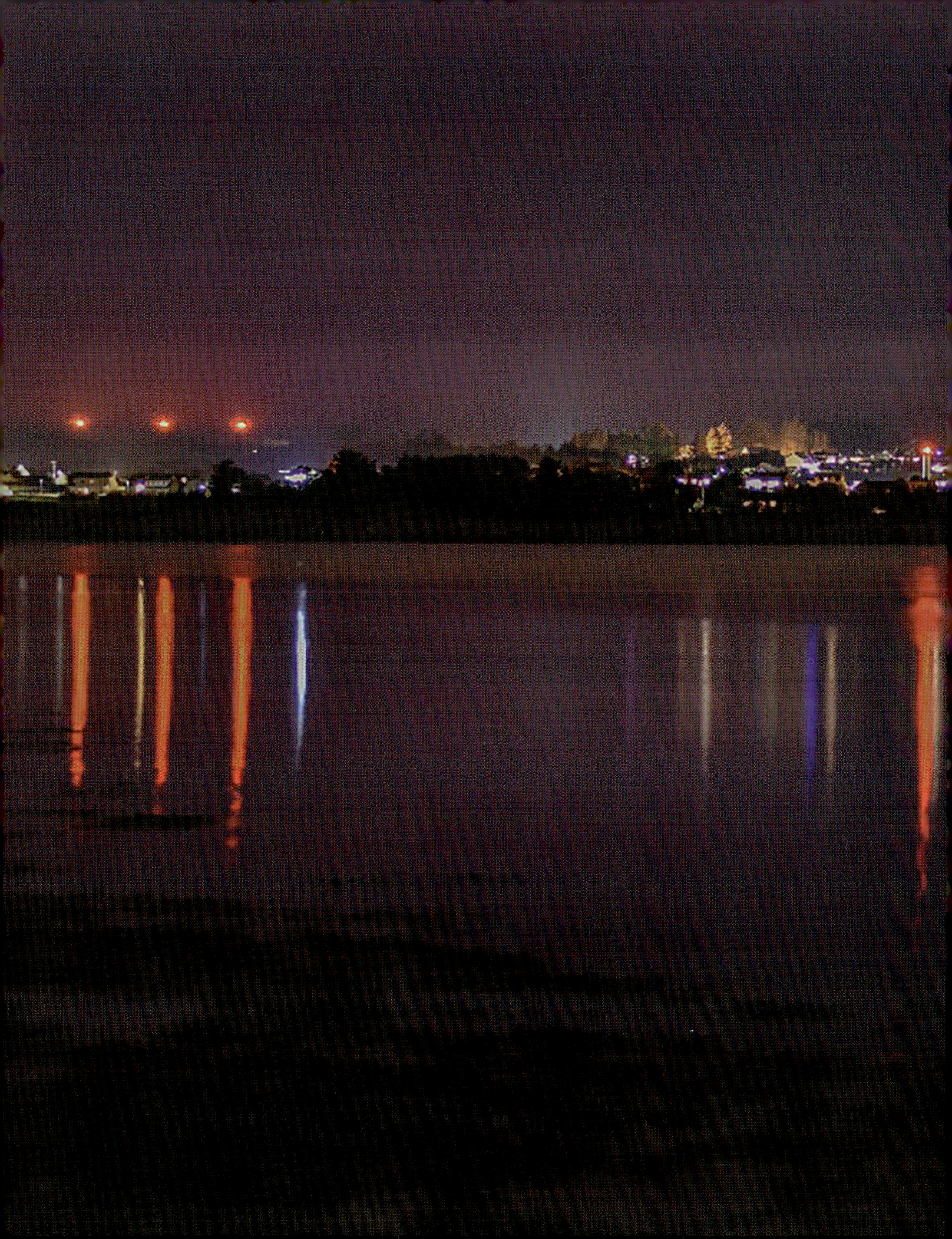

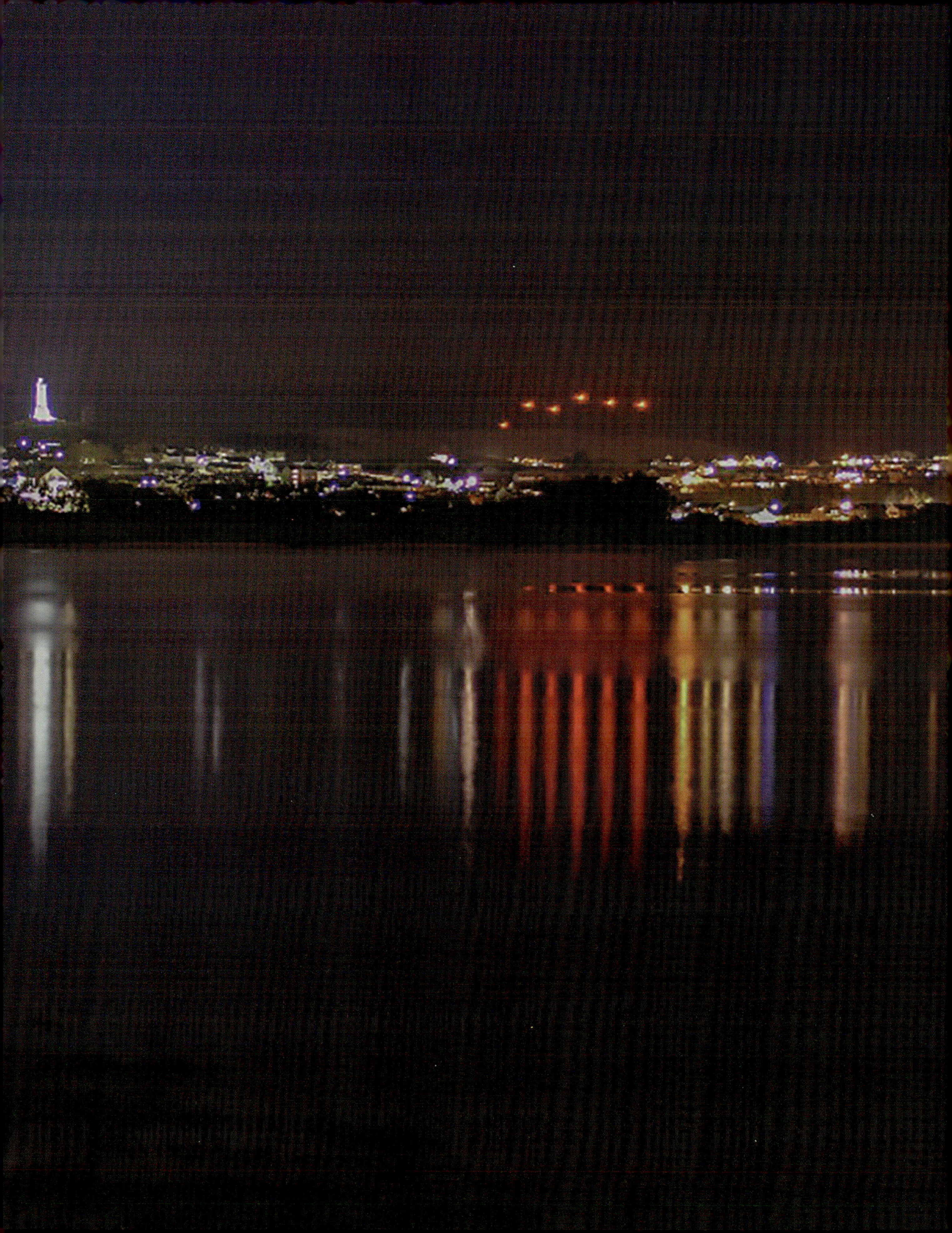

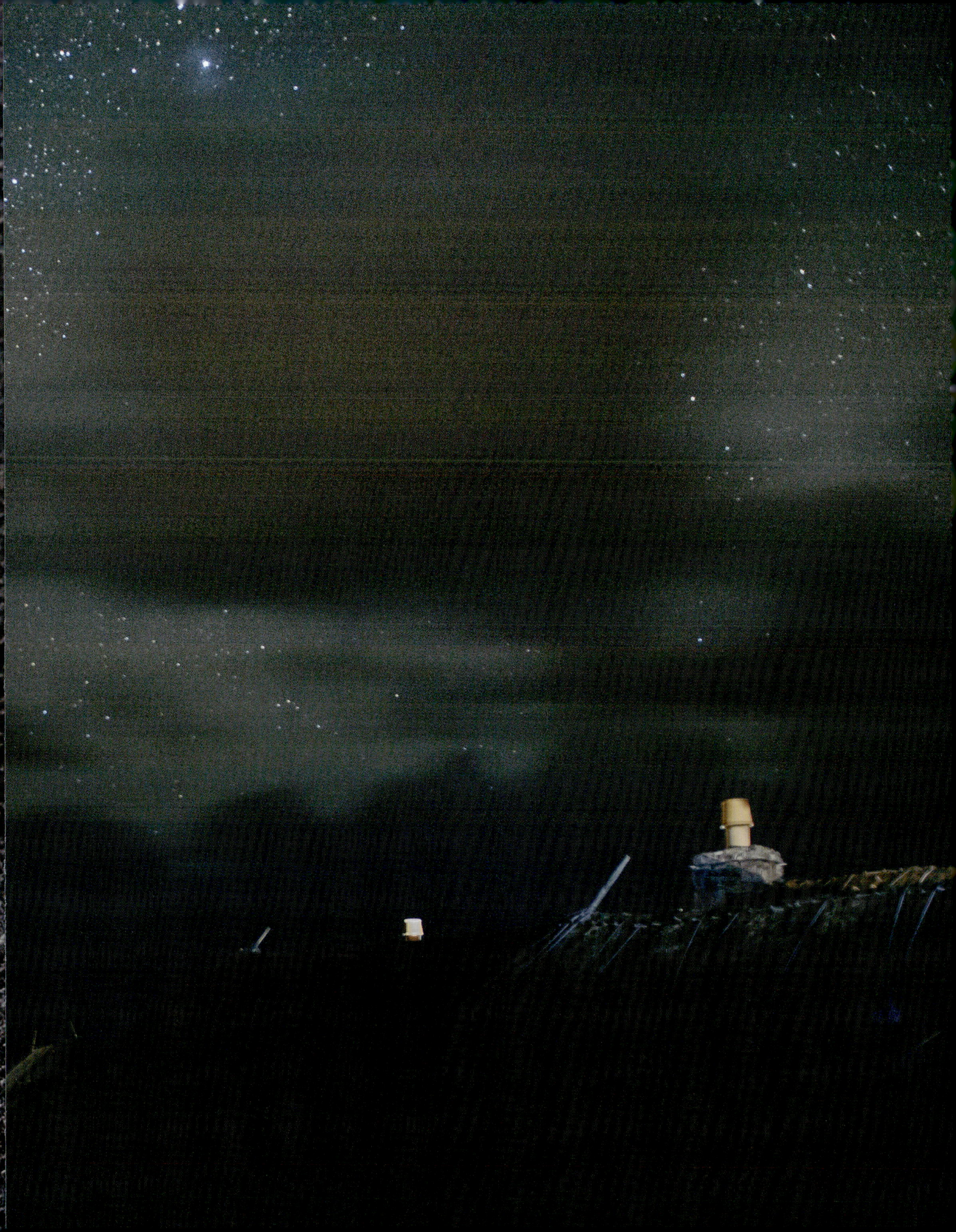

BARLEY BANNOCKS

Aran-eòrna is a traditional Hebridean bannock with the barley flour adding a distinctive flavour. Traditionally it would be cooked on a griddle. Delicious eaten hot with fresh crowdie or butter.

BONNAICH EÒRNA

'S e bonnach traidiseanta a th' ann an aran-eòrna, leis an eòrna a' toirt blas sònraichte dha. Gu h-àbhaisteach bhiodh e air a dhèanamh air greideal. Tha e blasta air ithe teth le gruth ùr no ìm.

225g barley flour
50g plain flour
1 tsp cream of tartar
1 tsp salt
1 tsp bicarbonate of soda
250ml buttermilk

Pre-heat the oven to 180°C.

Mix barley, flour, cream of tartar and salt together. Mix bicarbonate soda with buttermilk and pour into the dry ingredients. Mix to a soft dough onto a floured board and press down to make dough 1cm thick.

Cut into four or six segments halfway down and place on an oiled baking sheet. Bake in the oven for about 15 minutes. Wrap up in cloth to keep soft.

DULSE AND BEER BREAD

A tasty bread with the dulse adding that perfect salty hint from the sea and the beer giving it a lovely depth of flavour.

ARAN LE DUILEASG AGUS LEANN

Aran blasta leis an duileasg a' toirt dha fiamh de bhlas saillte na mara agus an leann a' toirt doimhneachd blais dha.

600g strong white flour
200g wholemeal bread flour
200g malted bread flour
40g finely chopped dulse
500ml Colonsay beer
100ml water (approx)
20g instant yeast
20g salt
60g butter

Put everything into a bowl and mix until it comes together. Don't add all the water at once in case it becomes too sticky. Tip the mixture onto an oiled surface and knead for 10 minutes until the dough is no longer sticky but nice and elastic. Cover in a bowl until it doubles in size.
Knock back and shape into two loaves, cover with a plastic bag and prove for at least one hour or until doubled in size. Dust with flour.
Bake at 200°C for 45 minutes, with ice cubes added to the oven to give it a nice crust.

RASPBERRY AND WHISKY SCOTTISH MACAROON

Another memory from the van, this is my take on the Scottish macaroon, flavoured with whisky and coated in dried raspberries.

MACARÙN ALBANNACH LE SÙBHAN-CRAOIBHE AGUS UISGE-BEATHA

Cuimhneachan eile air a' bhan. Seo mo thionndadh-sa air a' mhacarùn Albannach air a bhlasachadh le uisge-beatha agus air a chòmhdach le sùbhan-craoibhe air an tiormachadh.

Macaroon
1 large potato
450g icing sugar
1 tsp whisky

Peel and boil potato until soft enough to mash. Drain and mash the potato. Use a potato ricer or a sieve to get a really smooth texture. Add the icing sugar a little at a time, mixing well as you go. You want the mixture to become a stiff paste. Add the whisky.
Roll the macaroon mix into long rectangular shapes and place on a tray lined with greaseproof paper. Freeze for about an hour to set.

Chocolate Covering
225g dark chocolate
110g dried raspberries

Melt chocolate in a bowl over a pan of simmering water. Remove mix from freezer and cut into small rectangular pieces. Dip each bar into chocolate and coat in dried raspberries.
Place on a tray lined with greaseproof paper until the chocolate has set.

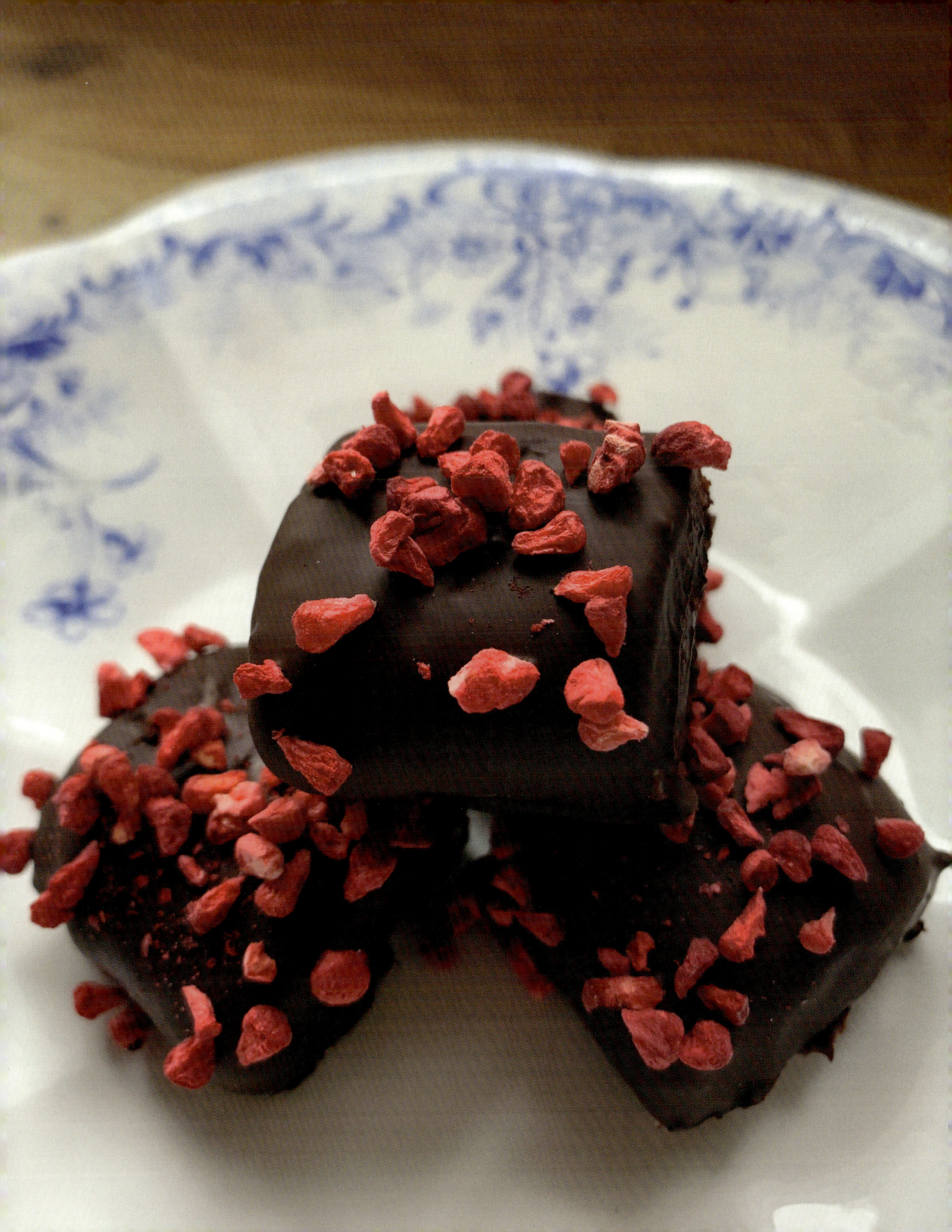

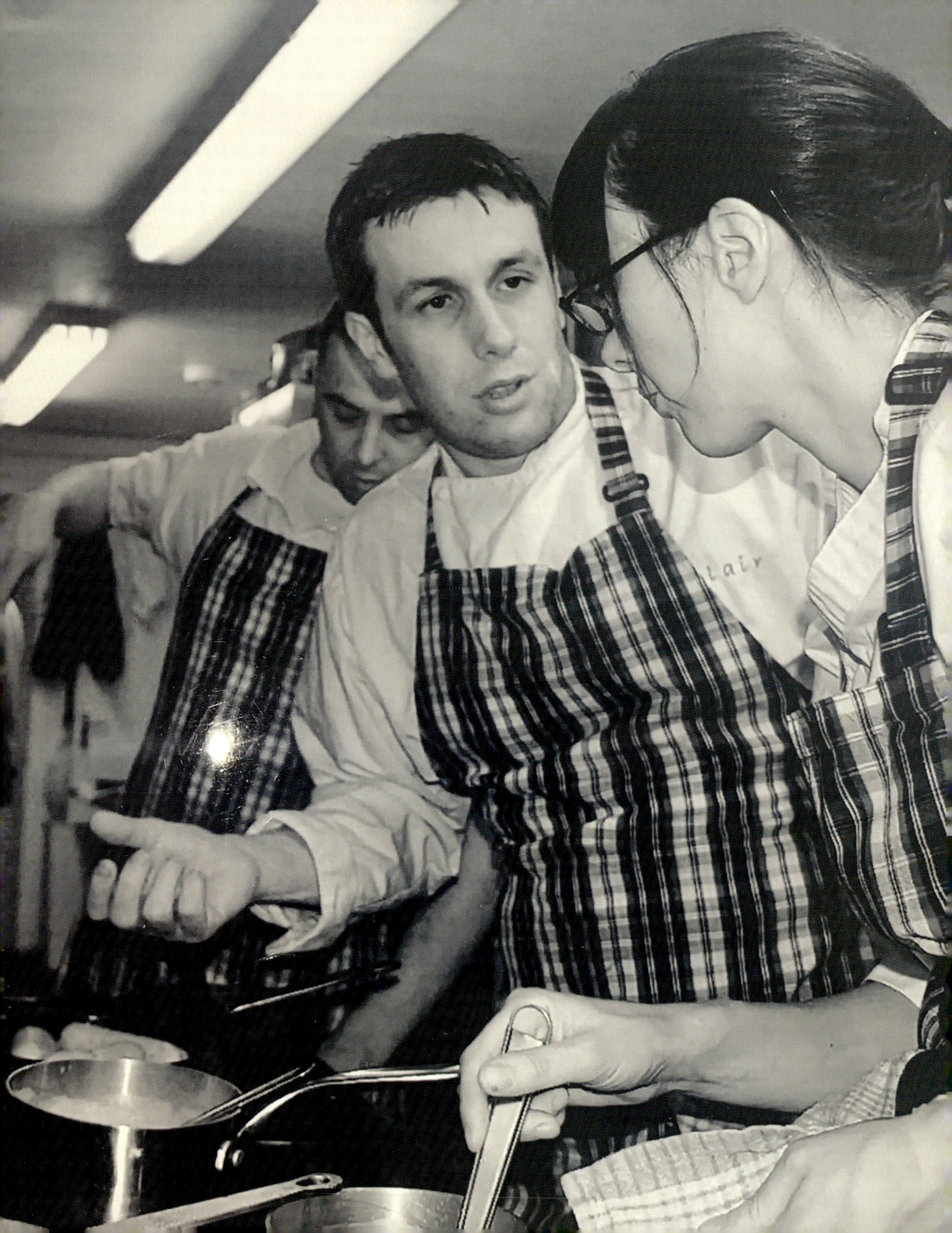

Sùlair

Sulair Restaurant - Stornoway

A taste of the Isle of Lewis Summer menu

Friday 21st May 2010

Ronnie Scotts hot & cold smoked salmon / crowdie / wasabi / orange / beetroot

~

Loch Leurbost oyster

~

Carloway brown crab / dashi seaweed / avocado / cucumber

~

Uig wild rabbit tortelloni / Eishkin langoustine / carrot / vanilla / pickled apple

~

Loch Roag diver caught scallop / apple / kohlrabi / hazelnut

~

Habost hogget loin & flank / peas / wild garlic / broad bean & tomato jus / potato fondant

~

Barvas moor gorse flower & citrus panna-cotta

~

Steinish strawberry cheesecake / hibiscus jelly / different textures of strawberry

~

Chocolates from the Hebridean Chocolate Company

10 courses   £25

Local Suppliers Used

Uig Seafare - Hand dived scallops
Douglas Craigie - Creel caught langoustines & brown crab
Islander Shellfish - Smoked salmon
Simon Hunt - Wild rabbit
Lewis Oysters - Oysters
A & C Maclean - Hogget
Tigh Uaine - Beetroot, wild garlic, peas, broad beans, tomato, carrots, kohlrabi, salad
Steinish Strawberries - Strawberries
Hebridean Chocolate Company - Chocolates

Sulair Restaurant – Stornoway
Early summer A la carte menu

Starters

Isle of Lewis Crab	Avocado ice cream / dashi seaweed / cucumber gelee / lime dressing	£8
Creel caught Langoustines	Pressed pork belly / butternut squash / pickled apple / sage / leaves	£9
Hand Dived Uig Scallops	Spice roasted / cauliflower / golden raisin / caper / cumin / pea shoots	£12
Wild Machair fed Rabbit	Cooked 5 ways / celeriac puree / verjus / prune / celery / radish	£7
Pea & Smoked Ham	Summer pea & marjoram soup / smoked ham hock tortelloni / quails eggs	£7

Mains

Aberdeen Angus Beef	Fillet, tongue & cheek / shitake mushrooms / shallots / red wine / tarragon	£24
Loch Duart Salmon	Langoustines / asparagus / lemongrass / crème fraiche / linguine	£17
Lamb	Loin / belly / ras el hanout / red pepper / smoked aubergine / basil	£18
Gartmorn Farm Duck	New season peas / black pudding / morels / pomme anna / Madeira	£19
Halibut	Smoked salmon / sorrel / Jersey Royals / horseradish / confit lemon	£22
English Asparagus	Poached duck egg / shitake mushrooms / charlotte potatoes / chervil	£16

Cheese — French cheeses - Reblouchon / delice d' cremier / mimolette tomme savoie / fourme d'ambert / Almond and ginger chutney oatcakes / fruit — £9

Desserts

Baked Chesecake	Vanilla / Brillat Savarin / nutmeg / rhubarb sorbet / hibiscus jelly	£7
Sticky Toffee Pudding	Medjool date & walnut pudding / apple terrine / salted caramel ice cream	£7
Chocolate Fondant	Warm chocolate and anise fondant / tonka bean ice cream	£7
Lemon Meringue	Iced lemon meringue & pistachio mousse / basil ice cream / lemon curd	£7

Coffee — Fresh tea or coffee with our handmade petit fours — £3

Sulair Restaurant, 11 James Street, Stornoway, Isle of Lewis, Hs1 2up, 01851 709090
www.sulair.co.uk

Sùlair Restaurant

There have been a few requests for my fish pie recipe, so here it is. The key is, firstly, not to overcook the fish and, secondly, not to miss out the vermouth, as this is what gives the sauce its intense flavour, and thirdly, a good fish stock.

Fish Pie Ingredients:
500ml fish stock
500g skinned fish fillets (mixture of salmon, monkfish, turbot or brill, cod and smoked haddock)
12 langoustines, peeled and de-veined
a knob of butter
4 Shallots, finely chopped
125ml dry white wine
125ml Noilly Prat vermouth
2 sprigs tarragon
250ml double cream
200g new season peas, blanched
2 tsp freshly chopped tarragon
1kg Maris Piper potatoes
2 egg yolks
a large pinch of paprika and a pinch of nutmeg

Method:
Pre-heat oven to 200°C/gas 6. Bring the fish stock to the boil in a large pan. Add the fish and prawns and simmer until they are just slightly undercooked. Remove with a slotted spoon to a pie dish, reserving the poaching liquor. Melt the butter in a pan over a medium heat. Add the shallots and cook until softened. Turn up the heat and add the wine and Noilly Prat. Boil until reduced by half.

Pour in half of the fish poaching liquor and add the tarragon sprigs and reduce by half again. Stir in the cream and simmer until the sauce is the consistency of pouring cream. Season the sauce and strain.

Scatter over the blanched peas and chopped tarragon and pour over the sauce.

For the topping, peel the potatoes and cut them into equal chunks. Cook in boiling water until tender. Mash with the egg yolks and season with salt, pepper and nutmeg.

Spoon the mash over the pie dish and sprinkle with some paprika. Bake for 30 minutes until golden and bubbling.

(From Fios Nis 10th April 2009)

Sùlair Restaurant

Chocolate and cheesecake!
What more could you ask for? This is a baked cheesecake and normally I'm not a fan of baked cheesecakes, but this one I've been working on over the last couple of weeks and finally got it how I want. If you don't like heather honey you could substitute it for star anise or lavender. When you take it out of the oven you may think that it is not quite cooked in the middle but that's how you want it because once it cools down it will have a nice smooth texture unlike many other baked cheesecakes that have a dry texture.

Baked Chocolate and Heather Honey Cheesecake
Ingredients:
225g digestive biscuits, crushed
150g butter, melted
2 tbsp sugar
400g cream cheese
75g caster sugar
3 eggs, lightly beaten
25g unsweetened cocoa powder
90g dark chocolate, 70% cocoa solids, melted
1 tbsp heather honey.

Method:
Preheat the oven to 170°C/gas 3.
Make the biscuit base by mixing together the crushed digestives, melted butter, sugar and 15g of the melted chocolate.
Press into a 20cm spring-form tin.
In a large bowl, whisk the cream cheese and caster sugar until smooth and fluffy. Using a large metal spoon, fold in the eggs one at a time. Mix in the cocoa powder, melted chocolate and heather honey. Pour the mixture over the biscuit base. Place in the oven and bake for 45-50 minutes until slightly springy. Allow to cool in the tin before turning out.

(From Fios Nis 13th March 2009)

Suppliers /Solaraichean

Black Puddings
Cross Stores, 7 Cross Skigersta Rd, Ness, HS2 0TD,
01851 810241

Charles Macleod, Ropework Park, Matheson Road,
Stornoway, HS1 2LB
01851 702445
charlesmacleod.co.uk

Macleod & Macleod, 45 Westview Terrace,
Stornoway, HS1 2HP
01851 703384
macleodandmacleod.co.uk

Blackhouse Tea
Hebridean Tea Store, 22 Cromwell Street,
Stornoway, HS1 2DD
08002289294
hebrideanteastore.co.uk

Colonsay Honey
Andrew Abrahams, Pollgorm, Isle of Colonsay,
Argyll, PA61 7YR
01951 200365

Flour; wholemeal, oatmeal and beremeal
Golspie Mill, Durobin, Golspie, Sutherland,
KW10 6SF
01408 633278,
golspiemill.co.uk

Hebridean Cheese
Isle of Mull Cheese, Sgrìob-ruadh Farm, Tobermory,
Isle of Mull, PA75 6QD
01688 302627
isleofmullcheese.co.uk

Highland Beef
Brue Highlanders, 19 Brue, Isle of Lewis, HS2 0QW
01851 840377
bruehighlanders.co.uk

Isle of Harris Gin
Isle of Harris Distillery, Tarbert, Isle of Harris, HS3 3DJ
01859 502212
harrisdistillery.com

Organic Vegetables
Horshader Community Development,
North Shawbost, Isle of Lewis, HS2 9BD
01851 701225
horshader.com

Pork
Donald 'Sweeny' Macsween, Air an Lot
19 North Dell, Isle Of Lewis, Outer Hebrides, HS2 0SW
07796415097
airanlotshop.co.uk

Rapeseed Oil
Cullisse, CSS Estates, Cullisse, Nigg, Tain,
Ross-Shire, IV19 1QN
01862 863108
cullisse.com

Scallops
Sandy Gillies, Stornoway, Isle of Lewis

Shellfish
The *Carlsbay*

Skye Sea Salt
Isle of Skye Sea Salt Company, Gaeltec Building,
Glendale Rd, Dunvegan, IV55 8GU
isleofskyeseasalt.co.uk

Smoked Trout
The Tobermory Fish Co., Unit 7, Baliscate,
Tobermory, Isle of Mull, PA75 6QA
01688 302120
tobermoryfish.co.uk

MACLEOD & MACLEOD
STORNOWAY
BLACK PUDDING
Family Butchers
Since 1929
1.3 kg e

Isle of Colonsay
Wildflower Honey

CULLISSE
HIGHLAND RAPESEED
OIL

THE TOBERMORY FISH Co
THE TOBERMORY FISH COMPANY IS FAMOUS FOR WONDERFUL PRODUCE AND CAREFULLY CRAFTED RECIPES, INCLUDING OUR RENOWNED TOBERMORY SMOKED TROUT
KEEP ALL FISH REFRIGERATED AND BELOW 5°C
WWW.TOBERMORYFISH.CO.UK

ISLE OF
HARRIS
GIN
INFUSED WITH
SUGAR KELP

Flavoured Black Tea
An Taigh Dubh
Blackhouse Tea
A lovely, smoky tea with heather blossoms and honey and a hint of whisky
Ingredients :China and Ceylon black teas, heather blossoms, flavouring
1 teaspoon per cup, boiling hot water, steeping time 3.5 minutes
Hebridean
The Hebridean Tea Store
8 Church Street, Stornoway, HS1 2DH
www.hebrideanteastore.co.uk
phone : 0800 228 9294
TEA
TEE

ISLE OF MULL
Isle of Mull Cheese
Handmade Traditional
Farmhouse Cheese

STORNOWAY
BLACK
PUDDING
HANDMADE BY:
Charles Macleod
Ropework Park
Stornoway
01851 702445
Ingredients: Beef Suet, Vegetable Fat, Oatmeal, Pork Blood, Onions, Salt, Spices.
Keep Refrigerated (1- 4 c)
Contains: Gluten

ISLE of SKYE
SEA SALT
COMPANY
Pure Sea Salt Crystals

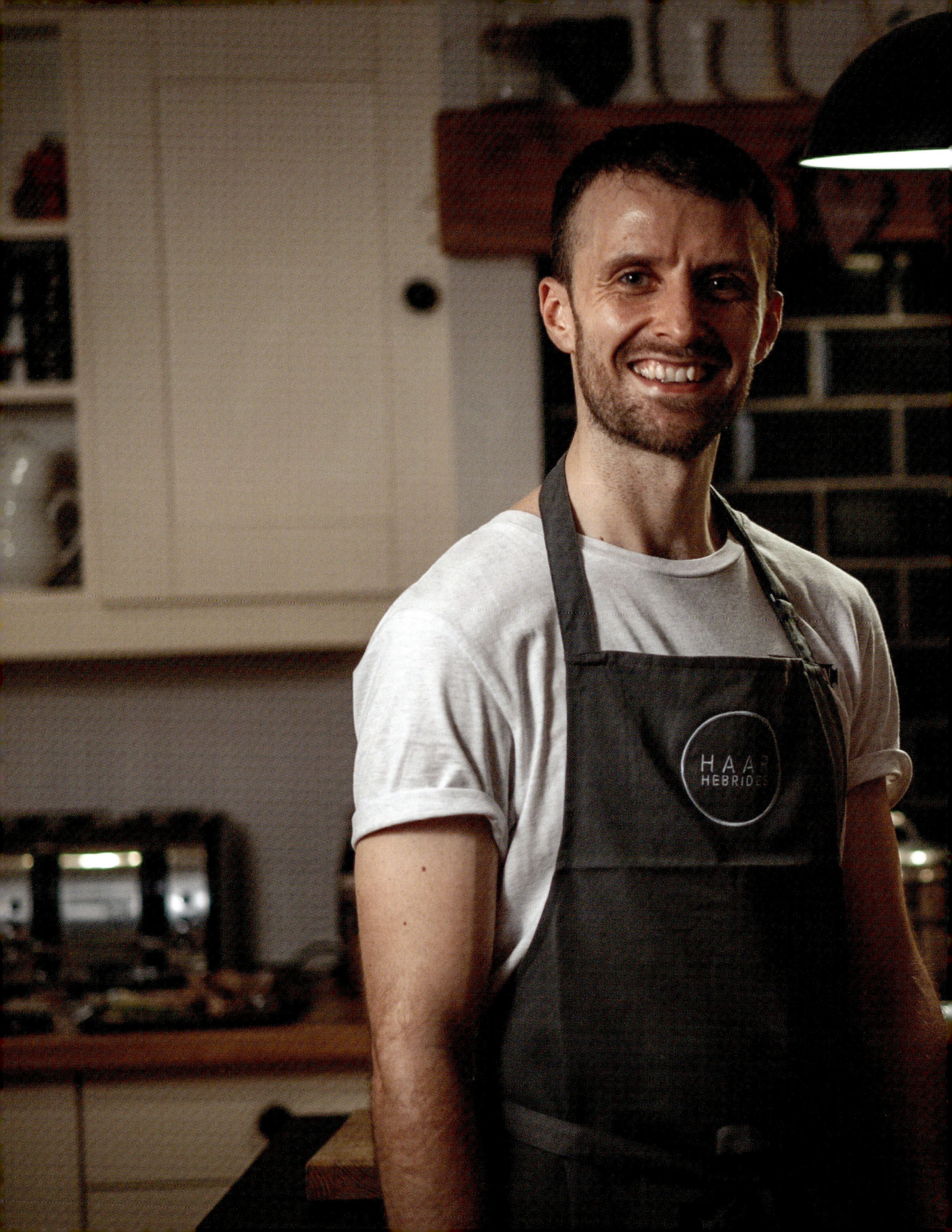
HAAR
HEBRIDES

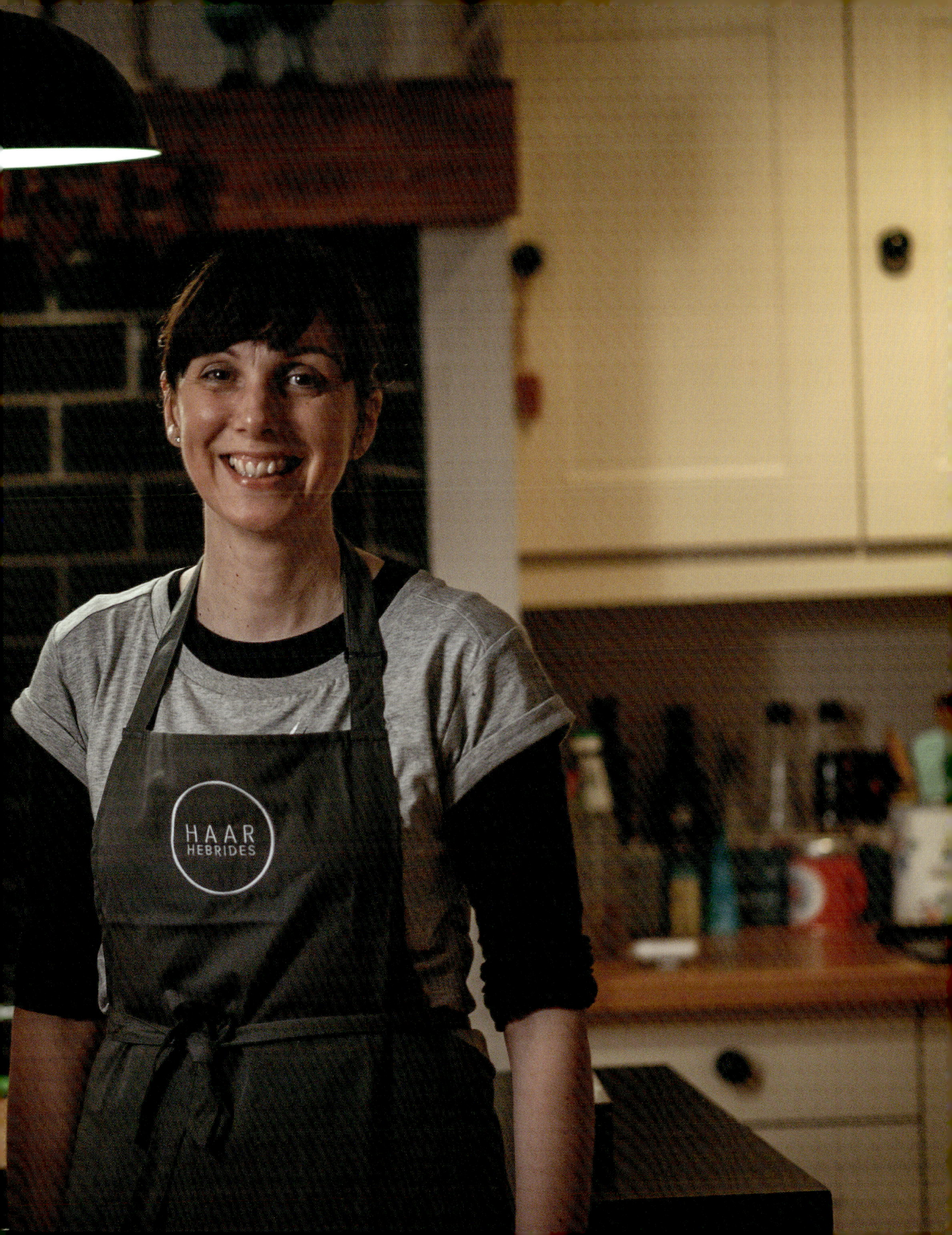
HAAR
HEBRIDES

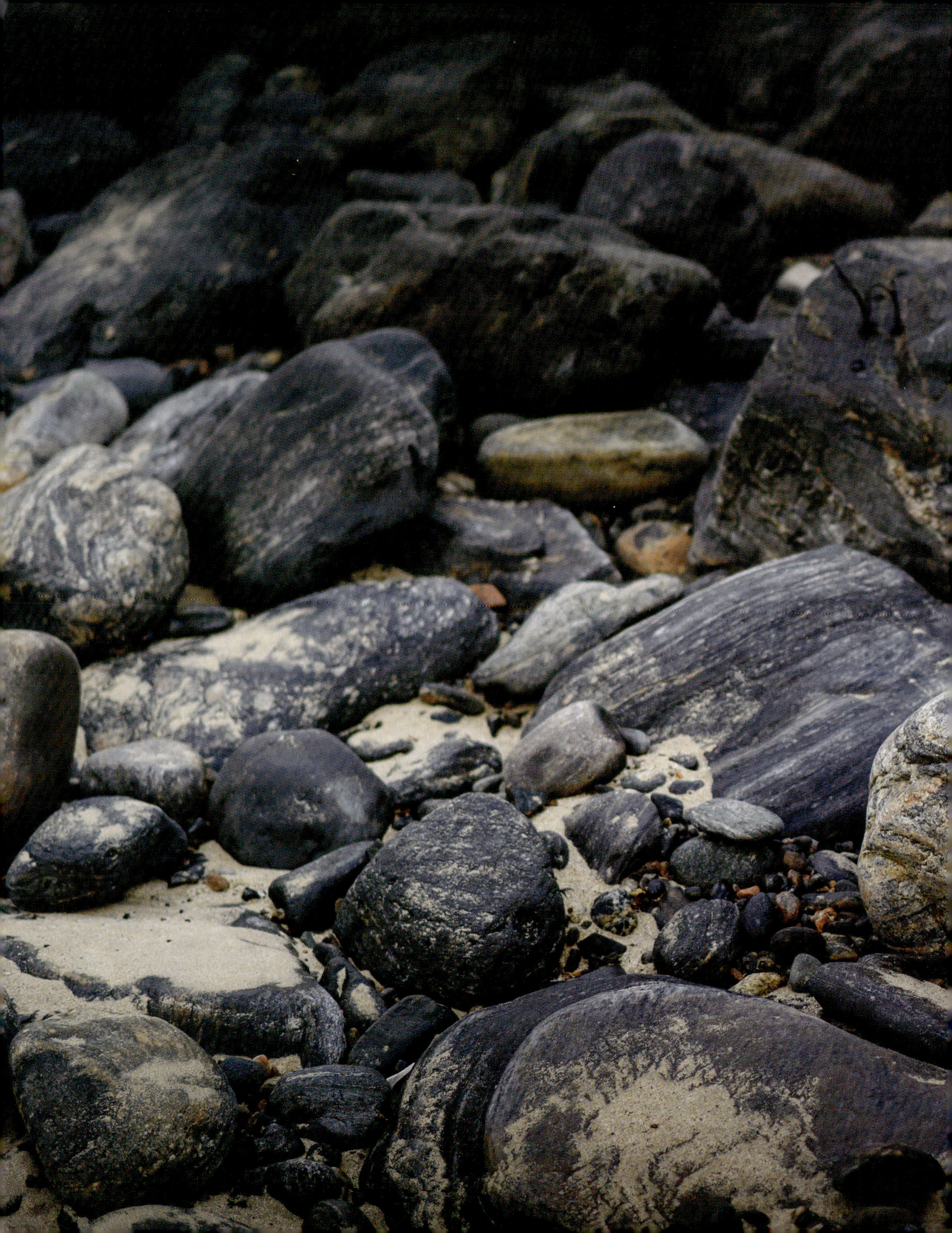

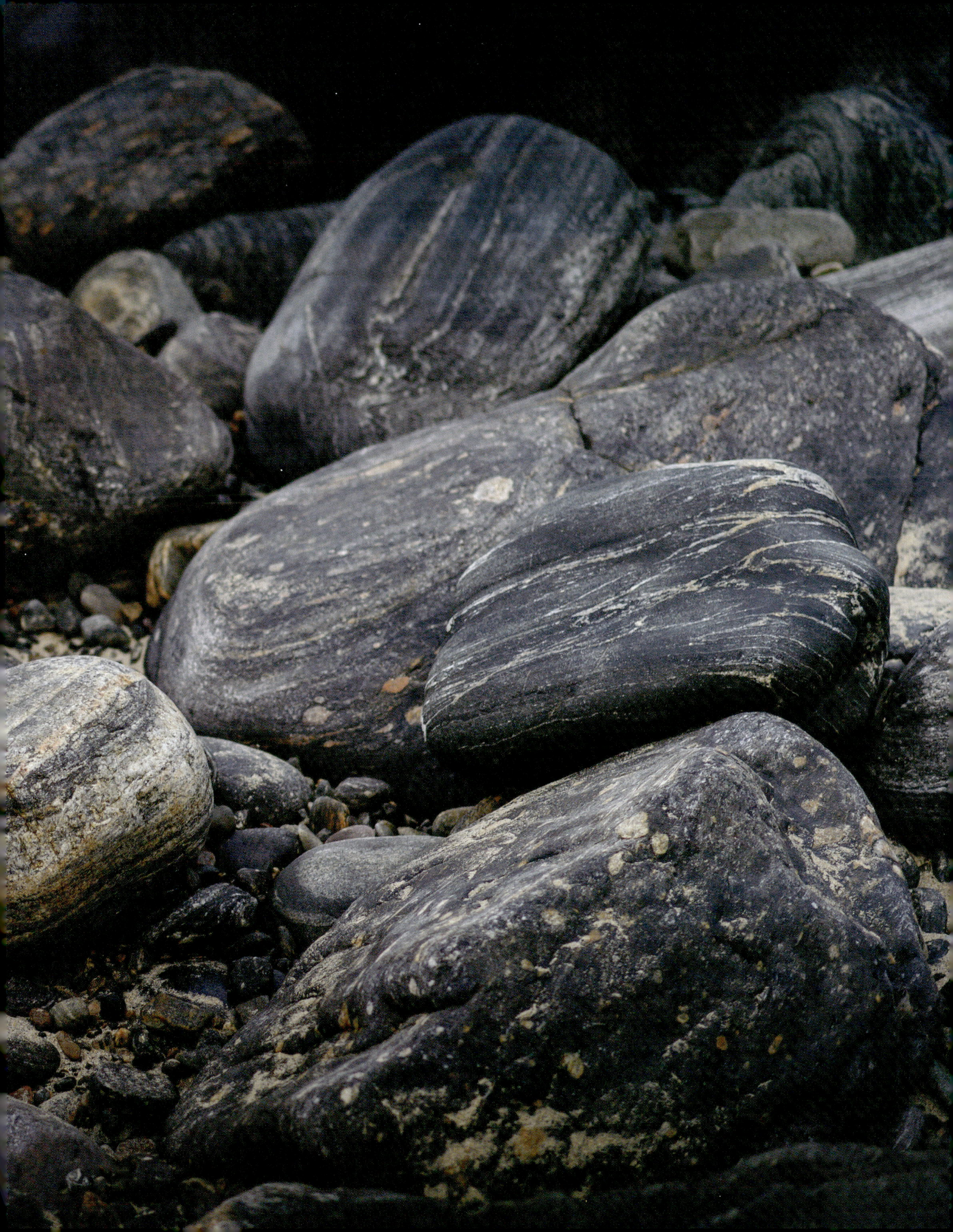

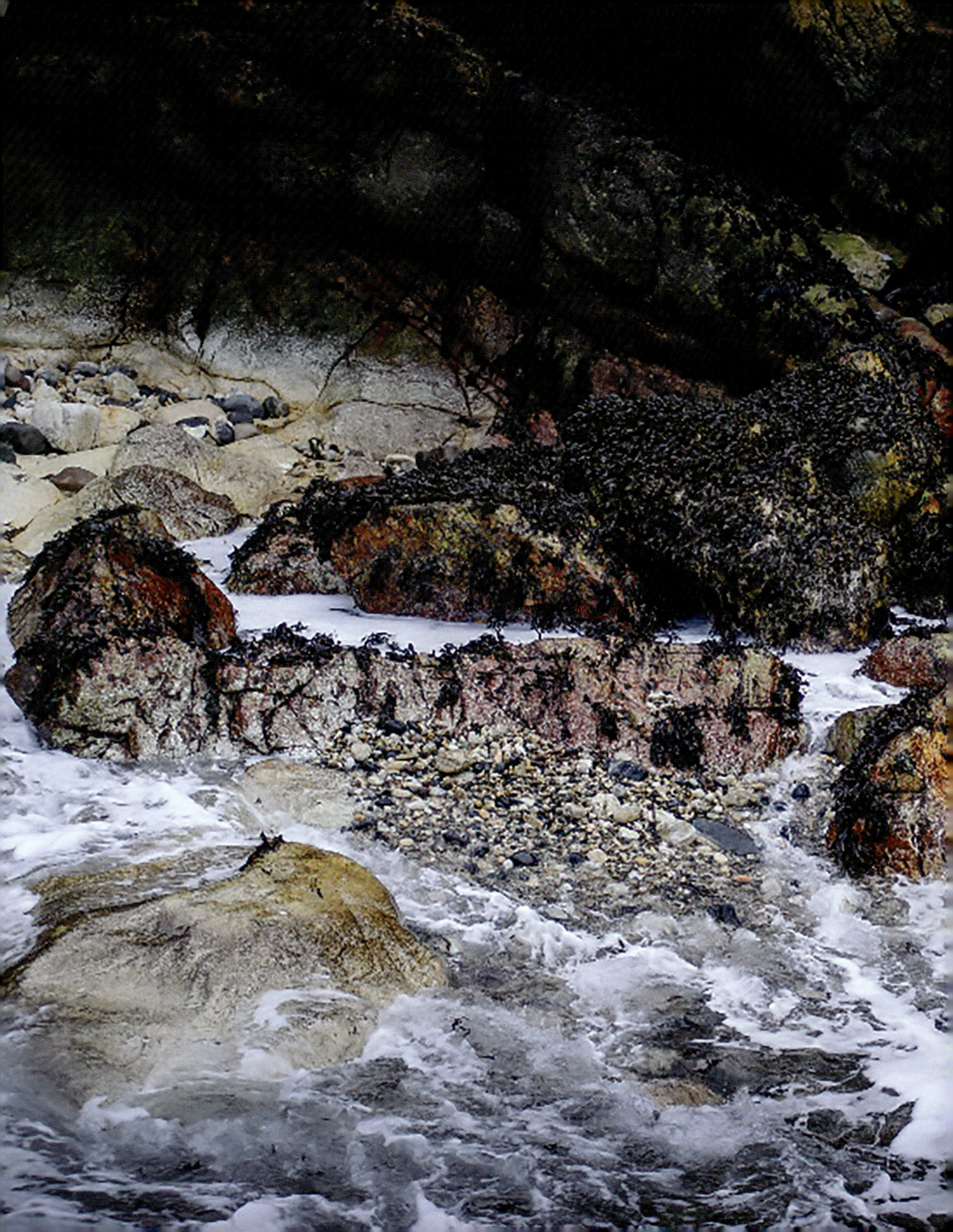

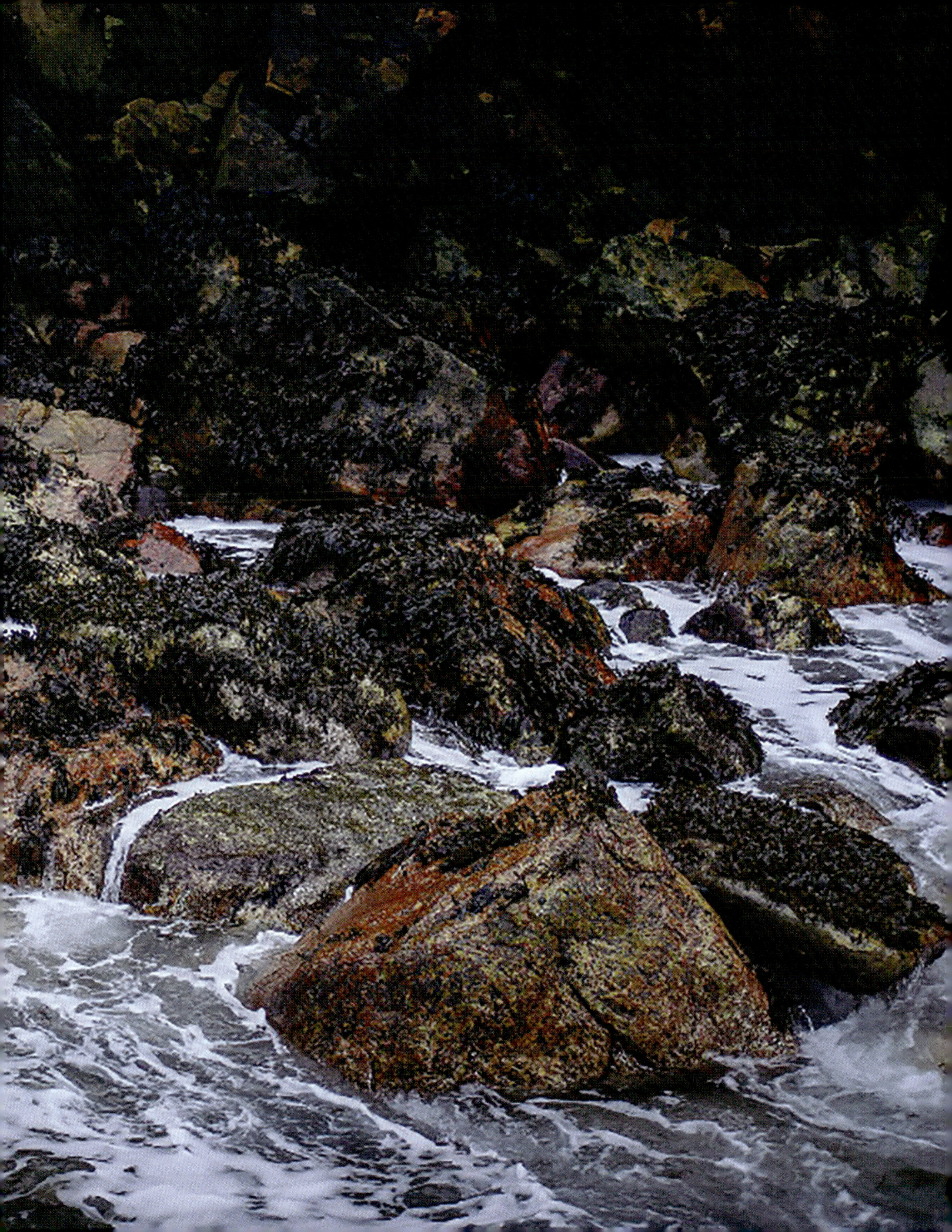

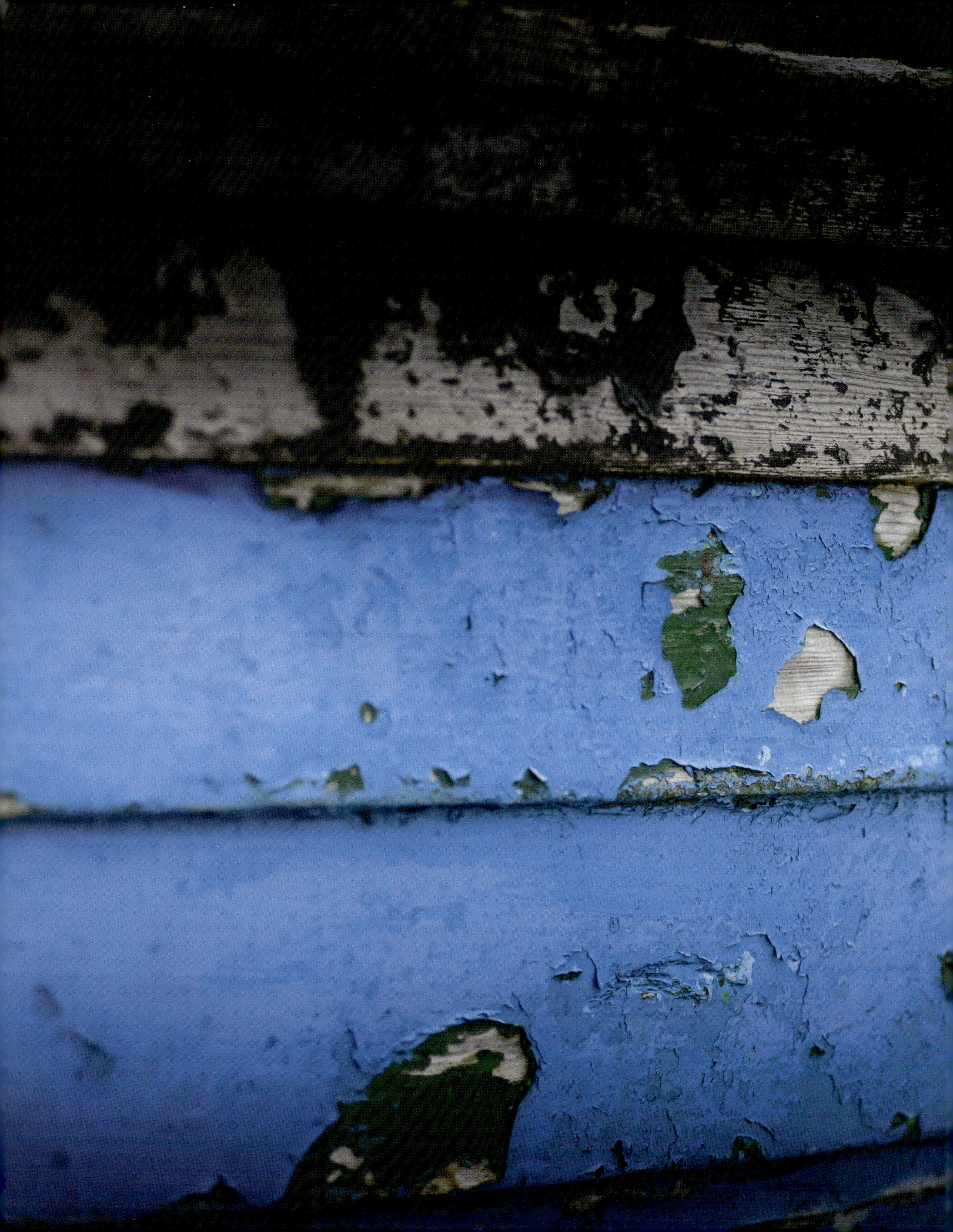

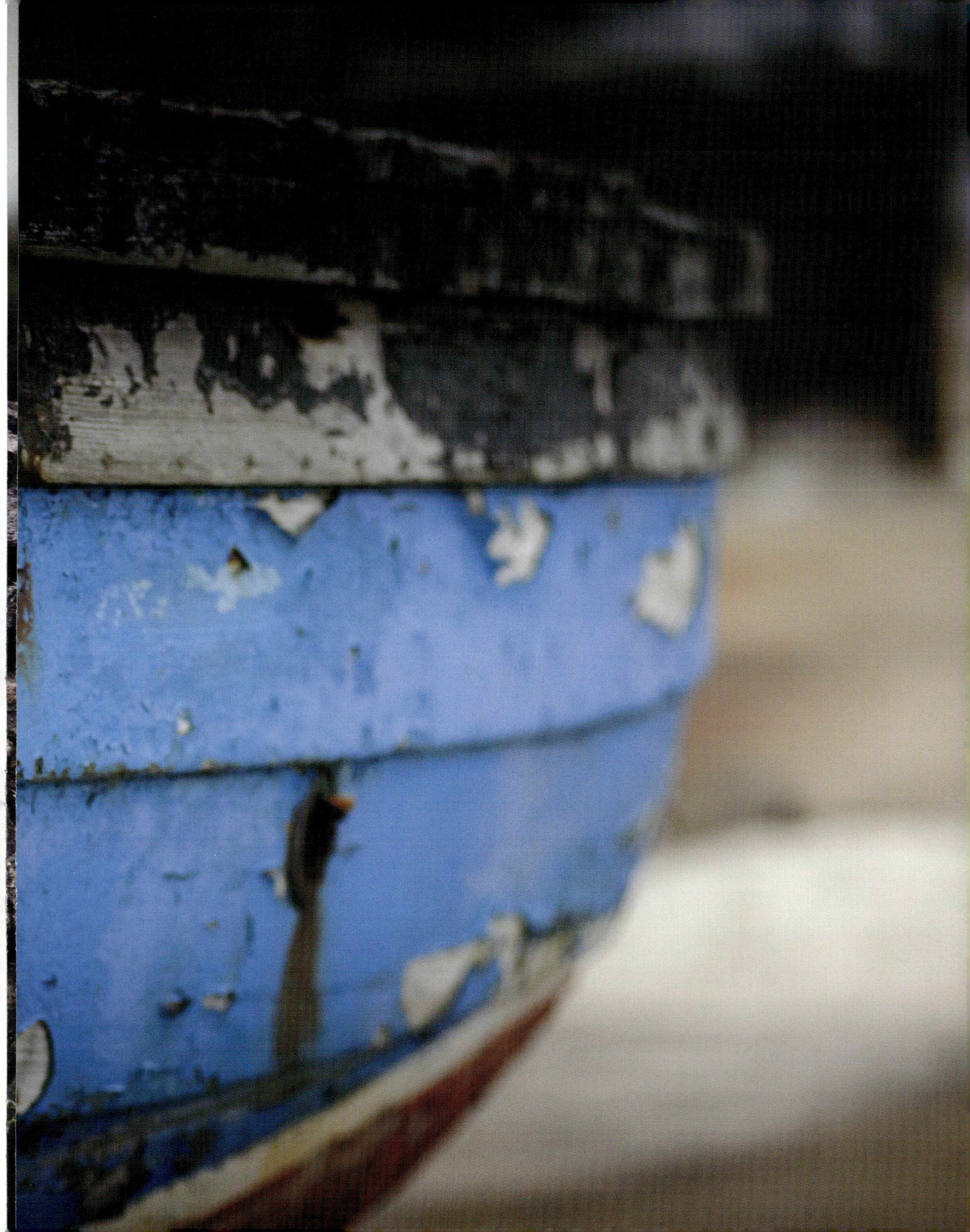

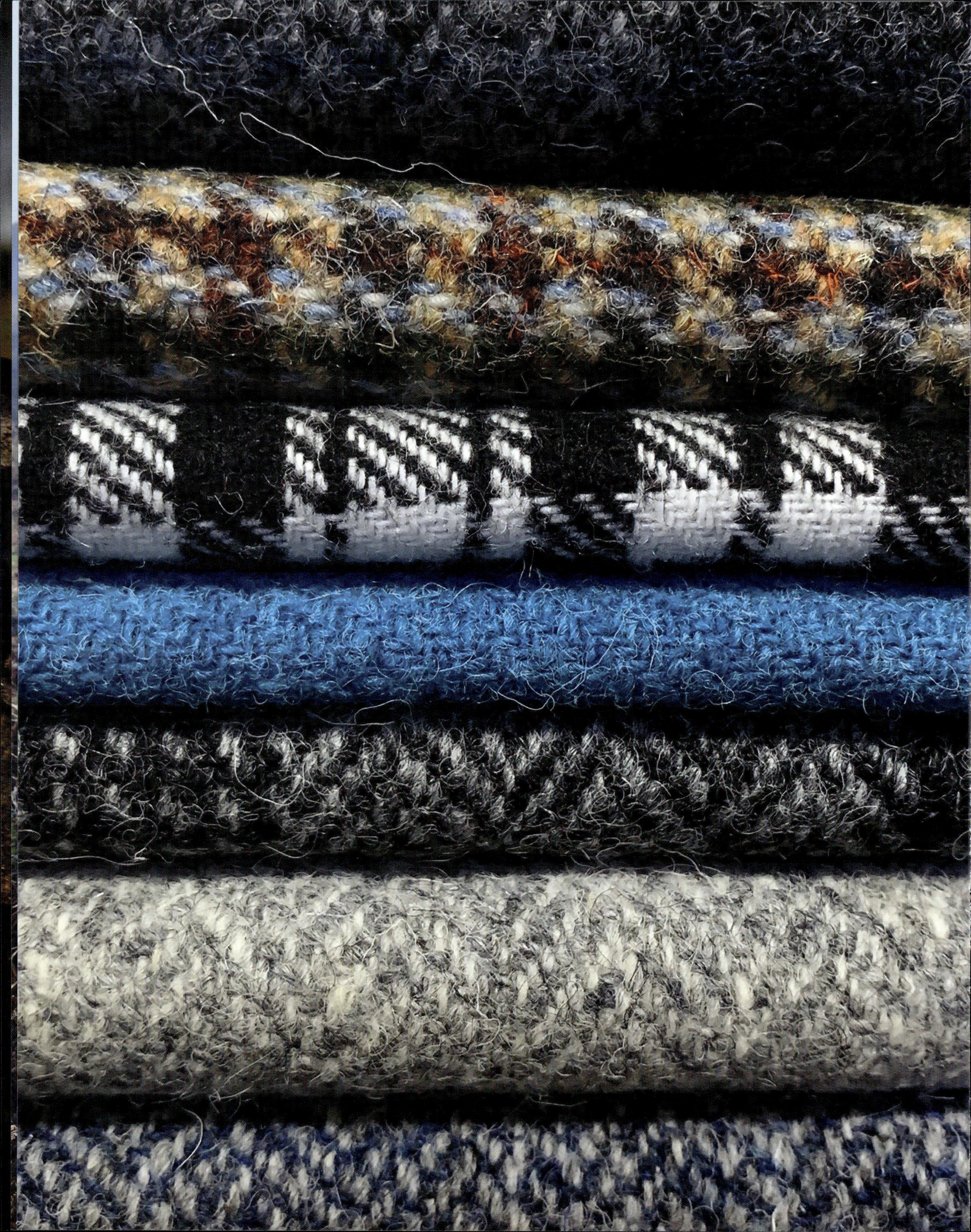

OSCR
Scottish Charity Regulator
www.oscr.org.uk
Registered Charity
SC047866

Riaghladair Carthannas na h-Alba
Carthannas Clàraichte/Registered Charity SC047866

First published in 2022 by Acair
An Tosgan, Seaforth Road, Stornoway, Isle of Lewis, Scotland HS1 2SD
www.acairbooks.com
info@acairbooks.com
© text Murdo Alex Macritchie 2022
© introduction text Kathleen MacDonald 2022
© an teacsa Gàidhlig Jo MacDonald 2022

All rights reserved.

The right of Murdo Alex Macritchie to be identified as the author of the work has been asserted by him in accordance with the Copyright, Designs and Patent Act 1998.

No part of this publication may be reproduced, stored in a retrieval system nor reproduced or transmitted by any means, electronic, mechanical, photocopying or otherwise, without the prior permission of the publisher.

Original design & concept by Murdo Alex Macritchie
Typeset and designed in-house at Acair by Margaret A. MacLeod

Chuidich Comhairle nan Leabhraichean am foillsichear
le cosgaisean an leabhair seo.

A CIP catalogue record for this title is available from the British Library
Printed by Hussar Books, Poland.
ISBN 978-1-78907-135-1

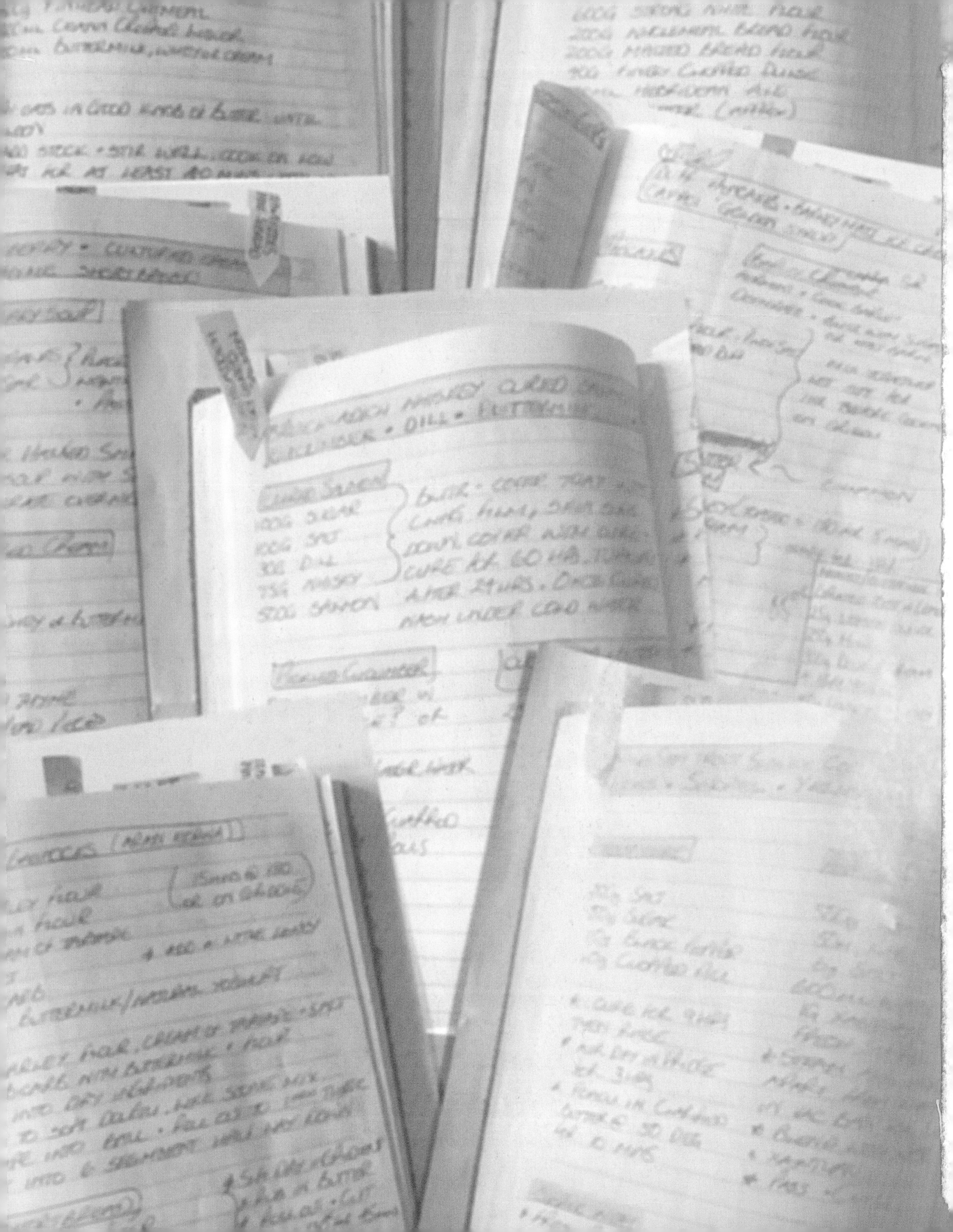